Madres del Verbo/
Mothers of the Word

Madres del Verbo/
Mothers of the Word

Early Spanish–American Women Writers
A Bilingual Anthology

Edited, Translated, and with an Introduction by
NINA M. SCOTT

University of New Mexico Press
Albuquerque

Library of Congress Cataloging-in-Publication Data
Madres del verbo - Mothers of the word : early Spanish-American
  women writers : a bilingual anthology / edited, translated, and
  with an introduction by Nina M. Scott.
      p.   cm.
  Includes bibliographical references and index.
  ISBN 0-8263-2145-3 (cloth : alk. paper).—ISBN 0-8263-2144-5
  (pbk. : alk. paper)
    1. Spanish American literature—Women authors—Translations
  into English.   2. Spanish American literature—Women authors.
  I. Scott, Nina M.   II. Title: Mothers of the word.
  PQ7087.E5M23   1999
  860.8'09282—dc21   99-37410
                                                            CIP

To Jim

Contents

Acknowledgments

During the many years I worked on this anthology, I often affectionately called it my "old girls" project, with no disrespect meant to the authors whose works I have included. On the contrary—the older I get, the more I respect the wit and wisdom of older women, and here I want to pay tribute to four very special "old girls" in my life: my mother, Hildegard Koppermann Budde, my mother-in-law, Elizabeth Tompkins Scott, and two aunts, Hertha Hamdorff Koppermann and Barbara Tompkins Stowell.

Many people have helped me directly and have inspired me with their scholarship. I owe a great deal to the generosity of Cristina González, Mary Berg, Kathryn McKnight, Montserrat Ordóñez, Asunción Lavrin, Kathleen Myers, and Frederick Luciani. My former graduate students Raúl Marrero-Fente and Carolina Alzate-Cadavid were also most generous in sharing their research. I continue to be enriched by the work of Stephanie Merrim, Doris Sommer, Jean Franco, Georgina Sabàt-Rivers, Mabel Moraña, Emilie Bergmann, Walter Mignolo, Rolena Adorno, Margarita Zamora, Rosa Perelmuter, Electa Arenal, Stacey Schlau, Susan Kirkpatrick, and Marie-Cécile Bénassy-Berling. Amanda Powell, Frances López-Morillas, Luis Harss, Margaret Peden, and Alan Trueblood are my model translators. I have major debts to scholars in Mexico: Elías Trabulse, Margo Glantz, Josefina Muriel, Clara Bargellini, Aureliano Tapia-Méndez, Sara Poot-Herrera, and Antonio Alatorre and the special friendship of Elena Poniatowska and Elena Urrutia. My list would not be complete without Márgara Russotto and Luisa Campuzano. To my many wonderful graduate students at the University of Massachusetts: *gracias por todo*.

My translation of Sor Juana's letter to her confessor was previously published in 1988. It is reprinted with permission from *Women's Studies International Forum,* vol. 11, Nina M. Scott, "'If You Are Not

Pleased to Favor Me, Put Me Out of Your Mind . . . ': Gender and Authority in Sor Juana Inés de la Cruz" and "Translation of Her Letter to the Reverend Father Maestro Antonio Núñez of the Society of Jesus," Copyright 1988, Pergamon Press Ltd, Headington Hill Hall, Oxford, OX3 OBW, United Kingdom.

I am especially grateful to Barbara Guth of the University of New Mexico Press, who was unfailingly kind, patient, and helpful. My greatest thanks go to my husband, Jim, whose constant help, encouragement, and computer skills really brought this book to fruition.

Nina M. Scott
Amherst, Massachusetts, 1999

# Introduction

This anthology has been many years in the making—far more than I had anticipated when the idea for it first occurred to me. A number of years ago I developed an advanced seminar dealing with the literature of Spanish-American women writers from colonial times to the end of the nineteenth century and found it difficult to obtain the texts I wanted my students to read. Many of them were rare and practically unavailable, so I put together my own anthology of photocopied materials, garnered through Inter-Library Loan or the generosity of friends and colleagues. I had so many requests for these materials that I felt I should try to publish an anthology in order to provide a useful text for classroom use in Spanish-American Literature. The editors at the University of New Mexico Press suggested that a bilingual anthology would be an even better idea, as many of these authors and their texts are unknown to non-Spanish speakers. This almost quadrupled my work in producing this book, but I hope that the final result will prove useful for courses in Women's Studies, Cultural Studies, Hemispheric American Studies, to name a few, as well as enjoyable for the general reader.

At the turn of the twenty-first century, it is difficult to remember how few women's voices and texts were recorded in the colonial era of Spanish America, and even those that have managed to reach our times were for years ignored or denigrated by literary historians and critics as peripheral, unworthy, uninteresting, second-rate literature. Feminist, cultural, and interdisciplinary studies have taught us new ways to approach traditional canons, to read and appreciate texts by women, slaves, indigenous peoples—all those heretofore relegated to the margins of the margins. As Kathleen Myers points out,

> The recuperation, translation, and publication of texts that had
> been lost or devalued as nonliterary characterize the current sta-

tus of the field as much as the new theoretical and interdisciplinary readings. Often for the first time, scholars are studying works by previously marginalized indigenous, mestizo, and women writers. The definition of what is considered a literary text has radically changed. . . . As a result, the canon continues to be drastically altered and expanded. (260)

The selections I have chosen range from Isabel de Guevara (first half of the sixteenth century) to Soledad Acosta de Samper (1833–1913). I have taught all of the texts included in this anthology on a number of occasions, and with great success. I have included four writers from the colonial period and five from the nineteenth century; the majority of the texts are autobiographical, and many are epistolary. All of the authors belonged to the middle or upper class and all are white, for in the past these were the only women who were literate or had access to publication. For the colonial era there is material from one married woman, one transvestite, and two nuns who were very famous in their time. For the nineteenth century I have given particular emphasis to networks of friendship and support among women writers, as well as to their roles in nation building (*el proyecto nacional*). In all cases I have tried to show that in spite of the limited roles society allowed women to play in their respective times, many of these writers still managed to assert their individuality and their talent.

Isabel de Guevara participated in the exploration and settlement of what is now Buenos Aires, Argentina, and Asunción, Paraguay. She arrived with Pedro de Mendoza's expedition in 1535. Hundreds of people died from hunger and disease on that ill-fated venture, and when the survivors, among whom were a number of women, realized that they would also die unless they went to a healthier location with better sources of food, the group made its way up the Paraná River to what is now Asunción. Twenty-one years later Doña Isabel wrote a letter to Princess Juana of Castile describing this trek and especially the role of the women in saving the lives of the remaining men; just as innumerable male explorers had, she asked for a land grant in return. This letter is one of the only published documents to record the experiences of a woman in the earliest years of Spanish America.

Catalina de Erauso, known as "la Monja Alférez" (the Ensign Nun), was born in Spain of Basque origin in 1592(?); her family placed her in a convent at the age of four, from which she escaped eleven years later, before taking her final vows. She shed her habit in favor of men's clothing, changed her name, and embarked for the New World, where she held a number of professions, including trader and mercenary soldier. Catalina gambled, brawled, dueled (she allegedly killed her own brother), and seduced other women until she confessed her identity to a clergyman. She was sent back to Spain, and her case became notorious. After she appeared before the king of Spain and the pope, she was granted permission to continue cross-dressing and returned to the New World; when last heard of she was a muleteer in Mexico. Erauso's autobiographical account may have been tampered with by subsequent authors, for much of it sounds fantastic, but then so was her life.

The largest body of writing in the initial years of the Spanish-American colonies was by nuns, as most convents accepted only women from the white elite, and many of these were literate. I have chosen two of the best-known nuns: Sor Juana Inés de la Cruz (1648/51?–95) from Mexico and La Madre Castillo (1671–1742) from Colombia. I have chosen to pair them because they are such diametrically opposite women: the brilliant intellectual and the devout mystic, each tormented by her own set of demons.

Sor Juana is such a gigantic figure that it is hard to choose just a few selections from her vast oeuvre. I have included some of her better-known poems, as well as others that are less familiar, especially the religious poems, often ignored by our more secular age. I have also included an autobiographical letter to her confessor that was discovered only in 1981; in it she exercised a nun's right to dismiss her confessor and spiritual father but did it in such a rebellious and insolent fashion that it shocks even today. The letter is a measure of the rage she felt at the unequal treatment of women by the male Church hierarchy, and, given the circumstances under which this letter was written, for once she was able to vent her anger openly.

The selections from Madre Castillo's *Vida* (Life) illustrate not only her religious vocation and mystical experiences but also some of the infighting among the nuns of her convent, the harsh treatment by her confessors, and the very ambivalent attitude she had about writing her autobiography. Whereas Sor Juana lived to write and used her pen to carve out as much intellectual freedom as was possible in her day, Madre Castillo was tormented by her confessors' order to write about herself. As was the case with many spiritual autobiographies by nuns, this text followed certain set parameters of hagiographic writing: early religious vocation and desire for the monastic life; an experience that makes the nun reject marriage; descriptions of an ascetic life filled with doubts, joys, self-accusations of sinfulness, and the striving toward union with her mystical bridegroom, Christ. Madre Castillo's autobiographical writing has neither the brilliance nor the assurance of Sor Juana's authorial voice, but it gives us a good record of life within a colonial convent and of the psychological processes of a woman bound to perpetual enclosure and self-sacrifice.

The jump to Gertrudis Gómez de Avellaneda and nineteenth-century writers is a quantum one, but the neoclassical poetry and essays of the eighteenth–century writers offer neither the stylistic interest nor the thematic concerns of the rest of this anthology. Enormous changes had taken place, not only politically, in that most Spanish-American countries achieved independence in the early part of the nineteenth century, but also with respect to women's place in literature. Many more women were now literate, meaning that there was a female reading public and women writers who wrote for this market. Although women were now writing and publishing, they still experienced anxiety of authorship, only for different reasons. In her analysis of women writers during the Romantic era, Susan Kirkpatrick has shown that the male ideal of womanhood was that of a modest, self-effacing, and self-sacrificing person (the "angel in the house," as Virginia Woolf called her), yet male Romantics simultaneously extolled the importance of human sentiments and emotions, long identified by Western society as the particular preserve of women. Women writers were thus caught in a paradoxical situation: how could they express powerful emotional selves and still remain modest and angelic?

Gertrudis Gómez de Avellaneda (1814–72) was one of the most successful writers of her day, one who lived by her pen and was famous both in Spain and in her native Cuba. (Cuba was an anomaly in the nineteenth-century Americas in that it was still a Spanish colony.) For this anthology I have chosen excerpts from her private correspondence, which show to perfection how she was trying to bridge the chasm between the conflictive roles of woman and writer. Avellaneda's love letters to Ignacio de Cepeda and Antonio Romero Ortiz oscillate between promising the men of her heart love and abject obedience and then fighting tooth and claw for her creative freedom. In her correspondence Avellaneda also made some incisive observations on nineteenth-century gender roles.

Juana Manuela Gorriti (1816–92) came from an upper-class Argentinian family. Because her father fought against the dictator Juan Manuel de Rosas in the civil wars of the early nineteenth century, the family had to go into exile in Bolivia, where their headstrong daughter insisted on marrying a Bolivian army officer when she was only fourteen. Manuel Isidoro Belzú eventually became president of Bolivia, but the marriage was a disaster and Gorriti ultimately moved to Lima, where she supported herself by teaching and writing. Gorriti's literary talents and her prolific writings on many subjects, from short stories to personal memoirs, make her Argentina's leading woman writer of the nineteenth century. The melodramatic novella included here records the horrors of Rosas's death squads and is eerily reminiscent of the literature that has recently come out of Argentina, especially by women authors who graphically recorded the torture and violence of the so-called Dirty War (1976–82).

Gorriti had a circle of women friends who made their living in much the same way that she did, such as the Peruvian novelist and essayist Mercedes Cabello de Carbonera (1845–1909) and Teresa González de Fanning (1835–?) who also wrote novels and was headmistress of a school. Gorriti did not have much money, but she hosted a literary salon at her house that attracted the leading intellectuals of Lima, both male and female, and provided a place for the exchange of ideas, musical performances, and the reading of new pieces of literature. I have selected two short essays written for these gatherings by Cabello de Carbonera and González de Fanning which illustrate topics of great interest to them and to other women of the nineteenth century: the merits of beauty versus intelligence and the need to give women sufficient professional training so that they could achieve economic in-

dependence. Although these topics might appear banal today, and the essays are not literary masterpieces, the topics presented were of vital interest to women like themselves—widows coping with straitened financial circumstances once their husbands had passed away. Male essayists of the nineteenth century produced ringing prose that spoke to heroic futures and national identity, yet "in their search for an Americanist equation of cultural authenticity, male essayists—even self-declared liberals—were virtually oblivious to the one-sided nature of their discourse" (Meyer 3). For example, it never seemed to have occurred to any of them what their wives and families would do if they died first. Women, too, wrote essays—most completely ignored until recently—that addressed problems that were to them more immediate and vital than national identity.

Soledad Acosta de Samper was, like Gorriti, the daughter of a general and a highly prolific author; in Colombia she is considered the leading nineteenth-century woman writer, yet she is little known in the United States. I have chosen her novella "Dolores" (1867) for two reasons: it is stylistically interesting in the alternation between male and female narrative voices; and her descriptions of the psychological processes for facing terminal illness, in this case leprosy, are strikingly modern. As opposed to many novels of the time written by males, in which terminally ill women expire beautifully and uncomplainingly, Dolores exhibits both rage at her fate and callousness toward those around her. This story is another example of the way early women writers resisted the roles and values that a male-dominated society imposed on them.

A word of explanation about the title of this anthology. It comes from Sor Juana's reference to the Virgin Mary as "Madre del Verbo" (Mother of the Word), an attribute based on the Gospel according to Saint John: "In the beginning was the Word, and the Word was with God, and the Word was God" (John 1.1). In Saint John's context, "Word" referred to the Greek *logos*: "in Greek thought the divine principle of reason that gives order to the universe and links the human mind to the mind of God" (*HarperCollins Study Bible* 2013). This reference to Mary is not original with Sor Juana; it existed not only in literature but also in the visual arts, as for example in the portraits of Mary as Mother of the Word by the Renaissance painter Giovanni Bellini (Kimbell Museum, Ft. Worth) and by Sandro Botticelli (Museo Poldi Pezzoli, Milan). However, given the nun/poet's reverence for language, Mary as Mother of the Word takes on a radical meaning. We must not forget that for a long time women had been considered a source of evil and corruption, to be kept both silent and enclosed. Just a century before, in 1583, the Spanish cleric Fray Luis de León wrote a highly popular manual entitled *La perfecta casada* (The Perfect Wife), in which he laid out the rules: "it is right that all women should strive to be silent, those for whom it is best to hide the little knowledge they have, as well as those who might without shame proclaim what they know, for in all women to be silent and to say little is not only an agreeable condition but proper virtue" (123). Sor Juana used Mary as her ally in countering this code of ignorance and silence for women. Besides seeing Mary as Mother of the Word, Sor Juana often extolled the Virgin's intellectual properties, hailing Mary as poet and even as Doctor of Divine Studies. As the critic Jean Franco so aptly observed,

> Sor Juana's celebration of the Virgin allows her to envisage female power and intellect. She describes Mary as Mother of the Word. When this is taken literally, it means that the female body is the matrix that gives birth to the logos. The womb is not only the sullied and impure repository of original sin but the source of redemption without which there would be neither life nor meaning. (52–53)

It is this prioritizing of women's voices I want to underscore in this anthology. Until very recently the curricula of courses dealing with Spanish America's early literary production might include Sor Juana and Avellaneda but usually ignored the many other significant women writers who also form part of this heritage. With this book their voices will now be available to both a Spanish- and an English-speaking public, so that their remarkable stories will not be forgotten.

A Note on Translation: As all of the introductory biographies to these writers are in English, I have translated all Spanish citations into English. All translations in this book, unless otherwise noted, are mine. Given the long, often-convoluted syntax that characterized the Spanish of earlier centuries, I have sometimes altered the punctuation, or made two sentences out of what was originally one, hoping to make the translations more readable without altering the original meaning.

Isabel de Guevara

*T*he letter that Isabel de Guevara wrote to Princess Juana, asking to be rewarded for services rendered, is one of the only published documents to record the participation of Spanish women in the settlement of the Americas.[1] As we have no information on Doña Isabel apart from her letter, I thought this introduction would be very brief, but the more I thought about her, the more I wanted to know the answers to some very basic questions. When did Spanish women begin to come to the Americas? What was the context in which Isabel de Guevara made these initial voyages? Was she unusual in asking for a *repartimiento,* or share, for herself; that is, were these privileges ever given to women? And finally, why did she wait twenty years after her arrival in Asunción before asking for this reward?[2]

Consuelo Varela, in her edition of Columbus's four voyages, notes that women sailed for the New World as early as his second voyage (20, esp. n. 5). The colonial historian Samuel Eliot Morison has only two references to women in his famous biography of Columbus, *Admiral of the Ocean Sea,* but even these are contradictory. He states that he could find no record of women on the island of Hispaniola before 1498 (397) yet maintains that women and children had come in 1494 with Antonio de Torres, who was bringing provisions to Columbus and his Spanish settlers on the north coast of that island (490). According to Morison, in 1498 Columbus was given permission to recruit one woman for every ten male emigrants (397), and as of that date Spanish women appeared to have come in greater numbers. In 1509 the first woman's name appeared on the passenger lists, which at that time were compiled by the Casa de Contratación, the administrative center in Seville that kept all records having to do with the American colonies (Schurz 286). As James Lockhart and Enrique Otte note, the wives and female relatives of the conquerors "begin to appear in the new country almost before the fighting was over" (14).

At the beginning of the sixteenth century women were expressly barred from expeditionary voyages (as opposed to establishing settlements), and there was a real effort made to control female emigration. As it was felt that the presence of single women aboard the ships to the colonies would prove troublesome on the voyages, at first only married women were legally allowed to embark, but there is little doubt that from the beginning such rules were bent with fair regularity. In her delightful book, *Algunas mujeres de la conquista* (Some Women of the Conquest), the Paraguayan writer Josefina Plà maintains that there must have been many single women, some quite respectable and others not very, who successfully smuggled their way across the Atlantic, because the captain looked the other way, or they hid as stowaways, or they dressed as men. Historians agree that cross-dressing was not as implausible as it may sound, and we have an example of it in Catalina de Erauso. Many of the soldiers of the time were teenagers, so that a woman's beardless face and slender build would not necessarily have attracted attention (Lopreto 45). Supposing women were discovered during a voyage? Tongue in cheek, Plà suggests that a captain would have three options: marry them off, return to port, or throw them overboard. Since none of these made real sense, most likely the women continued with the ship (13–14).

What about Isabel de Guevara's own journey to the Americas? In 1534 Pedro de Mendoza, a Spanish nobleman of great wealth, was granted permission to organize one of the largest and most ambitious expeditions to explore the Americas. A fleet of eleven ships transported some twelve hundred men, a few of them with their wives, and a hundred horses to the estuary of the River Plate, the site of present-day Buenos Aires. Settlement began in 1536, in a location that proved to be just as bad as Jamestown was for John Smith and his English compatriots some seventy years later. Disease, hunger, and hostile Indians decimated the group in short order, leaving a starving group of settlers who were reduced to eating "rats, mice, snakes, lizards, even their shoes, and all available hides. Some gorged on the bodies of those who had died" (Crow 131).

As Pedro de Mendoza was incapacitated during these events by a virulent case of syphilis, one of his lieutenants, Capt. Juan de Ayolas, took a group of the starving settlers up the Paraná River in 1537; in the following year they established Asunción, Paraguay. When Ayolas was killed by a group of Indians, Domingo Martínez de Irala was elected governor of the colony, Mendoza having died on his way back to Spain. Irala is considered the founder of present-day Paraguay. In 1580 a group of Spaniards from Asunción retraced the journey down the Paraná, and their leader, Blas de Garay, established the second, successful settlement of Buenos Aires.

Isabel de Guevara was one of the women who joined Mendoza's expedition. Even though it was apparently illegal, this being clearly an exploratory voyage, eight women are mentioned in the documents of this venture. The Argentine historian Gladys Lopreto, who has studied the history of this expedition, found no Isabel de Guevara among the eight listed but did notice a certain "Carlos de Guevara and Isabel de Laserna," though the relationship between the two was unclear (46). Guevara died in the same skirmish with the Indians in which Ayolas perished.

Isabel de Guevara participated in the trek upriver from Buenos Aires, as she records in the letter that was written some twenty years after this group arrived in Asunción. She waited until 1556 to write because in 1555 Governor Irala was granted permission by the Crown to distribute sizable *encomiendas* to the Spaniards residing in Asunción, and Isabel de Guevara had not received one (Lopreto 48; Marrero 4–5). It was not unusual for a woman to ask for a repartimiento for herself. Luis Marín has shown that women were indeed the beneficiaries of such privileges: "One of the first Spanish women to obtain an encomienda in America was Doña María de Toledo, the daughter-in-law of the discoverer, who with her husband, Diego Colón, arrived in Hispaniola in 1509. This precedent was followed later in Panamá and Mexico, where women encomenderas date back to the early days of the conquest" (46). Another example of this is María de Estrada, a Spanish woman who participated in Hernán Cortés's campaign, and perhaps foreshadows the exploits of Catalina de Erauso:

[She] was already noted for her readiness to take up arms with the men. After the fall of Tenochtitlán [the Aztec capital] she participated in an attack on a mountain town in the foothills of Popocatepetl. Charging on horseback with lance in hand and shouting the war cry of Santiago, enemy of the heathen, she frightened the defenders out of their wits. In recognition of her valor, certified by Cortés, she and her husband were awarded a grant of Indian service there. (Karttunen 17)

At some point in her life Isabel de Guevara married Pedro de Esquivel, a Sevillian who had come to Paraguay with Alvar Núñez Cabeza de Vaca (Tieffemberg 287), and thus had not been with her on the trek from Buenos Aires to Asunción. Isabel de Guevara and her husband may have been left out because Esquivel was not a supporter of Irala's; he was later jailed and beheaded, leaving Isabel a widow (Plà 26). In any event, Isabel de Guevara felt slighted by Irala, took pen in hand, and wrote to Juana of Austria, the emperor Charles V's youngest daughter, who was governor of Castile and of Spain's overseas possessions from 1554 to 1559 (Tieffemberg 288).[3] Did it make a difference to her that the recipient of her letter was a woman? Most likely, as Guevara bypassed all intermediary functionaries to write directly to Princess Juana (Lopreto 44).

As the letter is in fact a petition for a specific reward, it was necessary for Isabel de Guevara to tell her story to justify the grant by Princess Juana.[4] Letters from male explorers and colonizers to the Crown requesting a reward for their actions in subjugating the Americas were not unusual, but the insertion of a female protagonist's voice certainly was. In her narration she consistently foregrounds the heroic actions of the women and obscures the ratio of women to men to such a degree that the activities of the latter become completely secondary. A number of critics (Lopreto, Tieffemberg, Alzate-Cadavid) have remarked on the fact that Guevara almost always uses the third-person plural, "las mugeres," "ellas" (the women, they), when she refers to their participation in the upriver journey, switching to the first person only in the last paragraph, in which she asks for her personal reward. Silvia Tieffemberg also points out an alternation between an objective narrative and a more intimate, "woman-to-woman" tone that Guevara adopted in addressing the princess (289–90). It is important to note that she requests that the repartimiento be granted to her, not to her husband, and that it be given in perpetuity, as her actions had warranted it. In so doing Isabel de Guevara gives us a glimpse of a stalwart woman, one with a strong sense of self and worth. As was the case with many other documents of this kind, the letter she wrote articulated not only her personal frustration but also a common complaint among Spain's immigrants to the Americas: the resentment of the established colonists toward the newcomers, who were enriching themselves without having suffered the dangers and hardships of the original settlers.

Notes

1. Mary G. Berg has done research in the Archives of the Indies in Seville and has found other letters by women asking for redress of wrongs, but none of them tell as complete a story as Isabel de Guevara's. Berg is planning to publish some of her finds, which will add greatly to what we know about European women in the early colonial years.

2. The repartimiento she requested was given by the Spanish Crown under a system called *encomienda* (the entrusting of one person to another). A repartimiento was not a land grant per se—although in practice it turned out to be tantamount to one—but the right to the tribute and labor of a determined number of Indians on a specific parcel of land, given either for a limited time or in perpetuity. In return for this tribute or labor the Indians were entrusted to the Spanish *patrón* for instruction in the Christian faith. The two terms, *repartimiento* and *encomienda,* are often used interchangeably.

3. Juana governed in the absence of her brother Philip II, who was away in England for several years, having married Mary Tudor in 1555.

4. Raúl Marrero-Fente points out that her letter followed legal models for establishing a claim: she first narrates the facts, then denounces the injustice done her, and subsequently asks that her grievance be addressed.

Carta a la princesa doña Juana

Carta de doña ISABEL DE GUEVARA á la princesa gobernadora doña JUANA, exponiendo los trabajos hechos en el descubrimiento y conquista del Rio de la Plata por las mugeres para ayudar á los hombres, y pidiendo repartimiento para su marido.[1]

Muy alta y muy poderosa señora:

A esta probinçia del Rio de la Plata, con el primer gouernador della, don Pedro de Mendoça, avemos venido çiertas mugeres, entre las quales a querido mi ventura que fuese yo la vna; y como la armada llegase al puerto de Buenos Ayres, con mill é quinientos hombres, y les faltase el bastimento, fué tamaña la hambre, que, á cabo de tres meses, murieran los mill; esta hambre fué tamaña, que ni la de Xerusalen se le puede ygualar, ni con otra nenguna se puede conparar. Vinieron los hombres en tanta flaqueza, que todos los travajos cargavan de las pobres mugeres, ansi en lavarles las ropas, como en curarles, hazerles de comer lo poco que tenian, alimpiarlos, hazer sentinela, rondar los fuegos, armar las vallestas, quando algunas vezes los yndios les venien á dar guerra, hasta cometer á poner fuego en los versos, y á levantar los soldados, los questavan para hello, dar arma por el canpo á bozes, sargenteando y poniendo en orden los soldados; porque en este tienpo, como las mugeres nos sustentamos con poca comida, no aviamos caydo en tanta flaqueza como los hombres. Bien creerá V. A. que fué tanta la soliçitud que tuvieron, que, si no fuera por ellas, todos fueran acabados; y si no fuera por la honrra de los hombres, muchas más cosas escriviera con verdad y los diera á hellos por testigos. Esta relaçion bien creo que la escrivirán á V. A. más largamente, y por eso sesaré.

Pasada esta tan peligrosa turbunada, determinaron subir el rio arriba, asi, flacos como estavan y en entrada de ynvierno, en dos vergantines, los pocos que quedaron viuos, y las fatigadas mugeres los curavan y los miravan y les guisauan la comida, trayendo la leña á cuestas de fuera del navio, y animandolos con palabras varoniles, que no se dexasen morir, que presto darian en tierra de comida, metiendolos á cuestas en los vergantines, con tanto amor como si fueran sus propios hijos. Y como llegamos á vna generaçion de yndios que se llaman tinbues, señores de mucho pescado, de nuevo los serviamos en buscarles diversos modos de guisados, porque no les diese en rostro el pescado, á cabsa que lo comian sin pan y estavan muy flacos.

Despues, determinaron subir el Parana arriba, en demanda de bastimento, en el qual viaje, pasaron tanto trabajo las desdichadas mugeres, que milagrosamente quiso Dios que biviesen por ver que hen ellas estava la vida dellos; porque todos los serviçios del navio los tomavan hellas tan á pechos, que se tenia por afrentada la que menos hazia que otra, serviendo de marear la vela y gouernar el navio y sondar de proa y tomar el remo al soldado que no podia bogar y esgotar el navio, y poniendo por delante á los soldados que no desanimasen, que para los hombres heran los trabajos: verdad es, que á estas cosas hellas no heran apremiadas, ni las hazian de obligaçion ni las obligaua, si solamente la caridad. Ansi llegaron á esta çiudad de la Asunçion, que avnque agora está muy fertil de bastimentos, entonçes estaua dellos muy neçesitada, que fué nesesario que las mugeres boluiesen de nuevo á sus trabajos, haziendo rosas con sus propias manos, rosando y carpiendo y senbrando y recogendo el bastimento, sin ayuda de nadie, hasta tanto que los soldados guareçieron de sus flaquezas y començaron á señorear la tierra y alquerir yndios y yndias de su serviçio, hasta ponerse en el estado en que agora está la tierra.

E querido escrevir esto y traer á la memoria de V. A., para hazerle saber la yngratitud que comigo se a vsado en esta tierra, porque al presente se repartió por la mayor parte de los que ay en ella, ansi de los antiguos como de los modernos, sin que de mí y de mis trabajos se tuviese nenguna memoria, y me dexaron de fuera, sin me dar yndio ni nengun genero de serviçio. Mucho me quisiera hallar libre, para me yr á presentar delante de V. A., con los serviçios que á S. M. e hecho y los agravios que agora se me hazen; mas no está en mi

mano, por questoy casada con vn cauallero de Sevilla, que se llama
Pedro d'Esquiuel, que, por servir á S. M., a sido cabsa que mis trabajos quedasen tan oluidados y se me renovasen de nuevo, porque tres
vezes le saqué el cuchillo de la garganta, como allá V. A. sabrá. A
que suplico mande me sea dado mi repartimiento perpétuo, y en
gratificaçion de mis serviçios mande que sea proveydo mi marido
de algun cargo, conforme á la calidad de su persona; pues él, de su
parte, por sus serviçios lo merese. Nuestro Señor acreçiente su Real
vida y estado por mui largos años. Desta çibdad de la Asunçion y de
jullio 2, 1556 años.

Isabel
de Guevara
11

> Serbidora de V. A. que sus Reales manos besa
> Doña Ysabel de Guevara.

[Sello] Sobre.—*A la muy alta y muy poderosa señora la Princesa doña
Joana, Gouernadora de los reynos d'España, etc.—En su Consejo de Yndias.*

Notas

1. Es interesante ver cómo los que clasificaron este documento leyeron
mal su mensaje central: Doña Isabel pide recompensa principalmente
para sí misma, y no tanto para el marido.

Letter to the Princess Doña Juana

Letter from Doña ISABEL DE GUEVARA to the Governing Princess Doña JUANA, explaining the hardships endured in the discovery and conquest of the River Plate by the women in order to help the men, and asking for a land grant for her husband.[1]

Very High and Very Powerful Lady:

   To this province of the River Plate, with Don Pedro de Mendoza being the first governor thereof, there came certain women, of whom my destiny willed it that I should be one, and as the fleet arrived at the port of Buenos Aires with fifteen hundred men and they were in need of food, the starvation was so great that after three months a thousand of them died. So great was the famine that not even in Jerusalem could it have been worse, nor can it be compared to any other. The men became so weak that all the work fell on the poor women: from washing their clothes to caring for the sick, making them eat the little they had, cleaning them, standing guard, tending the watch-fires, arming the crossbows when sometimes there were Indian attacks and even firing the culverins; we would sound the alarm to the soldiers with loud voices, we drilled them and put them in order, for at that time we women could get by with less food and had not fallen into such a state of weakness as the men. Your Highness will understand that had it not been for the care and concern we had for them, all of them would have been finished, and were it not for the honor of the men, I might truly write a great deal more and offer the [men] as witnesses. I am sure they will write this report to Your Highness in greater detail, and for that reason I will desist.

   When this terrible time was over the few who remained alive determined to go upriver in two brigantines, as weak as they were and with winter about to begin. And the exhausted women cared for them and watched over them and cooked their food, lugging firewood onto the ships on their backs, and encouraging them with manly words not to let themselves die, that soon they would get to lands where there would be food, and carrying them aboard the brigantines on their backs with as much love as if they had been their own children. And when we came to a tribe of Indians called Timbues, lords of good places to fish, again we served the men by thinking up different ways of preparing the fish so that it would not disgust them, for they had to eat it without bread and were very feeble.

After that they decided to go up the Paraná River in search of food, on which journey the unfortunate women underwent such hardships that God determined that they should survive miraculously because He saw that the men's lives were in their hands, for the women took all the labors on board so to heart that one would feel affronted if she did less than another, so they all worked at handling the sails and steering the ship, taking soundings at the bow and taking over the oar from a soldier unable to row, and bailing the ship and encouraging the soldiers not to lose heart; this was men's work, and in truth the women were not rewarded for it, nor did it out of obligation, but only out of love. So they got to this city of Asunción which, although now it produces a great deal of food, was then very much in need of it, and thus it was necessary for the women to set to work again, clearing the land with their own hands, digging, weeding, sowing, and harvesting the food with no help from anyone until the soldiers had recovered from their weakness and began to govern the land and acquire Indian men and women as their servants, until the land came to be in the state it is now.

I have wanted to write and bring this to Your Highness's attention, to let you know the ingratitude that has been shown me in this country, because by now the greater part of it has been granted to those who reside here, the old colonists as well as the new, without any acknowledgment whatsoever of me and of my work, and I was left out, not having been given an Indian or any other kind of reward. I would dearly love to be free to go and appear before Your Highness, and tell you about the many services I have rendered His Majesty and the injuries now being done to me, but this is not in my power because I am married to a gentleman of Seville named Pedro d'Esquivel, whose services to His Majesty have caused mine to be quite forgotten, and they should be told again, because thrice I have saved his life when he had a knife at his throat, as Your Highness over there must know. And so I beg you to order that my repartimiento be given me in perpetuity and that in appreciation of my services my husband be assigned a position worthy of his person, as he for his services also merits this. May Our Lord God increase your royal life and state for many years. From this city of Asunción and on July 2, 1556.

> Your Highness's servant who kisses your royal hands
> Doña Ysabel de Guevara.

[Seal] Envelope— *To the very high and very powerful lady the Princess Doña Juana, Governor of the kingdoms of Spain, etc. — At her Council of the Indies*

Notes

1. It is interesting to see how the person who classified this document misread her central message: Doña Isabel's request is principally for herself, not so much for her husband.

Catalina de Erauso

Catalina de Erauso from The Nun Ensign. *James Fitzmaurice-Kelly (London: T Fisher Unwin, 1907).*

*T*he scandalous story of Catalina de Erauso, a transvestite with marked homoerotic tendencies, known in her day as the "Ensign Nun," has shock value even today. She was born in 1592 into a prominent family in the city of San Sebastián, in the Basque country in northern Spain. As a child Catalina was placed in a convent where her aunt was abbess, and was fully expected to take the veil; instead, she fled her convent when a teenager (she was a novice at the time), dressed as a boy, and lived a wandering life in Spain for about three years. She then embarked for the New World and joined the throngs of Spaniards looking for a way to make their fortunes. She lived as a man for more than twenty years, as merchant's apprentice, soldier, muleteer, constantly switching employers, clothes, jobs, names, and countries. She seduced women, brawled, cheated, stole, gambled, fought in major battles against the fierce Araucanian Indians in Chile, and killed her own brother in a duel. In Peru Catalina finally met a saintly bishop who showed her great kindness, and to him she confessed her true gender and identity, thus becoming instantly notorious. The bishop insisted that she return to the religious life until it could be proven that she indeed had not taken her final vows; while she waited for this information she lived in convents in Peru for about three years, once again wearing the habit she had discarded so many years earlier. When she returned to Spain, she appeared before King Philip IV, who was extremely curious to meet her. The king not only did not punish her, but gave her money, a land grant, and permission to continue dressing as a man. As the pope wanted to see her as well, Catalina subsequently went to Rome, where His Holiness, too, granted her permission to retain her male attire. In 1630 she returned to America and lived out her life as Antonio de Erauso, a teamster who, like many of his fellow Basques, transported the New World's goods by mule train. She died in Mexico in about 1650.

Catalina was a legend in her own time, and her story took many forms. She was so notorious on her return to Spain that at least one play, *La monja alférez* (The Ensign Nun), was written about her and performed on the Madrid stage—not after her death, but in 1626, the very year she was on her way to see the pope. If anything more of note happened to her, the playwright, Juan Pérez de Montalbán, promised a sequel. Catalina's portrait was painted twice, once by Francisco Pacheco, the father-in-law of Diego Velázquez. Her story—albeit somewhat sanitized—was incorporated into the colonial history of Chile (Merrim 190) and circulated in three versions on broadsheets in Mexico. Catalina purportedly wrote her own autobiography—or dictated it to someone—when she was in Seville, waiting to return to the New World, but the original manuscript has been lost.[1]

Although Catalina continued to exist in the legends of Mexico and Chile, not to mention her own Basque country, her autobiography had never been published. A fellow Basque, Joaquín María Ferrer, obtained a version of the manuscript in the early nineteenth century and, after some careful archival research, published it in Paris in 1829. It was an immediate sensation and was translated into German and French the following year. The first English translation was done by James Fitzmaurice-Kelly in 1908, but has long been out of print; another translation was published in 1996. Two films have been made about the life of the Ensign Nun: a Mexican one in 1940, starring María Félix in the title role, and a Basque one, made in Spain.[2] There is no doubt that Catalina de Erauso's story has continued to exert a powerful appeal.

Social and literary historians, especially those working on matters of sexuality and gender roles in early modern Europe, have long been aware of the story of Catalina de Erauso; especially good studies on this topic are those by Stephanie Merrim (1993) and Mary Elizabeth Perry (1990). In Catalina's day, and indeed in her own family, "the men served the king; the women entered religion" (Fitzmaurice-Kelly xvii). Four of the Erauso brothers went to the New World; three sisters became nuns, and only one married (Stepto xxvii). Catalina straddled these gender roles in a way that was both peculiar and successful. Perry underscores her primary desire to live a man's free and adventurous existence: "Catalina, in fact, refused feminization and embraced only masculine qualities. . . . Aware of the restrictions that gender imposed on her life, she did not try to change the inequity between the sexes. Instead, she chose to change herself, to deny her body, to repudiate the convent, habit, and submission expected of her as a woman, and to construct for herself a male persona who would completely obliterate her identity as a woman" (134). She was not punished for these transgressions—indeed she was rewarded—because she knew how to present her case: on the one hand, once her identity as a woman was revealed to the bishop, she proved that she was still a virgin: on the other, she presented herself before king and pope as exemplary for having renounced her femininity and aspired to become something superior, a man (Perry 134–35; Merrim 180, 188).

Catalina's autobiography is a problematic document for many reasons. There are many discrepancies with respect to the dates mentioned within it, including the date of her birth, which she gives as 1585 while her baptismal certificate is dated 1592, and we know that Catholic children are routinely baptized as soon after birth as possible. Then there is the question of authorship. Most trained readers immediately notice a familiar "literary" quality in her text. As Fitzmaurice-Kelly noted, "The dividing line between the personal narrative and certain specimens of picaresque romance is faint and shifting" (xxxix). Merrim feels that there are essentially three positions one can take on this issue: (a) Catalina actually wrote the entire document herself; (b) she dictated it to a trained author, who may have given it literary form; or (c) a later author changed the original version or inserted material of his own (196). This puzzle has not been resolved.

While the autobiography is certainly full of adventure and stirring action, a modern reader may long for some sort of introspection or psychological explanation in the narration. This is conspicuously absent, yet Catalina's tale keeps us in suspense because of "the constant risk that her 'secret' will be discovered" (Garber xii). In terms of gender, the narrative voice in Spanish is particularly distinctive, given the shifting masculine and feminine adjectives Erauso uses with respect to herself.[3] Social historians such as Rudolf Dekker and Lotte van de Pol, Diane Dugaw, and Perry have all called attention to the importance of

Erauso's story as it pertains to gender roles prevalent in her time. Although the Bible specifically forbade cross-dressing (Deut. 22.5), in sixteenth- and seventeenth-century Europe women who dressed as men were not infrequent, both in literature and in real life. What makes Erauso's case unique, however, is the bravado and skill with which she presents her story, how, in modern terms, she "markets" herself before the world. As Merrim so perceptively observed, she has "a keen awareness of the worth of a singular and prodigious tale" (192) in an age — much like ours today — in which the bizarre and the peculiar were appreciated and applauded.

Notes

1. This would have been sometime between 1626, when she left Rome, and 1630, when Erauso reembarked for the Americas.

The whole convoluted story of the manuscript is too complex and long to be told in its entirety here. Merrim (179–80) gives a concise summary of its vicissitudes; a complete account is in Rima de Vallbona's edition of *Vida i sucesos de la Monja Alférez escrita por ella misma*.

2. Adrienne Martin, "Catalina de Erauso: The Undressing of a Golden Age Transvestite," lecture at Mt. Holyoke College, South Hadley, MA, April 9, 1996.

To cast the sensuously beautiful María Félix in the title role was taking considerable visual license with the protagonist: contemporaries who knew her described Catalina as tall, of strong build, neither handsome nor ugly, a little stooped, with some facial hair, and the general appearance of a eunuch (Fitzmaurice-Kelly xxii–xxiii).

3. Critics have called attention to the fact that Basque, Catalina's native language, has no grammatical gender (Merrim 183), and thus she may have been unsure when using gender-inflected adjectives in Spanish. Ferrer's version (which I have used in this anthology) differs from Vallbona's transcription of the manuscript with respect to the gendered adjectives (Merrim 203 n. 7).

Vida i sucesos de la monja alférez

CAPÍTULO I

Su patria, padres, nacimiento, educación, fuga y correrías por varias partes de España.

Nací yo, doña Catalina de Erauso, en la villa de San Sebastián, de Guipúzcoa, en el año de 1585, hija del capitán don Miguel de Erauso y de doña María Pérez de Galarraga y Arce, naturales y vecinos de aquella villa. Criáronme mis padres en su casa, con otros mis hermanos, hasta tener cuatro años. En 1589 me entraron en el convento de San Sebastián el Antiguo, de dicha villa, que es de monjas dominicas, con mi tía doña Ursula de Unzá y Sarasti, prima hermana de mi madre y priora de aquel convento, en donde me crié hasta tener quince años, en que se trató de mi profesión.

Estando en el año de noviciado, ya cerca del fin, me ocurrió una reyerta con una monja profesa llamada doña Catalina de Aliri, que, siendo viuda, entró y profesó. Era ella robusta y yo muchacha; me maltrató de mano y yo lo sentí. A la noche del 18 de marzo de 1600, víspera de San José, levantóse el convento a media noche a maitines. Entré en el coro y hallé allí arrodillada a mi tía, la cual me llamó, y dándome la llave de su celda, me mandó traerle el breviario. Yo fuí por él. Abrí y lo tomé, y viendo en un clavo colgadas las llaves del convento, dejéme la celda abierta y volvíle a mi tía su llave y breviario. Estando ya las monjas en el coro y comenzados los maitines con solemnidad, a la primera lección llegué a mi tía y le pedí licencia, porque estaba mala. Mi tía, tocándome con la mano en la cabeza, me dijo: "Anda, acuéstate." Salí del coro, tomé una luz y fuíme a la celda de mi tía; tomé allí unas tijeras, hilo y una aguja; tomé unos reales de a ocho que allí estaban, y tomé las llaves del convento y me salí. Fuí abriendo puertas y emparejándolas, y en la última dejé mi escapulario y me salí a la calle, que nunca había visto, sin saber por dónde echar ni adónde ir. Tiré no sé por dónde, y fuí a dar en un castañar que está fuera y cerca de la espalda del convento. Allí acogíme y estuve tres días trazando, acomodando y cortando de vestir. Híceme, de una basquiña de paño azul con que me hallaba, unos calzones, y de un faldellín verde de perpetuán que traía debajo, una ropilla y polainas: el hábito me lo dejé por allí, por no saber qué hacer con él. Cortéme el pelo, que tiré, y a la tercera noche, deseando alejarme, partí no sé por dónde, calando caminos y pasando lugares, hasta venir a dar en Vitoria, que dista de San Sebastián cerca de veinte leguas, a pie, cansada y sin haber comido más que hierbas que topaba por el camino.

Entré en Vitoria sin saber adónde acogerme. A los pocos días encontré al doctor don Francisco de Cerralta, catedrático de allí, el cual me recibió fácilmente, sin conocerme, y me vistió. Era casado con una prima hermana de mi madre, según luego entendí; pero no me dí a conocer. Estuve con él cosa de tres meses, en los cuales, viéndome él leer bien el latín, se me inclinó más y me quiso dar estudio; pero como yo rehusara, me porfió y me instaba hasta ponerme las manos. Yo, con esto, determiné dejarle, e hícelo así. Cogíle unos cuartos, y concertándome en doce reales con un arriero que partía para Valladolid, que dista cuarenta y cinco leguas, partí con él.

Entrado en Valladolid, donde estaba entonces la Corte, me acomodé en breve por paje de don Juan de Idiáquez, secretario del rey, el cual me vistió luego bien. Allí me llamé Francisco Loyola y estuve bienhallado siete meses. Al cabo de ellos, estando una noche a la puerta con otro paje compañero, llegó mi padre, preguntándonos si estaba en casa el señor don Juan.

Respondió mi compañero que sí. Dijo mi padre que le avisase que estaba él allí, y subió el paje, quedándome yo con mi padre, sin hablarnos palabra ni él conocerme. Volvió el paje, diciendo que subiese, y subió, yendo yo tras de él. Salió don Juan a la escalera, y, abrazándole, dijo: "¡Señor capitán, que buena venida es ésta!" Mi padre habló de modo que él conoció que traía disgusto, y despidiendo una visita con que estaba, volvió y sentáronse, preguntándole qué había de nuevo. Mi padre dijo cómo se le había ido del convento aquella muchacha, y esto le traía por los contornos en su busca. . . .

Yo, que oí la conversación y sentimiento de mi padre, salíme atrás y fuíme a mi aposento. Cogí mi ropa y salí, llevándome cosa de ocho doblones con que me hallaba, y fuíme a un mesón, donde dormí aquella noche y donde entendí a un arriero que partía por la mañana a Bilbao. Ajustéme con él, y partimos a otro día, sin saberme yo qué hacer ni adónde ir, sino dejarme llevar del viento como una pluma. . . .

De allí, luego que salí, me pasé a Estella, de Navarra, que distará veinte leguas a lo que me parece. Entré en Estella, donde me acomodé por paje de don Carlos de Arellano, del hábito de Santiago,[1] en cuya casa y servicio estuve dos años, bien tratado y bien vestido. Pasado este tiempo, sin más causa que mi gusto, dejé aquella comodidad y me pasé a San Sebastián, mi patria, diez leguas distante de allí, y donde me estuve, sin ser de nadie conocido, bien vestido y galán. Y un día oí misa en mi convento, la cual misa oyó también mi madre, y vide que me miraba y no me conoció, y acabada la misa, unas monjas me llamaron al coro, y yo, no dándome por entendido, les hice muchas cortesías y me fuí. Era esto entrado ya el año de 1603.

Paséme de allí . . . a Sanlúcar. Hallé allí al capitán Miguel de Echarreta, natural de mi tierra, que lo era de un patache de galeones, de que era general don Luis Fernández de Córdoba, y de la armada, don Luis Fajardo, año 1603, que partía para la Punta de Araya. Senté plaza de grumete en un galeón del capitán Esteban Eguiño, tío mío, primo hermano de mi madre, que vive hoy en San Sebastián, y embarqué y partimos de Sanlúcar, Lunes Santo, año de 1603.

CAPÍTULO II

Parte de Sanlúcar para Punta Araya, Cartagena, Nombre de Dios y Panamá.

Pasé algunos trabajos en el camino por ser nuevo en el oficio. Inclinóseme mi tío sin conocerme, y haciéndome agasajos, oído de dónde era y el nombre supuesto de mis padres, que yo di, tuve en él gran arrimo. Llegamos a Punta de Araya y hallamos allí una armadilla enemiga fortificada en tierra, y nuestra armada la echó. Arribamos finalmente a Cartagena de las Indias, y estuvimos allí ocho días.

Híceme borrar de la plaza de grumete y pasé a servir al dicho capitán Eguiño, mi tío. De allí pasamos a Nombre de Dios, donde estuvimos nueve días, muriéndosenos en ellos mucha gente, lo cual hizo dar mucha prisa a salir.

Estando ya embarcada la plata y aprestado todo para partir de vuelta a España, yo le hice un tiro cuantioso a mi tío, cogiéndole quinientos pesos. A las diez de la noche, cuando él estaba durmiendo, salí y dije a los guardas que me enviaba a tierra el capitán a un negocio. Como me conocían, dejáronme llanamente pasar, y salté a tierra; pero nunca más me vieron. De allí a una hora dispararon pieza de leva y zarparon hechos a la vela.

Levada ya la flota, me acomodé allí con el capitán Juan de Ibarra, factor de las cajas de Panamá, que hoy vive. De allí a cuatro o seis días nos partimos para Panamá, donde él residía y donde estuve con él cosa de tres meses. Hacíame poca comodidad, que era escaso, y hube allí de gastar cuanto de mi tío había traído, hasta no quedarme ni un cuarto, con lo cual me despedí para buscar por otra parte mi remedio.

Haciéndome mi diligencia descubrí allí a Juan de Urquiza, mercader de Trujillo, y acomodéme con él, y con él me fué muy bien, y estuvimos en Panamá tres meses.

CAPÍTULO III

De Panamá pasa con su amo Urquiza, mercader de Trujillo, al puerto de Paita y a la villa de Saña.

De Panamá partí con mi amo Juan de Urquiza, en una fragata, para el puerto de Paita, donde él tenía un gran cargamento. Llegando al puerto de Manta, nos cargó un tiempo tan fuerte que dimos al través, y los que supimos nadar, como yo, mi amo y otros, salimos a tierra: los demás perecieron. En el dicho puerto de Manta nos volvimos a embarcar en un galeón del rey que allí hallamos y costó dinero, y en él partimos y llegamos al puerto de Paita, donde halló mi amo toda su hacienda, como esperaba, cargada en una nao del capitán Alonso Cerrato, y dándome a mí orden de que toda, por sus números, la fuese remitiendo allá, partió.

Yo puse luego por obra lo que me mandó, y fuí descargando la hacienda por sus números, y por ellos fuíla remitiendo. Mi amo, en Saña, que dista de Paita unas sesenta leguas, fué recibiéndola, y a lo último, con las últimas cargas, yo partí de Paita y llegué a Saña.

Llegado a Saña, me recibió mi amo con gran cariño, mostrándose contento de lo bien que lo había hecho, y con todo buen trato, hízome luego al punto dos vestidos muy buenos, uno negro y otro de color. Púsome en una tienda suya, entregándome por géneros y por cuenta mucha hacienda, que importó más de ciento treinta mil pesos, poniéndome por escrito en un libro los precios a cómo había de vender cada cosa. Dejóme dos esclavos que me sirviesen y una negra que me guisase, señalándome tres pesos para el gasto de cada día, y hecho esto, cargó él con la demás hacienda y se fué con ella a Trujillo, distante de allí treinta y dos leguas.

También me dejó escrito y advertido en el dicho libro las personas a quienes podía fiar la hacienda que pidiesen y quisiesen llevar, por ser de su satisfacción y seguras, pero con cuenta y razón y asentando cada partida en el libro. Y especialmente me advirtió esto, para en cuanto a mi señora doña Beatriz de Cárdenas, persona de toda su satisfacción y obligación. Fuése él a Trujillo y yo me quedé en Saña con mi tienda, vendiendo conforme a la pauta que él me dejó, y cobrando y asentando en mi libro, con día, mes, y año, género, varas, nombre de compradores y precios: de la misma suerte con lo fiado.

Comenzó mi señora doña Beatriz de Cárdenas a sacar ropas, prosiguió y fué sacando tan largamente, que yo llegué a dudar, y sin dárselo a ella a entender, se lo escribí todo por extenso al amo a Trujillo. Respondióme que estaba muy bien todo, y que en este particular de la señora, si toda la tienda entera me la pedía, se la podía entregar; con lo cual, y guardando yo esta carta, proseguí . . .

[Catalina de Erauso tiene más problemas con la justicia y tiene que dejar a este amo.]

CAPÍTULO V

Parte de Trujillo a Lima.

Partido de Trujillo a Lima, y andadas más de ochenta leguas, entré en la ciudad de Lima, cabeza del opulento reino del Perú . . .

Di mi carta a Diego de Solarte, mercader muy rico, que es ahora cónsul mayor de Lima, y a quien me remitió Juan de Urquiza, el cual me recibió luego en su casa con mucho agrado y afabilidad, y a pocos días me entregó su tienda, señalándome seiscientos pesos al año, y allí lo fuí haciendo muy a su agrado y contento.

Al cabo de nueve meses me dijo que buscase mi vida en otra parte, y fué la causa que tenía en casa dos doncellas, hermanas de su mujer, con las cuales, y sobre todo con una que más se me inclinó, solía yo jugar y triscar. Y un día, estando en el estrado peinándome acostado en sus faldas y andándole en las piernas, llegó acaso a una reja, por donde nos vió y oyó a ella que me decía que fuese al Potosí[2] y buscase dineros y nos casaríamos. Retiróse, y de allí a poco me llamó, me pidió y tomó cuentas, y despidióme y me fuí.

Hallábame desacomodado y muy remoto de favor. Estábanse allí entonces levantando seis compañías para Chile; yo me llegué a una y senté plaza de soldado, y recibí luego doscientos ochenta pesos, que me dieron de sueldo. Mi amo, Diego de Lasarte, que lo supo, lo sintió mucho, que parece que no lo decía por tanto. Ofrecióme hacer diligencias con los oficiales para que me borrasen de la plaza y volver el dinero que recibí; pero no vine en ello, diciendo que era mi inclinación andar y ver mundo. En fin, asentada la plaza en la compañía del capitán Gonzalo Rodríguez, partí de Lima en tropa de mil seiscientos hombres, de que iba por maestro de campo Diego Bravo de Sarabia, para la ciudad de la Concepción, que dista de Lima quinientas cuarenta leguas.

CAPÍTULO VI

Llega a la Concepción de Chile y halla allí a su hermano. Pasa a Paicabí, y hallándose en la batalla de Valdivia, gana una bandera. Vuelve a la Concepción, mata a dos y a su propio hermano.

Llegamos al puerto de la Concepción en veinte días que se tardó en el camino. Es ciudad razonable, con título de *noble y leal*, y tiene obispo. Fuimos bien recibidos por la falta de gente que había en Chile. Llegó luego orden del gobernador, Alonso de Ribera, para desembarcarnos, y trájola su secretario, el capitán Miguel de Erauso. Luego que oí su nombre me alegré y vi que era mi hermano, porque aunque no le conocía ni había visto porque partió de San Sebastián para estas partes siendo yo de dos años, tenía noticias de él, si no de su residencia. Tomó la lista de la gente, fué pasando y preguntando a cada uno su nombre y patria, y llegando a mí y oyendo mi nombre y patria, soltó la pluma y me abrazó y fué haciendo preguntas por su padre, y su madre, y hermanos, y por su querida Catalina, la monja. Yo fuí a todo respondiendo como podía, sin descubrirme ni caer él en ello. Fué prosiguiendo la lista, y en acabando me llevó a comer a su casa y me senté a comer. Díjome que aquel presidio que yo llevaba de Paicabí era de mala pasadía de soldados; que él hablaría al gobernador para que me mudase de plaza. En comiendo subió a ver al gobernador, llevándome consigo. Dióle cuenta de la gente que venía y pidió de merced que mudase a su compañía a un mancebito que venía allí de su tierra, que no había visto otro de allá desde que salió. Mandóme entrar el gobernador, y en viéndome, no sé por qué, dijo que no me podía mudar. Mi hermano lo sintió y salióse; pero de allí a un rato llamó a mi hermano el gobernador, y díjole que fuese como pedía.

Así, yéndose las compañías, quedé yo con mi hermano por su soldado, comiendo a su mesa casi tres años sin haber dado en ello. Fuí con él algunas veces a casa de una dama que allí tenía, y de ahí, algunas otras veces, me fuí sin él, y alcanzó a saberlo y concibió mal y díjome que allí no entrase. Acechóme y me cogió otra vez, y esperándome, al salir me embistió a cintarazos y me hirió en una mano. Fué forzoso defenderme, y al ruido acudió el capitán Francisco de Aillón, y metió paz; pero yo me hube de entrar en San Francisco por temor al gobernador, que era fuerte y lo estuvo en esto, aunque mi hermano intercedió, hasta que vino a desterrarme a Paicabí, y sin remedio hube de irme, y estuve allí tres años.

Hube de salir a Paicabí y pasar allí algunos trabajos por tres años, habiendo antes vivido alegremente. Estábamos siempre con las armas en la mano, por la gran invasión de los indios que allí hay, hasta que vino finalmente el gobernador Alonso de Sarabia con todas las compañías de Chile. Juntámonos otros cuantos con él y alojámonos en los llanos de Valdivia, en campaña rasa, cinco mil hombres, con harta incomodidad. Tomaron y asaltaron los indios la dicha Valdivia. Salimos a ellos, y batallamos tres o cuatro veces, maltratándolos siempre y destrozándolos; pero llegándoles la vez última socorro, nos fué mal y nos mataron mucha gente, y capitanes, y a mi alférez, y se llevaron la bandera. Viéndola llevar, partimos tras ella yo y dos soldados de a caballo, por medio de gran multitud, atropellando y matando y recibiendo daño. En breve cayó muerto uno de los tres. Proseguimos los dos y llegamos hasta la bandera; pero cayó de un bote de lanza mi compañero. Yo, con un mal golpe en una pierna, maté al cacique[3] que la llevaba, se la quité y apreté con mi caballo, atropellando, matando e hiriendo a infinidad; pero malherido y pasado de tres flechas y de una lanza en el hombro izquierdo, que sentía mucho; en fin, llegué a mucha gente y caí luego del caballo. Acudiéronme algunos, y entre ellos mi hermano, a quien no había visto y me fué de consuelo. Curáronme y quedamos allí alojados nueve meses. Al cabo de ellos, mi hermano me sacó del gobernador la bandera que yo gané, y quedé alférez de la compañía de Alonso Moreno, la cual poco después se dió al capitán Gonzalo Rodríguez, el primer capitán que yo conocí y holgué mucho. . . .

A este tiempo, y entre otros, vino un día don Juan de Silva, mi amigo, alférez vivo, y me dijo que había tenido unas palabras con don Francisco de Rojas, del hábito de Santiago, y lo había desafiado para aquella noche, a las once, llevando cada uno a un amigo, y que él no tenía otro para eso sino a mí. Yo quedé un poco suspenso, recelando si habría allí forjada alguna treta para prenderme. El, que lo advirtió, me dijo: "Si no os parece, no sea; yo me iré solo, que a otro no he de fiar mi lado." Yo me dije que en qué reparaba, y acepté.

En dando la oración, salí del convento y me fuí a su casa. Cenamos y parlamos hasta las diez, y en oyéndolas tomamos las espadas y capas, y salimos al puesto señalado. Era la obscuridad tan suma que no nos veíamos las manos; y advirtiéndolo yo, hice con mi amigo, para no desconocernos en lo que se pudiera ofrecer, que nos pusiéramos cada uno en el brazo atado su lenzuelo.

Llegaron los dos, y dijo el uno, conocido en la voz por don Francisco de Rojas: "¿Don Juan de Silva?" Don Juan respondió: "¡Aquí estoy!" Metieron ambos mano a las espadas y se embistieron, mientras estábamos parados el otro y yo. Fueron bregando, y a poco rato sentí que se sintió mi amigo la punta que le había entrado. Púseme luego a su lado, y el otro al lado de don Francisco. Tiramos dos a dos, y a breve rato cayeron don Francisco y don Juan; yo y mi contrario proseguimos batallando, y entréle yo una punta, según después pareció, por bajo de la tetilla izquierda, pasándole, según sentí, coleto de dos antes, y cayó. "¡Ah, traidor—dijo—, que me has muerto!" Yo quise reconocer el habla de quien yo no conocía; preguntéle quién era, y dijo: "El capitán Miguel de Erauso." Yo quedé atónito. Pedía a voces confesión, y pedíanla los otros. Fuí corriendo a San Francisco, y envié dos religiosos, que los confesaron. Dos expiraron luego; a mi hermano lo llevaron a casa del gobernador, de quien era secretario de guerra. Acudieron con médico y cirujano a la curación, e hicieron cuanto alcanzaron; luego hízose lo judicial, preguntándole el nombre del homicida; y como él clamaba por un poco de vino y el doctor Robledo se lo negaba, diciendo que no convenía, él porfió, el doctor negó y él dijo: "Más cruel anda usted conmigo que el alférez Díaz"; y de ahí a un rato expiró. . . . Muerto el capitán Miguel de Erauso, lo enterraron en el dicho convento de San Francisco, viéndolo yo desde el coro, ¡sabe Dios con qué dolor! . . .

CAPÍTULO XX

Entra en Guamanga, y lo que allí le sucedió hasta descubrirse al señor obispo.

Entré en Guamanga y fuíme a una posada. . . . Salí a ver la ciudad, que parecíame bien, de buenos edificios: los mejores que vide en el Perú. Vi tres conventos, de franciscanos, mercedarios y dominicos; uno de monjas y un hospital; muchísimos vecinos indios y muchos españoles; bello temple de tierra, fundada en un llano, sin frío ni calor; de grandes cosechas de trigo, vino, frutas y semillas, buena iglesia, con tres dignidades y dos canónigos y un santo obispo, fraile agustino, don fray Agustín de Carvajal, que fué mi remedio; aunque faltó, muriendo de repente el año veinte, y decían que lo había sido allí desde el año doce.

Estuve allí unos días, y quiso mi desgracia que me entrara unas veces en una casa de juego, donde estando un día entró el corregidor, don Baltasar de Quiñones, y mirándome y desconociéndome, me preguntó de dónde era. Dije que vizcaíno. Dijo: "¿De dónde viene ahora?" Dije: "Del Cuzco." Suspendióse un poco mirándome, y dijo: "Sea preso." Dije: "De buena gana"; y saqué la espada, retirándome a la puerta. El dió voces pidiendo favor al rey, y hallé en la puerta tal resistencia que no pude salir. Saqué una pistola de tres bocas, y salí y desaparecíme, entrando en casa de un amigo que me había hallado. Partió el corregidor y embargóme la mula y no sé qué cosillas que tenía en la posada. Estúveme allí unos días, habiendo descubierto que aquel amigo era vizcaíno. Entretanto no sonaba ruido del caso ni sentía que la justicia tratase de ello; pero todavía nos pareció ser forzoso mudar tierra, pues tenía allí lo mismo que en otra parte. Resuelto a ello, salí un día a boca de noche, y a breve rato quiere mi desgracia que tope con dos alguaciles. Pregúntanme: "¿Qué gente?" Respondo: "Amigos." Pídenme el nombre, y digo, que no debí decir: "El diablo." Vanme a echar mano, y saco la espada, armándose gran ruido. Ellos dan voces diciendo: "¡Favor a la justicia!," y acude gente. Sale el corregidor, que estaba en casa del obispo; avánzanme más ministros, hállome afligido, disparo una pistola y derribo a uno. Crece más el empeño, y hállome al lado aquel vizcaíno mi amigo y otros paisanos con él. Daba voces el corregidor que me matasen; sonaron muchos traquidos de ambas partes, hasta que salió el obispo con cuatro hachas y entróse por medio, encaminándolo hacia mí su secretario, Juan Bautista de Arteaga. Llegó y me dijo: "Señor alférez, déme las armas." Dije: Señor, hay aquí muchos contrarios." Dijo: "Démelas, que seguro está conmigo, y le doy palabra de sacarle a salvo, anuque me cueste cuanto soy." Dije: "Señor ilustrísimo, en estando en la iglesia[4] besaré los pies a V. S. [Vuestra Señoría] ilustrísima." En esto me acometen cuatro esclavos del corregidor, y me aprietan, tirándome ferozmente, sin respeto a la presencia de su ilustrísima; de modo que, defendiéndome, hube de entrar la mano y derribar a uno. Acudióme el secretario del señor obispo con espada y broquel, con otros de la familia, dando muchas voces, ponderando el desacato delante de su ilustrísima, y cesó algo la puja. Asióme su ilustrísima por el brazo, quitóme las armas, y poniéndome a su lado, me llevó consigo y entróme en su casa. Hízome luego curar una pequeña herida que llevaba, y mandóme dar de cenar y recoger, cerrándome con llave, que se llevó. Vino luego el corregidor, y tuvo su ilustrísima larga conversación y alteraciones con él sobre esto, lo cual después entendí.

A la mañana, como a las diez, su ilustrísima me hizo llevar a su presencia, y me preguntó quién era y de dónde, hijo de quién, y todo el curso de mi vida y causas y caminos por donde vine a parar allí. Y fuí en esto desmenuzando tanto, mezclando buenos consejos y los riesgos de la vida y espantos de la muerte y contingencias de ella, y el asombro de la otra si no me cogía bien apercibido, procurándome sosegar, y reducir, y arrodillarme a Dios, que yo me puse tamañito. Y viéndolo tan santo varón, pareciéndome estar ya en la presencia de Dios, descúbrome y dígole: "Señor, todo esto que he referido a V. S. ilustrísima no es así. La verdad es ésta: Que soy mujer, que nací en tal parte, hija de Fulano y Zutana; que me entraron de tal edad en tal convento, con Fulana mi Tía; que allí me crié; que tomé el hábito y tuve noviciado; que estando para profesar, por tal ocasión me salí; que me fuí a tal parte, me desnudé, me vestí, me corté el cabello, partí allí y acullá; me embarqué, aporté, trajiné, maté, herí, maleé, correteé, hasta venir a parar en lo presente, y a los pies de su señoría ilustrísima."

El santo señor, entretanto que esta relación duró, que fué hasta la una, se estuvo suspenso, sin hablar, ni pestañear, escuchándome, y después que acabé se quedó también sin hablar, llorando a lágrima viva. Después me envió a descansar y a comer. Tocó una campanilla, hizo venir a un capellán anciano, y envióme a su oratorio, donde me pusieron la mesa y un trasportín, y me encerraron; yo me acosté y me dormí. A la tarde, como a las cuatro, me volvió a llamar el señor obispo, y me habló con gran bondad de espíritu, conduciéndome a dar gracias a Dios por la merced usada conmigo, dándome a ver el camino perdido que llevaba derecho a las penas eternas. Exhortóme a recorrer mi vida y hacer una buena confesión, pues ya por lo más la tenía hecha y me sería fácil; después, Dios ayudaría para que viésemos lo que se debía hacer. Y en esto y en cosas ocurrentes se acabó la tarde. Retiréme, diéronme bien de comer, y me acosté.

A la mañana siguiente dijo misa el señor obispo, que yo oí, y después dió gracias. Retiróse a un desayuno, y me llevó consigo. Fué moviendo y siguiendo su discurso, y vino a decirme que tenía éste por el caso más notable, en este género, que había oído en su vida, y re-mató diciendo: "En fin, ¿esto es así?" Dije: "Sí, señor." Replicó: "No se espante que su rareza inquiete a la credulidad." "Señor" —dije—, "es así, y si quiere salir de dudas V. S. ilustrísima por experiencia de matronas, yo me allano." Dijo: "Conténtame oírlo, y vengo en ello." Y retiréme por ser la hora del despacho. A medio día comí, después reposé un rato, y a la tarde, como a las cuatro, entraron dos matronas y me miraron y se satisficieron, y declararon después ante el obispo, con juramento, haberme visto y reconocido cuanto fué menester para certificarse, y haberme hallado virgen intacta, como el día en que nací. Su ilustrísima se enterneció, despidió a las comadres y me hizo comparecer, y delante del capellán, que vino conmigo, me abrazó enternecido, en pie, y me dijo: "Hija, ahora creo sin duda lo que me dijisteis, y creeré en adelante cuanto me dijereis; os venero como una de las personas notables de este mundo, y os prometo asistiros en cuanto pueda y cuidar de vuestra conveniencia y del servicio de Dios."

Mandóme poner cuarto decente, y estuve en él con comodidad y ajustando mi confesión, la cual hice en cuanto pude, y después, su ilustrísima me dió la comunión. Parece que el caso se divulgó, y era inmenso el concurso que allí acudió, sin poder excusar la entrada a personajes, por más que yo lo sentía y su ilustrísima también.

En fin, pasados seis días, acordó su ilustrísima entrarme en el convento de monjas de Santa Clara de Guamanga, que allí de religiosas no hay otro, [y] púsome el hábito. Salió su ilustrísima de casa, llevándome a su lado, con un concurso tan grande, que no hubo de quedar persona alguna en la ciudad que no viniese; de suerte que se tardó mucho en llegar allá. Llegamos finalmente a la portería, porque a la iglesia, donde pensaba su ilustrísima entrar antes, no fué posible; entendido así, se había llenado. Estaba allí todo el convento, con velas encendidas, y otorgóse allí, por la abadesa y ancianas, una escritura en que prometía el convento volverme a entregar a su ilustríssima o prelado sucesor cada vez que me pidiesen. Abrazóme su ilustrísima, echóme su bendición, y entré. Lleváronme al coro en procesión e hice oración allí. Besé la mano a la señora abadesa, fuí abrazando y fuéronme abrazando las monjas, y lleváronme a un locutorio, donde su ilustrísima me estaba esperando. Allí me dió buenos consejos y exhortó a ser buena cristiana y dar gracias a Dios Nuestro Señor y frecuentar los sacramentos, ofreciéndose su ilustrísima a venir a ello, como vino muchas veces, y ofrecióme largamente todo cuanto hubiese menester. Corrió la noticia de este suceso por todas partes, y los que antes me vieron y los que antes y después supieron mis cosas en todas las Indias, se maravillaron. Dentro de cinco meses, año 1620, repentinamente, se quedó muerto mi santo obispo, que me hizo gran falta.

[Catalina de Erauso se va a Lima y pasa los dos años siguientes en un convento allí hasta que llegan las noticias de España que nunca había sido monja profesa; por eso puede salir del convento y dejar su hábito monjil. Se va a España y se presenta ante el Rey Felipe IV, que le otorga una pensión de 800 escudos de por vida; le vuelve a ver en Barcelona, después de que la hayan robado en el camino, y el rey le vuelve a regalar dinero. Luego viaja a Italia para ver al papa.]

CAPÍTULO XXV

Parte de Barcelona a Génova, y de allí, a Roma.

. . . Partí de Génova a Roma. Besé el pie a la Santidad de Urbano VIII, y referíle en breve y lo mejor que supe mi vida y correrías, mi sexo y virginidad. Mostró Su Santidad extrañar tal cosa, y con afabilidad me concedió licencia para proseguir mi vida en hábito de hombre, encargándome la prosecución honesta en adelante y la abstinencia de ofender al prójimo, teniendo la *ulción* [venganza] de Dios sobre su mandamiento *non occides* [no mates]. Hízose el caso allí notorio, y fué notable el concurso de que me vi cercado: personajes, príncipes, obispos, cardenales. Dondequiera me hallé lugar abierto, de suerte que en mes y medio que estuve en Roma fué raro el día en que no fuese convidado y regalado de príncipes; y especialmente un viernes fuí convidado y regalado por unos caballeros, por orden particular y encargo del Senado romano, y me asentaron en un libro por ciudadano romano. El día de San Pedro, 29 de junio de 1626, me entraron en la capilla de San Pedro, donde vi los cardenales y las ceremonias que se acostumbran aquel día. Todos, o los más, me mostraron notable agrado y caricia y me hablaron muchos. A la tarde, hallándome en rueda con tres cardenales, me dijo uno de ellos, que fué el cardenal Magalón, que [yo] no tenía más falta que ser español, a lo cual le dije: "A mí me parece, señor, debajo de la corrección que se debe a vuestra señoría ilustrísima, que no tengo otra cosa buena."

CAPÍTULO XXVI

De Roma viene a Nápoles.

Pasado mes y medio que estuve en Roma, me partí de allí para Nápoles, el día 5 de julio de 1626. Embarcamos en Ripa.

En Nápoles, un día, paseándome en el muelle, reparé en las risotadas de dos damiselas que parlaban con dos mozos. Me miraban, y mirándolas, me dijo una: "Señora Catalina, ¿adónde se camina?" Respondí: "Señoras p . . . , a darles a ustedes cien pescozones y cien cuchilladas a quien las quiera defender." Callaron y se fueron de allí.

FIN

Notas

1. La orden de Santiago era una de las órdenes militares de más prestigio en España.

2. Potosí era una ciudad riquísima en el virreinato del Perú (hoy Bolivia) donde se descubrió una fabulosa mina de plata en 1545, la cual enriqueció a muchos hombres.

3. "Cacique" era la palabra indígena para "jefe" o "capitán."

4. Erauso aquí se refiere al derecho de santuario, bajo el cual las autoridades seculares no podían llevarse a los criminales y fugitivos de la justicia que se refugiaban en una iglesia.

Life and Adventures of the Ensign Nun

CHAPTER I

Her homeland, parents, birth, education, flight, and journeys throughout various parts of Spain.

I, Doña Catalina de Erauso, was born in the town of San Sebastián, in Guipúzcoa, in the year 1585, the daughter of Captain Don Miguel de Erauso and of Doña María Pérez de Galarraga y Arce, natives and residents of that town. My parents brought me up at home with my other siblings until I was four years old. In 1589 they put me in the convent of San Sebastián el Antiguo, in said town, which belongs to Dominican nuns, with my aunt Doña Ursula de Unzá y Sarasti, my mother's cousin and the abbess of that convent; there I was raised until I was fifteen, when the matter of my profession came up.

When I was almost at the end of my year of the novitiate, I had a quarrel with a professed nun named Doña Catalina de Aliri, who, being a widow, had professed and entered the convent. She was strong and I but a girl; she slapped me, and I resented it. On the night of March 18, 1600, the eve of St. Joseph, the convent arose at midnight for Matins. I went into the choir and found my aunt kneeling there; she called me over, gave me the key to her cell, and told me to bring her her prayer book. I went to get it. I unlocked [the cell] and took it, and, seeing all the keys to the convent hanging from a nail, I left the cell open and gave my aunt her key and the prayer book. The nuns were already in the choir and had solemnly begun Matins; at the first lesson I went up to my aunt and asked her permission to withdraw, as I was feeling ill. My aunt put her hand to my forehead and said, "Go lie down." I left the choir, took a lamp, and went to my aunt's cell; there I took a pair of scissors, thread, and a needle; I took some coins (*reales de a ocho*) that were lying there and took the convent keys and left. I went along opening doors and shutting them behind me, and at the final one left my scapulary and went out into the street, which I had never seen, with no idea which way to turn or where to go. I don't remember where I went, but I came on a stand of chestnut trees that was outside [of town] but close behind the convent. There I hid, and spent three days designing, fitting, and cutting out clothes. I made myself a pair of breeches from a blue cloth petticoat I was wearing, and from an underskirt of coarse green wool, a sleeved doublet and leggings; I left the habit there because I didn't know what to do with it. I cut off my hair, which I threw away, and on the third night, since I wanted to get away from there, I left for parts unknown, slogging over roads and skirting villages until I came to Vitoria, which is about twenty leagues from San Sebastián, on foot, weary and without having eaten anything but plants I found along the way.

I entered Vitoria with no idea where to stay. A few days later I met Dr. Don Francisco de Cerralta, a professor there, who, without knowing me, took me in with no difficulty and gave me some clothes. He was married to a cousin of my mother's, as I found out later, but I did not reveal who I was. I was with him for about three months, during which time, as he saw that I read Latin well, he liked me more and wanted to educate me, but when I refused he insisted and even laid hands on me. When that happened I made up my mind to leave him, and did so. I took some of his money, agreed to pay twelve *reales* to a muleteer who was leaving for Valladolid, forty-five leagues away, and departed with the latter.

When I got to Valladolid, where the Court was at that time, I soon got a position as a page to Don Juan de Idiáquez, the king's secretary, who clothed me well. There I called myself Francisco Loyola, and was very comfortable for seven months. At the end of that time, while I was standing in the doorway one evening with a fellow page, my father arrived and asked us if Señor Don Juan was at home.

My comrade said he was. My father said to let him know that he was there, and the page went upstairs while I stayed with my father; we said nothing to each other and he did not recognize me. The page came back and said that he should go upstairs, so up he went and I behind him. Don Juan came out on the staircase and, embracing him, said, "Señor Captain, what a welcome visit!" My father spoke in such a way that the Señor knew he was annoyed, so Don Juan sent away another visitor, then came back and they sat down. He asked what was the matter. My father told how that girl of his had left the convent, and the search for her had brought him to that region. . . .

I, when I heard my father's conversation and feelings, withdrew and went to my room. I took my clothes and left, taking with me some eight doubloons which I happened to have, and went to a tavern; I slept there that night, and heard a muleteer say that he was leaving for Bilbao in the morning. I came to terms with him and we left the next day; with no idea as to what to do or where to go, I simply let myself be borne by the wind like a feather. . . .

After I got out I went to Estella, in Navarre, which I think is about twenty leagues away. I reached Estella, where I became the page of Don Carlos de Arellano, who belonged to the order of Santiago,[1] in whose house and service I remained for two years, well treated and well attired. Afterward, for no other reason than my fancy, I left that comfortable position and went to my native San Sebastián, where I, a well-dressed dandy, spent some time without anyone recognizing me. One day I went to mass at my convent, the same service my mother attended, and saw that she looked at me without recognizing me; when mass was over, some nuns called me over to the choir, but I pretended not to understand, paid them many compliments and left. This was well into the year 1603.

From there I went to . . . Sanlúcar. There I found Captain Miguel de Echarreta, another Basque, who commanded a tender to the galleons under General Don Luis Fernández de Córdoba, part of Don Luis Fajardo's armada, which was sailing for Punta de Araya. I signed on as a cabin boy in Captain Esteban Eguiño's galleon—he was my uncle, my mother's cousin, and today lives in San Sebastián. I went aboard and we left Sanlúcar on Holy Monday in the year 1603.

CHAPTER II

She leaves Sanlúcar for Punta Araya, Cartagena, Nombre de Dios, and Panama.

As I was new to the job, I had some difficulties on the voyage. Without knowing who I was my uncle was kind to me, and thought very highly of me; when he heard where I was from, and my parents' fictitious name, I had in him a great protector. When we got to Punta Araya we came upon a small enemy force entrenched on the shore and our fleet drove it away. We finally reached Cartagena de las Indias, and were there eight days.

I had my name taken off the list as cabin boy, and went into the service of the said Captain Eguiño, my uncle. From there we went to Nombre de Dios, where we stayed for nine days; many of our men died, which made us leave there very quickly.

When the silver was already aboard and everything was ready for our return voyage to Spain, I played a major trick on my uncle, making off with five hundred of his pesos. At ten at night, when he was asleep, I went on deck and told the sentries that the captain was sending me ashore on an errand. As they knew me, they let me pass with no trouble and I jumped ashore, but they never saw me again. An hour later they fired the departure gun and weighed anchor, ready to sail.

When the fleet had left, I took employment with Captain Juan de Ibarra, the agent for the Panama treasury, who is still alive today. Four to six days later we left for Panama, where he lived and where I stayed with him for about three months. He did not treat me well, for he was miserly, and I had to spend all the money I had lifted from my uncle until I had not a penny left; thereupon I departed in order to look for better employment elsewhere.

When I looked around I found Juan de Urquiza there, a merchant from Trujillo, and reached an agreement with him; things went well for me with him, and we were in Panama three months.

CHAPTER III

From Panama she goes with her master Urquiza, a merchant from Trujillo, to the port of Paita and the town of Saña.

I sailed from Panama in a frigate with my master Juan de Urquiza, bound for the port of Paita, where he had a large cargo. When we got to the port of Manta the ship was hit broadside by a tremendous storm, and those who knew how to swim, like me, my master, and some others, made it ashore; the rest perished. In the said port of Manta we reembarked in one of the king's galleons we found there, for a handsome price; we sailed on this ship and got to the port of Paita, where, just as he expected, my master found all of his property loaded onto Captain Alonso Cerrato's vessel. Giving me instructions to dispatch all of it in numbered order, he left.

I immediately did as he had ordered, unloading the merchandise by number, and sending it along to him. My master, who was in Saña, some sixty leagues away, received it and at the end, along with the last shipments, I left Paita for Saña.

When I got to Saña, my master greeted me very affectionately, for he was very pleased with the good job I had done; right away he ordered two suits to be made for me, one black and one colored, and treated me very well. He employed me in one of his shops, entrusting me with a considerable amount of both goods and cash, which amounted to more than one hundred thirty thousand pesos in value, and in a ledger annotated the prices at which I was to sell each item. He gave me two slaves to serve me and a negress to cook for me, setting aside three pesos for each day's expenses, and when he had done that, he took the rest of the merchandise and departed with it for Trujillo, about thirty-two leagues away.

He also left written instructions in the said ledger as to the people who could buy merchandise they wanted on credit and take it away, because they were people he trusted and whose credit was good, but I was to annotate and justify each transaction in the ledger. And he particularly stressed this with respect to Doña Beatriz de Cárdenas, a person he held in the highest regard. He left for Trujillo and I stayed in Saña with my shop, selling things according to the instructions he had left with me, collecting the money and noting it down in my book with the day, month, year, type and yards of cloth sold, names of the buyers, prices charged, etc., and the same procedure with merchandise bought on credit.

Then my lady doña Beatriz de Cárdenas began to buy material, and kept on doing so, and charged so much that I began to have my doubts; without informing her I wrote at length to my master in Trujillo. He replied that everything was just fine, and that with respect to this particular lady, should she ask for the entire shop I should let her have it; with those instructions, and holding on to the letter, I went on with my work.

[Catalina de Erauso has another brush with the law and has to leave this employer.]

CHAPTER V

She leaves Trujillo for Lima.

Having left Trujillo for Lima and having gone more than eighty leagues, I entered the city of Lima, capital of the prosperous realm of Peru. . . .

I gave my letter to Diego de Solarte, a very wealthy merchant who is now chief consul of Lima, and to whom Juan de Urquiza had recommended me; he immediately took me into his home with great courtesy and kindness, and a few days later entrusted his shop to me, assigning me a salary of six hundred pesos a year, and there I did my job much to his satisfaction and pleasure.

At the end of nine months he told me that it was time to make my living elsewhere, and the reason for this was that there were two young girls in his house, his wife's sisters, with whom I used to play and romp about, especially with one who showed a decided liking for me. And one day, while I was in the drawing room with my head in her lap and caressing her legs, while she was combing my hair, he happened to look in through the grille and see us, and heard her say to me that I should go to Potosí[2] to get some money and we would be married. He withdrew, soon after that summoned me, asked me to explain myself, discharged me, and I left.

I found myself unemployed and very out of favor. At that time six companies of men were being assembled to go to Chile; I went to one of them and enlisted as a soldier, for which I immediately received eighty pesos in wages. My employer Diego de Lasarte, who found out about it, was very sorry, for it seemed that he had not wanted it to come to this. He offered to intercede with the officers so that they would take me off the muster roll and return the money I had been given, but I refused, telling him that I had a taste for roving and seeing the world. Finally, having been assigned to the company of Captain Gonzalo Rodríguez, whose camp-master was Diego Bravo de Sarabia, I left Lima in a detachment of sixteen hundred men for the city of Concepción, which is five hundred forty leagues from Lima.

CHAPTER VI

She arrives in Concepción, Chile, and finds her brother. She goes to Paicabí and, while participating in the battle of Valdivia, captures a standard. She returns to Concepción and kills two men and her own brother.

It took us twenty days traveling time to get to the port of Concepción. It's a fair-sized city, with the title of *noble and loyal*, and has a bishop. Because of the scarcity of people in Chile we were well received. Soon an order came from the governor, Alonso de Ribera, that we should disembark, and it was brought by his secretary, Captain Miguel de Erauso. As soon as I heard his name I was delighted, and saw that he was my brother; even though I didn't know him, nor had seen him—because he left San Sebastián for these parts when I was two years old—I had had news of him, but not of his whereabouts. He took the list of soldiers, read it off, and asked each one his name and place of origin; when he got to me and heard my name and place of birth, he threw down the pen, embraced me, and asked many questions about his father and mother and siblings, and about his beloved Catalina, the nun. I answered everything as best I could, without betraying my identity, nor he guessing it. He went through the list, and when he finished he took me to his home for dinner and I sat down to eat. He told me that the garrison at Paicabí to which I was assigned was a terrible place for soldiers and that he would speak to the governor to have me transferred. During the meal he went over to see the governor, taking me along. He reported on the recent arrivals, and asked as a favor that a young lad from his part of the country be transferred to his company, for since his departure he had come across no others from there. The governor had me come in, and when he saw me, I don't know for what reason, he said that he could not transfer me. My brother was upset and left, but a short while later the governor called my brother back again and told him that things could be the way he wanted them.

And so, when the troops left, I stayed with my brother as his soldier, eating at his table for almost three years without having him guess a thing. A few times I accompanied him to his mistress's house; afterward I went a few other times without him, and he found out and took offense and told me not to go back. He spied on me, and caught me at it again; he waited for me when I came out, and whipped me with a belt, injuring my hand. I was forced to defend myself. When he heard the altercation Captain Francisco de Aillón showed up and made peace, but I had to slip into [the church of] San Francisco because I feared the governor, [known to be] a severe man, as he proved to be in this instance, although my brother interceded. Ultimately he banished me to Paicabí; there was no recourse but to go, and I stayed there for three years.

I was obliged to go to Paicabí and suffer hard times for three years, after having lived such a carefree life earlier. Because of the great Indian invasion there, we always lived with our weapons at the ready, until finally Governor Alonso de Sarabia and all the Chilean troops arrived. We all joined forces with him, and five thousand men camped on the open plains of Valdivia with a great deal of discomfort. The Indians captured and attacked said Valdivia. We went out to meet them and fought them three or four times, always besting and destroying them, but in the last battle their reinforcements came, things went badly for us, and they killed many of our men, our captains, and my ensign; they also took our standard. Seeing them make off with it, I and two other mounted soldiers went after them through a great multitude, charging and killing and being wounded in turn. Soon one of the three fell dead. The two of us kept on, and we got to the standard, but a lance thrust felled my companion. I, with a bad wound in one leg, killed the cacique[3] who had it in his possession, took the standard away and spurred my horse, charging, killing and wounding indiscriminately; badly injured, pierced by three arrows and with a very painful lance wound in the left shoulder, I finally reached our men and then fell from my horse. Several rushed to my help, among them my brother, whom I had not seen, and this was a great consolation to me. They dressed my wounds, and we stayed in camp there for nine months. At the end of that time my brother got the standard I had captured away from the governor and I became the ensign of Alonso Moreno's company, which was subsequently assigned to Captain Gonzalo Rodríguez, the first captain I had known, and I was very pleased. . . .

At this time, and among others, one day there appeared my friend Don Juan de Silva, a lively ensign, and he told me he had had an altercation with Don Francisco de Rojas, of the order of Santiago, and had challenged him to a duel that night at eleven. Each man was to bring a friend, and he had no one else but me. I was a little reluctant, wondering if this was some ruse to trap me. He noticed this and said, "If you do not wish to, don't do it; I will go alone, for I trust no one else at my side." I asked myself what was he thinking of, and accepted.

I left the convent when the bells rang for devotions, and went to his house. We dined and talked until ten, and when we heard it strike the hour, took our swords and cloaks and went to the designated spot. The darkness was so intense that we could not see our hands in front of our eyes, and when I noticed this I made a pact with my friend that each of us would tie a pocket handkerchief around his arm, so that we would know each other no matter what happened.

The other two arrived and one, whose voice we knew to be that of Don Francisco de Rojas, said, "Don Juan de Silva?" Don Juan answered, "Here I am!" They both drew their swords and began to fight, while the other man and I stood on the side. They fought on, and a little while later I sensed that my friend had been injured by a thrust he had received. Then I took my place at his side, and the other man joined Don Francisco. We fought two by two, and soon thereafter both Don Francisco and Don Juan fell; my opponent and I continued, and I wounded him with a thrust, which, as it subsequently turned out, pierced his chest underneath the left nipple. I felt my sword go through a double jerkin and he went down. "Oh, traitor," he said, "you have killed me!" I wanted to identify the voice of the unknown man; I asked him who he was, and he said, "Captain Miguel de E-rauso." I was astounded. He loudly called for confession, and the others did as well. I ran to San Francisco and sent two priests, who confessed them. Two men subsequently died; my brother was taken to the house of the governor, whose secretary of war he was. A doctor and a surgeon were brought to aid him, and they did what they could. Later on legal matters were attended to, and my brother was asked for the name of his assailant. He begged for a little wine, but Dr. Robledo refused to give it to him, saying it would do him harm; when he insisted the doctor refused again, and he said, "You're worse to me than Ensign Díaz," and shortly afterward he died. . . . After Captain Miguel de Erauso had expired, he was buried in the said monastery of San Francisco, I witnessing it from the choir with God alone knows what sorrow! . . .

CHAPTER XX

She goes to Guamanga, and what happened to her there, until she reveals her identity to the Bishop.

I got to Guamanga and went to an inn. . . . I went to look at the city, and liked it, as it had handsome buildings, the best I had seen in Peru. I found three monasteries (Franciscan, Mercedarian, and Dominican), a convent and a hospital, many Indian and Spanish residents, [and] a wonderful climate for settling this plain, neither hot nor cold. There are great harvests of wheat, wine, fruits, and grain, a fine church with three prebendaries, two canons and a saintly bishop, an Augustinian friar [named] Don Agustín de Carvajal, who people said had been there since 1612, and who was my salvation, though he was taken from me by his sudden death in 1620.

I was there for a few days, and my ill luck would have it that I sometimes visited a gaming house. One day when I was there, the magistrate, Don Baltasar de Quiñones, entered; he looked at me, and as he did not recognize me, asked me where I was from. I said I was Basque. He said, "Where have you come from just now?" I answered, "Cuzco." He hesitated a moment while observing me, and said,

"You're under arrest." I said, "Fine with me," drew my sword and retreated toward the door. He shouted for help in the king's name, and I found the door so blocked that I was unable to leave. I drew a three-barreled pistol, got away and disappeared, finding refuge in the house of a friend I had made there. The magistrate thereupon seized my mule, and some other trifles I had left in the inn. I spent a few days in hiding, having discovered that my friend was a Basque. Meanwhile there was no word of the matter, nor did I feel that the authorities were doing anything about it, but it still seemed a good idea to us for me to move to another place, for I had the same problem there as I did everywhere. Determined to do this, I left one day at nightfall, and, as my misfortune would have it, immediately ran into two constables. They ask me, "Who goes there?" I reply, "A friend." They demand my name, and I answer, "The devil," which I shouldn't have said. They begin to lay hands on me, and I take out my sword, causing a great commotion. They cry out, "Help us in the name of the Law!" and people gather. The magistrate comes out of the Bishop's house, where he had been, more constables come, I find myself in a desperate situation, fire my pistol, and one goes down. The brawl gets bigger, and I find my Basque friend and some of his compatriots at my side. The magistrate shouted that I should be killed, and shots were exchanged on both sides, until the Bishop came out with four torch-bearers, and stepped into the middle of the fray, directing his secretary Juan Bautista de Arteaga my way. This man stepped up to me and said, "Ensign, give me your weapons." I said, "Sir, there are many enemies here." He said, "Hand them over, for you are safe with me, and I give you my word that I will get you out of this, cost me what it may." I said, "Exalted Sir, when I get into the church[4] I will kiss your illustrious feet." As I was saying this, four of the magistrate's slaves fell upon me and put me into a tight spot, pulling at me ferociously with no regard for His Lordship's presence, so that I had to defend myself and knock one of them down. The Bishop's secretary, with sword and shield, along with others of his retinue, came to my aid, shouting loudly and denouncing the disrespect shown the Bishop, after which the brawling abated somewhat. His Lordship seized my arm, took away my weapons, and, placing me at his side, took me with him into his house. He had a slight wound of mine dressed, and ordered some dinner brought to me; thereupon he told me to go to bed, locked me in, and took the key with him. The magistrate subsequently arrived, and, as I later heard, had a long conversation and high words with His Lordship concerning this matter.

In the morning about ten, His Lordship summoned me into his presence, and asked me who I was and from where, who my parents were, and the whole course of my life: the hows and the whys of how I came to be there. I embellished my tale considerably, mixing in good advice, the perils of life, my fear of death and the consequences thereof, and how I terrified I was lest the afterlife catch me unawares; I tried to calm and humble myself and to kneel before God, which made me feel very small. And when I saw what a saintly man he was, it seemed that I was already in the presence of God, so I took off my hat and said to him: "Sir, all I have just told Your Lordship is false. The truth is this: I am a woman, I was born in such-and-such a place, the daughter of so-and-so, and at a certain age was placed in a certain convent with my aunt so-and-so. There I grew up, put on the habit and was a novice. When I was about to profess, for such-and-such a reason I left. I went to such-and-such a place, took off my habit, put on other clothes, cut my hair, went hither and thither; went aboard ship, put into port, went to and fro, killed, wounded, cheated, ran around, and finally landed here, at the feet of Your Most Illustrious Lordship."

During the time it took to tell this story, which took until one o'clock, the saintly man was all ears: he listened to me without speaking or batting an eyelash, and when I finished he said not a word, but wept bitterly. Afterward he sent me off to rest, and to eat something. He rang a bell, bid an old chaplain come, and sent me to his oratory where they put a table and a mattress for me, and locked me in. I lay down and slept. In the afternoon about four, the Bishop called me to him again, and spoke to me with great kindness of spirit, beseeching me to give thanks to God for the great favor He had shown me by making me see the path of perdition, which leads one straight to everlasting torment. He exhorted me to go back over my past and to make a proper confession, for I had already come a long way, and it would be easy for me. After this God would lend His help so that we could figure out what to do next. In these and other matters the afternoon drew to a close. I withdrew, was given a good meal, and went to bed.

The next morning the Lord Bishop said Mass, which I attended, and afterward he gave thanks. He withdrew to have breakfast, and took me with him. He expounded on his sermon, and told me that mine was the most curious case of this sort he had heard in his life, and finally said, "But is it really true?" I said, "Yes, Sir." He replied, "Don't be affronted if its peculiar nature strains the imagination." "Sir," I said, "it really is true and if Your Lordship wants to make sure by having me examined by some women, I am willing to do it." He said, "I'm glad to hear you say that, and I agree." I withdrew because it was his reception time. At noon I ate, then rested a bit, and in the afternoon about four, two matrons came in, examined me, and were convinced; later they swore before the Bishop that they had examined me to a sufficient degree to be sure, and had found me as intact a virgin as the day I was born. His Lordship was touched, dismissed the women and had me sent for; in the presence of the chaplain, who had come with me, he stood up and tenderly embraced me, saying, "My daughter, now I believe what you told with no doubts whatsoever, and will henceforth believe anything you tell me. I respect you as one of the amazing people of this world, and promise to help you in any way I can, to take care of your needs, and to do that to serve God."

He ordered me put in a suitable room, where I was comfortable and prepared my confession, which I made as soon as possible, and afterward His Lordship gave me communion. Apparently my story got around, and the number of people that came was huge; we were unable to keep them out, as much as I minded it, and His Lordship as well.

Finally, six days later, His Illustrious Lordship ordered me to go into the convent of the Poor Clares of Guamanga, as there was no other, and to put on the habit. His Lordship left his house with me at his side, surrounded by such a mob of people that I don't think there was anyone in the city who didn't come, and for that reason it took a long time to get there. We finally got to the porter's lodge, because going into the church, as His Lordship had initially intended, was out of the question, for it was completely full. The whole convent was there, bearing lit candles, and the abbess and senior nuns signed a document in which the convent promised to hand me over to the Bishop or a prelate who might succeed him, any time they gave the word. His Lordship embraced and blessed me, and I went in[to the convent]. I was escorted in procession to the choir, and prayed there. I kissed the lady abbess's hand, was embraced by and in turn embraced the other nuns; they then took me to a locutory where His Lordship awaited me. There he gave me good advice, and exhorted me to be a good Christian woman, to give thanks to Our Lord God and to make frequent use of the sacraments; His Lordship offered to come and administer them personally, as he indeed did many times, and generously offered me anything at all I might need. News of this event spread everywhere very quickly, and people who had seen me before, and people, both before and after, who heard my story all over the Indies, were amazed. In 1620, within five months, my saintly bishop suddenly died, and I felt his loss keenly. . . .

[Catalina de Erauso goes to Lima and spends the next two years in a convent there, until word arrives from Spain that she was never a professed nun, and can therefore leave the convent and take off her nun's habit. She goes to Spain and presents herself before King Philip IV, who grants her a life pension of 800 escudos; she sees him again in Barcelona, having been robbed along the way, and he gives her another gift of money. She subsequently travels to Italy to see the pope.]

CHAPTER XXV

She goes from Barcelona to Genoa and thence to Rome.

   . . . I left Genoa for Rome. I kissed the foot of His Holiness Urban VIII and told him succinctly, and as best I could all about my life, adventures, gender, and virginity. His Holiness appeared to be astonished thereby, and graciously gave me permission to continue to lead my life dressed as a man, urging me to lead an honest life from now on, and to refrain from offending my fellow man, reminding me of God's justice with reference to His commandment "Thou shalt not kill." My case became well known there and I was constantly surrounded by a throng of illustrious persons: princes, bishops, and cardinals. Every door was open to me, so that in the month and a half that I was in Rome, rarely a day went by that I was not invited and made much of by princes. One Friday in particular, on specific request by the Roman Senate, I was invited and entertained by some gentlemen who entered my name in a book as a Roman citizen. On St. Peter's Day, June 29, 1636, I was taken to St. Peter's chapel, where I saw the cardinals and the usual ceremonies they hold on that day. All—or most—of them were extremely courteous and kind, and many spoke to me. In the afternoon, while three cardinals stood around me, one of them, Cardinal Magalón, told me that I had no other flaw than being a Spaniard, to which I replied, "It seems to me, Sir, keeping in mind the deference one owes your illustrious person, that it is the only good thing I have."

CHAPTER XXXVI

From Rome she goes to Naples.

When I had been in Rome for a month and a half, I left to go to Naples on June 5, 1626. We went aboard in Ripa.

One day in Naples, as I was strolling on the wharf, I heard the guffaws of two wenches who were talking to two lads. They stared at me, and when I stared back, one of the women said, "Lady Catalina, where are you going?" I replied, "My lady whores, to give you a hundred whacks on the head, and a hundred knife thrusts to any who would defend you." They fell silent and went off.

THE END

Notes

1. The order of Santiago (Saint James) was one of the most prestigious military orders in Spain.

2. Potosí was the colonial boomtown in the viceroyalty of Peru

(today this region is in Bolivia) where a fabulously rich hill of silver ore was discovered in 1545 and made many men very wealthy.

3. *Cacique* was the indigenous word for a chieftain.

4. Erauso here refers to the right of sanctuary, whereby criminals and fugitives from justice who took refuge in a church could not be removed by secular authorities.

Sor Juana Inés de la Cruz

Sor Juana Inés de la Cruz, by Juan de Miranda. Courtesy of Patrimonio Universitario of the National Autonomous University of Mexico.

"*I* became a nun, even though I knew that that state entailed many things . . . that were repugnant to my nature, but with all that, given the total antipathy I felt toward marriage, it was the least unsuitable and most seemly [state] I could choose in light of the assurance I desired with respect to my salvation. . . . [When I became a nun] I thought I was fleeing from my self, but oh, misery! I brought my self along, and brought my greatest foe in this inclination [to study], for I cannot determine if Heaven bestowed it on me as a gift or as a punishment."

So spoke Sor Juana Inés de la Cruz in an autobiographical letter ("La Respuesta a Sor Filotea") she wrote in 1691, four years before her death. The greatest poet of colonial Spanish America was born in either 1648 or 1651 (most scholars prefer the latter date) in the hamlet of Nepantla, in the valley of Mexico, the illegitimate daughter of Isabel Ramírez and a Spanish officer, Pedro Manuel de Asbaje. Isabel was a *criolla,* a term that denoted someone of Spanish blood who was born in the New World. Sor Juana was thus of pure Spanish extraction and belonged to the white elite of New Spain, though her family was not wealthy and her social status was somewhat impaired for having been born out of wedlock. As Asunción Lavrin has shown, illegitimacy was a fairly common occurrence in colonial America, even among the upper classes (154 ff.). Isabel Ramírez bore six "natural" children, three to Asbaje and three to another Spaniard, Diego Ruiz de Lozano. Asbaje seems to have disappeared from his daughter's life when she was about eight, and soon afterward she was sent to Mexico City to live with a maternal aunt, who was both rich and socially prominent. Mexico City at the time was a city of some four hundred thousand inhabitants and the capital of the Viceroyalty of New Spain. Its cultural center was the glittering viceregal court, with which Juana was soon to have contact.

Juana had had a minimal education in a girl's school in Nepantla but had devoured the books in her grandfather's library and begun writing poetry at the age of eight. In her autobiographical letter she states that when she was six or seven and heard of the existence of a university in Mexico City, she begged her mother to let her dress as a boy in order to attend but that this request was denied. Many people in the capital knew of her prodigious intelligence and her poetic genius, and soon the viceroy, the Marquis of Mancera, and his wife, Leonor Carreto, asked to meet her. The vicereine was so taken with the pretty, bright girl that Juana was appointed one of her ladies-in-waiting, something that placed her in the center of court life. She continued her poetic activities, and her fame grew apace.

When Juana turned eighteen she had to make a decision as to her future, and for girls of her class there were only two options: marriage or the convent. According to Octavio Paz, at that time there were twenty-two convents in Mexico City (165), reserved for the legitimate daughters of the white elite, who paid a considerable dowry to become members of a prestigious group of women. What attracted the worldly court lady to choose the veil over marriage? Juana's consuming passion was her intellectual life, and she knew very well that once she married she would most likely face yearly pregnancies, as well as a husband who would have total control over her person and could easily forbid her studies and her writing. The convent offered her far more control over her personal life; many nuns were literate, and the Church encouraged study and writing, as long as it was in the service of God. The convent also offered her social prestige and economic security, no small matters for a woman in her position.

Another factor in the decision to profess was her confessor, the powerful Jesuit Antonio Núñez de Miranda, who was also the confessor of the viceroys. Given her fame at court, coupled with her considerable physical attraction, Father Núñez feared for Juana's future and desired nothing more fervently than to remove her from the public eye and have her safely enclosed by the walls of a convent; he also felt that she should devote her God-given intellect solely to her Creator. Her own inclinations, Núñez's influence, and a wealthy relative's willingness to pay her dowry decided her. Juana initially chose the order of the Barefoot Carmelites, the reformed order founded by Saint Teresa of Avila, but the severity of their lifestyle was too much for her. After falling ill, she withdrew and opted for the far more worldly and relaxed order of the Hieronymites. In 1669 Juana took the veil, taking vows of chastity, obedience, poverty, and perpetual enclosure. The vow of obedience would give her the most trouble; the vow of poverty was quite relative.

The convent of Saint Paula was one of the most prestigious in Mexico. It still stands in the historic center of the city, and has now been converted into a small private university. The dimensions of its two-story cloister, the spacious, flower-filled patio, and attendant church all attest to its wealth and prominence. The nuns who lived there in Sor Juana's time had luxurious quarters, with far more private space than any married woman of the time. They wore elegant habits of fine cloth and, as portraits of the time show, even wore jewelry; servants and slaves tended to their needs, and they could—and did—receive many visitors in the convent locutory. Given Sor Juana's fame before she became a nun, succeeding viceroys sought her out and requested that she continue to write verses for them. This explains why fully a third of her prolific output is secular poetry, much of it written for the court. As a reward for composing these poems, Sor Juana received gifts of money, books, musical or scientific instruments, and the like. Her private library in her convent cell was one of the finest in New Spain. In spite of her continuing connection to the viceregal court, however, the main body of her work is religious: prayers and devotions in honor of the Virgin or the saints, religious drama, carols to be sung at popular religious festivals. These carols, known as *villancicos,* are receiving a good bit of critical attention at the moment, as they are excellent examples of the popular culture of seventeenth-century Mexico. Sor Juana, in spite of living in perpetual enclosure, remembered the polyglot accents of the streets of the capital: the speech of the black street vendors, the soft sounds of indigenous Nahuatl, voices of Portuguese immigrants, even the fractured Latin of poorly educated clerics and students.

Núñez's two wishes, to remove Juana from the public eye and to have her devote herself completely to God, were not being realized, and relations between them became strained. Sor Juana had chosen the convent to be able to continue her intellectual life, but she was ambitious in her goals and definitely transgressing the parameters the Church permitted her. The other religious superior who frowned on her was the archbishop of Mexico, Francisco de Aguiar y Seijas, a Jesuit like Núñez. Aguiar y Seijas had arrived in Mexico in the early 1680s, about the same time as a new viceregal couple, the Marquis of la Laguna and his wife, María Luisa, the Countess of Paredes, both of the highest Spanish nobility. Sor Juana and the countess soon became intimate, if not passionate friends, and during the eight years these viceroys were in Mexico (1680–88), the nun skillfully played off the power of the State against that of the Church to assure herself maximum creative freedom. This was her happiest and most productive time.

From her earliest years Sor Juana was a consummate poet. The baroque was an age splendidly suited to her talents: she loved the play of dialectical opposites, puns and double entendres, labyrinthine syntax and imagery, much of it derived from classical mythology. She was skilled at all the poetic forms in use at the time and enjoyed showing her mastery in them. Not that all her poetry is uniformly great: she wrote a number of occasional verses that are quite forgettable or simply do not interest the modern reader. She excelled at the sonnet, and the best of these are among the masterworks of the Spanish language.

Although Sor Juana was always dutiful about her responsibilities as a nun, there is no doubt that in her writing she gave her superiors much to criticize. That a nun should write love poetry, satiric verses aimed at the double standard men imposed on women, some bawdy burlesque sonnets, and dramas of romantic intrigue, in one of which a male servant cross-dresses as a woman, certainly exceeded permissible boundaries and brought her relentless criticism. As long as María Luisa and her husband were there to protect her, Sor Juana was fairly safe, and she made the most of this. So safe did she feel that in 1681 she wrote a letter of dismissal to her confessor Núñez, a step not many nuns dared to take, but his public criticism of her had long rankled. The nun composed many affectionate, even impassioned verses to her benefactress (whom she addressed as "Lysi" in her poetry), leading

some *sorjuanistas* to wonder if there was ever a sexual attraction between the two women. In Alan Trueblood's opinion, what Sor Juana
felt was "a mixture of love and friendship in which affection, devotion, gratitude, respect, and a Neoplatonically accented idealization all
have a part" (13). Had it been more than that, it would have been a
very serious transgression, for "until the end of the eighteenth century
the existence of sexual feelings of women for other women was
nearly inconceivable."[1] Whatever the nature of their personal relationship, the vicereine played a decisive role in the nun's life in another
way: she assured the publication of Sor Juana's verses in Spain. We
must remember that her poems circulated among court and religious
circles in manuscript form and were essentially dispersed all over the
capital. Before her departure for Spain in 1688 the countess commanded Sor Juana to give her copies of as much material as she could
gather together and, once back in Europe, used her wealth and influence to have these verses published. *Inundación castálida* (Castalian
Flood) came out in 1689 and was so successful that by 1725 it had been
republished nine times. As I discussed in a previous study ("Ser mujer
. . . "), without the intervention of the countess, and especially in light
of subsequent Church persecution of Sor Juana, it is possible that much
of her poetry might have been lost forever.

After the departure of the viceroys in 1688, storm clouds began to
gather on Sor Juana's horizon. Pressure from the archbishop escalated,
and general criticism of her worldliness increased while there were few
powerful allies to fight for her. And, given the religious sentiment of
the times, Sor Juana could indeed be censored for vanity, the undue attention to the ephemeral attractions of the world. In 1691 the bishop
of Puebla, who admired the nun very much, made what appears to be
a very contradictory gesture: on the one hand, he published a critique
she had written of a sermon by the Portuguese Jesuit Antonio de
Vieyra, entitling it "A Letter Worthy of Athena" (the Greek goddess
of wisdom); on the other, he sent Sor Juana a more or less open letter
of censure, in which he reminded her that her amazing intelligence
was God's gift, a talent she should thus devote exclusively to His service, risking eternal damnation if she did not do so. To make this letter appear less harsh, he signed it "Sister Philotea," making it appear

as if it came from a sister nun instead of from a male superior, though everyone knew the real identity of the signatory.

Sor Juana's famous "Reply to Sister Philotea" is one of the unique documents of the seventeenth century, for it is one of the only ones to record so eloquently a woman's cry for intellectual freedom. Sor Juana used every argument at her disposal to make her case, beginning with the bishop's main premise. If God Himself had given her the gift of intelligence, then how could it logically follow that to use it was a sin? Sor Juana knew perfectly well that the crucial issue for the Church was her gender. Why was she being accused of censoring Vieyra, when he had written against several of the Fathers of the Church? "Is not my reason, such as it is, as free as his, seeing that both emanate from the same source?" she asked. The answer was, of course, no.

Events both inside and outside Sor Juana's convent walls conspired to make the atmosphere around her apocalyptic. There was famine in the land, and hungry bands of the poor rioted in the streets of the capital. The archbishop stepped up his campaign to bring her to heel. The nun at this point stood totally alone, and could hold out no longer against the power of the institutionalized Church. About two years before her death she underwent a radical change: she recalled Núñez as her confessor, appeared to stop all intellectual activity, and engaged in long hours of prayer and mortification of the flesh. Under pressure from the archbishop, she sold her library and other treasures and gave the money to the poor. She renewed her vows of profession several times, calling herself "the worst in the world" and signing them in her own blood. Other nuns did this as well, so it was not a unique gesture, but all of this was so uncharacteristic for Sor Juana that critics have long debated what brought on this radical change in her. Some believed that she had had a true religious conversion, had recognized the folly of her worldliness, and had thrown herself into acts of penitence to atone for her past. Others were just as convinced that she cracked under the pressure, perhaps had a nervous breakdown, and saw no alternative but to obey her superiors. Octavio Paz, for his part, conjectured that perhaps she was pretending remorse while waiting for better times (598, 601). Up until 1995, the tercentenary of Sor Juana's death, no one had resolved this mystery, but then the historian Elías Trabulse of the Colegio de México made some startling new finds. One is a poem, ostensibly written by one "Sor Serafina de Cristo," which attacked Núñez and supported Sor Juana—and which Trabulse believes Sor Juana herself composed.[2] His other find, no less startling, came when he reviewed the account books of the convent. Sor Juana had been elected treasurer of her convent twice, and oversaw the myriad economic transactions involved in the administration of her large community. Her account books, which had to be checked yearly by a Church official, showed that in the midst of her persecution by the archbishop she was clandestinely investing some of her own funds with a wealthy banker, probably to replace what she had been forced to give Aguiar y Seijas. A third find, by the historian Teresa Castello, was an item scholars had wanted to unearth for years: the inventory of Sor Juana's cell when she died. Although Aguiar y Seijas had made her divest herself of all her books and manuscripts, the inventory shows that at the time of the nun's death there were some 170 books and 180 bundles of manuscripts in her cell.[3] All of the above has given us final proof of what many Sor Juana scholars had hoped all along: she did, in fact, never surrender to the Church authorities.

In 1695 an epidemic of some highly contagious disease appeared in Mexico City and did not spare the Hieronymite convent. Sor Juana nursed her sisters until she herself succumbed to the disease. She died on April 17, 1695, and is buried in the chapel of her convent.

Notes

1. Rudolf M. Dekker and Lotte C. van der Pol, *The Tradition of Female Transvestism in Early Modern Europe* (New York: St. Martin's Press, 1989) 69. The intimate relationship between Sor Juana and the countess is the subject of María Luisa Bemberg's film *Yo, la peor de todas* (I, the Worst of All).

2. See his *El enigma de Serafina de Cristo: Acerca de un manuscrito inédito de Sor Juana Inés de la Cruz* (1691) (Toluca: Instituto Mexiquense de Cultura, 1995); and "La guerra de las finezas," *Memoria del Coloquio Internacional Sor Juana Inés de la Cruz y el pensamiento novohispano 1995* (Toluca: Instituto Mexiquense de Cultura, 1995): 483–93. Noted scholars who do not agree with Trabulse are Antonio Alatorre and Martha Lilia Tenorio. See their

Serafina y Sor Juana (con tres apéndices) (México: El Colegio de México, 1998).

3. Trabulse's and Castello's discoveries were presented at the November 1995 conference, "Sor Juana y su mundo," which was held at the Universidad Claustro de Sor Juana in her convent in Mexico City. Publication of the papers presented at this conference is forthcoming.

Carta al R. P. M. Antonio Núñez

Carta de la Madre Juana Inés de la Cruz escrita al R. P. M. Antonio Núñez, de la Compañía de Jesús.

Pax Xpti. [Christi]

Aunque ha muchos tiempos que varias personas me han informado de que soy la única reprensible en las conversaciones de V. R. [Vuestra Reverencia], fiscalizando mis acciones con tan agria ponderación como llegarlas a *escándalo público*, y otros epítetos no menos horrorosos, y aunque pudiera la propia conciencia moverme a la defensa, pues no soy tan absoluto dueño de mi crédito, que no esté coligado con el de un linaje que tengo, y una comunidad en que vivo, con todo esto, he querido sacrificar el sufrimiento a la suma veneración y filial cariño con que siempre he respetado a V. R. queriendo más aína que cayesen sobre mí todas las objeciones, que no que pareciera pasaba yo la línea de mi justo, y debido respeto en redargüir a V. R. en lo cual confieso ingenuamente que no pude merecer nada para con Dios, pues fue más humano respeto a su persona, que cristiana paciencia; y esto no ignorando yo la veneración y crédito grande que V. R. (con mucha razón) tiene con todos, y que le oyen como a un oráculo divino y aprecian sus palabras como dictadas del Espíritu Santo, y que cuanto mayor es su autoridad tánto más queda perjudicado mi crédito; con todo esto nunca he querido asentir a las instancias que a que responda me ha hecho, no sé si la razón o si el amor propio (que éste tal vez con capa de razón nos arrastra) juzgando que mi silencio sería el medio más suave para que V. R. se desapasionase; hasta que con el tiempo he reconocido que antes parece que le irrita mi paciencia, y así determiné responder a V. R. salvando y suponiendo mi amor, mi obligación y mi respeto.

La materia, pues, de este enojo de V. R. (muy amado Padre y

Señor mío) no ha sido otra que la de estos negros versos de que el cielo tan contra la voluntad de V. R. me dotó.[1] Estos he rehusado sumamente el hacerlos y me he excusado todo lo posible no porque en ellos hallase yo razón de bien ni de mal, que siempre los he tenido (como lo son) por cosa indiferente, y aunque pudiera decir cuántos los han usado santos y doctos, no quiero entrometerme a su defensa, que no son mi padre ni mi madre: sólo digo que no los haría por dar gusto a V. R. sin buscar, ni averiguar la razón de su aborrecimiento, que es muy propio del amor obedecer a ciegas; demás que con esto también me conformaba con la natural repugnancia que siempre he tenido a hacerlos, como consta a cuantas personas me conocen; pero esto no fue posible observarlo con tánto rigor que no tuviese algunas excepciones, tales como dos villancicos a la Santísima Virgen que después de repetidas instancias y pausa de ocho años, hice con venia y licencia de V. R., la cual tuve entonces por más necesaria que la del Sr. Arzobispo Virrey mi Prelado,[2] y en ellos procedí con tal modestia, que no consentí en los primeros poner mi nombre, y en los segundos se puso sin consentimiento ni noticia mía, y unos y otros corrigió antes V. R.

A esto se siguió el Arco de la Iglesia.[3] Esta es la irremisible culpa mía a la cual precedió habérmel[o] pedido tres o cuatro veces y tántas despedídome yo, hasta que vinieron los dos señores jueces hacedores que antes de llamarme a mí, llamaron a la Madre Priora y después a mí, y mandaron en nombre del Excmo. Señor Arzobispo lo hiciese porque así lo había votado el Cabildo pleno y aprobado Su Excelencia.

Ahora quisiera yo que V. R. con su clarísimo juicio, se pusiera en mi lugar y consultara ¿qué respondiera en este lance? ¿Respondería que no podía? Era mentira. ¿Que no quería? Era inobediencia. ¿Que no sabía? Ellos no pedían más que hasta donde supiese. ¿Que estaba mal votado? Era, sobre descarado atrevimiento, villano y grosero desagradecimiento a quien me honraba con el concepto de pensar que sabía hacer una mujer ignorante, lo que tan lucidos ingenios solicitaban: luego no pude hacer otra cosa que obedecer.

Estas son las obras públicas que tan escandalizado tienen al mundo, y tan [d]edificados a los buenos y así vamos a l[a]s no

públic[a]s: apenas se hallará tal o cual coplilla hecha a los años, al ob-
sequio de tal o tal persona de mi estimación, y a quienes he debido
socorro en mis necesidades (que no han sido pocas, por ser tan pobre
y no tener renta alguna). Una loa a los años del Rey Nuestro Señor
hecha por mandato del mismo Excmo. Señor Don Fray Payo, otra
por orden de la Excma. Sra. Condesa de Paredes.[4]

Pues a[h]ora Padre mío y mi señor, le suplico a V. R. deponga por
un rato el cariño del propio dictamen (que aun a los muy santos a-
rrastra) y dígame V. R. (ya que en su opinión es pecado hacer versos)
¿en cuál de estas ocasiones ha sido tan grave el delito de hacerlos?
Pues cuando fuera culpa (que yo no sé por qué razón se le pueda
llamar así) la disculparan las mismas circunstancias y ocasiones que
para ello he tenido, tan contra mi voluntad, y esto bien claro se
prueba, pues en la facilidad que todos saben que tengo, si a ésa se
juntara motivo de vanidad (quizá lo es de mortificación) ¿qué más
castigo me quiere V. R. que el que entre los mismos aplausos que
tanto [l]e duelen, tengo? ¿De qué envidia no soy blanco? ¿De qué
mala intención no soy objeto? ¿Qué acción hago sin temor? ¿Qué
palabra digo sin recelo?

Las mujeres sienten que las exceda, los hombres, que parezca
que los igualo;[5] unos no quisieran que supiera tánto, otros dicen que
había de saber más, para tánto aplauso; las viejas no quisieran que
otras supieran más, las mozas que otras parezcan bien, y unos y otros
que viese conforme a las reglas de su dictamen, y de todos juntos
resulta un tan extraño género de martirio cual no sé yo que otra
persona haya experimentado.

¿Qué más podré decir ni ponderar? que hasta el hacer esta forma
de letra algo razonable me costó una prolija y pesada persecución, no
por más de porque dicen que parecía letra de hombre, y que no era
decente, con que me obligaron a malearla adrede, y de esto toda esta
comunidad es testigo; en fin, ésta no será materia para una carta,
sino para muchos volúmenes muy copiosos. Pues ¿qué dichos son
estos tan culpables? ¿los aplauses y celebraciones vulgares los solicité?
y los particulares favores y honras de los Excelentísimos Señores
Marqueses que por sola su dignación y sin igual humanidad me
hacen ¿los procuré yo?

Tan a la contra sucedió que la Madre Juana de San Antonio, Priora de este Convento y persona que por ningún caso podrá mentir, es testigo de que la primera vez que Sus Excelencias honraron esta casa, le pedí licencia para retirarme a la celda y no verlos, ni ser vista (como si Sus Excelencias me hubiesen hecho algún daño) sin más motivo que huir el aplauso, que así se convierte en tan pungentes espinas de persecución, y lo hubiera conseguido a no mandarme la Madre Priora lo contrario.

¿Pues qué culpa mía fue el que Sus Excelencias se agradasen de mí? Aunque no había por qué ¿podré yo negarme a tan soberanas personas? ¿podré sentir el que me honren con sus visitas?

V. R. sabe muy bien que no; como lo experimentó en tiempo de los Excmos. Sres. Marqueses de Mancera, pues oí yo a V. R. en muchas ocasiones quejarse de las ocupaciones a que le hacía faltar la asistencia de Sus Excelencias sin poderlas no obstante dejar; y si el Excmo. Sr. Marqués de Mancera entraba cuantas veces quería en unos conventos tan santos como Capuchinas y Teresas, y sin que nadie lo tuviese por malo ¿cómo podré yo resistir que el Excmo. Sr. Marqués de la Laguna entre en éste? De más que yo no soy prelada, ni corre por mi cuenta su gobierno.

Sus Excelencias me honran porque son servidos, no porque yo lo merezca, ni tampoco porque al principio lo solicité.

Yo no puedo, ni quisiera aunque pudiera, ser tan bárbaramente ingrata a los favores y cariños (tan no merecidos, ni servidos) de Sus Excelencias.

Mis estudios no han sido en daño ni perjuicio de nadie, mayormente habiendo sido tan sumamente privados que no me he valido ni aun de la dirección de un maestro, sino que a secas me lo he habido conmigo y mi trabajo, que no ignoro que el cursar públicamente las escuelas, no fuera decente a la honestidad de una mujer, por la ocasionada familiaridad con los hombres, y que ésta sería la razón de prohibir los estudios públicos;[6] y el no diputarles lugar señalado para ellos, será porque como no las ha menester la República para el gobierno de los magistrados (de que por la misma razón de honestidad están excluídas) no cuida de lo que no le ha de servir; pero los privados y particulares estudios ¿quién los ha prohibido a las mujeres? ¿No tienen alma racional como los hombres? Pues ¿por qué no gozará el privilegio de la ilustración de las letras como ell[o]s?[7] ¿No es capaz de tanta gracia y gloria de Dios como la suya? Pues ¿por qué no será capaz de tántas noticias y ciencias, que es menos? ¿Qué revelación divina, qué determinación de la Iglesia, qué dictamen de la razón hizo para nosotras tan severa ley?

¿Las letras estorban, sino que antes ayudan a la salvación? ¿No se salvó San Agustín, San Ambrosio, y todos los demás Santos Doctores? Y V. R., cargado de tántas letras ¿no piensa salvarse?

Y si me responde que en los hombres milita otra razón, digo: ¿No estudió Santa Catalina, Santa Gertrudis, mi Madre Santa Paula[8] sin estorbarle a su alta contemplación, ni a la fatiga de sus fundaciones, el saber hasta griego? ¿El aprender hebreo? ¿Enseñada de mi Padre San Jerónimo, el resolver y el entender las Santas Escrituras, como el mismo santo lo dice? Ponderando también en una epístola suya en todo género de estudios doctísima a Blesilla, hija de la misma santa, y en tan tiernos años que murió de veinte?

Pues ¿por qué en mí es malo lo que en todas fue bueno? ¿Sólo a mí me estorban los libros para salvarme?

Si he leído los profetas y oradores profanos (descuido en que incurrió el mismo Santo [Jerónimo]) también leo los Doctores Sagrados y Santas Escrituras, demás que a los primeros no puedo negar que les debo innumerables bienes, y reglas de bien vivir.

Porque ¿qué cristiano no se corre de ser iracundo a vista de la paciencia de un Sócrates gentil? ¿Quién podrá ser ambicioso a vista de la modestia de Diógenes Cínico? ¿Quién no alaba a Dios en la inteligencia de Aristóteles? Y en fin ¿qué católico no se confunde si contempla la suma de virtudes morales en todos los filósofos gentiles?

¿Por qué ha de ser malo que el rato que yo había de estar en una reja hablando disparates, o en una celda murmurando cuanto pasa fuera y dentro de casa, o pelea[ndo] con otra, o riñendo a la triste sirviente, o vagando por todo el mundo con el pensamiento, lo gastara en estudiar? Y más cuando Dios me inclinó a eso y no me pareció que era contra su ley santísima, ni contra la obligación de mi estado. Yo tengo este genio, si es malo, yo [no] me hice,[9] nací con él y con él he de morir.

V. R. quiere que por fuerza me salve ignorando. Pues amado

Padre mío, ¿no puede esto hacerse sabiendo? Que al fin es camino para mí más suave. Pues, ¿por qué para salvarse ha de ir por el camino de la ignorancia, si es repugnante a su natural?

¿No es Dios como suma bondad, suma sabiduría? Pues, ¿por qué le ha de ser más acepta la ignorancia que la ciencia?

Sálvese San Antonio con su ignorancia santa, norabuena, que San Agustín va por otro camino, y ninguno va errado. .

Pues ¿por qué es esta pesadumbre de V. R. y el decir "que a saber que yo había de hacer versos no me hubiera entrado religiosa, sino casádome?"

Pues, Padre amantísimo (a quien forzada y con vergüenza insto lo que no quisiera tomar en boca), ¿cuál era el dominio directo que tenía V. R. para disponer de mi persona y del albedrío (sacando el que mi amor le daba y le dará siempre) que Dios me dio?

Pues cuando ello sucedió había muy poco que yo tenía la dicha de conocer a V. R., y aunque le debí sumos deseos y solicitudes de mi estado, que estimaré siempre como debo, lo tocante a la dote,[10] mucho antes de conocer yo a V. R. lo tenía ajustado mi padrino el Capitán D. Pedro Velázquez de la Cadena, y agenciádomelo estas mismas prendas, en las cuales, y no en otra cosa, me libró Dios el remedio. Luego no hay sobre qué caiga tal proposición, aunque no niego deberle a V. R. otros cariños y agasajos muchos que reconoceré eternamente, tal como el de pagarme maestro, y otros; pero no es razón que éstos no se continúen, sino que se hayan convertido en vituperios, y en que no haya conversación en que no salgan mis culpas, y sea el tema espiritual el celo de V. R. [por] mi conver[sión].[11]

¿Soy por ventura hereje? Y si lo fuera ¿había de ser santa a pura fuerza? Ojalá y la santidad fuera cosa que se pudiera mandar, que con eso la tuviera yo segura; pero yo juzgo que se persuade, no se manda, y si se manda, prelados he tenido que lo hicieran; pero los preceptos, y fuerzas exteriores, si son moderados y prudentes, hacen recatados y modestos, si son demasiados, hacen desesperados; pero santos, sólo la gracia y auxilios de Dios saben hacerlos.

¿En qué se funda, pues, este enojo? ¿En qué este desacreditarme? ¿En qué este ponerme en concepto de escandalosa con todos? ¿Canso yo a V. R. con algo? ¿Héle pedido alguna cosa para el socorro de mis necesidades? ¿O le he molestado con otra espiritual ni temporal?

¿Tócale a V. R. mi corrección por alguna razón de obligación, de parentesco, crianza, prelacía, o tal que cosa?

Si es mera caridad, parezca mera caridad, y proceda como tal, suavemente, que el exasperarme, no es buen modo de reducirme, ni yo tengo tan servil naturaleza que haga por amenazas lo que no me persuade la razón, ni por respetos humanos, lo que no haga por Dios, que el privarme yo de todo aquello que me puede dar gusto, aunque sea muy lícito, es bueno que yo lo haga por mortificarme, cuando yo quiera hacer penitencia; pero no para que V. R. lo quiera conseguir a fuerza de represiones, y éstas no a mí en secreto como ordena la paternal corrección (ya que V. R. ha dado en ser mi padre, cosa en que me tengo ser muy dichosa) sino públicamente con todos, donde cada uno siente como entiende y habla como siente.

Pues esto, Padre mío ¿no es preciso yo lo sienta de una persona que con tánta veneración amo y con tánto amor reverencio y estimo?

Si estas represiones cayeran sobre alguna comunicación escandalosa mía, soy tan dócil, que (no obstante que ni en lo espiritual, ni temporal he corrido nunca por cuenta de V. R.), me apartara de ella y procurara enmendarme y satisfacerle, aunque fuera contra mi gusto.

Pero, si no es sino por la contradicción de un dictamen que en sustancia tánto monta hacer versos como no hacerlos, y que éstos los aborrezco de forma que no habrá para mí penitencia como tenerme siempre haciéndolos ¿por qué es tánta pesadumbre?

Porque si por contradicción de dictamen hubiera yo de hablar apasionada[mente] contra V. R. como lo hace V. R. contra mí, infinitas ocasiones suyas, me repugnan sumamente (porque al fin, el sentir en las materias indiferentes es aquel *alius sic, et alius sic*) pero no por eso las condeno, sino que antes las venero como suyas y las defiendo como mías; y aun quizá las mismas que son contra mí, llamándolas buen celo, sumo cariño, y otros títulos que sabe inventar mi amor y reverencia cuando hablo con los otros.

Pero a V. R. no puedo dejar de decirle que rebosan ya en el pecho las quejas que en espacio de los años pudiera haber dado; y que pues tomo la pluma para darlas redarguyendo a quien tánto venero, es porque ya no puedo más, que como no soy tan mortificada como otras hijas en quien se empleara mejor su doctrina, lo siento demasiado.

Y así le suplico a V. R. que si no gusta ni es ya servido favorecerme (que eso es voluntario) no se acuerde de mí, que aunque sentiré tánta pérdida mucho, nunca podré quejarme, que Dios que me crió y redimió, y que usa conmigo tántas misericordias, proveerá con remedio para mi alma, que esper[o] en su bondad no se perderá, aunque le falte la dirección de V. R., que [al] cielo hacen muchas llaves, y no se estrechó a un solo dictamen, sino que hay en él infinidad de mansiones para diversos genios, y en el mundo hay muchos teólogos, y cuando faltaran, en querer más que en saber consiste el salvarse, y esto más estará en mí que en el confesor.

¿Qué precisión hay en que esta salvación mía sea por medio de V. R.? ¿No podrá ser otro? ¿Retringióse y limitóse la misericordia de Dios a un hombre, aunque sea tan discreto, tan docto, y tan santo como V. R.?

No por cierto, ni hasta ahora he tenido yo luz particular ni inspiración del Señor que así me lo ordene; conque podré gobernarme con las reglas generales de la Santa Madre Iglesia, mientras el Señor no me da luz de que haga otra cosa, y elegir libremente Padre espiritual el que yo quisiere: que si como Nuestro Señor inclinó a V. R. con tánto amor y fuerza mi voluntad, conformara también mi dictamen, no fuera otro que V. R. a quien suplico no tenga esta ingenuidad a atrevimiento, ni a menos respeto, sino a sencillez de mi corazón con que no sé decir las cosas sino como las siento, y antes he procurado hablar de manera que no pueda dejar a V. R. rastro de sentimiento o quejas.

Y no obstante, si en este manifiesto de mis culpas hubiere alguna palabra que haya escrito mala, [será] inadvertencia que la voluntad no sólo digo de ofensa, pero de menos decoro a la persona de V. R., desde luego la retracto, y doy por mal dicha y peor escrita, y borrara desde luego si advirtiera cuál era.

Vuelvo a repetir que mi intención es sólo suplicar a V. R. que si

no gusta de favorecerme, no se acuerde de mí, si no fuere para en-
comendarme al Señor, que bien creo de su mucha caridad lo hará
con todas veras.

Yo pido a Su Majestad me guarde a V. R. como deseo.   *Sor Juana Inés*
De este convento de mi Padre San Jerónimo de México.   *de la Cruz*
Vuestra   *69*
Juana Inés de la Cruz[12]

Notas

1. Hay varios errores en el texto de la carta, debidos o al descuido de
parte de Sor Juana, o a los errores de transcripción del amanuensis en
cuestión. Como nota Paz con mucha razón, la intención de Sor Juana aquí
no es sugerir que son los *versos* los que son desafortunados, sino el talento
que Dios le dio para componerlos (634). Para una versión anotada y co-
rregida del texto de la carta, véase Antonio Alatorre, "La *Carta* de Sor
Juana al P. Núñez," *Nueva Revista de Filología Hispánica* 15 (1987): 591–673.

2. Esto se refiere a Fray Payo Enríquez de Rivera, que fue primero Arzobispo de México, y luego virrey de 1674 a 1680.

3. Lo que ella llama "el Arco de la Iglesia" era una alegoría poética
a Neptuno, compuesta para acompañar un provisional arco triunfal
erigido para celebrar la llegada en 1680 de los nuevos virreyes, el Marqués
de la Laguna y su esposa. Sor Juana escogió la referencia mitológica a Neptuno para aludir al apellido acuático del virrey. Este arco, que consistía de
un *collage* de pintura y poesía, lo comisionaron por orden directa el Capítulo de la Catedral y el Arzobispo Fray Payo, mencionado arriba.

4. María Luisa Manrique de Lara y Gonzaga, Condesa de Paredes y
Virreina de México, fue la amiga más íntima de Sor Juana y la que hizo
publicar la poesía de la monja en Sevilla en 1689.

5. El texto original es algo diferente: "Las mujeres sienten que las excedan los hombres, que parezca que los igualo," una frase muy confusa de
sintaxis por el subjuntivo de "parecer"; estoy de acuerdo con la opinión
de Marie-Cécile Bénassy-Berling, que cree que debe decir "Las mujeres
sienten que las exceda, los hombres que parezca que los igualo," y así lo
he traducido (Carta personal, 28 de febrero de 1987).

6. En el original el verbo es "publicar los estudios públicos," que no
tiene sentido alguno y probablemente es un error; lo he cambiado a "prohibir." El segundo error ocurre con "disputarles lugar," cuando debe ser

"diputarles lugar señalado," o sea "designar lugar especial" para estudiar esta materia. Le agradezco a Antonio Alatorre señalarme este punto.

7. Otra vez el original tiene poco sentido: "¿Pues por qué no gozará el privilegio de la ilustración de las letras con ellas?" Bénassy-Berling sugiere que debe ser "como ellos" que me parece más razonable.

8. Aquí Sor Juana se refiere a la legendaria Santa Catarina de Alejandría (s. III), famosa por su belleza y su erudición, martirizada por el Emperador Maximino II cuando ella rehusó casarse con él. Gertrudis "la Magna" (s. XIII) era monja benedictina que redactó trozos del "Legatus Divinae Pietatis," una de las obras más destacadas del misticismo alemán, y también es santa patrona de las Indias; Santa Paula (s. V), adinerada matrona romana, era una de las discípulas más devotas de San Jerónimo; él la nombró superiora de una de las comunidades monásticas gemelas que él fundó en Belén. Era la santa patrona del convento de Sor Juana.

9. El original dice "yo me hice," que parece contradecir todo el mensaje de este pasaje; Tapia Méndez ya lo cambió en su texto (*Carta* 25) y yo le seguí en mi traducción, pero Alatorre (623) y Paz (643) mantienen "yo me hice," que también tiene sentido. Que decidan los lectores.

10. Aparentemente la gente pensaba que Núñez le había procurado la dote a Sor Juana, y que por eso ella le debía algo. Este punto—antes desconocido—es uno de los más importantes descubrimientos biográficos que el hallazgo de esta carta ha aportado a los estudios sorjuaninos.

11. El original dice "conversación," en vez de "conversión," que sería mucho más verosímil; parece ser otro error de transcripción. Tapia Méndez está de acuerdo que el término correcto debe ser "conversión" (*Carta* 25).

12. El texto aquí reproducido se basa en tres versiones anteriores de la carta descubierta por Aureliano Tapia Méndez: en la *Carta*, publicada por este último; en la versión incluida en el apéndice de la 3ª edición de *Sor Juana Inés de la Cruz o Las trampas de la fe* de Octavio Paz, y en la versión de Antonio Alatorre en "*La Carta* de Sor Juana al P. Núñez (1682)." Para facilitar la lectura de este texto para los lectores modernos he alterado algo la puntuación y los párrafos.

Letter to the R. F. M. Antonio Núñez

*Letter of Mother Juana Inés de la Cruz written to the Reverend Father
Maestro Antonio Núñez of the Society of Jesus.*

The Peace of Christ.

Although for a long time now various persons have informed me
that I am the only one to blame in Your Reverence's conversations,
as you criticize my actions with such bitter criteria so as to classify
them as a *public scandal* and other epithets no less dreadful, though it
would be only natural for me to defend myself, as I am not the absolute mistress of my reputation, linked as it is to the state in which
I exist and the community in which I live, in spite of all that I have
wanted to sacrifice my suffering to the highest veneration of filial
affection with which I have always respected Your Reverence, desiring sooner that all these objections fall on me rather than that it
seem that I were deviating from just and proper respect by engaging
in a counterargument with Your Reverence; in this matter I confess
openly that my actions do not merit divine reward because it was
more a matter of human respect for your person than of Christian
patience; [I say] this not ignoring the veneration and great esteem
which Your Reverence (with good reason) receives from everyone,
for they listen to you as to a divine oracle and value your words as
though dictated by the Holy Spirit, so that the greater your authority, the more my reputation suffers; yet even so, in view of all of
this, I have never wished to yield to the desire to answer that has
impelled me, I know not whether it was a matter of reason or of
self-esteem (for perhaps the latter in the guise of reason sways us),
judging that my silence would be the gentlest means whereby Your
Reverence might be restored to calm, until in time I came to realize
that it appears that my patience irritates you, and so I resolved to

reply to Your Reverence, all the while certifying and implying my love, my duty, and my respect.

The focus, then, of Your Reverence's anger (most beloved Father and Sir) has been none other than those unfortunate verses which Heaven—most contrary to Your Reverence's wishes—has bestowed on me.[1] I have always tried mightily to refrain from writing them and I have excused myself from doing so as much as possible, not because I found in them either good or evil, as I have always held them (as indeed they are) as something quite indifferent, and though I could tell you how many holy and learned persons have made use of them, I do not want to get involved in defending them for they are not that important (they are neither my father nor my mother); I only say that in order to please Your Reverence I would refrain from composing them without even searching for or attempting to ascertain the reason for your displeasure, for one of the characteristics of love is to obey blindly; furthermore, by doing this I would also be able to give in to the natural aversion which I have always felt while writing them, as is well known to all who know me; however, it was not possible to do this so rigorously as not to admit some exceptions, as for example two pieces to the Most Holy Virgin which, after repeated requests and an interval of eight years, I composed with the permission and leave of Your Reverence, which at the time I thought more important even than those of my Prelate, the Lord Archbishop and Viceroy,[2] and proceeded with them with such modesty that I refused to sign my name to the first, and as to the second, my name appeared on it with neither my consent nor prior notice to me, and both the former as well as the latter were first submitted to Your Reverence for correction.

These [pieces] were followed by the Church's Arch.[3] This is my unforgivable fault, which was preceded by my having been asked to write it three or four times and I having refused as many until two lay magistrates went to the Mother Superior before coming to me and summoned me to do it in the name of His Excellency the Lord Archbishop, because the entire municipal council had voted in favor and His Excellency had approved it.

Now I ask that Your Reverence, with your great clarity of judgment, put yourself in my position and ask yourself what you would have done under similar circumstances? Would you have answered that you were unable to comply? That would be a lie. That you did not want to? That would be disobedience. That you did not know how? They did not ask me to go beyond the extent of my knowledge. That they had voted badly? That would be bold-faced impudence, base and rude ingratitude toward those brilliant minds who honored an ignorant woman with their request. Therefore I could do no less than to obey.

These are the public works which have so scandalized the world and contributed to the detriment of good souls, so let us go on to those works which are private: one will find perhaps a couplet here or there written to honor the birthday of some person whom I esteemed and who has helped me with things I needed (which were not a few, given the fact that I am very poor and have no income whatever). A panegyric on the occasion of the birthday of Our Lord the King, written by order of His Excellency Don Fray Payo, another by order of Her Excellency the Countess of Paredes.[4]

Well, then, my Father and good Sir, I beg Your Reverence to suspend for a while the affection you feel for your own advice (even the most holy are swayed by this tendency) and tell me, Your Reverence (since in your opinion it is a sin to write poetry), in which of these occasions was it a grave sin to compose verses? And even supposing it was a sin (though I cannot conceive for which reason it would be deemed such), the same circumstances and occasions which forced me do it so much against my will would excuse it, and this can be clearly proved, for should the gift which all know I possess be joined to vanity (perhaps it is actually chagrin), what greater punishment could Your Reverence envision for me than the pain which this very applause occasions me? Of what envy am I not the target? Of which evil intention am I not the object? What action do I take without quailing? What word do I utter without misgiving?

Women take offense that I surpass them, men that I seem to equal them;[5] some wish that I did not know quite so much, others say I should know more to merit such praise; old women do not want others to know more than they do, young women resent those who attract more attention and one and all want me to comply with the rules of their judgment; all these sources together produce such a strange kind of martyrdom that I know of no one else who has undergone the like.

What more can I say or think? Why, even writing a more or less reasonable hand has cost me lengthy and difficult persecution only because they say my writing looked like a man's and that was unseemly, so I was purposely made to alter it and to this the whole community can bear witness; in short, this is a matter not just for a letter but for a number of very lengthy volumes. For what have I said that is so sinful? Did I ask for praise and common approval? And the special favors and honors which Their Excellencies the Lords Marquesses bestow on me only by their favor and unequaled kindness, did I strive to obtain these?

So differently did it happen that Mother Juana de San Antonio, Prioress of this convent and a person incapable of lying under any circumstances, is witness to the fact that the first time that Their Excellencies honored this house with their visit, I asked her permission to withdraw to my cell and neither see them nor be seen (as though Their Excellencies had done me some harm), with no other motive than to flee from the praise that subsequently is turned into most painful barbs of persecution, and I would have been able to do it had the Mother Superior not commanded me otherwise.

What fault is it of mine that Their Excellencies find my company pleasant? Even if there were no reason for this, can I refuse to see such highborn persons? Should I regret the honor they do me with their visits?

Your Reverence knows very well I should not, as you yourself experienced in the times of Their Excellencies the Lords Marquesses of Mancera, for many was the time that I heard Your Reverence complain of the occupations you had to put aside in order to attend Their Excellencies without being able to do otherwise, and if His Excellency the Lord Marquis of Mancera entered convents as saintly as those of the Capuchins and the Barefoot Carmelites any time he wished without anyone thinking ill of it, how can I prevent His Excellency the Marquis of Laguna from visiting this one? Besides, I am not the one in charge here, nor is the governance of this convent my responsibility.

Their Excellencies do me honor because they wish to, not because I deserve it nor because I originally courted it.

I cannot, and would not wish to even if I could, be so barbarously ungrateful for the favors and affection of Their Excellencies (favors so undeserved and so unmerited).

My studies have not been undertaken to hurt or harm anyone and have principally been so private that I have not even made use of the guidance of a teacher but have relied solely upon myself and my work, for I know that studying publicly in schools is unseemly to a woman's modesty because of the hazardous familiarity with men and this would be the reason for keeping women[6] from public studies; not delegating a special place for their study is probably because as the Republic has no need of women for the government of magistrates (from which area, for the same reasons of propriety, the former are also excluded), [the state] is not concerned with that of which it has no need, but who has forbidden women to engage in private and individual studies? Have they not a rational soul as men do? Well, then, why cannot a woman profit by the privilege of enlightenment as they do?[7] Is her soul not as able to receive the grace and glory of God as that of a man? Well, then, why should she not be just as capable in matters of information and knowledge which are of less import? What divine revelation, what rule of the Church, what reasonable judgment formulated such a severe law for us women?

Does learning now prevent, when in other times it furthered salvation? Were not Saint Augustine, Saint Ambrosius and all the other Doctors of the Church saved? And Your Reverence, bowed down under the weight of so much learning, do you not plan to be saved?

And if you answer that men are governed by other rules I say: did not Saint Catherine, Saint Gertrude and my mother Saint Paula[8] study without harming their lofty contemplations, and was the latter's travail in the founding of convents impeded by her knowledge even of Greek? By having learned Hebrew? By having been instructed by my Father Saint Jerome to understand and interpret

Holy Writ, as the Saint himself tells us? Who also, in one of his epistles dealing with all manner of knowledge, praised Saint Paula's daughter Blesilla as being extremely learned, [and this] when the latter was very young indeed, dying as she did when she was twenty?

Then why is that, which in all others was considered good, judged to be evil in my case? Is it only I whose salvation is hindered by books?

If I have read the prophets and secular orators (a lapse of which Saint Jerome himself was guilty), I also read the Holy Doctors and Scripture and cannot deny that to the former I owe countless gifts and rules of good conduct.

For which Christian will not avoid wrath when confronted by the patience of a pagan Socrates? Who can be ambitious in view of the modesty of the Cynic Diogenes? Who does not praise God in Aristotle's intelligence? And finally, what Catholic can fail to be astonished when contemplating the sum of moral virtues in all of the pagan philosophers?

Why should it be judged evil that the time which I might spend in foolish chatter at the grille, or in a cell sniping at everything that goes on in and out of this house, or fighting with someone or shouting at a poor servant or wandering idly through the world with my thoughts, be invested in studying?

And all the more so since God disposed me to be this way and it does not appear to me to be against His most holy law nor contrary to the obligations of my profession; I have this inclination and if it is evil I am not the one who formed me thus[9]—I was born with it and with it I shall die.

Your Reverence wishes that of necessity I should be saved in a state of ignorance, but my beloved Father, can one not accomplish this end and be learned? In the final analysis, for me it is the easier path. Because why should one be led to salvation by the way of ignorance if this is repugnant to one's nature?

Is not God as ultimate goodness also ultimate wisdom? Well, then, why should ignorance be more pleasing to Him than learning?

Let Saint Anthony achieve salvation with his holy ignorance and well and good, while Saint Augustine goes by a different path and neither one of the two is wrong.

Then from whence comes Your Reverence's displeasure and your saying that "had you known I was going to write poetry you would not have made me a nun but would have arranged for me to marry"?

Well, dearly beloved Father (to whom, obliged and with all modesty, I say that which I would prefer not to utter), what direct authority (leaving aside that which my love gave and always will give you) did you have to dispose of my person and my God-given free will?

Because when all that happened I had only very recently had the pleasure of knowing Your Reverence, and although I was indebted to you for your very great concern and interest in my condition, for which I will always be very grateful as indeed I ought to be, as to the matter of my dowry,[10] long before I got to know Your Reverence my sponsor Captain Pedro Velázquez de la Cadena had already set it aside and in making the arrangements for this same sum, and in no other way, God gave me the means [to enter the convent], for which reason I do not know on what your assumption is based, though I do not deny that I owe Your Reverence other kindnesses and favors for which I will be eternally grateful, such as having paid for a teacher of mine, and others; there is no reason that these might not continue except that they have been converted into insults and there seems to be no conversation in which my faults are not mentioned and in which my conversion[11] is not the topic of Your Reverence's zeal.

Am I perchance a heretic? And even if I were, could sheer force make me a saint? Would that saintliness were something to be commanded, for then I would be sure to possess it, but I feel that one must be persuaded of it, not ordered, and if it were a matter to be commanded I have had prelates who have done it; if external precepts and pressures are tempered and prudent they make a person circumspect and modest, but if they are excessive, result in despair. Only the grace and assistance of God are capable of producing saints.

On what, then, is this anger based? Why this descrediting of my person? Why this attitude of making me out to be scandalous in front of everyone? Do I annoy Your Reverence in some way? Have I asked you to help me in remedying any of my needs? Or have I importuned you with any other spiritual or temporal request?

Has Your Reverence any stake in my betterment by reason of obligation, blood relation, upbringing, Church authority, or anything else?

If it is pure charity, let it seem pure charity and have it proceed as such, gently, because exasperating me is not a good way to bring me around, for I do not possess such a servile nature that I will do something when threatened which reason would not persuade me to do; neither would I do for human respect that which I would not do for God, for to give up everything that might give me pleasure —even though it might be very just—is good if I do it to humble myself when I might want to do penance, but it is not when Your Reverence wishes to obtain it by dint of reprimands, and these not in secret as befits paternal correction (given that Your Reverence has decided to be my Father, something for which I consider myself to be very fortunate) but publicly, in front of everyone, where each one reacts to a situation to the extent of his understanding and speaks as he may feel.

Then in all this matter, my Father, is it not natural that I should be hurt by a person whom I love with such veneration and whom with such love I esteem and revere?

If these admonishments were to fall upon some scandalous statement of mine, I am so obedient that (in spite of the fact that neither in matters secular nor spiritual have I been answerable to Your Reverence) I would desist from it and would try to reform and please you, even though it went against my will.

But this not being the case, as our dispute centers on the fact that it amounts to the same thing whether I write verses or not and, considering that I dislike them intensely, so that for my penance there could be no greater punishment than constantly to oblige me to write them, why then do you feel such troublesome affliction?

Because if, to contradict this opinion, I were to speak as passionately against Your Reverence as Your Reverence does against me, countless actions of yours have displeased me (because, after all, in different matters feeling is a question of one doing it this way, the other that), but I do not condemn them for that but instead revere them for being yours and defend them as though they were my own, and perhaps even those same ones which are directed against me, calling them laudable zeal, supreme affection and other merits which my love and reverence are able to invent when I converse with others.

But I cannot refrain from telling Your Reverence that my heart is bursting with the recriminations which for years I might have uttered, and if now I take up the pen to vent them and reply to one I venerate so highly, it is because I can bear no more, for as I am not as submissive as others of your daughters in whom you might better employ your doctrine, [I do it] because I am too deeply affected by this.

And so I beg Your Reverence that if you no longer wish or are disinclined to favor me (for this is voluntary), put me out of your mind, for though I will regret so great a loss, I will have no grounds for complaint, for the God who created and redeemed and bestows so many mercies on me will provide a means whereby my soul, which trusts in His goodness, will not go astray even if it be without Your Reverence's guidance, for Heaven has many keys and is not restricted to one judgment only, but there are many mansions for diverse temperaments and in the world there are many theologians and even if these were lacking, salvation consists more in the desiring than in the knowing and the former depends more on me than on a confessor.

What rule dictates that this salvation of mine must be by means of Your Reverence? Cannot it be someone else? Is God's mercy restricted and limited to one man, even if he be as prudent, as learned and as saintly as Your Reverence?

Surely not, nor have I had up to now particular enlightenment or inspiration of the Lord that He has so ordained and so I will be able to govern myself by the general rules of the Holy Mother Church— as long as the Lord does not enlighten me otherwise—and thus freely choose the spiritual Father I wish, for just as our Lord has disposed Your Reverence to feel such love for me, were He to influence my heart and help me arrive at a firm judgment, I would choose none other than Your Reverence. I beg you not to judge this candor as boldness or lack of respect but as simplicity of heart, as I do not know how to say things other than how I feel them, for which reason I have attempted to speak so that Your Reverence would not have a shred of regret or complaint. Notwithstanding, if in this declaration of my faults there be any word which I have written by inadvertent oversight rather than intentionally and which might be not only offensive but discourteous to Your Reverence's person, consider it retracted and judge it to be ill said and worse written and if I could discern which phrase might cause offense, I would immediately expunge it.

I repeat once again that my intention is solely to beg Your Reverence that if you are not pleased to favor me that you put me out of your mind, unless it be to entrust me to the Lord, as I truly believe that in your great charity you will do this most fervently.

I entreat God's Majesty to keep you.

From this my Father St. Jerome's convent in Mexico.

Your

Juana Inés de la Cruz[12]

Notes

1. There are a number of errors in the text of the letter, caused either by carelessness on Sor Juana's part or through errors of transcription of the original letter by the amanuensis involved. As Paz rightly notes, Sor Juana's intention here is not to suggest that it is her *verses* that are unfortunate but her God-given talent for composing them (634). For a corrected and extensively annotated version of the letter's text, see Antonio Alatorre, "La *Carta* de Sor Juana al P. Núñez," *Nueva Revista de Filología Hispánica* 15 (1987): 591–673.

2. This is a reference to Fray Payo Enríquez de Rivera, who was first archbishop of Mexico and subsequently viceroy from 1674 to 1680.

3. What she calls "the Church's Arch" was a poetic allegory on Neptune, composed to accompany a temporary triumphal arch erected to celebrate the arrival in 1680 of the new viceroys, the Marquis de la Laguna and his wife. Sor Juana chose the mythological reference to Neptune to allude to the water-related last name of the viceroy (Laguna = lake). This

arch, which consisted of a collage of painting and poetry, was commissioned by direct order of the Cathedral's Chapter and of Archbishop Payo, mentioned above.

4. María Luisa Manrique de Lara y Gonzaga, Countess of Paredes and Vicereine of Mexico, was Sor Juana's most intimate woman friend and the one who arranged for the publication of the nun's poetry in Seville in 1689.

5. The original text here reads somewhat differently: "Las mujeres sienten que las excedan los hombres, que parezca que los igualo," a syntactically confusing sentence because of the subjunctive form of "parecer"; I agree with the opinion of Marie-Cécile Bénassy-Berling, who believes it should read "Las mujeres sienten que las exceda, los hombres que parezca que los igualo," which is how I have translated it (Personal letter, February 28, 1987).

6. In the original the verb used is "publicar los estudios públicos," which in context makes no sense and is in all likelihood an error; I have translated it as "prohibir. " The second error is in the phrase "disputarles lugar," when it should read "diputarles lugar señalado," that is, "designate a special place" for women to study these matters. I am grateful to Antonio Alatorre for pointing this out.

7. Again the original makes very little sense: "¿Pues por qué no gozará el privilegio de la ilustración de las letras con ellas?" Bénassy-Berling suggests it should read "como ellos," which also seems more plausible to me.

8. Sor Juana here refers to the legendary Saint Catherine of Alexandria (third century), famous for her beauty and learning, who was martyred by the Emperor Maximin II when she refused to become his bride; Saint Gertrude "the Great" (thirteenth century) was a Benedictine nun who wrote parts of the "Legatus Divinae Pietatis," one of the most important works of German mysticism, and is also the patron saint of the West Indies; Saint Paula (fifth century) was the wealthy Roman matron who was one of Saint Jerome's most devoted disciples; he named her head of one of the twin monastic communities he founded in Bethlehem. She was the patron saint of Sor Juana's convent.

9. The original text reads "yo me hice" (I made myself), which appears to contradict the whole thrust of this passage; Tapia Méndez changed it in his text (*Carta 25*), and I followed him in my translation, but Alatorre (623) and Paz (643) keep "yo me hice," which is also plausible. Let the readers decide.

10. People were apparently under the impression that Núñez had procured Sor Juana's dowry for her and that she was therefore beholden to him. This is one of the most important points of heretofore unknown biographical information that the discovery of this letter has contributed to Sor Juana studies.

11. The original text says "conversación" instead of the more plausible "conversión," which again appears to be an error of transcription. Tapia Méndez is also persuaded that the correct term should be "conversión" (*Carta* 25).

12. I wish to express my sincere thanks to David Lagmanovich and to Antonio Alatorre for their help in this translation.

Poesía religiosa

361
Dos letras sueltas para cantar en la solemnidad del nacimiento [de Cristo].

LETRA I
Estribillo
¿Cómo será esto, mi Dios,
que yo creo en Vos,
y aunque creo lo que veo
no veo todo lo que creo?

Coplas
Si la Fe y la vista son
tan encontradas, ¿por qué
aquí ha de hacer fe la vista
y no hacer vista la Fe?

Niño os miro, y que lo sois
es necesario creer;
mas también sé que sois Grande,
y mis ojos no lo ven.

Cuando allá en la Eucaristía
estáis, más fácil me es,
porque ya sé que al contrario
de la vista he de creer.

Pero aquí, ¿qué me mandáis?
Que crea mi sencillez
lo que veo y que no veo,
lo que es y que no es.

Hombre parecéis, y sois,
Señor, lo que parecéis;
pero lo Dios no se os mira,
y sé que sois Dios también.

En fin, el sentido aquí
no se engaña, pero es
Infinito más lo que hay
que lo que se alcanza a ver.

219

Compuesto para la fiesta de la Asunción de la Virgen 1676.

VILLANCICO III

La soberana Doctora
de las Escuelas divinas,
de que los Angeles todos
deprenden sabiduría,

por ser quien inteligencia
mejor de Dios participa,
a leer la suprema sube
Cátedra de Teología.

Por Primaria de las ciencias
es justo que esté aplaudida,
quien de todas las criaturas
se llevó la primacía.

Ninguno *de Charitate*
estudió con más fatiga,
y la materia *de Gratia*
supo aun antes de nacida.

Después la *de Incarnatione*
pudo estudiar en sí misma,

con que en la *de Trinitate*
alcanzó mayor noticia.

Los soberanos Cursantes
que las letras ejercitan
y de la Sagrada Ciencia
los secretos investigan,

con los Espíritus puros
que el eterno Solio habitan
(e Inteligencias sutiles,
Ciencia de Dios se apellidan),

todos la votan iguales,
y con amantes caricias,
le celebran la victoria
y el triunfo le solemnizan.

Estribillo
Y con alegres voces de aclamación festiva,
hinchen las raridades del aire de alegrías,
y sólo se percibe en la confusa grita:
—¡Vítor, vítor, vítor, vítor María,
a pesar del Infierno y de su envidia!
¡Vítor, vítor, vítor, vítor María![1]

Poesía cortesana

Soneto 167

Continúa [del soneto 166]² el mismo asunto y aun le expresa con más viva elegancia.³

Feliciano me adora y le aborrezco;
Lisardo me aborrece y yo le adoro;
por quien no me apetece ingrato, lloro,
y al que me llora tierno, no apetezco.

A quien más me desdora, el alma ofrezco;
a quien me ofrece víctimas, desdoro;
desprecio al que enriquece mi decoro,
y al que le hace desprecios, enriquezco.

Si con mi ofensa al uno reconvengo,
me reconviene el otro a mí, ofendido;
y a padecer de todos modos vengo,

pues ambos atormentan mi sentido:
aquéste, con pedir lo que no tengo;
y aquél, con no tener lo que le pido.

Soneto 168

Prosigue el mismo asunto, y determina que prevalezca la razón contra el gusto.

Al que ingrato me deja, busco amante;
al que amante me sigue, dejo ingrata;
constante adoro a quien mi amor maltrata;
maltrato a quien mi amor busca constante.

Al que trato de amor, hallo diamante,
y soy diamante al que de amor me trata;
triunfante quiero ver al que me mata,
y mato al que me quiere ver triunfante.

Si a éste pago, padece mi deseo;
si ruego a aquél, mi pundonor enojo:
de entrambos modos infeliz me veo.

Pero yo, por mejor partido, escojo
de quien no quiero, ser violento empleo,
que, de quien no me quiere, vil despojo.

*Sor Juana Inés
de la Cruz*

87

Poesía satírica

Epigrama 95[4]
Que dan el Colirio merecido a un soberbio.

El no ser de Padre honrado,
fuera defecto, a mi ver,
si como recibí el ser
de él, se lo hubiera yo dado.

Más piadosa fue tu Madre,
que hizo que a muchos sucedas:
para que, entre tantos, puedas
tomar el que más te cuadre.

Poemas a la Virreina (la Condesa de Paredes)

82

ENDECHAS REALES

Expresa su respeto amoroso: dice el sentido en que llama suya a la Señora Virreina Marquesa de la Laguna.

Divina Lysi mía:
perdona si me atrevo
a llarmarte así, cuando
aun de ser tuya el nombre no merezco.

Y creo, no osadía
es llamarte así, puesto
que a ti te sobran rayos,
si en mí pudiera haber atrevimientos.

Error es de la lengua,
que lo que dice imperio
del dueño, en el dominio,
parezcan posesiones en el siervo.

Mi rey, dice el vasallo;
mi cárcel, dice el preso;
y el más humilde esclavo,[5]
sin agraviarlo, llama suyo al dueño.

Así, cuando yo mía
te llamo, no pretendo
que juzguen que eres mía,
sino sólo que yo ser tuya quiero.

Yo te vi; pero basta:
que a publicar incendios
basta apuntar la causa,
sin añadir la culpa del efecto.

Que mirarte tan alta,
no impide a mi denuedo;
que no hay Deidad segura
al altivo volar del pensamiento.

Y aunque otras más merezcan,
en distancia del Cielo
lo mismo dista el valle
más humilde, que el monte más soberbio.

En fin, yo de adorarte
el delito confieso;
si quieres castigarme,
este mismo castigo será premio.

Soneto 195[6]

A la excma. Sra. Condesa de Paredes, Marquesa de la Laguna, enviándole estos papeles que su excia. Le pidió y que pudo recoger Soror Juana de muchas manos, en que estaban no menos divididos que escondidos, como tesoro, con otros que no cupo en el tiempo buscarlos ni copiarlos.

El hijo que la esclava ha concebido,
dice el Derecho que le pertenece
al legítimo dueño que obedece
la esclava madre, de quien es nacido.

El que retorna el campo agradecido,
opimo fruto, que obediente ofrece,
es del señor, pues si fecundo crece,
se lo debe al cultivo recibido.

Así, Lysi divina, estos borrones
que hijos del alma son, partos del pecho,
será razón que a ti te restituya;

y no lo impidan sus imperfecciones,
pues vienen a ser tuyos de derecho
los conceptos de una alma que es tan tuya.

*Ama y Señora mía, besa los pies de V. Excia., su criada
Juana Inés de la Cruz.*

Poesía filosófica

Soneto 149
Encarece de animosidad la elección de estado durable hasta la muerte.

Si los riesgos del mar considerara,
ninguno se embarcara; si antes viera
bien su peligro, nadie se atreviera
ni al bravo toro osado provocara.

Si del fogoso bruto ponderara
la furia desbocada en la carrera
el jinete prudente, nunca hubiera
quien con discreta mano lo enfrenara.

Pero si hubiera alguno tan osado
que, no obstante el peligro, al mismo Apolo[7]
quisiese gobernar con atrevida

mano el rápido carro en luz bañado,
todo lo hiciera, y no tomara sólo
estado que ha de ser toda la vida.

Soneto 145
Procura desmentir los elogios que a un retrato de la poetisa[8] inscribió la verdad, que llama pasión.

Este que ves, engaño colorido,
que del arte ostentando los primores,
con falsos silogismos de colores
es cauteloso engaño del sentido;

éste, en quien la lisonja ha pretendido
excusar de los años los horrores,
y venciendo del tiempo los rigores
triunfar de la vejez y del olvido,

es un vano artificio del cuidado,
es una flor al viento delicada,
es un resguardo inútil para el hado:

es una necia diligencia errada,
es un afán caduco, y, bien mirado,
es cadáver, es polvo, es sombra, es nada.

Soneto 146

Quéjase de la suerte: insinúa su aversión a los vicios, y justifica su diverti-
miento a las Musas.

En perseguirme, Mundo, ¿qué interesas?
En qué te ofendo, cuando sólo intento
poner bellezas en mi entendimiento
y no mi entendimiento en las bellezas?

Yo no estimo tesoros ni riquezas;
y así, siempre me causa más contento
poner riquezas en mi pensamiento
que no mi pensamiento en las riquezas.

Y no estimo hermosura que, vencida,
es despojo civil de las edades,
ni riqueza me agrada fementida,

teniendo por mejor, en mis verdades,
consumir vanidades de la vida
que consumir la vida en vanidades.

1. El tradicional grito triunfal de "Vítor" que Sor Juana emplea aquí se usaba cuando un estudiante aprobaba sus exámenes doctorales, o cuando un profesor ganaba una serie de exámenes muy rigurosos y competitivos, *las oposiciones*, para ocupar una cátedra.

2. En un ciclo de tres sonetos, de los cuales he escogido el segundo y el tercero, Sor Juana trabaja con el tema de las "encontradas correspondencias," o sea las antítesis triangulares amorosas. Esta era una convención popular en la poesía cortesana de la época.

3. Sor Juana no redactó estos breves resúmenes al principio de sus versos; los puso algún editor.

4. Alguién debe de haber aludido al nacimiento ilegítimo de Sor Juana, para que ella respondiera con tal poema. En su época se les echaba la culpa de la bastardía a los hijos, lo cual a ella le parece ilógico e injusto. ¿Cómo se puede culpar a la criatura de la forma en que fue concebida? Son los padres los responsables de sus hijos. Por eso, razona Sor Juana, la única manera por la cual le pueden echar la culpa a ella por su estado social es ser ella la progenitora de su propio padre (que sea él el hijo de ella).

5. Sor Juana se considera "esclava" de amor y de gratitud de la Virreina.

6. Este soneto funcionaba como prefacio a la *Inundación castálida*, el primer libro impreso de Sor Juana, gracias a los esfuerzos y la influencia de la condesa.

7. Sor Juana aquí hace referencia al destino de Faetón, hijo de Apolo. El rey sol le había prometido a su hijo cumplir cualquier deseo suyo, y Faetón eligió conducir el carro de su padre, que llevaba el ardiente disco solar a través del cielo. Apolo le advirtió a su hijo que el joven carecía de fuerza para controlar a los caballos que tiraban del carro, pero Faetón no le hizo caso. Efectivamente, poco después de comenzar a regir el carro, perdió el control, y el sol empezó a girar tan violentamente por el cielo que amenazaba destruir la tierra y el Monte Olimpo, hogar de los dioses. Para evitar el desastre, Júpiter mató al conductor con un rayo, y el joven se precipitó al mar y a la muerte. Sor Juana aludía a Faetonte con mucha frecuencia en sus escritos, destacando su atrevimiento y su voluntad de arriesgarlo todo; es obvio que ella se identificaba con este mismo deseo.

8. Los críticos, basándose en la sinopsis del editor, siempre han interpretado este poema como si Sor Juana estuviera hablando de un retrato de sí misma, pero una cuidadosa lectura del soneto no nos indica tal cosa.

Religious Poems

361

Two separate lyrics to sing on the solemn occasion of the birth of Christ.

SONG I

Refrain
How can this be, my God,
That I believe in You,
And though I believe what I see
see not all I believe?

Verses
If Faith and sight are
so opposite, why must sight
be taken on faith, and not
Faith on sight?

I see You as Child,
and must believe that You are such,
yet I also know You are Great,[1]
though this my eyes cannot see.

Things are easier for me
When You are present in the Eucharist,
for then I know I must believe
the opposite of what I see.

But here, what do You wish me to do?
That my simplicity may believe
what I see and do not see,
that which is and yet is not.

You seem a Man, and You are,
My Lord, that which You seem.
But that You are God is not obvious,
Yet I know You are God as well.

In any case, sense here
cannot be fooled, for what there is
is Infinitely more
than that which is possible to see.

219
Composed for the feast of the Assumption of the Virgin 1676.

VILLANCICO III

The unsurpassed Doctor
of divine Doctrine,
from whom all the Angels
learn wisdom,

for as she is the one who best
shares in God's intelligence,
she rises to lecture
from the highest Chair[2] of Theology.

It is right to praise her
as First [in her class] in knowledge,
she who has won
first place among all creatures.

No one studied *Charity*
with greater effort than she,
while she mastered the course on *Grace*
even before her birth.

The assignment on the *Incarnation*
she could study in her own person,

in the matter of the *Trinity*
even greater acclaim was hers.

The sovereign Students [3]
whose business is literature
research the secrets
of Divine Knowledge,

along with the pure Spirits
who dwell in the eternal Throne of Heaven
(and the subtle Minds
who call themselves God's Knowledge),

all these together cast their vote for her,
and with loving affection
celebrate her victory
and solemnize her triumph.

Refrain
And with happy voices of festive acclaim
the highest spheres with joy do swell,
in the confused uproar one hears but this:
"Vítor, vítor, vítor, vítor, Mary,
in spite of Hell and its envy!
Vítor, vítor, vítor, vítor, Mary!"[4]

Courtly Poems

Sonnet 167

She continues the same topic [from Sonnet 166]⁵ and expresses it with even livelier elegance.⁶

Feliciano adores me, and I loathe him;
Lisardo loathes me, and I adore him;
I weep for him who ungratefully shuns me,
and shun him who tenderly weeps for me.

To him who most debases me, I offer my soul;
he who offers me [sacrificial] victims, I debase;
I scorn him who enriches my good name,
and enrich him who shows me scorn.

If, by my offense, I rebuke the one,
the other, offended, rebukes me;
and either way I come to suffer,

for both torment my judgment:
the one, by pleading for what I do not have;
and the other, by not having that for which I plead.

Sonnet 168

She continues the same theme and determines that reason must prevail over desire.

He who ungratefully leaves me, I lovingly long for;
he who lovingly pursues me, I ungratefully leave;
steadfastly I adore him who abuses my love;
abusing him who steadfastly seeks my love.

He, to whom I would speak of love, I find diamond-obdurate,
obdurate as diamond am I with him who speaks of love;
he who slays me, I would see triumphant,
yet would I kill the one who longs to see me triumph.

If I please the latter, my desire suffers;
if I beg the former, I vex my honor:
both ways lead to my unhappiness.

But I, as the better option, choose
to be the constrained object of him I do not love,
than for him who does not love me, degraded plunder.

Sor Juana Inés
de la Cruz

99

Satiric Poems

Epigram 95[7]

Where eyewash is administered to an arrogant man who needs it.

As I see it, not to be born of an honorable father,
Might indeed be judged a flaw,
If, instead of receiving my life from him,
[My father] had received his life from me.

Far more charitable was your mother
with you, the successor of many:
So that among infinite fathers
You might choose the sire you liked.

Poems to the Vicereine (the Countess of Paredes)

82

ENDECHAS REALES

*She expresses her loving respect: she explains the sense in which she calls the
Vicereine Marchioness of la Laguna her own.*

My divine Lysi:
forgive me if I dare
to call you thus, when as yet
I do not deserve to be called yours.

It is not too bold, I think,
to call you thus
for you have thunderbolts to spare,
with which to blast any boldness of mine.

It is an error of the tongue,
when what it calls the lord's realm
appears instead to be
the property of the servant.

My King, says the vassal;
my prison, says the prisoner,
and the humblest of slaves,[8] with no insult intended,
calls the master his as well.

And so, when I call you
my own, I do not claim
that others should judge you mine;
For I only wish to be yours.

I saw you—but enough:
when one shouts "Fire,"
it is enough to point out the cause,
without adding blame to the effect.

Seeing you there so high,
does not affect my daring;
there is no Deity who is safe
from thought's proud flight.

Though others may be more worthy,
when one measures distance from Heaven,
the humblest valley is just as far
as the proudest mountain of all.

And so, I confess
to the crime of adoring you;
should you desire to punish me
that same punishment would be glory.

Sonnet 195[9]

To Her Excellency the Countess of Paredes, Marchioness of la Laguna, on sending her these papers which Her Excellency requested of her and which Sor Juana was able to collect from many hands, where they were no less scattered than hidden, like treasure, along with others which for lack of time she could neither find nor copy over.

The child the slave woman has conceived,
the Law says belongs
to the rightful master [whom] the slave mother
—from whom the child is born—obeys.

The lush harvest the grateful earth
obediently returns to its master,
should by rights be his, for if the earth bears fruit,
[the earth] owes it to the care it has received.

So then, divine Lysi, these scribbles,
which are my soul's children, births of my heart,
are rightfully restored to you;

no matter their imperfections,
by right they belong only to you,
the concepts of a soul which is utterly yours.

My Mistress and My Lady, your servant kisses
Your Excellency's feet.
Juana Inés de la Cruz.

Philosophical Poems

Sonnet 149

She ponders the choice of a state that lasts until death.

If one considered the dangers of the sea,
no one would embark; if first one clearly saw
one's peril, no one would dare
to bravely provoke the raging bull.

If the prudent rider
would ponder the wild steed's fury
no guiding hand would ever be found
to check his headlong frenzy in the race.

But were there one of such daring
that, mindless of the danger, he would
with fearless hand aspire

to steer the sun-bathed chariot of Apollo himself:[10]
he would risk all, and would not deign
to accept a state that bound him all his days.

Sonnet 145

She attempts to prove false the praise which truth inscribed on a portrait of the poetess,[11] which she terms enthusiasm.

This, which you see, a colored deception,
displaying art's exquisite beauties
with false syllogisms of color,
is a guileful deception of sense;

this, in which flattery has attempted
to exonerate the years' ravaged traces,
and, overcoming time's harsh sentence,
to triumph over old age and oblivion,

is a vain artifice of care,
is a delicate flower exposed to the wind,
is a useless defense against fate:

is a foolish, misguided effort,
is a fruitless desire, and, truly seen,
is corpse, dust, shadow, naught.

Sonnet 146

*She bemoans her fate; she suggests her aversion to vices and justifies her
diversion with the Muses.*

In persecuting me, World, what is your intention?
How do I offend you, when all I desire
is to place beauty in my mind
instead of focusing my mind on worldly beauty?

I esteem neither treasures nor riches,
and thus, am always more content
to put riches into my thoughts
than to waste my thoughts on riches.

I esteem not that beauty which, vanquished,
is the ravaged prey of passing years,
nor do false riches please me;

for I prize more to consume
the vanities of life with my truths
than to have my life consumed by vanity.

Notes

1. Sor Juana here is playing with the double meaning of *grande* in Spanish, where it can mean both "great" and "adult."

2. In the Middle Ages professors read from a high chair and podium (*cátedra*) on a level above the student body. "Chair" and "professorship" later became synonymous terms.

3. The Students, Spirits, and Minds to which Sor Juana refers all dwell in Heaven.

4. The Spanish cheer "Vítor" that Sor Juana uses here was, and is today, the traditional shout of triumph when a student passed his doctoral examinations, or a professor attained a coveted professorship after winning a series of *oposiciones* (highly competitive academic examinations).

5. In a cycle of three sonnets, of which I have selected the second and third, Sor Juana addresses the subject of "encontradas correspondencias" or triangular antitheses on the subject of love. This was a popular convention in the courtly love poetry of the time.

6. Sor Juana did not write these brief synopses that precede her poems; they were added by an editor.

7. Someone must have alluded to Sor Juana's illegitimate birth in order for her to write such a response. In her time children were blamed for the stain of illegitimacy, which to her seems illogical and unjust. How can the child help the way he or she is conceived? It is the parents who are responsible for their children. Therefore, Sor Juana reasons, the only way she could be blamed for her social status is for her to have given birth to her own father.

8. Sor Juana considers herself the Vicereine's "slave," chained by feelings of love and gratitude.

9. This sonnet functioned as a preface to the *Inundación castálida* [Castalian Flood], Sor Juana's first published work, thanks to the effort and influence of the countess.

10. Sor Juana here refers to the fate of Apollo's son Phaeton; the Sun God had promised to fulfill any wish of his, and Phaeton chose to drive his father's chariot, which pulled the sun's burning disk across the sky. Apollo warned his son that he lacked the strength to control the horses that drew the chariot, but Phaeton would not listen. Soon after he began to drive the chariot he indeed lost control, and the sun careened wildly across the sky, threatening to burn the earth and Mount Olympus, the

home of the gods. Jupiter killed Phaeton with a thunderbolt to prevent this from happening, and the young man fell headlong into the sea to his death. In her writing Sor Juana frequently alluded to Phaeton's daring and willingness to risk all; it is obvious that she identified with this desire.

11. Although critics have always read this poem as though Sor Juana were speaking to a portrait of herself, basing themselves on the editor's synopsis, a careful reading of the sonnet itself shows no such reference.

Madre Francisca
Josefa de Castillo

*Madre Francisca Josefa de Castillo, courtesy
of Biblioteca Luis Angel Arango, Bogotá.*

*F*rancisca Josefa de la Concepción de Castillo y Guevara was born in Tunja, Colombia—known as New Granada during the colonial era—in 1671, to a family that wielded a great deal of influence in the small, provincial city. Her father was from Spain, from the province of Toledo, and her mother was a criolla. Francisca learned to read from her mother, and although she never had any formal education, the fact that she was literate at all made her different from many of her peers. Religious life attracted her from a very early age; she shared with Sor Juana a distinct aversion to marriage, but her family was totally opposed to her desire to enter a convent. They offered her space in their house to use for her devotions and agreed to let her wear a religious habit (*Obras* 1: 15–17), but it was not enough: Francisca ran away from home to join the Real Convento Franciscano de Santa Clara. This was the first religious community for women established in New Granada (1572), and the founders were directly related to Francisca.

In spite of her deep commitment to the religious life, Francisca was never happy in her community. Her autobiography chronicles many conflicts with her sister nuns, some of whom were verbally and others even physically abusive. There were several reasons for this. As upper-class women had only two life choices, marriage or the veil, convents housed many women who had little or no religious vocation (McKnight, "Voz" 86; Mújica 7), who spent their time gossiping about each other, and who may well have resented someone as devout, socially powerful, and literate as Francisca. Her own personality may also have put them off, so that when she claimed to have experienced mystical unions with God, many of the nuns reacted not with joy but with disbelief and envy.[1] The community also resented the many members of her family who joined the order, including her widowed mother and sister. In Madre Castillo's writings the Tunja convent often comes across more as a snake pit than a house of God. In spite of these frictions, however, she was elected abbess on three different occasions, though rumor had it that she had been somewhat heavy-handed in wielding her influence to get elected. During her terms she appears to have run the convent very efficiently, once even saving it from bankruptcy.

Madre Castillo is known for two very different works: the *Afectos espirituales,* devotional meditations on a variety of themes, and *Su Vida,* the spiritual autobiography that covers her life from about 1713 to 1723. Her confessors were aware of her piety and encouraged her to write down her thoughts and mystical experiences. She began to write the *Afectos* very soon after entering the convent in 1689 (she professed in 1694) and continued to work on them for most of her life. These meditations are considered of better literary quality than her autobiography: lyrical, positive, the product of an assured authorial voice that derived deep spiritual satisfaction from this activity. For the modern reader, however, it is her autobiography that is of greater interest.

Although she wrote some of the *Afectos* and the *Vida* more or less at the same time, the *Vida* is so different that, as Elisa Mújica says, "it seems that they could not have come from the same pen" (30). One explanation may be that the time covered by the *Vida* was a particularly difficult one for the nun (McKnight, "Sister Acts" 91). Another is that whereas she *wanted* to write the *Afectos,* she composed her autobiography under duress. As happened with many nuns who were renowned for their piety, Madre Castillo's confessors compelled her to relate her life story, and her trepidation at doing this is palpable in the text. It is no wonder that it should be so (many other nuns made to write their autobiographies expressed similar feelings): having been trained to subject, even annihilate all personal will and volition in the service of God, a nun who was ordered to write her life, the most self-affirming form of writing there is, would often react with confusion, resistance, and fear. While Madre Castillo composed the *Afectos* for the greater glory of God, recounting the particulars of her own life must have seemed out of place and even sinful to her. Thus there is a marked difference in authorial voice: in the *Afectos* she is serving as a conduit for *God's* voice, not as principal author of the text, as was the case in her autobiography. Hence she is surer of herself, and less nervous about narrative responsibility.

The *Vida* is not particularly pleasant reading, but it offers fascinating insights into the life of an exceptionally devout nun and into the nature of her mystical experiences as a Bride of Christ. It records a life of ascetic discipline, morbid mortification of her own body, celestial visions and erotic nightmares, recurrent ill health, and the ongoing enmity of her community. Although Madre Castillo casts herself into the role of perpetual sinner and victim, she also insists that all her suffering is for the sake of her beloved Bridegroom. What is so interesting in the *Vida* is the author's strategy of subjectivity, which is less obvious than it seems. Madre Castillo presents herself in a dual role: she may be a vile sinner, yet she is also the chosen Bride of Christ (McKnight, "Voz" 80). Her narrative strategy is elusive and paradoxical: her very humility is simultaneously self-affirming.

The *Afectos* should also be read with care. After the ecclesiastical reforms of the sixteenth-century Council of Trent, nuns were forbidden to read the Bible in the vernacular or to teach religious matters. They had always been forbidden to preach. Madre Castillo had somehow learned Latin, and was familiar with the Bible in this language. Though the *Afectos* appear to fall squarely within the mainstream of what a nun was permitted to write, McKnight shows that in many of these meditations Madre Castillo was actively paraphrasing and interpreting Scripture, as well as adopting an instructional tone while purportedly only preaching to her own soul ("Nexos" 249). Her humility thus was not quite what it appeared to be. Stacey Schlau noted a similar strategy in the nun's writing: while insisting on her total obedience to Catholic tradition and dogma, the Madre is nevertheless affirming her own uniqueness (166). Madre Castillo's strategies in the formation of her subjective voice are thus much more complex and transgressive than first meets the eye.

The other aspect of her narrative self we must not forget is that in spite of her affinity for spiritual withdrawal, Madre Castillo as abbess had to deal with the outside world on a daily and direct basis. This was especially true in the administration of the convent's finances and property, which led to frequent lawsuits (McKnight, "Voz" 75–76).

She herself came under fire from her community when she inherited her late sister's extremely valuable jewelry. Just like Sor Juana with her "nest egg," Madre Castillo did not donate these assets directly to her convent: she gave most of the inheritance to fashion a beautiful and costly *custodia* (monstrance), a ceremonial piece of altar plate used to exhibit the consecrated Host. This monstrance, known as "La Custodia de los Andes," is made of eight pounds of gold, emeralds, amethysts, topazes, diamonds, and the like; considered a major national treasure, it now reposes in the vaults of Colombia's Banco de la República (Mújica 18).[2] Just as in her writing, Madre Castillo has engaged in a double-edged act: she neatly bypassed her sister nuns while exalting her own name as pious donor.

The manuscripts of both the *Afectos* and *Su Vida* are in the Luis Angel Arango Library in Bogotá. There is also a third manuscript known as "El cuaderno de Enciso" (The Enciso Notebook), an accounting ledger given to Madre Castillo by her brother-in-law, José Enciso; as paper was always very scarce, she used the blank pages to rework some of the "Afectos," or to copy works of other authors she admired. Among these was Sor Juana, several of whose verses Madre Castillo copied without recording her source; for a while these poems were attributed to the Colombian nun until the mistake was rectified. It is fortunate that this mix-up occurred, as it established a direct link between the two most famous nuns of Spanish America.

After the Madre died in 1742, the Clarissan nuns gave her writings to the Castillo family. *Su Vida,* curiously enough, was first published in Philadelphia in 1817 by one of her descendants because Colombia was undergoing a period of political instability that made publishing there difficult (Mújica 21–22). The *Afectos* were published in 1843.

There is no doubt that in temperament and in religious vocation the Madre Castillo is very different from Sor Juana, but both left their mark on the colonial literature of their respective countries. They are but the tip of the iceberg: many more life stories of religious women lie in the archives of libraries and convents, waiting for the critical attention that has been denied them for so many centuries.[3]

Notes

1. As Electa Arenal and Stacey Schlau show, hers was not the only text to record such reactions by other nuns, many of whom were openly hostile to claims of mystic experiences.

2. Sor María del Niño Jesús relates that other nuns contributed what they could to the monstrance, but Madre Castillo gave the lion's share (389).

3. Arenal and Schlau's *Untold Sisters* is an invaluable resource in this area. Kathleen Myers has also recently published the writings of a Mexican nun who was Sor Juana's contemporary: *Word from New Spain: The Spiritual Autobiography of Madre María de San José (1656–1719)* (Liverpool: Liverpool University Press, 1993). See also Kathryn McKnight, *The Mystic of Tunja: The Writings of Madre Castillo, 1671–1742* (Amherst, MA: U of Massachusetts Press, 1997).

Su Vida

Padre mío: Hoy día de la Natividad de Nuestra Señora, empiezo en su nombre a hacer lo que vuestra paternidad me manda y a pensar y considerar delante del Señor todos los años de mi vida en amargura de mi alma, pues todos los hallo gastados mal, y así me alegro de hacer memoria de ellos, para confundirme en la divina presencia y pedir a Dios gracia para llorarlos, y acordarme de sus misericordias y beneficios, y uno de ellos he entendido fue el darme padres cristianos y temerosos de Dios, compasivos y recatados; tánto, que a mi padre jamás se le oyó una palabra menos compuesta, ni se le vió acción que no fuera; siempre nos hablaba de Dios, y eran sus palabras tales, que en el largo tiempo de mi vida aún no se me han olvidado; antes, en muchas ocasiones, me han servido de consuelo y aliento, y también de freno. En hablando de Nuestra Señora (de quien era devotísimo) o de la pasión de Nuestro Señor, siempre era con los ojos llenos de lágrimas, y lo mismo cuando daba limosna a los pobres, que se juntaban todos los de la ciudad en casa los viernes, y yo lo vía, porque lo acompañaba a repartir la limosna, y vía la ternura, humildad y devoción con que la repartía, besando primero la que daba a cada pobre; y aun con los animales enfermos tenía mucha piedad, de que pudiera decir cosas muy particulares. Asimismo, mi madre era tan temerosa de Dios, cuanto amiga de los pobres, y enemiga de vanidades, de aliños ni entretenimientos, y de tánta humildad, que habiendo enviudado y estando casi ciega, le dio una criada muchos golpes en una iglesia por que se quitara del lugar donde estaba, lo cual llevó con mucha mansedumbre, y se quitó medio arrastrando; y me lo refería alabando a Dios y bendiciéndolo, porque la había traído de tánta estimación a tiempo en que padeciera algo; de esto pudiera decir mucho, y de los buenos ejemplos que vía en mi niñez; sino que yo como las arañas volvía veneno aun las cosas más saludables.

Padeció mucho mi madre cuando yo hube de nacer al mundo, hasta que llamando a su confesor, que era el padre Diego Solano, de la Compañía de Jesús, para confesarse y morir, que ya no esperaba otra cosa, confesándose y teniéndose del bordón del padre, nací yo—y lo que al decir esto siente mi corazón, sólo lo pudieran decir mis ojos hechos fuentes de lágrimas. Nací, Dios mío, Vos sabéis para qué, y cuánto se ha dilatado mi destierro, cuán amargo lo han hecho mis pasiones y culpas, Nací, ¡ay Dios mío!, y luego aquel santo padre me bautizó y dio una grande cruz, que debía de traer consigo, poniéndome los nombres de mi padre san Francisco y san José; dándome Nuestro Señor desde luégo estos socorros y amparos, y el de los padres de la Compañía de Jesús, que tánto han trabajado para reducirme al camino de la verdad. Quiera Nuestro Señor que éntre por él, antes de salir de la vida mortal.

Nací día del bienaventurado san Bruno, parece quiso Nuestro Señor darme a entender cuánto me convendría el retiro, abstracción y silencio en la vida mortal, y cuán peligroso sería para mí el trato y conversación humana, como lo he experimentado desde los primeros pasos de mi vida, y lo lloro, aunque no como debiera. A los quince o veinte días, decían que estuve tan muerta, que compraron la tela y recados para enterrarme, hasta que un tío mío, sacerdote, que despúes me aconsejó (sólo él, que en los demás hallé mucha contradicción) que entrara monja; éste me mandó, como a quien ya no se esperaba que viviera, aplicar un remedio con que luégo volví y estuve buena. En esto sólo la voluntad de Dios me consuela, pues, ¿a quién no pareciera mejor que hubiera muerto luégo quien había de ser como yo he sido?

Siendo aún tan pequeña, que apenas me acuerdo, me sucedió que uno de los niños que iban con sus madres a visita (como suele acaecer, según después he visto), me dijo había de casarse conmigo, y yo sin saber qué era aquello, a lo que ahora me puedo acordar, le respondí que sí; y luégo me entró en el corazón un tormento tal, que no me dejaba tener gusto ni consuelo; parecíame que había hecho un gran mal; y como con nadie comunicaba el tormento de mi corazón, me duró hasta que ya tendría siete años; y en una ocasión hallándome sola en un cuarto donde habían pesado trigo, y quedado el lazo pendiente, me apretó tánto aquella pena, y debía de ayudar el enemigo, porque luégo me propuso fuertemente que me ahorcara, pues sólo este era remedio; mas el santo ángel de mi guarda debió de favorecerme, porque a lo que me puedo acordar, llamando a Nuestra Señora, a quien yo tenía por madre y llamaba en mis aprietos y necesidades, me salí de la pieza, asustada y temerosa; y así me libró Nuestro Señor de aquel peligro, cuando no me parece que tendría siete años. Hasta esta edad, y algún tiempo adelante, todo mi recreo y consuelo era hacer altares y buscar retiros; tenía muchas imágenes de Nuestro Señor y de Nuestra Señora, y en componerlas me pasaba sola y retirada. . . .

Pues el temor que digo despertaba Nuestro Señor en mí, algunas noches en sueños vía cosas espantosas. En una ocasión me pareció andar sobre un entresuelo hecho de ladrillos, puestos punta con punta, como en el aire, y con gran peligro, y mirando abajo vía un río de fuego, negro y horrible, y que entre él andaban tántas serpientes, sapos y culebras, como caras y brazos de hombres que se vían sumidos en aquel pozo o río; yo desperté con gran llanto, y por la mañana vi que en las extremidades de los dedos y las uñas tenía señales de fuego: aunque yo esto no pude saber cómo sería. Otras veces, me hallaba en un valle tan dilatado, tan profundo, de una oscuridad tan penosa, cual no se sabe decir, ni ponderar, y al cabo de él estaba un pozo horrible de fuego negro y espeso; a la orilla andaban los espíritus malos haciendo y dando varios modos de tormentos a diferentes hombres, conforme a sus vicios. Con estas cosas y otras me avisaba Dios misericordioso, para que no le ofendiera, del castigo y pena de los malos; mas nada de esto bastó para que yo no cometiera muchas culpas, aun en aquella edad.

Criábame muy enferma, y esto, y el grande amor que mis padres me tenían, hacía que me miraran con mucho regalo y compasión, y aunque me habían puesto el hábito de santa Rosa de Lima,[1] que se lo prometieron a la santa porque me diera salud Nuestro Señor, mi madre se esmeraba en ponerme joyas y aderezos, y yo era querida de toda la casa, y gente que asistía a mis padres. Con todo eso, jamás tuve contento, ni me consolaba cosa ninguna de la vida, ni los entretenimientos de muñecas y juegos que usan en aquella edad; antes me parecía cosa tan sin gusto, que no quería entender en ello. Algunas veces hacía procesiones de imágenes o remedaba las profesiones y hábitos de las monjas, no porque tuviera inclinación a tomar ese estado; pues sólo me inclinaba a vivir como los ermitaños en los desiertos y cuevas del campo.

[Los trozos que siguen se refieren a su vida después de ser monja.]

En este tiempo vino a confesarme el padre Francisco de Herrera, a quien vuestra paternidad lo dejó encomendado, y yo procuré darme del todo al trato interior con Nuestro Señor, de quien recibía tánta luz; y me parece tenía tan embebida en sí mi alma, como si no viviera en esta vida. El padre me trataba con severidad, y hacía que trabajara de manos lo más del día, y si alguna vez le pedía licencia para gastar el medio día en oración, me la daba, con condición que a la tarde doblara el trabajo. Mandóme muchas veces que escribiera y le mostrara los sentimientos que Nuestro Señor me daba; fue grande mi pena y vergüenza en eso; mas al fin lo hice. . . .

Pocas noches podía irme a acostar, detenida de aquella fuerza de mi alma; parecíame que tenía en lo íntimo de mi corazón una brasa viva, que me enseñaba sin palabras, y encendía en un fuego más dulce que la vida. . . .

Así pasé casi dos años, pareciéndome todas las cosas de esta vida un sueño, y cosa de risa. Un día, estando recogida con Nuestro Señor, me parecía ver a mí misma con una vestidura encarnada que cogía del cuello a los pies, y que los cabellos tenía tan dilatados que llegaban hasta el suelo; dos espíritus malos andaban por allí en forma humana, echando y queriendo trabar con las puntas de aquellos cabellos, para enredarlos; yo me quedé confusa, sin saber qué sería aquello. De ahí a unos días le dijeron al padre algunas cosas de mí, que le causaron un grande enojo: decíame cosas muy sensibles, y me dejaba en el confesionario y se iba sin oírme, hasta que paró en dejarme de confesar, y yo, como quien no tiene fundamento en cosa buena, no hacía sino llorar y desconsolarme de muerte, y darme por engañada, pues mi confesor así me echaba de sí, y me daba por errada; bien veo ahora que el camino hubiera sido rogarle con humildad me enseñara y ayudara a la enmienda de aquellas faltas, y entrar por el camino que me mostrara. . . .

[La Madre Castillo luego obedece al P. de Herrera y redacta algunos de sus pensamientos sobre la verdadera devoción a Dios.]

Este papel como va aquí, vio mi confesor, el padre Francisco, cuando había pasado su enojo; y me respondió: que, aunque más lo miraba, no hallaba en él las señales que suele dejar la serpiente en las cosas por donde anda; que antes, a todo su entender, era Dios; que sólo lo que me aconsejaba era que, aunque más el confesor me azotara e hiriera, no huyera de él, etc.; y así, con la gracia de Dios, lo he procurado hacer en lo que después he vivido, pasando por esto grandes trabajos. . . .

Y así, un día, como yo rehusara mucho escribir lo que el padre Francisco me mandaba, me parecía que vía escribirse en el corazón de Nuestro Señor con su misma sangre, aquellos sentimientos que El mismo daba a mi alma, y los afectos que contenían aquellos papeles; aunque por entonces yo no entendí lo que esto significaba. . . .

Muchas veces, en pasando, aunque fuera de prisa, por donde está el Santísimo Sacramento, sentía, en lo más escondido de mi alma, estas su[a]vísimas palabras, como que salían de Su Divina Majestad: ¿*Quis nos separabit?* (Rom. 8.35). Eran estas palabras, como si dijera: "*ninguno será poderoso a apartarnos.*" Eran tan dulces, tan tiernas y tan suaves, que no sé yo quién, si no es mi corazón de tierra, ingrato y vil, pudiera volver a tener gusto en cosa que no fuera Dios; ni sé por qué gasto el tiempo corto de la vida en otra cosa que en llorar mis culpas e ingratitudes. Asimismo, me advirtió que El solo debía ser mi consuelo; porque un día, como hubiera venido mi confesor, y se fuera sin consolarme, yo quedé con pena y tristeza por esto, y luego entendí estas palabras: *Cur fles? et quare non comedis? et quam ob rem affligitur cor tuum? Numquid non ego melior tibi sum quam decem filii?* (I Sam. 1.8). Fueron estas palabras tan sentidas en mi alma, que me hicieron casi salir de mí con la alegría y amor que habían infundido en ella. No entendí, yo, que dejara de buscar el asilo y la enseñanza en el confesor, sino que el consuelo lo buscara en Dios.

[La Madre Castillo sueña con conversaciones iniciadas por el diablo.]

También había tomado Nuestro Señor otro medio para sacarme de aquellas conversaciones, y éste fue, en medio de ellas ver yo a vuestra paternidad junto a mí, no sé si dormida o despierta, reprendiéndome con severidad y caridad, y acordándome de lo que debía a Dios; con esto tomé más horror a aquellas cosas, aunque yo se lo tenía grande, y tánto, que para escribirle a vuestra paternidad (que ya había vuelto a Santa Fe) el desconsuelo en que me hallaba; me acuerdo que me puse a llorar sobre el tintero, para mojarlo con las lágrimas que lloraba, porque estaba seco, y temía yo tánto el abrir la celda, ni pedir nada, para no dar lugar a que entraran, que más quise mojarlo con mis lágrimas y escribir con ellas; cosa que podía hacer con facilidad, por lo mucho que lloraba.

Después que estuvo acá [mi confesor Juan Martínez], estaba yo un día en mi retiro, considerando en el paso de los azotes que dieron a Nuestro Señor, y pareciéndome caía al desatarlo de la columna, sentía lo mismo que la vez pasada, aquella ansia y deseo de ayudarlo a levantar, pero ahora, al contrario de lo que me sucedió la otra vez, sentía, al llegar mi alma a El, que se desaparecía su cuerpo, porque se hacía como espiritualizado, o yo no sé cómo me dé a entender: parece que se desaparecía de los ojos o conocimiento del alma, y la hacía quedar con gran pena. Esto me parece fue prevenirme para el trabajo, y trabajos que me vinieran. También me sucedió que habiendo entrado en ejercicios con la novicia, a quien yo deseaba encaminar lo mejor que pudiera, estando una tarde en oración, vi pasar el enemigo en hábito de religioso por la puerta de la celda, y que mirando, con unos ojos que daban horror, hacia donde estábamos, se entró en la celda de otra religiosa que estaba junto a la mía; yo no entendí qué sería aquello, mas quedé llena de pavor y tristeza.

Pues por aquel tiempo yo vía mi alma tan mudada, y tan renovados en ella los buenos deseos que en otro tiempo Nuestro Señor me había dado, que yo misma no me conocía, ni sabía con qué así me había encendido Nuestro Señor el alma. Estaba lo más del día retirada, previniendo mi confesión general de aquel año, cuando una noche, a las oraciones, que no se habían hecho maitines,[2] viene a la celda aquella religiosa en cuya celda vi entrar al enemigo, tan llena de furor, y dando gritos contra mí, que yo me quedé pasmada; hízome muchas amenazas, diciendo que no era la novicia mi criada, que ahora vería lo que hacía la madre abadesa. Dio tántas voces, y se levantó tal murmullo de criadas y gritos, que yo me hallé cortada, y no tuve más alivio que meterme en una tribuna, mas desde allí oía tales voces en el coro, tal algazara y cosas que se decían de mí, que estaba medio muerta de oírlas, y no saber en qué pararía aquel furor y gritos; cuando fueron a buscarme la madre vicaria, la religiosa que he dicho, y un tropel de criadas, con linternas y luces. Las cosas que allí me dijeron fueron sin modo, y la cólera con que iban. . . . Las cosas que me levantaron no son para dichas, yo no hallaba dónde acogerme, porque la celda había quedado llena sólo de pavor, y con el susto no me podía tener ya en pie. Mis criadas habían levantádose también contra mí, con que hube de acogerme a las puertas de una religiosa a quien le habían dicho cosas que la pudieran enojar mucho contra mí; mas viéndome en tan miserable estado, se movió a compasión, y fue la única que en toda la casa la tuvo de mí en mis trabajos. Luégo caí enferma de una enfermedad tal, que el sudor que sudaba me dejaba las manos como cocidas en agua hirviendo. La boca se me volvía a un lado, y me daban unos desmayos tan profundos que duraban tres y cuatro horas largas. En estos desmayos tiraba a ahogarme una criada que había allí, amiga de aquellas religiosas que digo, porque me tapaba la boca y las narices con toda fuerza; y si su ama, que era en cuya celda yo estaba no la advirtiera, según me decía después, no sé qué hubiera sido. Yo pienso que no tiraría a ahogarme, sino sólo a mortificarme. . . .

. . . y cuando se lo avisaban a la madre abadesa, que había tántas horas que [yo] estaba sin sentido, respondía: "darle unos cordeles bien fuertes, que la hagan reventar." Otras veces decía: "ya he estado amolando muy bien un cuchillo para enviárselo que se lo meta, y le enviaré soga para que se ahorque." Yo, en volviendo en mí de los desmayos, lloraba amargamente, y les preguntaba: "Señoras mías, madres mías, ¿qué motivo, qué causa les he dado?". . .

Las veces que yo salía al confesonario, o a esconderme en una parte muy sola y retirada de la casa, las criadas que me topaban, o me atropellaban, y otras me ponían nombres muy afrentosos y ridículos, diciéndomelos con gritos y repetidas veces a mí misma. La madre abadesa prometía cada día en comunidad, que me había de poner en un cepo, y brearme a azotes, que era una loca y que ella me haría cuerda . . . mas no dejaba por esto de valerme mucho de la Virgen Santísima, . . . y poniéndome en su presencia como la más enferma en lo espiritual, como la más pobre de virtudes, como la más ciega, baldada y llagada, llena de enfermedades incurables, sentía una grande consolación, esperando por mano de la Madre de las misericordias el remedio de mi alma, como por ella lo han recibido tántos. Aunque en esta ocasión, que voy contando a vuestra paternidad, estaba yo tan llena de turbación, confusión y congoja, que no me entendía.

[Después de esta temporada difícil, la Madre Castillo siente mayor comprensión.]

Otras muchas cosas entendí por entonces, que algunas escribí, por mandármelo mi confesor.

Andaba mi alma como una ligera pluma, que es llevada del viento suave; así me parecía que yo no tenía parte en mí, para nada, sino que andaba como sin alma, que mi alma se había entrado en su Dios, y que era gobernada por otro impulso, suave, dulce, amoroso y eficaz. Todo lo que vía y oía, era Dios, era sumo bien; y era un bien sobre todo sentido y conocimiento. No me estorbaba nada exterior; antes todo era como soplos que hacían arder aquella llama, y más ardía, con todo lo que era desprecio y humillación mía.

Mi confesor me mortificaba, cuanto alcanzaba su industria, y en esto se la daba Nuestro Señor muy grande, y tal, que a veces me decía: que había estado vacilando sobre qué modo hallaría de mortificarme; y que ya no se le ofrecía ninguno. Tratábame mal, cuanto se podía, de palabra, y me respondía ásperamente. A veces, y lo más ordinario, se enojaba tánto, y tan de veras, reprendiéndome sobre cosas que a mí me parecían buenas, que me quedaba temblando y temiendo, y después me decía que las prosiguiera, que bien iba. Algunas veces me echaba del confesionario, con tal enojo y desprecio, que parecía le había dado alguna grave causa; en particular en algunas ocasiones me escribió: "Que ya había echado de ver que yo y todas mis cosas, sólo para quemadas eran buenas y que estaba determinado a huir de mí, porque mi camino era perdición"; y otras cosas muy duras, a que parece concurría Nuestro Señor, porque me dejaba en una escuridad y confusión, que me parecía era así verdad que el padre lo decía de veras, y lloraba amargamente, sin más consuelo que la determinación que en mí hallaba, de hacer todo aquello que me dijera, era voluntad de Dios, fuera lo que fuera; mas, para hallar quién me guiara en esto, se me cerraba el camino, porque el padre me decía: no volvería más y que mis culpas lo desterraban. Pero luégo venía y me volvía a reñir y reprender, porque no había sabido llevar bien aquella mortificación y cruz. Con todo esto y otras muchas cosas, yo vía y conocía el cuidado que tenía de mi alma y el gran deseo de mi aprovechamiento; y así, aquel rigor era lo que más me animaba, porque me había puesto en sus manos con deseo de quitar de mí todo lo que fuera desagradable a los ojos de Dios. Dióme licencia muy larga para todo cuanto pudiera de mortificación y penitencia, y mientras más hacía, con más salud me hallaba; porque así lo debía de querer Dios, por entonces. . . .

Y así he llegado a los cuarenta y cuatro años de vivir en este mundo; y así le pido, padre mío, que pues con el favor de Nuestro Señor yo he vencido tánto y pasado tántas tribulaciones en escribir esto, y darle cuenta de toda mi vida, la mire bien, y los pasos que lleva mi alma, para que no se pierda; pues de nuevo la vuelvo a poner en sus manos, que miro en ellas las de Dios, para que, libre de mí misma, pueda llegar a conseguir el fin para que Nuestro Señor nos crió, y lo veamos allá, y lo alabemos; donde espero, por la misericordia de Dios y la intercesión de la Virgen Santísima, ver a vuestra paternidad.

Padecí en este tiempo enfermedades, trabajos y desconsuelos grandes, en lo exterior e interior, y como se fuera llegando la cuaresma, me parecía ver con los ojos del alma, un mar de aguas tan turbias y oscuras, que causaba el verlas una gran congoja, amargura, y aprieto interior. Parecíame que Nuestro Señor Jesucristo andaba en medio de aquel mar, y entendí significar algún grande padecer, que quería enviarme, y quedé con grande temor a esta cuaresma. . . . Junto con esto llevaba muchas pesadumbres y contradicciones, en las cosas más sensibles; padeciendo también la persecución del enemigo malo, no sólo con las tentaciones graves y continuas, sino también con espantos malos y aborrecibles. En llegando la noche, llegándose y cargándose sobre mí, etc., con figuras abominables, y sobre toda ponderación aborrecibles, etc. Teníame yo ya por perdida, y que toda mi vida había sido engañada, y sólo andaba a que me dejaran quemar aquellos papeles, que por obediencia había escrito. Y ahora conozco la astucia del enemigo, pues sólo aquello me acordaba por culpa. . . .

Con estas cosas y otras, que escribí en aquellos papeles, consoló y animó la infinita piedad de Dios, entonces, mis desconsuelos, y me detuvo a que no quemara lo que había escrito, según yo lo había muchas veces propuesto y pedido a vuestra reverencia. Especialmente, un día de Pascua de Espíritu Santo, habiendo comulgado, entendí con mucha claridad y razones que para ello me ofreció Nuestro Señor, que ninguna cosa de las que había escrito era mía, ni del demonio. . . .

Proseguiré, padre mío, obedeciendo por la voluntad de Dios, que es el único fin que yo en esto pueda tener para atropellar mi repugnancia y vergüenza, y las muchas cosas con que se aflige mi corazón en esta obediencia. Y si quisiera decir cuántas se me ofrecen para no proseguir, llenara mucho papel, y lo gastara en balde. . . .

También escribiré aquí algunas razones de consuelo que recibía el alma, no porque yo piense que me hablaba Nuestro Señor como a las almas justas, mas para explicarme, es como si dijera: "Pobrecilla, combatida por la tempestad, sin ninguna consolación, no temas, no morirás. Yo soy el Señor Dios tuyo, mira que yo te adornaré con piedras preciosas. Yo te daré aquella corona y diadema de diamantes, que es mi fiel, piadosa y amorosa Madre. Yo pondré en tu pecho aquella cruz de rubíes, que soy yo, tu esposo, humanado, amantísimo, y ensangrentado. Yo te daré aquella piedra que, siendo blanca, toda es fuego, que te adorne y abrase en el sacramento, y sea para ti un rico tesoro de esperanza y amor. . . .

"Sufre la vida, suspira por la muerte, sujeta siempre a mi voluntad, y encerrada en el fiel y fuerte muro de mi eterno querer. . . .

"¡Ea! alienta tu corazón, pobrecilla, mujer, anégate en el mar de las misericordias mías. Mira que vendrá la aurora, y se acabará la lucha y batalla, y se dará fin a las tinieblas, en entrando la aurora María, fuerte, suave, apacible y misericordiosa; terrible para los espíritus malos como un ejército bien ordenado. ¿No es tu Madre, y Madre de su esposo? ¿Pues, qué temes? ¿No es escogida, como el sol, para alegrar, beneficiar y vivificar, desde el águila real hasta la más pequeña avecilla, desde el león coronado hasta el animalito más pequeño, desde el cedro del Líbano hasta el hisopo y hierba más humilde? Pues, ¡oh gusanito pobre! también gozarás de las beneficencias de esta aurora y sol clarísimo, hermosísimo, y purísimo. Arrójate a sus pies, escóndete en este mar de piedades, bebe de esta fuente purísima, cuando recibas a su Hijo Sacramentado, etc." Con estas razones se alienta y respira mi corazón en la fuerza de los desconsuelos y angustias. . . .

Padre mío: hasta aquí he cumplido mi obediencia, y por el amor a Nuestro Señor le pido me avise si es esto lo que vuestra paternidad me mandó, o he excedido en algo, y si será este camino de mi perdición, como me afligen algunas veces terribles temores, que me parece me atan de pies y manos. Puede ser lo haga el enemigo para que no corresponda con el agradecimiento que debiera, a los beneficios de mi Señor y Dios. Me propone que todo son engaños e ilusiones mías; y estas noches que estaba escribiendo, me ha afligido el enemigo, poniéndose tres noches arreo: una, atajándome el oratorio, y riéndose mucho; otra, diciéndome hartos oprobios, y entre ellos, que era una habladora, que no callaba nada; otra, haciendo unas acciones de extraordinario desprecio y asco, y aunque de esto no hago caso, por ser en sueños, pero los modos que él tiene de afligirme y atormentarme, sólo Nuestro Señor lo sabe; y sólo El, por intercesión de su Santísima Madre, me puede librar y dar aliento y paciencia para no haber desfallecido. Bendito sea Dios, y alabado.

Notas

1. Santa Rosa de Lima (1586–1617), joven peruana muy devota, canonizada en 1668; es la primera santa americana.

2. Hora de oración al principio del día.

Her Life

My Father: Today, the day of the birth of Our Lady, I shall in her name begin to do what Your Reverence orders and to think and ponder all the years of my life before the Lord with grief in my soul, for I consider them ill spent. Therefore I rejoice to write them down, so that I may be shamed in the divine presence and to ask God's grace to lament them and to remember His mercies and benefits. One of these I understand was to give me Christian and God-fearing parents, compassionate and modest, to such a degree that my father never uttered a word nor took an action which was not circumspect. He always spoke to us of God, and his words were such that in my whole long life I have never forgotten them; more than that, on many occasions they have given me consolation and strength, and restraint as well. In speaking of Our Lady (to whom he was extraordinarily devoted) or of Our Lord's Passion, his eyes always filled with tears, just as they did when he gave alms to the city's poor, who would gather at our house on Fridays. I would watch him, for I used to accompany him to distribute the alms, and saw the tenderness, humility and devotion with which he distributed them, first kissing [the coin] before he gave it to each one of the poor; he was also very kind to sick animals, of which I could give some very specific examples. In the same way my mother was as respectful of God as she was a friend to the poor, and an enemy of [worldly] vanities, of fancy clothing and entertainments. She was so humble that when she was widowed and nearly blind, [one day] in church a servant woman hit her many times so that she would give up her place, all of which she bore with great meekness and left the church half limping. She told me about this while praising and blessing God Who had seen fit to think so highly of her that He had given her something to suffer. I could tell much more about this and about the good examples I observed in my childhood, but I, just as spiders do, was able to convert even the most wholesome things into poison.

My mother suffered terribly when I was about to be born, and even called her confessor, Father Diego Solano of the Jesuit Order, in order to make her last confession and to die, for she was convinced she would; while she was making her confession and holding on to the father's staff, I was born—and to describe what my heart feels when I say this, only my overflowing eyes could express. I was born, oh God, [and] You must know why, as You know how long my exile has been, and how bitter my passions and faults have made it. I was born, oh Lord! and afterward my saintly father baptized me and donated a large cross which he must have brought with him, giving me the names of my Father Saint Francis and of Saint Joseph, Our Lord bestowing on me henceforth this help and aid, as well as that of the fathers of the Company of Jesus who have worked so hard to compel me to the way of truth. May it be Our Lord's will that I find it before I depart this mortal life.

I was born on the day of the blessed Saint Bruno; it seems that Our Lord wished me to understand how much I would benefit from seclusion, introspection and silence in this mortal life, and how perilous dealings and conversations with people would be for me, just as I have experienced from the first stages of my life, and I regret this, though not as much as I should. People said that fifteen to twenty days [after my birth] I was so near death that the cloth and other trappings for my burial had been bought, until an uncle of mine, a priest, who later on advised me to become a nun (only he, for in the others I encountered much opposition), ordered that a certain remedy be given me, as to someone who was not expected to live, to which I responded and later got well. In this matter only the will of God consoles me, for who would not agree that it would have been better for me to die than to have become the person I am?

When I was still so young that I can hardly remember it, I had this experience: one of the little boys who used to come and visit with his mother (these things often happen, as I later realized) told me that he was going to marry me. I, as far as I can remember now, had no idea what that meant and agreed. Then such a torment afflicted my heart that it allowed me neither pleasure nor consolation and it seemed to me that I had committed a terrible evil, but as I told no one of this pain in my heart, it stayed with me until I must have been seven. On one occasion when I was alone in the room where grain was weighed and the rope had been left hanging, I felt so tormented and the Devil must have had a hand in it as well, because he strongly urged me to hang myself as the only solution. My guardian angel must have been looking out for me, because as far as I can recall I cried out to Our Lady, whom I regarded as a mother and on whom I called in my distress and affliction, [and] ran out of the room, startled and afraid. This is how Our Lord helped me out of that peril, when I don't think I was even seven years old. Until that age, and even a little beyond, all my amusement and consolation came from building altars and seeking seclusion; I had many images of Our Lord and Lady, and alone and secluded spent many hours arranging them. . . .

Because of the fear which I said Our Lord awoke in me, some nights I saw terrible things in my dreams. One time I thought I was walking on a raised floor made of bricks that were stood on end, as though up in the air and in great danger. Looking down I saw a fiery river, black and horrible, and within it a great number of serpents, frogs and snakes, as well as the faces and arms of men who were floating in that well or river. I awoke racked by sobs, and in the morning saw that the ends of my fingers and my nails bore marks of fire, although I had no idea how that could happen. Other times I was in a valley so wide, so deep and so wretchedly dark I cannot describe nor imagine it, and at the end was a horrible well of thick, black fire. On the bank evil spirits wandered about inflicting various torments on other people, in accordance with their sins. So that I would not offend Him, by means of these and other things God the Merciful warned me as to the punishment and the pain of evildoers, but none of this sufficed to keep me from committing many sins, even at that age.

I grew up a very sickly child, and this and the great love my parents had for me, caused them to look upon me with great affection and understanding. Although they dressed me in the habit of Saint Rose of Lima,[1] a promise they had made the saint so that Our Lord would give me good health, my mother took great pains in adorning me with jewels and finery, and I was the darling of the house and of all the people who served my parents. But in spite of this, I never derived pleasure or consolation from any of life's objects, neither playing with dolls nor games children engage in at that age; on the contrary, they held so little attraction for me that I wanted nothing to do with them. Sometimes I would organize processions of religious images, or imitate nuns' professions or customs, but not because I had any inclination to take the veil; all I wanted was to live the way hermits did in the desert and in caves out in the country.

[The following passages refer to events after Madre Castillo had become a nun.]

About this time Father Francisco de Herrera came to confess me, whom Your Reverence had recommended; I attempted to surrender myself completely to inner discourse with Our Lord, from Whom I received so much light, and it seemed to me that my soul was so innerly absorbed with this that it was as though I were not living in this life. The Father treated me harshly and made me do manual labor the greater part of the day; if at some time I asked his permission to spend half a day in prayer he would grant it, on the condition that I would do twice as much work in the afternoon. Many times he ordered me to write and to explain to him the feelings Our Lord produced in me. This caused me much suffering and shame, but I finally did it. . . . There were few nights I could sleep, being kept therefrom by that power in my soul; it seemed that I had live coals in the innermost part of my heart which showed me [things] without words, which ignited into a fire sweeter than life itself. . . .

I spent two years like this, in which all the things of this life seemed dreamlike and laughable to me. One day, while withdrawn with Our

Lord, I thought I saw myself dressed in a scarlet garment which went from my neck to my feet, and my hair was so long it reached the ground. Two evil spirits in human form were there, giving off sparks and wanting to play with the ends of my hair in order to snarl them. I was perturbed, not knowing what to make of it. Some days later some things were said to the Father about me which made him exceedingly angry. He said some very hurtful words to me; he would leave me in the confessional and go away without listening to me, until finally he stopped hearing my confession. I, as one who had no sure foundation, could only weep and become disconsolate unto death; I believed myself deceived and mistaken because my confessor rejected me in this way, but I see clearly now that what I should have done was to ask him humbly to instruct me, to help me to correct those faults and to take the path he would show me. . . .

[Madre Castillo subsequently obeys Father de Herrera and writes down some of her thoughts on true devotion to God.]

My confessor, Father Francisco, looked over this paper when his anger had abated and gave me his response: that the closer he examined it, the less he could find any of the marks the serpent [i.e., the Devil] leaves in matters in which he is involved; that, on the contrary, as far as he was concerned, it was God's work, and the only thing he advised me to do was not to flee from my confessor, no matter how much he chastised and hurt me, etc. In my later life, with God's grace, I have attempted to do this, suffering great travail because of it. . . .

And so one day, as I was strongly resisting writing what Father Francisco ordered, it seemed to me that I saw those same emotions which Our Lord instilled in my soul and the feelings which those pages expressed were being written on His heart with His very own blood, though at that time I did not understand what all this meant. . . .

Many times, as I hurried by the place where the Holy Sacrament was, I would feel in the innermost part of my soul these exceedingly gentle words as though emanating from His Divine Majesty: "Who shall separate us [from the love of Christ]?" (Rom. 8.35). Those were the words, as though He were saying, "No one will be strong enough to separate us." The words were so sweet, so tender and so gentle that I know not what, unless it be my stony, vile and ungrateful heart, would ever again take delight in anything that were not God, nor do I know why I waste the short span of my life in anything but lamenting my faults and ingratitude. In the same way He indicated that He alone should be my comfort, because one day, when my confessor had come and gone without consoling me, I was left with sorrow and sadness because of it and then I heard these words: "Why do you weep? And why do you not eat? And why is your heart sad? Am I not more to you than ten sons?" (1 Sam. 1.8). My soul felt these words so deeply that I was nearly beside myself with the joy and love they had instilled therein. I understood that I should not stop looking to a confessor for refuge and instruction but should look to God for consolation.

[Madre Castillo dreams about conversations instigated by the Devil.]
    Our Lord also devised another way to get me away from those conversations, and this was when in the midst of them I saw Your Reverence at my side (I know not if I was asleep or awake), reprimanding me with severity and kindness, and reminding me of what I owed God. Therewith those matters filled me with even greater horror, although it was already very bad, so much so that I began to write Your Reverence (who had already returned to Santa Fe) about the distress in which I found myself. I remember that I began to weep into the inkwell in order to moisten it with the tears I was shedding, for it was dry, and I was so afraid to open my cell or to ask for anything so that [the demons] couldn't enter, that I wished to fill up the inkwell with my tears and to write with them, something I could easily do because of the copious tears I shed.

After [my confessor Juan Martínez] was here, one day I was in my retreat thinking about the lashes Our Lord was given and it seemed to me that He fell when they untied Him from the column; I felt the same thing as the time before, that anxiety and desire to help Him rise, but now, as opposed to what happened to me the other time, I felt that when my soul reached Him that His body disappeared because it became somehow spiritualized—I don't know how to explain it: it seemed that He disappeared from view or from the soul's knowledge, leaving it feeling great sorrow. I think this was to warn me for what lay ahead, and for the trials that were destined for me. It also happened that when I had begun spiritual exercises with the novice, whom I wished to direct the best I could, we being at prayer one afternoon I saw the Devil go by the door of the cell dressed in a religious habit; he watched us where we were with eyes that horrified, then went into the cell of another nun which was next to my own; I did not understand what all that might be, but was filled with fear and sadness.

About then I saw that my soul was so changed, and so renewed with the good impulses that on another occasion Our Lord had bestowed on me, that I hardly knew myself, nor understood by what means Our Lord had kindled my soul. I had been in seclusion the better part of the day, anticipating my general confession for that year, when one night at prayers, because there had been no Matins,[2] the nun into whose quarters I had seen the Devil disappear entered my cell. She was so filled with rage and screamed at me that I was dumbfounded. She uttered numerous threats against me, saying that the novice was not my servant and that now we would see what the Mother Abbess would do. She shouted so loudly and there was such an outcry by the maids and general commotion that I was cut off and could find no refuge but that of slipping into a gallery, but from there heard such cries in the choir, such a tumult and things that were said about me that I was half dead with shame from hearing them. I had no idea where all this anger and shouting would end when the assistant mother superior, the nun I described earlier, and a throng of servant women with lanterns and lights came to find me. Their anger and what they said to me there were beyond description. . . . The things that they accused me of were unspeakable, and I didn't know where to hide, for anger had filled my cell and I could not stand up I was so afraid. My servant women had also rebelled against me so I was forced to knock at the door of a nun who had been told things that might make her feel angry toward me, but when she saw me in such an afflicted state she was moved to compassion, and she was the only one in the whole house who was on my side during my travails. Afterward

I fell ill with a sickness so grievous that the sweat which poured from my body left my hands as though scalded in boiling water. My mouth twisted to one side, and I had such terrible fainting spells that they would last three and four long hours. During those spells one of the servant women there, a friend of the nuns I described, tried to suffocate me because she covered my nose and mouth with all her might, and if her mistress, in whose cell I was, had not noticed it, who knows what might have happened to me, as she later told me. I think perhaps she wasn't trying to suffocate but only to torment me. . . .

When they told the Mother Abbess that I had been unconscious for so many hours she responded, "Give her some stout lashes, and let her drop dead." Other times she said, "I've been putting a good edge on a knife so that I can send it to her and she can stab herself, and I'll send her a rope so that she can go hang." And I, when I would regain consciousness, wept bitterly and asked them, "Good ladies, my mothers, what cause, what motive have I given you?" . . .

The times I would leave my room to go to the confessional or to withdraw to a solitary and out-of-the-way part of the house, the servant women I would meet would either knock me down or call me insulting and ridiculous names, screaming them at me repeatedly. The Mother Abbess would promise every day when we were in community that she was planning to put me in the stocks and mortify me with a whip, that I was a madwoman and that she would bring me to my senses. . . . But in spite of this I did not cease appealing to the Most Holy Virgin. . . . And when I presented myself before her as the sickest in spirit, the poorest in virtue, the blindest, most incapacitated and wounded being, stricken with incurable illnesses, then I would feel a great consolation, hoping for the healing of my soul at the hand of the Mother of mercies, from whom so many others have received help. However, on this occasion, which I am describing to Your Reverence, I was so filled with anxiety, confusion and distress that I did not understand myself.

[After this difficult time Madre Castillo experiences greater understanding.]

I understood many other things then, some of which I wrote down because my confessor bade me. My soul floated like a light feather which is carried on a gentle wind; in that way it seemed to me that I no longer belonged to myself for anything, but that I went about without a soul, for my soul had entered into its God and was ruled by another impulse that was gentle, sweet, loving and effective. All that I saw and heard was God; it was supreme good, a good beyond all feeling and knowledge. Nothing outward affected me; rather, everything was like little puffs which made that flame burn, and it burned higher, fed by all that was my scorn and my humiliation.

My confessor tormented me to the best of his ability, which Our Lord increased greatly in him, so much so that at times I speculated that he must have been having difficulty figuring out what new way he could devise to torment me, and that perhaps there weren't any left. He spoke to me as badly as he could, and answered me harshly. Usually he would get so profoundly angry, reproving me for things that to me seemed good, that I would end up trembling and afraid; then afterward I would think that perhaps he should go on doing them, that he was doing well. Sometimes he would throw me out of the confessional with such anger and scorn that it seemed I had given him some serious reason for doing so; at times he wrote to me specifically, "That he had seen that I and all my affairs were good only for burning, and that he had resolved to leave me because my path was that of perdition," and other very harsh things. And Our Lord must have agreed because He left me in such a state of darkness and confusion that I was convinced that things really were the way the Father had said and I would cry bitterly. I had no comfort but my own inner determination to do all that he bade me, for it was God's will, be what may. However, to find someone to guide me through this was almost impossible, because the Father told me that he was not coming back, that my sins drove him away. But then he would come back to scold and reprove me because I had not known how to bear that burden and mortification well. In spite of this and many other things, I saw and knew the care he felt for my soul and his great desire for my improvement, and thus his severity was what most spurred me on because I had put myself in his hands with the desire that all be taken from me that might be offensive in the sight of God. He gave me extended permission to do all I was able in the way of penitence and mortification, and the more I did, the better I felt, because that was what God must have wanted then. . . .

And thus I have reached the age of forty-four years of living in this world, and thus I beg you, my Father, that as with the help of Our Lord I have overcome so much and have endured so many trials in writing this and in telling you about my life, that you look on it with favor. [This also goes for] the steps my soul has taken in order not to lose its way, and again I place it in your hands, for to me they are the hands of God, so that, freed from myself, I may come to attain the end for which God has created us, where we shall see Him and praise Him. And there, through God's mercy and the intercession of the Most Holy Virgin, I hope to see Your Reverence.

About that time I was very ill and suffered from troubles and great distress, both interior and exterior, and as we were approaching Lent, I seemed to see in my soul's eye a sea with such muddy, dark waters that looking at it caused me great affliction, bitterness and inner pangs. I seemed to see Our Lord Jesus Christ walking in the midst of that sea and I understood that that meant that He wanted to send me a great trial and during that Lent I was very afraid. . . .

Along with this I bore many cares and contradictions in the most sensitive matters, suffering as well the persecution of the Devil, not only with grave and continuous temptations, but also with evil and loathsome fears. When night came they would come and throw themselves on me, etc., with abominable shapes and disgusting beyond all belief. I gave myself up for lost and felt that all my life I had been deceived, and only wanted permission so I could burn those papers which I had written for the sake of obedience. And now I know the enemy's astuteness, because only that occurred to me as a sin. . . .

By means of these and other things I wrote on those pages, the infinite mercy of God consoled and encouraged [me in] my disconsolateness, and kept me from burning what I had written, which is what I have so often proposed and asked Your Reverence to let me do. One Pentecost in particular, when I had just taken Communion, I understood very clearly and for many reasons which Our Lord showed me, that not one thing which I had written belonged either to me or to the Devil. . . .

I will go on [writing], Father, obeying by the will of God, which is the only goal which in all this I can have in order to overcome my loathing and my shame, and the many other things which afflict my heart in this obedience [to you]. And if I wanted to count up the reasons I can think of not to continue, I would fill up a great deal of paper and waste it. . . .

I will also write down some reasons for consolation which I received in my soul, not because I think that Our Lord spoke to me as to one of the just, but to explain that it is as though He said: "Poor thing, tossed about by the storm without any consolation, fear not, you will not die. I am the Lord your God and see, I will adorn you with jewels. I will give you the crown and diadem of diamonds that is my faithful, pious and loving Mother. I will place on your breast a cross of rubies which is I, your husband, made flesh, most loving and stained with blood. I will give you that stone, which, though white, is fire itself, that it may adorn you and sear you in the sacrament, and be for you a rich treasure of hope and love.

"Endure life, long for death, be subject always to my will and enclosed in the faithful and strong wall of my eternal love. . . .

"There! Cheer your heart, poor little one, woman, and drown in the sea of my mercies. Look, for the dawn will come, the strife and battle will be over and there will be an end to darkness when the dawn which is Mary, strong, gentle, mild and merciful, breaks, and she will be as terrible for evil spirits as a well-ordered army. Is she not your Mother, and the Mother of your Husband? Then what do you fear? Is she not chosen like the sun to cheer, to benefit and to bestow life, from the royal eagle to the smallest bird, from the crowned lion to the least little creature, from the cedar of Lebanon to the hyssop and the lowliest plant? And you poor little worm, you too will enjoy the rewards of this dawn and of the brightest, loveliest and purest sun. Throw yourself at her feet, hide in this sea of mercies, and drink of this purest of springs when your receive her Transsubtantiated Son, etc." When in the grip of discouragement and anguish, thoughts such as these restore my heart and it breathes anew. . . .

Father: up to this point I have met my obligations, and for love of Our Lord I beg you to tell me if this is what Your Reverence ordered me to do, or if I have done too much, and if this will be the path to my perdition, as sometimes I am afflicted with terrible fears which seem to bind me hand and foot. It may be that this is caused by the Devil so that I do not repay the benefits of my Lord and God with the gratitude I should. He suggests that all is deception and illusion on my part, and these past evenings as I have been writing the Enemy has tormented me, appearing on three successive nights. On one he headed me off on the way to chapel and laughed heartily; on another he said extremely disgraceful things, among them that I was a chatterbox, and could keep nothing to myself; and on yet another he made extraordinarily scornful and disgusting gestures (though I don't pay attention to this because it was in a dream). Only Our Lord knows the ways [the Devil] has of distressing and tormenting me, and only He, by the intercession of his Most Holy Mother, can free me from this and give me strength and patience so as not to weaken. Blessed and praised be God.

Notes

1. Saint Rose of Lima (1586–1617), a very devout young Peruvian woman, was canonized in 1668 and became the first American saint.

2. An early-morning hour of prayer.

Gertrudis Gómez
de Avellaneda

Gertrudis Gómez de Avellaneda from La Avellaneda y sus obras,
Emilio Cotarelo y Mori (Madrid: Tipografía de archivos, 1930).

*J*ust like Sor Juana and Madre Castillo, Gertrudis Gómez de Avellaneda was the daughter of a Spanish father and a criolla mother. She was born in the central Cuban city of Camagüey in 1814 and was raised in comfortable circumstances. She was very proud of her father's aristocratic lineage, and her mother, too, came from Cuba's landed gentry—which meant, of course, that they were slaveholders.

Cuba's white population in the early nineteenth century was an uneasy society, primarily because the successful slave uprising in nearby Haiti (1791) was seen as a direction Cuban blacks and mulattoes might take as well. Domingo del Monte, a wealthy Venezuelan planter who opposed the further importation of slaves to Cuba, organized a group of intellectuals to compose antislavery (but not abolitionist) literature; as the critics Ivan Schulman and Antonio Benítez Rojo have shown, these writings marked the beginning of a national Cuban literature. Avellaneda would play her part in this, albeit indirectly, as she lived in Spain most of her life.

She was eight when her father died, and within the year her mother married another Spaniard, Isidoro de Escalada, a handsome military officer who was part of Spain's colonial garrison on the island. Gertrudis (or Tula, as she was called) could not bear her stepfather—nor he her—but, true to the patriarchal nature of nineteenth-century families, she had no alternative but to obey him, especially because of her financial dependence on him. Tula's grandfather had disinherited her when she refused to marry a man he had chosen but whom she did not love, and all her life she remained sensitive to women's powerlessness due to a lack of money. This, as we shall see, is an issue that was also very important to other nineteenth-century writers in this anthology: Gorriti, Cabello de Carbonera, and González de Fanning.

Escalada was worried about the possibility of a Cuban slave uprising and in 1836 took the family back to Spain: Tula, her brother Manuel, and three new siblings. They went first to Galicia, Escalada's home. The strong-willed Tula detested both his conservative family and the gloomy, wet climate. With her mercurial temperament she must have made everyone's life so miserable that she and Manuel were subsequently allowed to go to Seville, her father's birthplace. Andalusia suited her a great deal better. She lost no time in joining Seville's literary circles and published both poetry and her first play. Tula was also writing *Sab,* her first and today most famous novel, which she published in Madrid in 1841. It was a radical story, especially for a Cuban woman author. Set on the island, it concerned the doomed love of a mulatto slave for his white owner's daughter. It was immediately banned in Cuba.

Tula was a talented writer, and she also knew how to present herself to her best advantage. As a Cuban in Spain, she was considered exotic, and she knew it; she was also very attractive and knew that as well. She was ambitious in her goal to become a recognized writer and knew that Seville was too small a pond for her. She moved to Madrid and parlayed her many contacts with writers and intellectuals into acceptance into their circles. Tula was now writing and publishing poetry, novels, and plays and was successfully supporting herself by her pen.

While she was still in Seville, Tula had fallen passionately in love with Ignacio de Cepeda, a local aristocrat about two years younger (she actively lied about her age all her life). The tempestuous emotions he aroused in her were definitely *not* reciprocated: Cepeda was socially and intellectually conservative, cool of temperament, dictatorial, and apparently often embarrassed by Tula's passion. They had an on-again, off-again relationship until 1854, when Cepeda married another woman. He fortunately kept all of Tula's letters to him, with instructions to have his wife publish them after his death, which she did.[1]

Today, with telephones, voice mail, e-mail, and the like, it is hard to appreciate what letters meant in the nineteenth century, and how much time people spent writing them—even if they saw each other almost daily, as was the case with Tula and Cepeda. The letters she wrote to her reluctant lover are not only compelling insights into her psyche, they are helpful in providing a background against which her literature developed. They are also, as Emil Volek noted, more appealing to modern readers than much of her other literature.

In the early stage of their relationship Cepeda had asked her to write him about her past, and she provided him with her epistolary autobiography.[2] At this juncture Avellaneda was twenty-five years old. Epistolary writing was one genre women had always been able to practice freely, and, in Susan Kirkpatrick's opinion, Tula's private writing was good training for her later career: "It was in letters and in diaries that the very young Gómez de Avellaneda, before she had the confidence to enter the man's world of publication, had cultural permission and precedent to construct and represent herself as a woman in writing" (135). Even as she attempted to construct a submissive, dutiful self who would appeal to someone like Cepeda, Tula also realized that that was not where she wanted to be: "The autobiography is of particular interest because it shows her working out in a very personal mode of writing an image of the self that draws on Romantic literary models while registering acute awareness that these models were antithetical to the cultural pattern of feminine existence" (Kirkpatrick 135). The same could be said of many of her other letters, not only to Cepeda but also later on to another suitor, Antonio Romero Ortiz. I have included examples of her correspondence with both of these men in this anthology.

After *Sab* Avellaneda wrote *Dos mugeres* (Two Women; 1842), another radical novel that took a sympathetic and tolerant view of adultery; it was also banned in Cuba. Tula also established herself as one of Madrid's most successful playwrights, in spite of some harsh criticism because of her gender. She took her writing very seriously, as can be seen in her correspondence with both Cepeda and Romero Ortiz, in which she would often alternate between phrases of endearment and very businesslike assessments of the reception her writing was receiving. After a blowup with Cepeda in 1840, for instance, she sent him a letter enumerating her numerous successes with *Sab* and a play and concluded by saying, "You see that I ought to be very satisfied with the brilliant success of my literary endeavors. God willing that when people get to know the novel and the play it will not affect their enthusiasm [for my poetry], and just because I want to be a playwright and a novelist, [I hope] they will not forget the reputation I have acquired as a lyric poet" (*Diario íntimo* 99).

We can see the same tendency in her letters to Romero Ortiz. Eight years her junior, he was a reporter for *La Nación,* and Tula thought nothing of writing him a steamy love letter ("I love you, Antonio; you are my lover; I know nothing else," etc.) and then, in a postscript, giving him precise instructions on how he was to write a review of one of her plays (*Cartas inéditas* 67–68).

In 1844 Tula had an affair with Gabriel García Tassara, a poet and diplomat, which resulted in a pregnancy and the birth of their daughter, Brenhilde. Tassara left her and would not acknowledge the child, who died before she was a year old. Two years later Tula married Pedro Sabater, who was already terminally ill with throat cancer and died within four months of their wedding. In 1853 came one of her cruelest disappointments: her failure to be elected a member of the Royal Spanish Academy. Her literary accomplishments certainly qualified her, and she had many *académicos* who supported her, but a majority of the all-male members of the Academy voted her down. When the poet Carmen Conde was elected an *académica* in 1977, it was reported that she was the first women to receive this honor, but this is not true. While doing research on Avellaneda's only essay, "La mujer," I noticed her reference to a "Doctora de Alcalá" and wondered about her identity. She was Doña María Isidra Quintina de Guzmán y de la Cerda (1768–1803), a very intelligent young noblewoman who had the favor of King Charles III and of his prime minister, Floridablanca. The king wanted her admitted to the Royal Academy and arranged for her to get a doctorate from the University of Alcalá to qualify her for admission. There was a great deal of resistance from the *académicos,* but the king was not to be denied, and in 1784, at the age of eighteen, she was admitted to their ranks. The most amazing part of her story, however, is that she was the granddaughter of María Luisa Manrique de Lara, Countess of Paredes—Sor Juana's friend and benefactress (Serrano y Sanz 493–95).

Avellaneda was deeply disappointed and embittered by this defeat. In the same year she began her relationship with Antonio Romero

Ortiz; just as had been the case with Cepeda, the lovers used romantic aliases to hide their affair and their correspondence.[3] This relationship also had its ups and downs. In her amorous correspondence Tula would use the familiar "tú" or the formal "Ud." in addressing her lovers, depending on the state of her feelings for them at the moment of writing. Just as she had done with Cepeda, in her letters Tula actively courted Romero Ortiz, which resulted in frightening both of them off. At one point Tula toyed with the idea of marrying Romero Ortiz but ultimately broke off their relationship.

She dallied briefly with Tassara again but in 1855 married Domingo Verdugo, who was close to Queen Isabel II of Spain and to her consort, King Francisco. The ceremony took place in the Royal Palace, with the monarchs as witnesses. Tula was now at the pinnacle of society and continued her successful career as a playwright. Unfortunately Verdugo had an altercation with a spectator who had attempted to disrupt one of his wife's plays; the man stabbed him in the chest, and although Verdugo survived, his health was permanently impaired.

Late in 1859 the couple went to Cuba with the new Spanish governor, and the famous Tula was celebrated in high style by her native country, though there were some Cuban patriots who criticized her alliance with the Spanish colonial administration. She was crowned with a diadem of gold laurel leaves in Havana's Teatro Tacón and lionized wherever she went—surely a source of great satisfaction after her exclusion from the Royal Academy. While in Cuba she founded the island's first journal for women, the *Album Cubano de lo Bueno y lo Bello* (The Cuban Album of the Good and the Beautiful). Though it lasted only a year, the issues are excellent examples of popular women's literature in the nineteenth century. Aside from a number of her poems, Tula contributed the essay "La mujer," some sketches of famous women of the past, and gave the *Album* the prestige of her name.

Verdugo died in 1863, after which Avellaneda returned to Spain via the United States. She lived first in Seville and then went back to Madrid, continuing her writing and preparing an edition of her complete works. The five volumes, published between 1869 and 1871, do not, however, contain either *Sab* or *Dos mugeres,* partly because she herself was now much more conservative than in her youth and also because these novels were banned in Cuba and she did not want to endanger sales in that country. Her real *Obras completas* were published in Havana in 1914.

Tula died of diabetes in February 1873. After Cepeda's death, her love letters to him were published (*Diario íntimo*), and the passion of her voice was heard again.

Cepeda! You have not understood me; you have not understood my love. I want your heart, your heart without any kind of ties. I am free and so are you; both of us should always be free; the man who acquires a right to humiliate a woman, the man who abuses his power, tears that woman's precious freedom away, because she who acknowledges a master is no longer free. (81)

I don't know if I am always prudent; sometimes I fear I will never be, but I dare anyone to prove that I am false or mean-spirited. My defects are of the same measure as my good qualities, and I have presented myself to you just the way I am. Did you love me the way I am? Do you think me worthy? . . . I don't know, but I do know that you will not find other women on this earth like me. They may be better or worse, but they will not be like

TULA. (119)

She was very right.

Notes

1. The letters to Cepeda were compiled and published by Lorenzo Cruz de Fuentes, who edited out certain parts. As the originals have disappeared, we have no idea what the editor suppressed. He also put the letters in the order in which they appear here, which may or may not be correct, as many of the letters were undated.

2. I translated this autobiography earlier, in *Sab* and *Autobiography*, for which reason I am not including it in this anthology.

3. Cepeda was from the small town of Almonte, and when writing to him, Avellaneda called herself "Doña Amadora de Almonte"; Romero Ortiz signed his first letters to her "Armand Carrel," and it took her a while to find out his real identity.

Cartas a Ignacio de Cepeda

CARTA I

Una hora de desvelo y melancolía en la noche del 13 de julio [1839].
Dedicada a mi "compañero de desilusión." Para él solo.
[Avellaneda empieza su carta con un largo poema que habla de su
desilusión personal con la vida, y cómo estos sentimientos la vinculan
a Cepeda; ella cree que él siente lo mismo.]

Me hace mal, mucho mal, oír a usted expresar sus ideas, dolores y
esperanzas. Ya ve usted por esta composición qué pensamientos me
inspira. Atienda usted a los versos y no a las ideas.

Efectivamente, a veces me abruma esta *plenitud de vida* y quisiera
descargarme de su peso. He trabajado mucho tiempo en minorar mi
existencia moral para ponerla al nivel de mi existencia física. Juzgada
por la sociedad, que no me comprende, y cansada de un género de
vida que acaso me ridiculiza; superior e inferior a mi sexo, me encuentro extranjera en el mundo y aislada en la naturaleza. Siento la
necesidad de morir, y, sin embargo, vivo y pareceré dichosa a los
ojos de la multitud. . . .

Usted me habla de amistad, y no ha mucho que sintió usted
amor. Yo no creo ni en una ni en otro. Busco en emociones pasa-
jeras, en afectos ligeros, un objeto en que distraer mis devoradores
pensamientos y me siento así menos atormentada, porque inconstante en mis gustos, cánsome fácilmente de todo, y los afectos
ligeros, que apenas me ligan, no me privan del derecho de seguir el
instinto de mi alma que codicia libertad. Alguna vez deseo hallar
sobre esta tierra un corazón melancólico, ardiente, altivo y ambicioso como el mío; compartir con él mis goces y dolores y darle este
exceso de vida, que yo sola no puedo soportar. Pero más a menudo

temo en mí esta inmensa facultad de padecer, y presiento que un
amor vehemente suscitaría en mi pecho tempestades, que trastor-
naría acaso mi razón y mi vida. Además, ¿llenaría aún el amor el

abismo de mi alma? Todo lo he probado y todo lo desecho: amor y
amistad. ¿Qué puedo, pues, ofrecer a usted, querido mío? ¡La compasión de un corazón atormentado! . . . y mis versos para distraerle
un momento de ocupaciones graves.

CARTA 2

[1° de agosto de 1839]

Estoy avergonzada, ¡Dios mío! ¿Qué habrá usted pensado de mí,
Cepeda, después de la extraña y ridícula conducta que tuve anoche?
Si fuese usted un fatuo presumido, uno de estos hombres vanidosos
de que abundan en la ciudad, ya sé lo que pensaría.

Aun no siéndolo usted, aun creyéndole a usted modesto y no
ligero en sus juicios, tiemblo al reflexionar en mis locuras el concepto que usted se formará y lo que usted supondrá. ¿Qué hombre
habrá bastante modesto que viendo en una mujer el arrebato indo-
minable que usted vió anoche en mí, no creyera que sólo los celos
. . . ? ¡Dios mío!, mi mano tiembla y mi frente se cubre de vergüenza
al pensarlo. He dado motivo para que usted no crea nada de cuanto
le he dicho hasta el presente acerca de la naturaleza de mis sentimientos para con usted; he dado motivo para que usted me crea
enamorada y celosa; he dado motivo para que usted me coloque en la
lista de esas cuatro o cinco a quienes inspiró, sin pretenderlo, una
pasión desgraciada. ¡Maldición! Yo sufro una humillación que no
creía estuviese en la lista de mis padecimientos. ¡Qué papel he
querido representar, o, mejor dicho, he representado involuntariamente! ¡El de enamorada celosa! ¡Yo, yo, Dios mío! No sé como no
muero sofocada de rabia. Es cierto que no hay en mí ni amor ni
celos; es bien cierto que ni le he mirado a usted como amante, ni le
deseo como tal, ni lo admitiría . . . ¡lo juro a Dios y por mi dignidad
de mujer! Juro que no lo admitiría a usted por mi amante, así como
hasta ahora no le he considerado a usted como a tal.

Es bien cierto todo esto y que el afecto mutuo que nos ha ligado hasta el alma, ha sido tan puro como desinteresado; y, sin embargo de esto, ¡qué papel hago desde anoche! ¡Cómo me he degradado por un capricho inconcebible, por una violencia pueril y extravagante! ¡A qué suposiciones humillantes he dado lugar! Ya lo ve usted probado; ya ve usted probado lo que yo le he dicho muchas veces: que hay en mi carácter algo de tan ligero, tan caprichoso y tan inconsecuente, que me ha de causar en mi vida muchas pesadumbres.

Las gentes me creen mujer de algún talento y mundo, y yo misma lo he pensado así; pero nos engañábamos: ya lo sé por experiencia. A los veinticuatro años[1] soy más niña que una de cinco. Yo no tengo talento ninguno, ni tengo mundo, ni tengo prudencia: no tengo más que una desgraciada cualidad, que yo maldigo: una ingenuidad que raya en necedad y en locura. Usted debe haberse reído de mí; ya lo creo. No puedo quejarme. Pero tenga usted la bondad de escucharme un momento, que aunque no pueda ni pretenda justificar la ligereza y extravagancia de mi conducta anoche, acaso haré comprender a usted sus verdaderos motivos y evitaré, ya que no sea el concepto de arrebatada y de indiscreta en que usted debe justamente tenerme, al menos el de *celosa*, que me humilla lo que no es decible y que ciertamente no merezco. . . .

. . . Mi dolor, mi sorpresa, mi exaltación eran efectos de una misma causa. No vi en usted en aquel momento el amigo de mi corazón, que asegurándome una *amistad grande, tierna y santa*, me había dicho: *"puedes aceptarla sin temor ni reserva, porque te la ofrece el más puro y ardiente de los corazones."*[2] En vez de este corazón *puro y ardiente*, yo no vi en aquel momento rápido de sorpresa y de dolor sino un corazón usado al extremo, un corazón dividido entre muchos objetos. . . .

Lo que dije, lo que hice, yo no lo sé exactamente. Sé que me volví loca nada más; loca de dolor, al ver destruida mi última y más querida ilusión: la ilusión divina que me hizo creer había hallado al fin un corazón sensible, puro, ardiente, capaz de grandes pasiones y acaso de grandes faltas, pero no capaz de tibios y multiplicados afectos. . . .

Todo esto, agolpándose súbitamente en mi cabeza, la trastornó en términos que ya no supe más lo que hice. Parecíame que me habían transportado a otro mundo, a un infierno, y aquella carta de usted, que tenía en mi seno, me quemaba como una ascua de fuego. Hice mil locuras, locuras que pudieron ser bien siniestramente interpretadas; y lo que más siento, lo que más me humilla, es el pensar que usted mismo, Cepeda, usted mismo, habrá creído ver un arrebato de celos en lo que no era más que un exabrupto de dolor. ¡Cuán avergonzada estoy, Dios mío! ¡Hubiera querido morir antes de salir anoche de mi casa! . . .

Por lo demás, nada me resta que decir. Retíreme usted su confianza; no la merezco; soy demasiado violenta y ligera. Soy también muy joven todavía para ser confidente de un hombre de la edad de usted y de sus méritos, y diré, aun más, de un hombre que se halla en posición tan delicada. No tengo ni la madurez, ni el talento necesario para aconsejar con acierto, y sólo podré afligirme o hacer locuras como anoche. Seré siempre su amiga de usted. . . .

¡Adiós, mi amable amigo, feliz viaje! Déjeme usted cuatro letras en el correo, acusándome recibo de ésta, pues no estaría tranquila si no supiese con certeza que usted la había recibido. Diviértase usted en Elmonte o Almonte, y consérvese bueno y estudioso para que le veamos pronto. Repito y ruego encarecidamente, de rodillas si es preciso, que olvide usted mis miserias de anoche. Si no puede usted impedirse el creer que sólo el amor, y un amor exaltado y celoso, pudo arrastrar a tales loca ni tonta, créalo usted; pero crea usted también en que, si existió, ya no existe, y que si existió, era sin conocerlo yo misma. En fin, lo que deseo, sobre todo, es que se olvide de todo lo pasado.

CARTA 6

Señor don Ignacio Cepeda:

He recibido la amable de usted, mi caro amigo, con tanta mayor satisfacción cuanto que informada por Concha[3] de que no estaba usted en Almonte, sino en otra parte que designó su hermano y de cuyo nombre no me acuerdo, temía hubiese padecido extravío mi carta. Varias veces mandé una criada al correo, y siempre me dijo que no había carta, hasta que ayer, siéndome imposible salir yo, me valí de Concha, la cual fué ella misma al correo y me trajo al momento la suspirada de usted.

Celebro que esté usted bueno, como en ella me dice, y menos melancólico que en ésta. Yo, por mi parte, quisiera poder decir otro tanto, pero, por desgracia, no es así, Mis dolores de estómago me han dado mucho que hacer, y mi melancolía se aumenta cada día. ¡Usted me pide que la venza! . . . Ciertamente, es grande el influjo que una súplica de usted ejerce en mi corazón; pero en este punto acaso no esté en mi poder el complacer la solicitud de su tierna amistad. Aparte de la ausencia de mi mejor, de mi único amigo, que es suficiente causa para melancolizarme, ¡tengo tantos otros motivos de tristeza! ¡La expectativa de una separación acaso próxima y larga de una madre que amo con ternura! ¡La indecisión en que batallo sin saber qué partido tomar ni qué suerte me espera! ¡La necesidad de independencia y el temor de la opinión, que me impide proporcionármelo! . . . En fin, tantas y tantas cosas me agitan al presente (en que según las apariencias se aproxima el día de la crisis), que la amistad misma, la dulce y lisonjera amistad de Cepeda no será poderosa a darme tranquilidad. Pero, ¡basta! Hablemos de otra cosa. ¡Yo quisiera que mis cartas fuesen tan risueñas! ¡Ah, ya lo veo, imposible! La amargura de mi corazón se mezcla en todas ellas. ¡Perdón!

Mandaré mi traducción por el conducto que me indica; pero será luego que tenga tiempo para escribirla, pues el borrador está ininteligible y la única copia leíble que tenía la he mandado a Cádiz por compromiso. Los señores redactores del nuevo periódico de literatura, que sale en dicha ciudad con el nombre de *La Aureola*, me han escrito una lisonjera carta rogándome cediese a su periódico algunas de mis composiciones, y aunque quise negarme, me he visto forzada a complacerles por haber intervenido en el asunto un paisano mío, a quien estimo, y que se ha empeñado de un modo que no podía yo, sin desairarle, mantener mi negativa. Así, pues, he cedido a *La Aureola* mi traducción, poniendo la condición de que no se imprimiera firmada con mi nombre sino enteramente anónima.

Ya enviaré a usted, tan pronto pueda, una copia, y de antemano reclamo su indulgencia. Preciso fuera que usted conociese el original, para que se formase un juicio exacto de la grandísima dificultad de la traducción. Lamartine, uno de los más grandes poetas de la moderna escuela, y acaso el más dulce y fácil, tiene, sin embargo, algo de vago y metafísico en su poesía y una manera de decir que es, ciertamente, intraducible. Sus ideas en muchas composiciones son tan delicadas, que se marchitan, por decirlo así, bajo la pluma del traductor, y sus giros son a veces tan atrevidos, que intimidan. He procurado en *La Fuente* traducir con la exactitud posible, penetrándome de los pensamientos e ideas del autor; pero estoy muy lejos de la satisfacción de creer que he logrado imitar con mediano acierto su versificación flúida y armoniosa y aquel colorido místico y melancólico que distingue sus composiciones.

Respecto a mi novela [*Sab*], he sometido sus diez primeros capítulos a la censura de mi compatriota, ya mencionado, hombre instruido y de gusto que, felizmente, se halla ahora en esta ciudad, y he tenido el gusto de que mereciese su aprobación. Él ha animado mi tímida pluma, asegurándome que la parte descriptiva está trazada con exactitud y variedad y que los caracteres están bien delineados y desenvueltos con vigor. Su bondad le ha hecho propasarse hasta dar al estilo elogios inmerecidos y juzgar de altamente interesante el plan de la novela. A pesar de mi amor propio, he conocido el favor de este juicio; pero me ha animado, sin embargo, a continuar haciendo esfuerzos para merecer lo mejor.

Ya ve usted, mi buen amigo, que le hablo de cosas que no son más que cosas; ya ve usted que evito un lenguaje que usted llama de la imaginación y que yo diría del corazón: usted lo juzga peligroso y lo destierra de nuestras cartas. Yo suscribo a su formidable sentencia; pero, ¿qué temes tú, amigo mío? ¿qué peligro quieres evitar? Acaso oyendo y empleando el idioma del corazón, ¿temerás no poder impedirle adelantarse demasiado? ¿Temerás sentir o inspirar un sentimiento más vivo que el de la amistad . . . ? Si es cierto, tranquilízate, yo te aseguro que no me amarás nunca sino como a tu hermana, y que en mi alma no hallarás jamás otros afectos que los que hoy día me envanezco de expresarte. Yo he meditado mucho en estos días sobre la naturaleza de nuestros sentimientos, y, te lo juro, este examen me ha tranquilizado. Yo perdería mucho si tú dejases de ser mi amigo para ser mi amante. ¡Amantes! . . . ¡Cercan tantos a una mujer joven y de tal cual mérito! Pero, ¿dónde hallar un amigo como tú? ¡Amantes! . . . Mira, me empalagan ya; esa cáfila de aduladores que asedian nuestro sexo, me parecen poca cosa aún para divertirse una un rato con sus necios galanteos. ¡Ni puedo yo creer que me amen! Uno me obsequia porque soy una forastera que no conoce, cuya clase acaso juzga dudosa, cuyas costumbres ignora y acaso puedan ser fáciles; cuya conquista no le parecerá dudosa, y me obsequia creyendo que puedo ser su capricho, su juguete, su pasatiempo, su placer de algunos días. Otro me obsequia porque hace profesión de obsequiante de cuantas mujeres bien parecidas se le presentan: sin ideas, sin cálculos, sin esperanzas, y sólo por el prurito de galantear y hacer de elegante. Otro me obsequia porque anda a la cuarta pregunta, como suele decirse, y oliendo donde guisan. Soy americana, y por ser americana supone que soy rica, lo cual basta para que forme sus cálculos de matrimonio. En fin, otro me hace el amor sólo por vanidad: porque se lisonjearía de ser mi novio, no porque yo le guste, sino porque cree darse importancia en la sociedad con la preferencia de una mujer que es celebrada, que dicen tiene algún talento. He aquí, querido Cepeda, los motivos que impulsan a la mayor parte de aquellos que me hacen la corte. Y estando yo en esta persuasión, ¿podré oírlos con otro objeto que el de burlarme de ellos?

¿Y usted qué hallará en más mujeres que digan amarle? Una dice que le ama, y no ama más que su colocación. Desea un marido, un estado, que es la ambición de las mujeres vulgares y lo busca en usted. Otra dice amarle, y sólo ama en usted a su pasatiempo, al que le regaló el oído y la lisonjea en la sociedad, al que satisface su vanidad y al que dejaría sin pesar por otro más galán, de más representación social, de más nombradía, etcétera, etcétera. Otra dice amarle, y sólo ama en usted sus propios placeres, y . . . ¡oh! —rubor causa decirlo—, pero lo vemos cada día para vergüenza nuestra. Vemos esta clase de mujeres que degradan la dignidad de su sexo, y son a mis ojos más despreciables que la escoria más vil de la tierra.

¡Y tal es el amor en nuestra triste y corrompida sociedad! ¿Cómo podía él existir entre nosotros? ¡Oh, no, jamás! Esos profanados nombres de amante y querida déjalos a otros y a otras. Tú serás mi amigo, yo tu amiga de toda la vida, y no debes temer que sea degradado nunca el santo carácter de nuestros vínculos. ¿Temerás tú cuando yo no temo? Todo lo dicho te prueba que nada arriesgas en dejar hablar tu corazón. No interpretará la vanidad tus palabras, ni puede tu amiga confundir la expresión de tus sentimientos con la jerga insípida del galanteo que llaman amor. En cuanto a mí, haré lo que quieras; no te expresaré si esto te hace mal, pero ¡me cuesta tanto este esfuerzo!

Cepeda: ya lo ve usted: mi pluma corre a pesar mío y dice más de lo que quiero decir. Yo debiera ofenderme en vez de halagarle a usted; pero mi orgullo, tan susceptible en otras, no lo es en esta ocasión. No tema usted, *vanidoso*, no tema usted, que yo le crea *enamorado* si usa conmigo un lenguaje tierno. ¿Me cree usted una niña o una vieja? No tema usted, repito, y para tranquilizarse enteramente, sepa usted que el día en que le creyese a usted *enamorado* de mí, ese día cesaría de amarle y no le vería a usted más. Con que con esta seguridad su libertad no corre ningún riesgo conmigo, ni tiene usted necesidad de alarmarse de mi ternura, como si viese en ella un lazo de hierro pronto a aprisionarlo. ¡Amable melancólico! ¡Qué poco mundo tiene usted! Perdóname, amigo, esta frase, pero me hace gracia, tanta gracia ver tu temor y adivinar tu corazón al través de ese velo con que piensas cubrirlo! Me temes, Cepeda, no lo niegues; temes que me posesione yo de tu corazón; temes los lazos de hierro que pudieran ser consecuencia de tu amor por mí, y crees evitar algo acogiéndote a la sagrada sombra de la amistad. ¡Oh!, eres un niño si tal crees. Cuánto te engañas, querido, cuánto, si crees que la amistad señalaría límites que el corazón respetara! ¿Qué importa el nombre a los sentimientos? ¿Dejan de ser los mismos? Lo que debe tranquilizarte no es eso, sino el saber que no hallas en mí *un enemigo de tu libertad* y que, por mi propio interés, cuidaré de no dar a tu corazón más vehementes afectos que los que hoy abrigue.

Raro, original es el papel que hago contigo. Yo, mujer, ¡tranquilizándote a ti del miedo de amarme! ¡Es cosa peregrina! Pero contigo no soy mujer, no: soy toda espíritu, y ninguna regla es aplicable a este cariño excepcional que me inspiras.

Muy larga es esta carta; pero no imitaré yo a los que acaban las suyas jurando (nada menos que jurando) ser más corto en lo sucesivo. Esta es larga; pero aún lo será más la que escriba cuando no se me ordene *no usar expresiones que conmuevan demasiado y hagan mucho daño.* . . .

¡Adiós, mi amado amigo! Cuídese usted, diviértase y vuelva pronto donde le llaman los votos más sinceros de una amistad tiernísima.

Expresiones de Concha, y mil afectos de su invariable TULA.

Sevilla, agosto 28 de 1839

P.D.: Ruego a usted disimule la incoherencia de ésta [carta] y su poca unidad y defecto de estilo. Veo que está rara; pero va según mi cabeza. ¡Tengo tanta confusión en ella! Y luego, mi humor hoy es malísimo.

CARTA 9

[Sin fecha—sobre noviembre de 1839]

Anteanoche te dije que había enviado a tu casa un libro, y no pude añadir, por los testigos que había, que dicho libro era, como lo es el que hoy te mando, un pretexto para escribirte sin que el portador se haga cargo. La fatalidad hizo que no te encontrase en tu casa el mensajero, y rasgué la carta en un momento de impaciencia contra la mala suerte, que la hizo volver por dos veces a mis manos cuando la suponía en las tuyas.

Nada, empero, contenía dicha carta de importancia; era solamente la expresión de mi tristeza en varios días, que no te veía, y una proposición que ahora voy a repetir en pocas palabras. Veremos si te agrada.

Pronto vas a graduarte, y creo que saliendo de eso podrás verme con más frecuencia: aún antes de graduarte nos hemos de ver algunas veces, porque, ¿cómo vivir así, querido amigo? ¿Quién tiene resistencia? La mía comienza a faltarme, no obstante todos mis propósitos. He pensado, pues, que debemos convenir en una cosa, y es que siempre que tú vengas y esté yo sola aprovechemos tales momentos para realizar un deseo, que tengo desde hace mucho tiempo, y que es el de leer contigo alguna obra interesante. Aun estando mamá podemos, si nos agrada, entretener un rato en la lectura, pues ningún inconveniente veo en ello si a ti no te desagrada mi proyecto. Con este objeto he hecho una lista de algunas obras de mi gusto, que voy a nombrarte para que tú escojas la que te parezca y me lo digas. Yo la tendré en casa inmediatamente, y la comenzaremos en la primera oportunidad. ¡Qué placer presiento, mi dulce amigo, en leer contigo una obra interesante!

En primer lugar, porque quiero que conozcas al primer prosista de Europa, el novelista más distinguido de la época. Tengo en lista: *El pirata*; *Los privados rivales*; *El Waverley* y *El anticuario*, obras del célebre Walter Scott.

Seguidamente, *Corina o Italia*, por Madame Staël. Novela descriptiva del más hermoso y poético país del mundo, y hecha esta descripción por la pluma de una escritora cuyo mérito conoces. Además, han dado algunos amigos en decirme que hay semejanzas entre mí y la protagonista de esta novela, y deseo por eso volver a leerla contigo y buscar la semejanza, que se me atribuye con este bello ideal de un genio como el de la Staël.[4]

Sigue la *Atala* del inmortal Chateaubriand, porque te agradan todas las escenas de la naturaleza, todos los *corazones primitivos*, en fin, el hombre en su estado normal; y esta linda obra te satisfará. Luego, las poesías de Lista, Quintana y Heredia, porque, como dice uno de estos poetas:

> . . . *Verás la poesía*
> *del corazón y mente descendiendo*
> *al corazón y mente arrebatarse.*

Esta es mi lista: escoge tú la obra que mejor te parezca y avísamelo. ¡Verás qué placer gozamos en los momentos que pasemos juntos! A tu elección dejo también tus visitas a casa, pero no quiero que dejemos de vernos por un motivo. . . . Leeremos juntos. ¿No es éste un placer? Adiós, mi bien.

CARTA 10

Señor don Ignacio Cepeda:

Hasta hoy sábado, que vino el correo general, no se ha traído la carta de usted, querido Cepeda, y para que ésta no duerma hasta el miércoles en la estafeta, determino enviarla directamente a su casa de usted.

Cuando anteanoche me dijo usted que mandase al correo, porque me había usted escrito, se olvidó advertirme que la carta venía a mi nombre y no al adoptado en nuestra correspondencia. Así, aunque ayer mandé, no me la trajeron, porque la persona encargada buscó a Doña Amadora de Almonte[5] y no a mi nombre. En fin, ya está en mis manos esta querida carta.

¡Una vez por semana . . . ! ¡Solamente te veré una vez por semana . . . ! Bien: Yo suscribo, pues así lo deseas y lo exigen tus actuales ocupaciones. Una vez por semana te veré únicamente: pues señálame, por Dios, ese día feliz entre siete para separarle de los otros días de la larga y enojosa semana. Si no determinases ese día, ¿no comprendes tú la agitación que darías a todos los otros? En cada uno de ellos creería ver al amanecer *un día feliz*, y después de muchas horas de agitación y expectativa pasaría el día, pasaría la noche, llevándose una esperanza a cada momento renovada y desvanecida, y sólo me dejaría el disgusto del desengaño. Dime, pues, para evitarme tan repetidos tormentos, qué día es ese que debo desear: ¿será el viernes? En ese caso comenzaremos por hoy; si no, será el sábado. ¿Qué te parece? Elige tú: si hoy, lo conoceré viéndote venir; si mañana, avísamelo para que yo no padezca esta noche esperándote, que tendrá para mí luz y alegría.

¡Ya lo ve usted, me arrastra mi corazón, no sé usar con usted el *lenguaje moderado*, que usted desea y emplea; pero en todo lo demás soy dócil a su voz de usted, como lo es un niño a la de su madre! Ya ve usted que suscribo a no verle sino semanalmente. Pero, ¿no irá usted al Liceo? ¿no al baile? Para decidirle a usted ¿no será bastante que yo le asegure no habrá placer para mí en estas diversiones si usted no asiste? . . .

¡Cepeda! ¡Cepeda! Debes gozar y estar orgulloso, porque este poder absoluto que ejerces en mi voluntad debe envanecerte. ¿Quién eres? ¿qué poder es ése? ¿quién te lo ha dado? . . . Tú no eres un hombre, no, a mis ojos. Eres el Angel de mi destino, y pienso muchas veces al verte que te ha dado el mismo Dios el poder supremo de dispensarme los bienes y los males que debo gozar y sufrir en este suelo. Te lo juro por ese Dios que adoro, y por tu honor y el mío; te lo juro que mortal ninguno ha tenido la influencia que tú sobre mi corazón. Tú eres mi amigo, mi hermano, mi confidente, y, como si tan dulces nombres aún no bastasen a mi corazón, él te da el de su Dios sobre la tierra. ¿No está ya en tu mano dispensarme un día de ventura entre siete? ¡Así pudieras también señalarme uno de tormento y desesperación, y yo lo recibiría, sin que estuviese en mi mano evitarlo! Ese día, querido hermano mío, ese día sería aquel en que dejases de quererme; pero yo lo aceptaría de ti sin quejarme, como aceptamos de Dios infortunios inevitables con que nos agobia.

No me haga usted caso; tuve jaqueca a medianoche y creo que me ha dejado algo de calentura: ¿no es verdad? Mi cabeza no está en su ser natural.

Adiós. Lo que es esta noche, si usted me ve, será en casa, porque C. ha quedado en venir, y no puedo ir a su casa sabiendo [que] viene ella a la mía.

Deseo leer a usted un himno patriótico, que acabo de componer, y otros versos a un jilguero.

Adiós otra vez, mi dulce amigo; no conserves ésta, rásgala, te lo ruego. Es una carta de dislates, que sólo la desconfianza de que todas las que escriba hoy salgan lo mismo me hace mandar ésta. Hay días en que está uno no sé cómo: días en que el corazón se rompería si no se desahogase. Yo tenía necesidad de decirte todo lo que te he dicho; ahora ya estoy más tranquila. No me censures, por Dios.

CARTA 12

Caro amigo: Aprovecho la visita, que ha venido a hacerme una de mis antiguas criadas, menos torpe que las que tengo actualmente, para ponerte estas líneas, encargándola de llevártelas.

No irás al baile, ya lo sé, y no quiero infringir mis propósitos importunándote con objeto de verte en él. Pero como deseo contarte qué tal estuvo y lo que hice, y lo que vi, y lo que hablé . . . ¡todo!: como deseo referirte las personas que estaban, los trajes de las señoras, en fin, todo, todo como ya dije, espero que tú tengas también alguna curiosidad de saberlo, y te invito (sin comprometerte) a que vengas mañana por la noche.

El baile, según parece, no estará demasiado concurrido, pues anoche mismo vimos despachando en el teatro billetes sueltos, y se nos dijo que había sido preciso hacerlo, porque no había más que 44 suscritores. Pero si usted estuviera, ¿no estaría harto concurrido para mí . . . ? ¡No será! ¡paciencia! Voy adquiriendo con usted una resignación admirable, de la que no me creía capaz: porque a la verdad, vida mía, puedo muy bien decirle a usted aquel verso de una comedia de Moreto:[6]

¡Qué tibio galán hacéis!

Y, sin embargo, yo lo sufro con un estoicismo heroico. ¿Sabes que a veces me pregunto a mí misma por qué he de querer a un hombre tan poco complaciente, tan poco asiduo, tan poco apasionado como tú? Me lo pregunto y no alcanzo respuesta de mi pícaro corazón, tan caprichoso. Pero, no, Ignacio mío, ¡no es verdad! El me responde siempre satisfactoriamente y me dice que te ama porque eres bueno, noble, sincero, porque eres el mejor hombre del mundo, y es justicia amarte cuando se ha tenido la dicha de conocerte.

Ya lo ves: aunque mis cartas comiencen algunas veces amargas o festivas, siempre las concluyo más tiernas que debieran ser, y tú abusas, ingrato, de esta ternura mía para hacer cuanto se te antoja y nunca lo que yo deseo. Ya me las pagará usted, señor mío, el día en que esté yo de humor de hacer desesperar a usted; digo, si acaso usted se desespera por alguna cosa. . . . Vaya esta heridita entre tantas flores como le prodigo, porque, a fe mía, no merece usted tanta bondad.

Adiós. — Mañana, ¿eh? . . . esto es, *si puede usted*, si se lo permiten sus estudios, visitas, etc.; y ahora acuérdate un momento de que te ama a pesar de tus *indocilidades* tu demasiada buena

G.

CARTA 13

Voy a probarte que no soy tan dócil, como anoche me reprochaste, a tu antigua orden. Voy a saludarte con la pluma, ya que verbalmente no puedo hacerlo hoy. ¡Vida mía! ¡qué mala noche he pasado, qué mala estoy, qué triste . . . ! No tengo vida sino para amarte; para todo lo que no es tu amor estoy insensible. Ni me agrada escribir, ni leer, ni bordar, ni la calle, ni mi casa. Si algún talento he tenido, creo positivamente que lo he perdido ya, porque me encuentro lo más necia y fastidiada. He leído no sé donde:

> *Un momento ha vencido*
> *mi audacia imprudente,*
> *este alma tan soberbia . . . ,*
> *¡vedla ya dependiente!*

Yo he mandado siempre en mi corazón y en mis acciones con mi entendimiento, y ahora mi entendimiento está subyugado por mi corazón, y mi corazón por un sentimiento todo nuevo, todo extraordinario.

¡Posible es, Dios mío, que cuando yo me creía libre ya del dominio de amor, cuando me persuadía de haberlo conocido, cuando me lisonjeaba de experta y desilusionada, haya caído como una víctima débil e indefensa en las garras de hierro de una pasión desconocida, inmensa y cruel! . . . !Posible es, Cepeda, que yo ame ahora con el corazón de una niña de trece años! . . . ¿Qué es esto que por mí pasa? ¿Qué es esto que yo siento? . . . Dímelo, dímelo, porque yo no lo sé. Es harto nuevo para mí, te lo juro. Y yo he amado antes que a ti, he amado, o lo he creído así, y, sin embargo, nunca, nunca he sentido lo que ahora siento. ¿Es amor esto? No, hay algo de más, a mi corazón. ¡Qué feliz era! ¡Cuán tiernamente te amaba! ¡Los ángeles me envidiarían! Y ahora, ahora, ¡cuán desgraciada! ¡Cuánto sufro! ¡Cuánto, querido mío! ¿Y por qué? ¿Qué ha sucedido? ¿Qué cosa me atormenta? Nada, yo no lo sé. ¿Es acaso que Dios castiga el exceso de amor, haciéndole un martirio? ¿Es que el corazón humano es estrecho y se rompe cuando está demasiado lleno? . . . ¿Es un presentimiento de desgracia? ¿Es una plentitud de felicidad? ¿Es un defecto de mi organización, o una inconsecuencia de mi espíritu? . . . Yo no lo sé, pero estoy abatida, padezco, soy desgraciada.

No te pido que vengas a menudo, no, ni aun el lunes, como has ofrecido. Mejor será más tarde: el martes, el miércoles, el jueves . . . en fin, cuando yo esté menos triste que ahora, porque tu presencia, tan cara, tan deseada antes, ahora aumentaría mi tristeza. ¡Cuidado,

Cepeda, cuidado! . . . Ten cuidado de mi corazón, tenlo . . . , mira que puedo morir. Tú no sabes, no puedes saber, que puedes matarme, no lo sabes. Pues bien, acaso te es muy fácil. Si quieres mi vida, si quieres conservar tu amiga, cuídala; dale tranquilidad, dale sosiego. Yo conozco que eres más prudente que yo, y me acuerdo de que alguna vez me has pedido *paz y olvido*. Olvido, no, pero paz, yo quiero dártela y quiero tenerla. Tú tenías razón, la tenías. ¡Paz, sí, paz! Yo la necesito como tú y como tú la demando. De hoy en adelante, de común acuerdo, nos daremos paz, bien mío. ¡Desgraciados los que quieren apretar el corazón hasta romperlo, los que dan impulso a una máquina sin saber si tienen fuerza para detenerla cuando quieren! Es santa, es sagrada la vida del corazón, y nos empeñamos en gastarla. ¡Porque todo se gasta, todo! ¡Hoy no puedo resistir, mi corazón me ahoga! Mañana acaso estará parado y frío. ¡Nada es inexhausto! Se deben respetar los sentimientos y se debe temerlos. Ellos pueden dar la dicha o la desgracia. Tú no querrás darme sino felicidad. Si para dármela al presente es preciso más. Es preciso que me compadezcas, y acaso . . . acaso que dejes de verme. ¡Cuánto me cuesta decírtelo! Rompe ésta, y adiós.

CARTA 32

Madrid, 25 de julio de 1845

Querido Cepeda: Perdona el innoble papel en que te escribo; se va el correo, estoy demudada y no encuentro otro papel a mano. Te ofrezco, antes de todo, mi nueva habitación, calle del Horno de la Mata, número 9, cuarto principal, y luego voy a contestar brevemente tu grata última. . . .

¡Conque piensas casarte? . . . No te lo censuro, ni lo apruebo. Para mí la verdadera felicidad no consiste en el estado que se tiene; así como no creo que la bondad de los gobiernos consista en su forma. El matrimonio es mucho o poco, según se considere; es absurdo o racional, según se motive.

Yo no me he casado, ni me casaré nunca; pero no es por un fanatismo de libertad, como algunos suponen. Creo que no temblaría por ligarme para toda la vida, si hallase un hombre capaz de inspirarme una estimación tal que garantizase la duración de mi afecto. Más; tengo la convicción de que no hay dicha en lo que es pasajero, y digo, como Chateaubriand, que si tuviese la locura de creer en la felicidad la buscaría en la costumbre. El matrimonio es un mal necesario del cual pueden sacarse muchos bienes. Yo lo considero a mi modo, y a mi modo lo abrazaría. Lo abrazaría con la bendición del cura o sin ella; poco me importaría; para mí el matrimonio garantizado por los hombres o garantizado por la recíproca de los contrayentes únicamente, no tiene más diferencia sino que el uno es más público y el otro más solemne: el uno puede ser útil a la impunidad de los abusos y el otro los dificulta; el uno es más *social* y el otro más *individual*. Para mí es santo todo vínculo contraído con recíproca confianza y buena fe, y sólo veo deshonra donde hay mentira y codicia. Yo no tengo ni tendré un vínculo, porque lo respeto demasiado; porque el hombre a quien me uniese debía ser no solamente amable, sino digno de *veneración*; porque no he hallado, ni puedo hallar un corazón bastante grande para recibir el mío sin oprimirlo, y un carácter bastante elevado para considerar *las cosas y los hombres* como yo los considero.

Tú no estás en ese caso; eres el hombre y puedes buscar felicidad en una mujer aun cuando ella no esté a tu altura. Créeme, sin embargo: no te cases con una tonta; la mayor virtud no compensa el defecto de talento, y aun me atrevo a decir que no hay virtud en la estupidez. Las ligerezas, las faltas mismas de una mujer son males más remediables que la incapacidad de comprender aun las mismas virtudes que acaso se practican. El talento se extravía, pero la tontería no sabe siquiera que sigue el buen camino, y si lo deja no lo recobra jamás. Cásate, si lo crees conveniente; pero acuérdate siempre de que una amiga te aconseja no juzgar nunca virtud la frialdad de las almas ineptas, ni pensar, como algunos, que la ignorancia garantiza el corazón.

Ésta es ya muy larga, y aun no te he dicho que pienso establecerme en París. Sí, amigo mío; parece que en aquella capital puedo prometerme mayores ventajas de mi pluma, y como no soy rica y quiero asegurarme una vejez sin privaciones, pienso irme *adonde mejor paguen*. Esto, sin embargo, aun no es cosa decidida. Veremos.[7]

Estoy cansada del mundo, de los obsequios, de las calumnias, de la adulación, de la gloria y hasta de la vida. Necesito otro espacio mayor o menor que éste, otra vida de más calma o de más agitación. El amor no existe ya para mí; la gloria no me basta; quiero *dinero*, pues quiero la vida de los viajes o la vida del *retiro muelle y lleno de goces del lujo.* Tampoco me sería ingrato irme a una pobre aldea a criar pichones; pero aun no puedo, porque necesito de mi pluma.

En fin, si tú te casas con una buena chica que tenga talento, que sea bonita para que no sea celosa, que te quiera mucho y merezca ser correspondida, suspenderé mi curso vagabundo para ir dondequiera que estéis a cantaros un lindo epitalamio y a pasar ocho días con vosotros. ¿Aceptas?

Adiós; acabo de publicar una oda, que ha alborotado a Madrid, y que me ha valido un gran regalo del Infante D. Francisco de Paula. Te la mandaré un día de éstos, y hoy me repito tu amiguísima,

TULA

P.D. . . . . Yo he dicho en una novela: "No acuséis al corazón de perder sus ilusiones; así como no se acusa al árbol por ceder sus hojas al inclemente soplo de viento." ¿Pero el árbol desnudo y el corazón desengañado no pueden llorar la pérdida de sus flores? Sin acusar a nadie se puede decir: han hecho a mi corazón un daño con voluntad o sin ella.

Carta a Antonio Romero Ortiz[8]

Día 5 de Mayo (1853)

Querido Antonio, parece que no tienes ni chispa de impaciencia por repetir tu visita à Eloisa. Nada me dices de eso; nada de vernos. Acaso haces bien: creo que el comunicarnos por cartas tiene grandes ventajas bien examinado. Por mi parte, aunque se me hacen muy largos los dias privada de tu presencia, con todo, conozco que mas bien nos conviene q^e. nos daña este [*sic*] lejania, que no me impide saber tus pensamientos y comunicarte los mios. El amor, ese tirano insaciable que con nada sé da por satisfecho, sabe ser tambien un niño dócil y hasta pueril, q^e. se entretiene con cualquier cosa, y se alegra y se reputa dichoso. He deseado algunas veces que Armand[9] hubiese continuado siendo por largo tiempo mi *invisible caballero*; que solo su pensamiento hubiese llegado à mi, siempre envuelto en esas nubes de rosa del misterio, como la eterna promesa de una felicidad nunca poseida p^o. incesantem^{te}. esperada. Al adquirir una forma, y un caracter determinado, mi fantástico caballero se ha hecho amar mucho, si ciertam^{te} . . . mucho! pero es indudable q^e. lo q^e. ahora me inspira es un sentimiento agitador y doloroso; mientras que todo era dulce, tranquilo, ideal en lo que esperimentaba por mi Armand.

Sin pensarlo, amigo mio, he contestado à la pregunta que me haces en tu carta de ayer. Si, Antonio, yo te amo, eso es una verdad: pero quieres tambien que te esplique *como te amo* y eso lo espresare mejor cuando no quiera q^e. cuando de intento me ponga à definirlo. Te amo, à lo que entiendo, de varios modos, y eso es lo que me disgusta: si te amase de uno solo ambos seriamos mas felices y nos entenderiamos mejor. Te amo cuando no te veo, cuando no te escucho, cuando solo llegan à mi tus cartas y no te veo mas q^e. en mi corazon, te amo entonces con un afecto en q^e. gozo; con un afecto q^e. me engrandece à mis propios ojos: Siento en tales instantes q^e. aunq^e. fueras viejo, de fea figura, despreciable p^a. todas las mujeres, serias bello p^a. mi por tu alma; joven por tu amor. Siento q^e. mi corazon noble y puro se lanza al tuyo por un movimiento de santa confianza y de casta simpatia, y que nos unimos con un vínculo sin nombre, pero augusto, indisoluble, eterno: por aquel consorcio de las inteligencias que he deseado tanto conocer y q^e. no he visto jamas. Entonces, Antonio, no dudo de ti, ni de mi: entonces no te llamo esposo, porq^e. no encuentro nombre que darte en el lenguaje humano: entonces eres p^a. mi *la esperanza*, q^e. es lo unico grande que puede gozar el hombre: entonces respiro contigo en una atmósfera tan pura, tan embalsamada, tan suave, que me parece imposible la puedan surcar jamas las pasiones terrenales. He aqui como te amo algunas veces; como quisiera amarte para siempre; como debo amarte si aspiro à ser feliz por el amor. Pero desgraciadam^{te}. en mi organizacion desventurada todos los estremos se tocan: cuando te veo, cuando te oigo, cuando respiro tu aliento, cuando me haces una caricia, me arrancas subitam^{te}. de mi region encantada, me haces desear delicias terrenales, me das fiebre, Antonio, una fiebre tal que quedo enferma por muchas horas; me transformas en una mujer vulgarisima; me haces avergonzar de mi misma y de la flaca naturaleza humana . . . en fin, te amo entonces con un amor tan violento como receloso, tan ambicioso como impotente: con un amor que logrando cuanto anhela no seria feliz; que dandolo todo no daria nada. Si, te amo entonces con pasion pero con cólera contra ti y contra mi, y contra la naturaleza: te amo dudando de tu corazon y del mio, porq^e. en tales momentos me parece muy dudoso que sea algo ese q^e. llamamos corazon: en esos momentos, querido mio, me pregunto con pavura si es cierto q^e. el hombre está llamado à mas alto destino que el q^e. vé en el bruto; si no ha nacido, lo mismo que este, para multiplicarse y morir . . . me parece entonces que lo q^e. llamamos alma, sentimiento, idea, acaso no son en suma sino seducciones que emplea la pícara naturaleza material p^a. llevarnos ciegos à cumplir sus leyes: esas leyes q^e. el bruto obedece por instinto, y q^e. el *animal pensador* cumple mas fatalm^{te}. todavia, arrastrado por la esperanza de un bien mentiroso, irrealizable.

Oh! no sabré nunca esplicarte lo que yo veo y siento y juzgo en

Gertrudis Gómez de Avellaneda

167

estas cosas: no podré por mas que diga hacerte comprender la lucha qᵉ. hay entre mi orgullo de inteligencia y mi naturaleza de mujer apasionada: no se definen estas contrariedades, Antonio: se sienten, no se pintan. ¿Quieres saber como te amo? . . . Como tu quieras: esta es la verdad. Con un afecto que no puede darte ninguna otra mujer; con una ternura y un idealismo infinito; con una felicidad íntima y duradera . . . y tambien puedo amarte como Safo à Faon:[10] tambien puedo decir como ella,

> Ante mis ojos desparece el mundo
> y por mis venas circular ligero
> el fuego siento de placer profundo . . .
> Trémula, en vano resistirte quiero,
> de ardiente llanto mi méjilla inundo,
> deliro, gozo, te bendigo, y muero!

Oh! si! desgraciadamᵗᵉ. hay en mí estas dos naturalezas poderosas del poeta y de la mujer: hay en mí idealismo bastante pᵃ. vivir toda la vida de un suspiro de tu amor, y bastante sangre pᵃ. agotar en un momento todo tu amor y el mio. Desgraciadamᵗᵉ. tambien, has tenido el poder de despertar à la vez ambas naturalezas, y se empeñan en una lucha cuyo exito ignoro. En los momentos en qᵉ. la victoria se inclina por la *naturaleza ideal*, entonces es cuando te amo con fé, en ti y en mi; cuando creo qᵉ. seré feliz y me hallo digna de serlo. En los momentos en qᵉ. gana terreno la *naturaleza terrestre*, entonces es cuando te amo dudando, cuando temo qᵉ. no podamos querernos ni estimarnos largo tiempo; cuando me desprecio à mi misma al mismo tiempo qᵉ. se revela mi insensato orgullo contra el fallo de mi propia conciencia: entonces sufro, y te hago sufrir, y soy caprichosa, y desigual, y llena de inconsecuencias. Entonces me parece qᵉ. ha sido ridículo todo mi idealismo de poeta, puesto qᵉ. había de parar por donde comienza el instinto de la bestia. Y sin embargo, en medio de aquellas tempestades de alma, qᵉ. se venga tan cluelmᵗᵉ.[*sic*], en mí, de los momentáneos triunfos de mi otra naturaleza terrestre, sucede qᵉ. te amo locamᵗᵉ. y te llamo *mon homme* [mi hombre], y me parece en aquel instante qᵉ. no hay dicha mayor qᵉ. ser tuya de todos modos; tuya por todos los vínculos posibles. Una hora despues, por cuanto existe en el orbe no querria que se me cumpliese semejante deseo: por cuanto hay no querria que me uniesen à ti lazos vulgares, fuese cualquiera su nombre: no querria dar un destino vulgar à este hermoso sueño que encanta à mi alma: à esta página de mi vida en q^e. has escrito con rasgos originales y nuevos el nombre de Armand; de Antonio. Pero otra hora despues vuelvo à verte y entonces . . . entonces digo q^e. solo à Dios se puede amar en *su esencia incomprensible*; q^e. tu eres mi amante, mi esposo, que mi idealismo es una locura, una profanacion . . . q^e. la felicidad del amor está en tus brazos y no en mis sueños: entonces, Antonio, quisiera inventar lazos todavia mas estrechos que los q^e. conocemos, y mas corpóreos, y mas sensibles, p^a. ligarme à ti con todos ellos. De todos estos modos te amo: yo no sé de mi corazón mas de lo q^e. te digo: te lo juro, Antonio. ¿Me haras feliz? no lo sé. ¿Lo soy ahora? No; estoy muy disgustada conmigo misma, y de rechazo contigo tambien. ¿Está en tu mano terminar mis disgustos? Creo q^e. no, por ahora al menos: ¿estará despues? Es muy probable. ¿De que modo? . . . Casi no lo alcanzo. Lo único q^e. veo claro es q^e. te quiero, que si sabes no escitar en mi estas luchas, mi amor puede hacerme mucho bien: que si te gozas en matar mi idealismo, acaso luego querras en balde hacerlo renacer. Si; tengo un poder terrible sobre mi corazón; es mi orgullo: respétalo siempre, Antonio: no me digas jamas una sola palabra que me haga sospechar q^e. me crees flaca y esclava de mis pasiones: con solo eso me harias fuerte, me harias invencible; pero ¡ah! ¿viviria mi amor despues de haber sido una vez violentam^{te}. ahogado?—Basta de esto p^a. siempre, amigo mio: te suplico que volvamos à ser por algunos dias Armand y Gertrudis: escríbeme como entonces: véme ò no me veas, segun te parezca conveniente: te dejo dueño absoluto de tu conducta en este punto. Recibiré tus cartas con placer intimo: te veré con felicidad siempre q^e. quieras; pero ni te exijo que dediques algun rato cada dia à hablar con tu amiga, ni me quejaré si dejas de verme mas ó menos tiempo. Sé libre, Antonio mio, sé siempre libre en tus relaciones conmigo, y cree q^e. aunq^e. tan celosa, tan exijente, tan inconstante en mi caracter, soy bastante firme en mis sentimientos, y no decaerá mi amor mientras tu seas noble, bueno, sincero, leal, aunq^e. seas menos apasionado si asi lo crees conveniente. ¿Que mas puedo decirte?

¿Dudaras aun? no me entenderas todavia? ¿Seguiras creyendo que no te amo lo q^e. tu deseas? Oh! serias bien injusto. Antonio, antes q^e. serlo pideme pruebas à tu placer. No es la primera vez q^e. te he dicho q^e. *serás arbitro de mi suerte:* te repito ahora q^e. *te amaré como tu quieras*; q^e. seré p^a. ti, hoy mismo si te place, *la q^e. tu quieras q^e. sea*; pero déjame creer, amigo mio, Armando mio, mi leal caballero, déjame creer q^e. tu no quieres sino mi felicidad, y q^e. comprendes que mi felicidad será grande si me haces sentir que tu la posees, y q^e. ambos la merecemos. Si soy una pobre sensitiva q^e. sufre con los cámbios atmosféricos, eso, ya lo ves, no es culpa mia. Si deseo verte y me enojo alguna vez porque no lo adivinas . . . tampoco es culpa mia. Se indulgente: sufre mis desigualdades y ámame siempre, como esposo, como hermano, como quieras, Antonio, pero estimandome siempre. La idea de q^e. tu amor era meram^{te}. fisico me haria mucho, muchisimo daño. Tuya.

T.

Notas

1. En realidad tenía un año más.

2. Estas son palabras de Cepeda, citadas de una carta que él le había mandado el 15 de julio de 1839.

3. Concepción Noriega, amiga de la Avellaneda.

4. Esta novela describe las frustraciones de la mujer como artista creadora a causa de los límites que la sociedad se la impone.

5. Cepeda era del pueblo de Almonte. "Amadora" era el nombre ficticio bajo el cual la Avellaneda se carteaba con Cepeda.

6. Agustín de Moreto y Cabaña (1618–69). Famoso dramaturgo.

7. Nunca lo hizo.

8. Para estas cartas, sí hay acceso a las que Tula escribió de su puño y letra. He conservado la ortografía original.

9. El nombre ficticio con el cual Romero Ortiz firmaba sus cartas iniciales a la Avellaneda.

10. Safo: poeta griega (600 *a.C.*). Hay una leyenda, probablemente ficticia, que dice que se enamoró de un hombre, Faón, y cuando él no le correspondió su amor, Safo se tiró de un precipicio. Se sabe muy poco de su vida.

Letters to Ignacio de Cepeda

During an hour of sleeplessness and melancholy on the night of July 13 [1839]. Dedicated to my "companion in disillusionment." For him alone.

[Avellaneda begins her letter with a lengthy poem that speaks to her personal disappointment with life and to how these feelings link her to Cepeda, who she thinks feels similarly.]

It disturbs me very, very much to hear you express your ideas, sufferings and hopes. You see by the above creation what thoughts this produces in me. Listen to the verses and not to the ideas.

In actual fact, sometimes this *fullness of life* oppresses me and I would like to be rid of its weight. I have worked for a long time to diminish my moral existence so as to bring it to the same level as my physical one. Judged by a society which fails to understand me, and weary of a lifestyle that perhaps makes me look foolish, superior and inferior to my sex, I feel like a stranger in the world and isolated in nature. I feel the need to die, yet nevertheless live and in the eyes of many must seem happy. . . .

You speak to me of friendship, and not long ago you felt love. I believe in neither one nor the other. In fleeting emotions, in superficial affections I look for something to distract my consuming thoughts, and in this way I feel less tormented, for [as I am] inconstant in my tastes I easily tire of everything, and superficial feelings which hardly bind me do not take away the right to follow the instinct of my soul, which longs for freedom. Sometime I hope to find on this earth a melancholy, ardent, proud and ambitious heart like my own, to share with him my pleasures and sorrows, and to give him this excess of life which alone I am unable to bear. But more often I fear this enormous capacity of mine for suffering, and have a foreboding that an impassioned love would arouse [such] storms in my breast that they might perturb my reason and my life. Besides, would even love fill my soul's abyss? I have tried everything and discarded it all: love and friendship. What, then, can I offer you, my dear? The compassion of a tormented heart! . . . and my verses to distract you for a bit from momentous cares.

LETTER 2

[August 1, 1839]

I am ashamed. My Lord! What must you have thought of me, Cepeda, after the strange and ridiculous conduct I displayed last night? If you were one of those conceited fools, one of those vain men who abound in this city, then I'd know what you were thinking.

Even though you are not one of those, even knowing that you are a modest man and not hasty in your judgments, I tremble when I reflect on what you must think of my foolishness, and the opinion you must have of me. What moderately modest man could there be, who, seeing the immoderate outburst you observed in me last evening, would not believe that only jealousy . . . ? My Lord! My hand trembles and I blush to think of it. I have given you cause not to believe anything I have told you up to now about the nature of my feelings toward you; I have given you cause to think that I am *in love and jealous*. I have given you cause to put me on the list of the four or five women in whom, without desiring it, you inspired an unfortunate passion. Damnation! I am feeling a humiliation which I did not think was on my list of afflictions. What kind of a role did I want to play, or, better yet, have I unwillingly played? That of the jealous woman! I, I, good Lord! I can't understand why I do not die choked with rage! I certainly feel neither love nor jealousy; it is absolutely certain that I have not regarded you as a lover nor want you as such, nor would I permit it . . . I swear this by God and my dignity as a woman! I swear that I would not have you as my lover, just as until now I have not thought of you as such.

All of this is absolutely true, as is the fact that the mutual affection which has linked us even unto our souls is as pure as it is selfless, yet in spite of this, what a role have I played since last night! How I have degraded myself for an inconceivable whim, for a childish and bizarre outburst! To what humiliating conjectures have I laid myself open! There you have the proof, the proof of what I have often told you: there is something in my character that is so frivolous, so capricious and unstable that it will cause me much sorrow in my life.

People think me a woman of some talent and sophistication, and I myself have felt this way, but we were wrong: I know this from experience. At the age of twenty-four[1] I have no talent, no sophistication, no prudence; I only have an unfortunate trait which I curse: an ingenuity which borders on stupidity and madness. You must have laughed at me; I do believe you must have. I cannot complain. But please be so good as to hear me out for a moment, for although I do not pretend to justify the frivolous and unrestrained nature of my conduct last evening, perhaps I can make you understand the true motivation thereof and will avoid, if not the impression you must justifiably have of me as rash and indiscreet, having you think of me as a *jealous woman*, which humiliates me beyond words and which I most certainly do not deserve.

. . . My pain, my surprise and my agitation were the result of the same cause. At that moment I could not see in you my heart's friend, who assured me of a *great, tender and holy friendship* and had told me: "you can accept it without fear or reservation, because the purest and most fervent of hearts offers it to you."[2] Instead of this "pure and fervent heart" at that instant of surprise and hurt I saw only a heart which had reached its limit, a heart torn between many alternatives. . . .

I don't recall exactly what I did or said. I know that I went mad, nothing more, mad with pain when I saw my last and dearest illusion shattered: the divine illusion which let me think that at last I had found a sensitive heart, pure [and] ardent, capable of great passions and perhaps of great mistakes, but not of lukewarm and multiple affections. . . .

All this, rushing suddenly to my head, upset it to such a degree that I no longer knew what I did. It seemed that I had been transported to another world, a hell, and that letter of yours which I had in my breast burned me like a glowing ember. I committed a thousand improprieties, improprieties which could be disastrously interpreted, and what I feel worst about, what most humiliates me, is to think that you, Cepeda, you thought you were seeing an outburst of jealousy when it was only a pained rebuff. My God, how ashamed I am! Would that I had died before going out last evening! . . .

Other than that I have nothing left to say. Withdraw your trust from me; I do not deserve it, for I am too violent and frivolous. I am also still very young in order to be the confidante of a man of your age and worth, and, I would even say of a man in such a delicate position. I have neither the necessary maturity nor the talent in order to give sound advice, and can only get upset or engage in foolishness like last night. I will always be your friend. . . .

Good-bye, my dear friend, bon voyage! Leave me a few lines at the post office, acknowledging receipt of this letter, for I would have no peace if I did not know for sure that you had received it. Have a good time in Elmonte or Almonte, take care of your health and be studious so that we will see you again soon. I repeat and fervently beg you, on my knees if necessary, that you forget my wretched behavior last night. If nothing can stop you from believing that only love, a jealous and exalted love at that, could drive a woman who normally is neither mad nor stupid to commit such foolishness, then believe it. But you must also believe that if such a love existed, it does so no longer, and if it existed, it was without my knowledge. In any case, what I most desire is that all that is past be forgotten.

LETTER 6

Mr. Ignacio Cepeda:

I have received your kind letter, my dear friend, with even greater satisfaction ever since Concha[3] informed me that since you were not in Almonte, but somewhere else your brother had men-

tioned and whose name I could not remember, I was afraid my letter might have gotten lost. I sent a maid to the post office several
times and she always told me that there was no letter, until yesterday, when it was impossible for me to go out and I availed myself of
Concha, who went to the post office herself and immediately
brought me the longed-for letter from you.

I am so glad that you are well, as you write me, and less melancholy than in your former [letter]. For my part I would like to be
able to say the same but, unfortunately, this is not the case. My
stomach pains have given me a great deal of trouble and my melancholy is worse every day. You tell me to get over it! . . . A wish of
yours certainly exercises strong influence on my heart, but in this
matter it is perhaps not within my power to accommodate the request made by your tender friendship. Besides the absence of my
best, indeed of my only friend, which is reason enough to make me
melancholy, I have so many other reasons to be sad! The prospect of
soon having to face a protracted separation from a mother I love
very dearly! The indecision with which I struggle without knowing
which side to take nor what life has in store for me! The need for
independence and the fear of public opinion which impedes my taking it! . . . In any event, so many, many things are upsetting me at
the present moment (during which time, if appearances are any indication, the day of crisis is approaching), that even Cepeda's friendship, that sweet and flattering friendship, will not be enough to give
me peace. But enough! Let's speak of other matters. I do wish my
letters were more cheerful! But oh, I see that that is impossible! The
bitterness of my heart becomes entangled in all of them. Do forgive
me!

I will send on my translation by the channels you indicated, but
it will have to be later on, when I have the time to do it, for the
rough draft is unintelligible and the only readable copy I had, I had
promised to send on to Cádiz. The editors of the new literary journal, which is published there under the name of *The Aureole*, sent me
a flattering letter asking me to let the journal publish some of my
works, and even though I wished to say no, I was obliged to do
them the favor because a relative of mine, of whom I think highly,

was so insistent in this matter that I could not refuse without insulting him. Therefore I have let *The Aureole* have my translation, under the condition that it not be published under my name, but entirely anonymously.

As soon as I can I will send you a copy, and from the outset beg your indulgence. You would really need to know the original to fully appreciate just how difficult the translation was. Lamartine, one of the greatest poets of the modern school, and perhaps the sweetest and easiest, nevertheless has something undefined and metaphysical in his poetry and a way of speaking that is really quite untranslatable. In many of his works his ideas are so delicate that they can wither, so to speak, under the translator's pen, and his expressions on occasion are so daring as to be intimidating. In *The Fountain* I have tried to translate with the greatest possible precision, letting the author's thoughts and ideas penetrate me, but I am still very far from the satisfaction of thinking that I have been able to imitate with even middling success his fluid and harmonious versification or that mystical, melancholy coloring which is characteristic of his works.

As far as my novel [*Sab*] is concerned, I have submitted the first ten chapters to the scrutiny of the compatriot whom I already mentioned, a cultivated man who fortunately is now here in this city, and have had the pleasure of gaining his approval. He has encouraged my timid pen, assuring me that the descriptive parts are rendered with precision and variety, and that the characters are well drawn and forcefully developed. His kindness has made him go so far as to bestow undeserved praise on my style and to judge the novel's organization extremely interesting. For all my self-esteem, I know that he has done me a good turn with his opinion, but in spite of that he has encouraged me to keep on trying in order to deserve the best.

So you see, my good friend, that I speak to you of things that are only things; you see that I am avoiding what you call the language of the imagination and I call the language of the heart: you judge it to be dangerous and banish it from our letters. I obey your formidable verdict, but what are you afraid of, my friend? What danger do you wish to avoid? Perhaps if you heard and used the language of the heart, are you afraid that you would be unable to prevent it getting away from you? Would you be afraid to feel or inspire a feeling stronger than that of friendship . . . ? If that is the case, calm yourself, for I assure you that you will never love me as anything but a sister, and that you will never find other affections in my soul other than those which today I am vain enough to express to you. These past few days I have thought a great deal about the nature of our feelings, and, I swear to you, this examination has given me peace. I would lose a great deal if you stopped being my friend in order to become my lover. Lovers! . . . So many of them besiege a young woman and what good are they? But where to find a friend such as you? Lovers! . . . Look, I'm fed up with them; that gaggle of flatterers that pesters our sex seems to me hardly worth bothering with, even to amuse oneself for a while with their idiotic compliments. I don't for a minute believe that they are in love with me! One man courts me because I'm an foreigner he hasn't met, whose class he perhaps judges as doubtful, whose customs he doesn't know and thinks are probably lax, of whose conquest he has no doubt and woos me with the idea that I could be his little whim, his toy, his amusement, his short-term pleasure. Another man courts me because he is a professional flatterer of any pretty women he meets: devoid of ideas, of sense, of prospects, just for the sake of courting and cutting an elegant figure. Yet another courts me because he hasn't got a plugged nickel, as the saying goes, and is sniffing around the fleshpots. I'm American, and because I am American he supposes I have money, which is reason enough for him to begin to make his matrimonial calculations. And last, there is the man who makes love to me only for the sake of vanity: it would flatter him to be my fiancé, not because I appeal to him, but because he could give himself airs in society that a woman with a modicum of fame and who people say has some talent has chosen him. Here, my dear Cepeda, you have the motives of the great majority of the men who come to pay me court. And given my frame of mind, can I even listen to them with any other motive but to make fun of them?

And what will you find in the majority of women who say they are in love with you? One declares she loves you and all she cares about is your profession. She wants a husband, a social position, which is the goal of common women, and they look for it in you. Another says she loves you and all she sees in you is her own amusement, a man who gives her his ear, who flatters her in public and who satisfies her vanity, and whom she would jilt without a second thought for another who is a more consummate flatterer, of higher social position, more distinguished name, etc., etc. Another says she loves you and all she loves in you is her own pleasure, and . . . Oh!— I blush to mention it—but we women see it every day, to our shame. We see that class of women which degrades the dignity of their sex, and which to my eyes are more despicable than the vilest scum of the earth.

Such is love in our unhappy and corrupt society! How could it even exist between us? Oh no, never! Let us leave the tainted words of lover and beloved for other men and women. You will be my friend and I yours all our lives, and you must never fear that the holy nature of our bonds will be degraded. Will you be afraid when I am not? All I have said proves to you that you risk nothing when you let your heart speak. Vanity will not interpret your words, nor can your friend confuse the expression of your sentiments with the insipid gibberish of courtship which is termed love. As far as I am concerned I will do whatever you wish; I won't express my feelings if this bothers you, but it's such an effort for me!

You see, Cepeda: my pen runs on in spite of me and says more than I want to say. I should be offended instead of showing my affection for you, but my pride, normally so sensitive in other matters, on this occasion is not affected. Don't be afraid, *you conceited person*, don't be afraid that I shall think you are *in love* when you use tender words with me. Do you take me for a little girl or an old woman? I repeat: do not be afraid, and so that you may have complete peace of mind, know that the day I believe you are *in love* with me is the day I stop caring for you and would never see you again. With this assurance your freedom runs absolutely no risk with me, nor have you any reason to be alarmed at my affection, nor need to envision it as an iron shackle ready to make you a prisoner. Dear melancholy man! How little sophistication you have! Forgive my using this sentence, my friend, but it tickles me, it really does, to see your fear and to try to find your heart under the veil with which you try to shroud it! You are afraid of me, Cepeda, don't deny it; you're afraid I will take possession of your heart, you fear the iron shackles that might be the consequences of your love for me and you think you can avoid things by clinging to the sacred protection of friendship. Oh, if you think that, you are a child. How much you deceive yourself, dear one, how very much, if you think friendship will delineate the limits the heart should respect! What difference does it make what you call feelings? Do they stop being what they are? It is not this that should calm you, but rather the knowledge that in me you do not have *a threat to your freedom*, and that, for the sake of my own interests, I will take care not to bestow on your heart more impassioned affection than that which I feel right now.

Strange and novel is the role I play with you. I, a woman, calming your fears of loving me! That's an odd thing! But with you I am not a woman; no: I am all spirit and there are no applicable rules for the exceptional affection you arouse in me.

This letter is very long, but I refuse to imitate those people who end their letters swearing (nothing less than swearing) to be briefer in subsequent ones. This letter is long, but longer still will be the one I write when I am not told to *avoid using expressions which are too moving and do a lot of harm. . . .*

Good-bye, my dear friend! Take care of yourself, have a good time and come back soon to where the sincerest desires of a most tender friendship call you.

Concha sends her best, and from me a thousand greetings from your unchanging

Tula ·

Seville, August 28, 1839

P.S. I beg you to disregard the incoherence, lack of organization and defective style of this letter. I realize that it's odd, but it follows my head. It's so confused! And besides, I'm in an awful mood today.

[Undated—about November 1839]

Night before last I told you that I had sent a book to your house, but because there were other people who were around, I couldn't add that the book in question (just like the one I am sending you today) was just a pretext so that I could write you without having the messenger be any wiser. Luck had it that the man didn't find you at home, so in a fit of pique I tore up the letter to protest the bad luck that sent it back to me twice when I supposed it was already in your hands.

Anyway, the letter contained nothing of importance; it was only an expression of my sadness at not having seen you for several days, and a proposition which I shall repeat in a few brief words. Let's see if you like it.

Soon you will be graduating, and I think that when you are out from under that you can see me more often. We have to see each other sometimes even before you graduate, because who can live like this, dear friend? Who can stand it? My own resistance is beginning to fail me, in spite of all my intentions. Anyway, I thought we should agree on one thing, and that is that whenever you come and I am alone, we should take advantage of such moments to satisfy one desire, and that is for me to read some interesting book with you. Even when Mother is around we could, if we feel like it, amuse ourselves a while by reading, as I see no problem with this if the idea appeals to you. With this in mind I've drawn up a list of some works I enjoy, which I will identify so that you can choose the one you like best and then tell me. I will have it here at home right away, and we can start the first chance we have. What pleasure I envision, my sweet friend, on reading an interesting book with you!

In the first place, I want you to get to know the most eminent European prose writer, the most distinguished novelist of our time. On the list I have *The Pirate*, *The Rival Favorites*,[4] *Waverley* and *The Antiquary*, works by the famous Walter Scott.

Right afterward, *Corinne or Italie*, by Madame Staël. A descriptive novel of the most beautiful and poetic country in the world, the descriptions written by the pen of a woman writer of whose worth you are aware. Besides, some friends have begun to say that there are similarities between me and the heroine of this novel, for which reason I would like to reread it with you and look for the similarity which people say I have with this lovely ideal created by the genius of Mme. Staël.[5]

Then there is *Atala*, by the immortal Chateaubriand, because you like all those nature scenes, all those *primitive hearts*, anyway, man in his natural state, and this lovely work will please you. Then poetry by Lista, Quintana and Heredia, because, as one of these poets says:

> . . . You will see that poetry
> which comes from the heart and the mind
> will carry the heart and the mind away.

That's my list: you choose the work that appeals to you the most and let me know. You'll see what pleasure we derive from the moments we spend together! I'll let you choose your visits to my house as well, but I don't want us to stop seeing each other for a reason. . . . We'll read together. Isn't that a pleasure? Good-bye, my love.

LETTER 10

Mr. Ignacio Cepeda:

There was no letter from you, my dear Cepeda, until today, Saturday, when the regular mail came, and so that this letter will not slumber in the post office until Wednesday, I have decided to send it directly to your house.

When night before last you told me to inquire at the post office because you had written me, you forgot to mention that the letter was addressed to my name and not to the one we adopted for our correspondence. So, even though I sent someone to inquire yesterday, they couldn't bring it to me because the messenger looked under Doña Amadora de Almonte and not under my name.[6] In any event, now the cherished letter is in my hands.

Once a week . . . ! I will see you only once a week! All right, I agree, because that's how you want it and your present occupations

demand. I will see you only once a week. For God's sake indicate to
me which one will be the happy day to separate it from the other
seven of the long and tedious week. If you don't select a day, don't

you understand the agitation you would cause on the other days?
On every one of them I would expect the dawn to bring me *a happy
day*, and after many hours of fretting and waiting the day would go
by, and the night would go by, taking away with it a hope continually renewed and fading, which would only leave me with the disappointment of disillusion. For that reason, and to spare me such repeated torments, tell me, then, which day is it to which I should
look forward? Shall it be Friday? In that case let's start with today; if
not, let it be Saturday. What do you think? You choose: if it's today,
I'll know it when I see you coming; if it's tomorrow, let me know
so that I don't suffer through the night waiting for you to come; it
will hold light and happiness for me.

You see, my heart sweeps me away; with you I don't know how
to use the *moderated language* you ask for and yourself employ, but in
all else I am docile to your voice, just as a child to the voice of his
mother! You see that I do agree not to see you more than once a
week. But won't you be going to the Lyceum? To the ball? So that
you can make up your mind, isn't it enough for me to assure you
that I will find pleasure in none of these activities if you aren't
there? . . .

Cepeda! Cepeda! You must be satisfied and very proud, because
this absolute power you have over my will must make you arrogant.
Who are you? What power is this? Who gave it to you? . . . In my
eyes you are not a man; no, you aren't. You are the Angel of my
fate, and many times when I see you I think that God Himself gave
you the supreme power to bestow on me the good and the evil I am
fated to enjoy and to suffer on this earth. I swear this to you by the
God I worship, by your honor and by mine; I swear that no mortal
has ever had the influence over my heart that you do. You are my
friend, my brother, my confidant, and if such sweet terms were not
enough for my heart, it gives you the title of its God on earth. Isn't
it in your hands to assure me one day of happiness among seven? ·
That way you could also designate one day of torment and despera-

tion, and I would accept it, for it is not in my hands to do otherwise. That day, my dear brother, that day would be the one on
which you stopped loving me, but from you I would accept this
without complaint, as we accept from God the inevitable misfor-
tunes by which He weighs us down.

Don't mind me; I had a splitting headache at midnight and I
think it's left me with a little fever, don't you think so? My head is
not in its normal state.

Good-bye. With respect to tonight, if you see me it will be at
home, because C. has arranged to come by, and I can't go to her
house knowing that she is coming to mine.

I'd like to read you a patriotic hymn I've just composed, and
some verses to a goldfinch.

Good-bye again, my sweet friend; don't keep this [letter], tear it
up, I implore you. It's a letter filled with nonsense, and only the sus-
picion that any others I might write today would come out the
same impels me to send you this one. There are days when one is in
I don't know [what kind of state], days in which one's heart would
break were it not able to vent its feelings. I needed to tell you
everything I have said; now I feel more composed. For God's sake,
don't censure me.

LETTER 12

Dear Friend: I am taking advantage of a visit by one of my former
maids, less dim-witted than the ones I have now, in order to write
you these lines, requesting her to deliver them to you.

I know you're not going to the ball, and I don't want to infringe
on my plans by pestering you with the purpose of seeing you there.
But since I want to tell you how it was and what I did, what I saw
and what I said . . . everything! Because I want to give you an account of the people who were there, the ladies' dresses, well, everything, just as I said, I hope that you are just a little curious to know
these things, and so I am inviting you (with no commitment on
your part) to come by tomorrow evening.

The way it looks not too many people will be going to the ball, because last night they were selling single tickets in the theatre, and we were told it was necessary to do so because there had been only 44 subscribers. But if you were there, wouldn't it be filled to overflowing for me? But it won't be! Patience! With you I am acquiring an admirable resignation, one of which I did not think myself capable, because in truth, my love, I really can quote you this line from a play by Moreto:[7]

What a lukewarm lover you are!

But nevertheless, I bear this with heroic stoicism. Do you know that sometimes I ask myself why I had to fall in love with a man who is as little agreeable, as little devoted, as little passionate as you? I pose this question and get no answer from my mischievous and fickle heart. But no, my Ignacio, it's not true! My heart always answers me very satisfactorily and tells me that it loves you because you are good, noble, sincere, because you are the best man in the world, and it is right to love you when one has had the pleasure of knowing you.

You see: even though my letters sometimes begin in a bitter or a joyful vein, I always end them more tenderly than they ought to be, and you, ingrate, take advantage of this tenderness to do whatever pleases you and never what I'd like. You'll pay for that someday, Mister, the day I'm in the mood to drive you to despair, that is, in the event that you ever despair of anything. . . . Let this little insult be sent along with all the compliments with which I shower you, because, on my oath, you don't deserve that much kindness.

Good-bye. — Tomorrow, right? . . . that is *if you can*, if your studies, company, etc. permit, and now recall for one moment that in spite of your *intractableness* you are loved by your too good

G.

LETTER 13

I am going to prove to you that I am not as docile as you reproached me for being last night, according to your old system. I shall use my pen to say hello to you, as I cannot do so verbally today. My dearest! What a ghastly night I had, how awful I feel, how sad. . . . I have no life but loving you; I am insensitive to anything that is not your love. I don't even care about writing, or reading, or embroidering or going out, or staying home. If ever I had any talent at all, I am positive that by now I have lost it, as I feel so foolish and irritated. Somewhere or another I read:

> [In] one instant
> this supremely proud soul
> has vanquished my reckless audacity . . .
> Look how dependent it has become!

I have always controlled my heart and my actions by means of my mind, yet now my mind is in thrall to my heart, and my heart to a feeling that is completely new and completely extraordinary.

It is possible, my God, that when I thought myself free at last from love's power, when I convinced myself that I knew what it was all about, when I flattered myself I was an expert and undeceived [thereby], I have fallen like a weak and defenseless victim into the iron claws of an unknown, immense and cruel passion! . . . It is possible, Cepeda, that I now love with the heart of a thirteen-year-old girl! . . . What is happening to me? What is this I feel? . . . Tell me, tell me, for I don't know. It is totally new to me, I swear to you. I have been in love before loving you, I have loved, or at least I thought I did, and nonetheless I have never, ever felt what I do now. Is this love? No, there's something more, it isn't just love. It is hell that has come to lodge in my heart. How happy I was! How tenderly I loved you! Angels would envy me! And now, now—how unhappy I am! How I suffer! How very much, my love! And why? What has happened? What is torturing me? I just don't know. Could it be that God punishes an excess of love, making it martyrdom? Is it that the human heart has a restricted capacity and bursts when it is too full? . . . Is it a foreboding of disaster? A deluge of happiness? Is it a defect in my makeup or an inconsistency in my spirit? . . . I have no idea, but I am dispirited, I suffer, I am unhappy.

I'm not asking you to come by often, no, not even on Monday, as you offered to do. It would be better a little later: Tuesday, Wednesday, Thursday . . . eventually, when I am less unhappy than now, because your presence, which was so dear and desired ere this, at present would heighten my sadness. Careful, Cepeda, careful! . . . Be careful of my heart, be . . . you know I might die. You don't know, you can't know, that you could kill me; you really don't know. Really, it might be quite easy for you. If you value my life, if you want to keep your friend, take care of her; give her peace, give her calm. I know that you are more prudent than I am, and I remember that once you asked me for *peace and forgetfulness*. Forgetfulness, no, but I want to give you peace and want it for myself as well. You were right, you were right. Peace, yes, peace! I need it and demand it just the way you do. From today on, by mutual agreement, my dearest, we will give each other peace. Woe to those who want to squeeze the heart until it breaks, and those who set a machine in motion without knowing if they are strong enough to stop it when they so desire! The life of the heart is holy and sacrosanct, and we insist on squandering it. Because everything gets squandered, everything! Today I can't bear it, my heart is choking me! Tomorrow perhaps it will have stopped and be cold. Nothing is inexhaustible! Feelings should be respected and feared. They can bring joy or misfortune. I know you only want to give me happiness. But it takes more to give this to me now. You must have pity on me and perhaps . . . perhaps you have to stop seeing me. How hard it is for me to tell you this! Tear this up and good-bye.

LETTER 32

Madrid, June 25 [1845]

Dear Cepeda: Forgive the poor quality of the paper on which I am writing you; the mail is about to go out, I am upset and can't find any other. First of all I want to give you my new address: Horno de la Mata Street, Number 9, fourth floor, and then I will briefly answer your last letter, which was greatly appreciated. . . .

. . . So you're going to get married? I neither approve, nor disapprove. For me true happiness does not depend on one's status, just as I don't believe that a government's goodness depends on its type. Matrimony is a lot or a little, depending on how you look at it; it is absurd or rational, depending on how it works.

I have not married, nor do I ever plan to, but this is not because of some kind of fanatic desire for freedom, the way some people suppose. I don't think I would hesitate to bind myself for a lifetime if I were able to find a man capable of inspiring in me such esteem as to guarantee the duration of my affection. Furthermore: I am convinced that there is no joy in what is temporary, and I say with Chateaubriand that were I mad enough to believe in happiness, I would look for it in what is habitual. Marriage is a necessary evil from which one can extract a number of benefits. I look at it my way, and in my way would embrace it. I would embrace it with or without benefit of clergy; [their blessing] matters very little to me because in my opinion there is no difference between a marriage that is vouched for by men and one that is vouched for solely by the reciprocal word of the parties involved. The only difference is that one is more public and the other more serious, one can facilitate the impunity of abuses and the other makes it more difficult, one is more *social* and the other more *individual*. In my opinion any bond is holy which is entered into with reciprocal trust and good faith, and I see dishonor only where there are lies and greed. I have not and will not enter into such a bond because I respect it too much; because the man to whom I bind myself must be not only kind but worthy of *veneration*; because I have not found and cannot find a heart great enough to accept mine without oppressing it, nor a character lofty enough to look at *things and men* as I do.

You are not in this position: you are the man and can look for happiness with a woman even when she is not on the same level as you. Nevertheless, believe me: don't marry a stupid woman; the greatest virtue does not make up for a lack of talent, and I would go so far as to say that there is no virtue in stupidity. A woman's indiscretions and even her mistakes are faults which are more easily remedied than the incapacity to understand the very virtues which might be put into practice. Talent may err, but stupidity doesn't even know that it is on the right path, and once off the path, will never find it again. Marry, if you think it's worthwhile, but always remember that a friend advises you never to judge as a virtue the coldness of inept souls, nor to think, as some do, that ignorance guarantees [the affections of] the heart.

This letter is already very long, and I haven't even told you that I am planning to take up residence in Paris. Yes, my friend, in that capital city it appears likely that I will be able to garner greater advantages from my pen, and as I am not wealthy and want to assure myself of an old age without privation, I plan to go *where they pay the best*. Nevertheless, this is not yet totally decided. We shall see.[8]

I am tired of the world, of its flattery, its slander, its adulation, its glory, and of life itself. I need another space either larger or smaller than this one, another life, either calmer or more exciting. Love no longer exists for me; glory isn't enough; I want *money* because I want to be able to travel or have *a comfortable retreat filled with luxurious pleasures*. I wouldn't even mind going to a poor village to raise pigeons, but I can't do that yet because I am dependent on my pen.

Anyway, if you are marrying a nice girl who has some talent, who is pretty so that she need not be jealous, who loves you a lot and deserves to be loved in turn, I will end my vagabond ways and go wherever you all may be to sing you a pretty wedding song and spend a week with you. Do you accept?

Good-bye. I have just published an ode which has put Madrid on its ear and earned me a substantial gift from Prince Francisco de Paula. I'll send you [the ode] one of these days, and today sign myself your very good friend,

Tula

P.S. . . . In one of my novels I said, "Don't blame the heart for losing its illusions, just as you can't blame the tree for surrendering its leaves to the inclement wind." But can't the bare tree and the disillusioned heart mourn the loss of their blossoms? Without accusing anyone it could be said that voluntarily or involuntarily my heart has been dealt a wound.

Letter to Antonio Romero Ortiz[9]

May 5 [1853]

Dear Antonio, it seems you don't feel the slightest bit of impatience to repeat your visit to Eloisa. You say nothing to me about it, nothing about seeing each other. Perhaps you do well: I think that for us to communicate by letter has, on close scrutiny, many advantages. For myself, although the days on which I am deprived of your presence are very long, nevertheless I understand that this distance is better for us, rather than doing us harm, as it does not stop me from knowing your thoughts or communicating mine to you. Love, that insatiable tyrant who is never satisfied with anything, also knows how to be a docile and even an immature child who can amuse himself with trifles, is content and considers himself happy. Sometimes I have wished that Armand[10] could have kept on being my *invisible gentleman*, that only his thoughts had reached me, always shrouded in those pink clouds of mystery, like the eternal promise of a happiness that is never possessed but incessantly hoped for. When he acquired a shape and a particular character, my fantastic gentleman became extremely cherished . . . that most certainly! But there is no doubt that what he produces in me now is an agitated and painful feeling, whereas what I felt for my Armand was completely sweet, tranquil and ideal.

Without intending to, my friend, I have answered the question you asked me in your letter of yesterday. Yes, Antonio, I love you, that is the truth, but you also want me to explain to you *how I love you*, and that I can express better when I'm not thinking about it than when I try to define it. As I understand it, I love you in different ways and that annoys me: if I only loved you one way both of us would be happier and we'd understand each other better. I love you when I don't see you, when I don't hear you, when only your letters reach me and I see you only in my heart. Then I love you

with an emotion that exalts me in my own eyes. At such moments I feel that even though you were old, ugly in body, worthless to all other women, to me you would be beautiful because of your soul, and young because of your love. I feel that my noble heart hurls itself toward yours in a gesture of sacred trust and chaste affection, and that we are united by a bond that is nameless, but august, indissoluble, eternal, by an intellectual partnership I have wanted so much to know and which I have never seen. Then, Antonio, I have no doubt either of you or of me; then I do not call you "husband," because in human speech I can find no name to give you. Then you are *hope* for me, which is the only great thing man can enjoy; then I breathe with you an atmosphere so pure, so sweetly scented, so soft, that it seems impossible to me that earthly passions could ever destroy it. This is how I sometimes love you, how I'd like to love you forever, how I ought to love you if I aspired to happiness through love. But unfortunately in my hapless makeup all extremes come together: when I see you, when I hear you, when I feel your breath, when you caress me, you suddenly tear me out of my enchanted region, you make me desire earthly delights, you inflame me, Antonio, with such a fever that I become ill for many hours. You transform me into a totally common woman, you make me ashamed of myself and of weak human nature . . . in short, then I love you with a love that is as violent as it is suspicious, as ambitious as it is powerless, with a love that were it to attain what it wishes, would not be happy, and giving all would give nothing. Yes, at those times I love you with passion, but also with rage at you, at me and at nature; I love you while doubting your heart and mine because in those moments it seems very doubtful to me that something we call a heart even exists. At those times, my darling, I ask myself with dread if it is true that man is called to a higher destiny than the one he sees in animals, if he has not been born, just like the latter, to multiply and die . . . then it seems to me that those things we call soul, feeling, idea, are all only seductions which mischievous material nature uses to get us blindly to fulfill her laws, those laws an animal obeys instinctively and which the *thinking animal* fulfills even more fatefully, dragged along by the hope of a deceptive, unattainable good.

Oh! I will never be able to explain to you what I see and feel and judge in these matters; no matter how much I say I will never be able to make you understand the battle that goes on between my pride in being intelligent and my nature as a passionate woman—these contradictions cannot be defined, Antonio, they are felt, not described. You want to know how I love you? . . . Any way you want, that's the truth. With an affection no other woman can give you, with infinite tenderness and idealism, with an intimate and lasting happiness . . . and I can also love you the way Sappho loved Phaon[11] and say as she did:

> The world disappears from before my eyes
> and lightly through my veins I feel
> the fire of a deep pleasure circulate . . .
> Trembling, I want vainly to resist you,
> my cheek is washed by ardent tears,
> I feel delirium, pleasure, I bless you, and die!

Ah, yes! Unhappily, there are within me these two powerful temperaments: that of the poet and that of the woman. I have enough idealism in me to live all my life on the breath of your love, enough blood to exhaust in one moment all of your love and mine. Unhappily, too, you have had the power to awaken both of these temperaments simultaneously, and they are locked in a struggle whose outcome I do not know. In those moments where victory seems to be on the side of *ideal nature*, that's when I love you with faith in you and in me, when I believe I will be happy and feel I deserve it. In those moments when *earthly nature* gains ground is when I love you uncertainly, when I am afraid we will be incapable of loving and respecting each other for long, when I hate myself while my foolish pride is rebelling against the errors of my own conscience. Then I suffer, and make you suffer, am capricious and difficult and full of inconsistencies. Then all of my idealism as a poet seems ridiculous, as it must end up where animal instinct begins. But nevertheless, in the midst of those tempests in my soul—which exacts such cruel revenge of me—[in the midst] of the short-lived triumphs of my other, earthly nature, it happens that I love you madly, and call you *my man*; at that instant it seems to me that there could be no greater joy than to be yours in every way, yours by any bonds whatsoever. An hour later, nothing in the world would induce me to wish for any such destiny; nothing on earth would want me to be bound to you by common bonds, whatever their name. I would not want a common destiny for this beautiful dream that bewitches my soul, for this my life's page on which you have written with a new and original script the name of Armand, of Antonio. Another hour later I see you again and then . . . then I say that one can only love God in his *incomprehensible essence*, that you are my lover, my husband, that my idealism is madness, desecration . . . that love's happiness is in your arms and not in my dreams and then, Antonio, I would like to think up even closer bonds than any we know of, more physical, more sensitive, to bind myself to you with them all. I love you in all these ways; I do not know more of my heart than what I say to you: I swear it, Antonio. Will you make me happy? I have no idea. Am I now? No: I am very annoyed with myself, and indirectly with you as well. Is it in your power to end my vexation? I don't think so, at least not now. Later perhaps? Quite probably. How? . . . I can hardly explain it. The only thing I see clearly is that I love you, that if you know how not to provoke these inner battles, my love can do me a great deal of good; if you enjoy destroying my idealism, perhaps later on you will try in vain to bring it back. Yes, I have a terrible power over my heart: my pride. Always respect it, Antonio: don't ever say a single word that would make me suspect that you think me weak and a slave to my passions. With that alone you would make me strong, you would make me invincible, but ah! Would my love survive once it had been violently extinguished?

Let us leave this matter forever, my friend; I beg you to let us be Armand and Gertrudis again for a few days. Write to me as you did then, see me or not, according to what even seems convenient for you; in this matter I leave you totally in charge of your conduct. I will receive your letters with intimate pleasure, I will happily see you whenever you wish, but I don't insist that you devote some part of every day to chat with your friend, nor will I complain if you see me a little more or a little less time. Be free, my Antonio, always be free in your relationship with me, and believe that although I am so jealous, so demanding, so inconstant in character, I am quite steadfast in my feelings, and my love will not fail as long as you are noble, good, sincere, loyal, though perhaps less passionate if you think it's best that way. What else can I tell you? Do you still doubt? Do you still not understand me? Will you keep on thinking that I don't love you as much as you wish? Oh! You would be very unjust, Antonio, and before you are, ask me for any proof you want. This is not the first time I have told you that *you will be the judge of my destiny*. I now repeat to you that *I will love you any way you want me to*, that I will be for you—today if that's what you want—*the woman you wish me to be*, but allow me to believe, my friend, my Armand, my loyal gentleman, allow me to believe that you only want my happiness, and that you understand that my happiness will be great if you make me feel that you have it in your hands, and that we both deserve it. If I am a poor woman who is sensitive to atmospheric changes, that, you see, is not my fault. If I want to see you and I sometimes get angry because you don't sense this . . . that isn't my fault, either. Be indulgent: bear with my inconsistencies and always love me, as a husband, a brother, any way you wish, Antonio, but always with respect for me. The idea that your love was only physical would hurt me very, very much. Yours,

T.

Notes

1. She was making herself out to be a year younger than she was.
2. These are Cepeda's own words, quoted from a letter he had sent her on July 15, 1839.
3. Avellaneda's friend, Concepción Noriega.
4. I have been unable to track down the correct title of this work in English.
5. This novel describes the frustrations of the woman as creative artist, because of the constraints that society places on her.

6. Almonte was the town from which Cepeda came; "Amadora" roughly means "the loving woman," the fictitious name under which Avellaneda wrote to Cepeda.

7. Agustín de Moreto y Cabaña (1618–69), a famous playwright.

8. She never did go to Paris.

9. For these letters, the originals in Tula's handwriting do exist.

10. A fictional name with which Romero Ortiz signed his initial letters to Avellaneda.

11. Sappho was a Greek woman poet who lived about 600 B.C.; the story of her unrequited love for Phaon, which caused her to throw herself off a cliff, is probably fictitious. Very little is known of her life.

Juana Manuela Gorriti

Juana Manuela Gorriti

*J*ust like Gertrudis Gómez de Avellaneda, Juana Manuela Gorriti could truly be said to have lived a "Romantic" life, this one marked by the dramatic constants of war, exile, violence, and almost perpetual movement.

Juana Manuela was born in 1818 in the northern Argentinian province of Salta, the daughter of a prominent landholding family. Her father, José Ignacio Gorriti, was a distinguished military officer who fought first in the wars of independence from Spain and later in the interminable, bloody civil wars that marked the early years of the Argentine Republic. General Gorriti opposed the rising power of Juan Manuel de Rosas, the tyrant who began to be a force in Argentine politics about 1829 and, when he became dictator, would impose a bloody reign of terror that lasted from 1835 to 1852. On the losing side in this struggle, the Gorriti family had to flee the country for Bolivia in 1831, leaving behind them their lands, their home, and their past. The critic Cristina Iglesia has pointed out very adroitly how the ruins of the paternal house are a leitmotiv in Gorriti's writing, both in the content and in the fragmented style (19).

The adolescent Juana Manuela—again like Avellaneda—was attractive, intelligent, and headstrong. She had had a minimal formal education but from the beginning had been an avid reader, and literature was her passion. She felt passion of a different kind for a dashing Bolivian officer, Juan Manuel Isidoro Belzú, and insisted on marrying him when she was fourteen. Belzú rose to power quickly and became president of his country on two different occasions, but the marriage was a rocky one and, in spite of the birth of two daughters, Edelmira and Mercedes, ended in separation and divorce. Gorriti chose to settle in Lima, Peru, and, as she had no personal funds, supported herself and her daughters by establishing the first coeducational primary school in Lima as well as a high school for girls. Besides teaching and administration, she founded several women's magazines and wrote prolifically. She also organized the leading literary salon in the city, where men and women of letters and the arts met, read their writings to each other, listened to music, and exchanged ideas. Mercedes Cabello de Carbonera and Teresa González de Fanning, the two writers who appear next in this anthology, were close friends and active participants in these literary and social activities.

Gorriti's personal life continued to be unconventional: she had a number of affairs and two children out of wedlock, but this did not appear to dissuade the parents of Lima's leading families from sending their daughters to her schools (Berg, "Rereading Fiction" 129). Belzú —who had demanded his girls' return to Bolivia—was assassinated in 1865, just when his wife happened to be in La Paz to visit her daughters; in spite of their past marital differences, Gorriti organized a formal wake and burial for her late husband and pronounced a stirring funerary oration before returning to Peru.

The following year was also a politically turbulent one: Callao, Lima's port city, was besieged by the Spanish fleet, and many people were killed or injured in the bombardments. Gorriti aided the victims so heroically that she was awarded a medal by the Peruvian government.

From then on Gorriti alternated living in Lima and Buenos Aires and became a famous literary figure in both countries. During her life she wrote essays, stories, personal reminiscences, novels, historical biographies, and much travel literature, publishing in newspapers, women's magazines, and books. She was an indefatigable traveler between Bolivia, Argentina, and Peru, crossing the Andes many times by horse or mule; she also rounded the Horn several times by ship. A glance at a topographic map of South America shows that these journeys were tremendously arduous and dangerous, but this never kept her at home. Not only did Gorriti often document her own journeys in her writing, she cast many of her literary protagonists as travelers or exiles in search of physical or spiritual homes (Berg, "Viajeras" 69–70).

As Gorriti was so closely tied to major political figures and events in all three of the countries in which she lived, it is no wonder that her writing should reflect this. In the nineteenth century many writers from the newly independent Spanish-American nations were preoccupied with nation building and the identification of a national self ("el proyecto nacional"), but, given women's domestic roles that precluded their involvement in the public sphere, this writing was almost exclusively from a male perspective. Gorriti, however, actively participated in her country's historical discourse, partially for economic reasons. On repeated occasions she made it a point to remind her Argentine readers of her father's role as soldier and patriot and of the fact that he (and hence she) had lost their sizable fortune as a result of his opposition to Rosas (Mizraje 48, 52, 58). She thus consciously kept her illustrious name before her reading public, and, near the end of her life, the Argentine government indeed awarded her a pension in recognition of her father's service to his country. Besides her personal reminiscences, she also wrote biographies of some of the heroic generals of her father's circle (Puch, Güemes), another way of inserting herself into the discourse of nation building. "Without a doubt," says Iglesia, "her greatest audacity consists in presenting herself as a *patriotic writer*, and from there to narrate the national legend" (8).

Gorriti was also unique in telling of the horrors of war and terrorism from a woman's perspective, as she does in this highly melodramatic tale, "La hija del mashorquero," and in several other stories as well. Many leading Argentine politicians and intellectuals (Sarmiento, Mitre, Echeverría, Mármol) used their pens to oppose Rosas, for which they suffered prison or exile. A whole school of anti-Rosas literature came into being during the long years of his tyranny; one of the most famous examples is Esteban Echeverría's harrowing short story, "El matadero," in which Rosas's government is equated to a bloody slaughterhouse. When one compares these two stories the gendered viewpoints are strikingly different. Whereas Echeverría deals with issues of class, race, and society, Gorriti describes what terrorism does to the family.[1] If one recalls that in the literature of the nineteenth century stories of love, matrimony, and the family were often used as allegories for reconciling national interests,[2] the metaphorical charge of her story becomes even greater. Seen through a woman's eyes, and from inside the home, institutionalized terrorism takes on new meanings: children rebel against parents; parents kill their children; children from rival bands may fall in love, but their relationships are aborted or truncated by violence.[3] According to Isabel Quintana, Gorriti's heroine, Clemencia, is not only a kind of ghost but also a voluntary celibate because in this kind of world it is madness to procreate (77); Quintana also points out the stylistic counterpoint between the brutality of the father's dialogue and the ameliorating, suffering female voices (87).

The original title of the story, "La hija del mashorquero" (1865), which I have translated as "The Executioner's Daughter," needs some explanation. It refers to the Mashorca, the secret police who had networks of spies among the population, and would engage in undercover acts of torture and terrorism. The term "mashorca" is a play on words: "horca" is the gallows, so "más horca" is "more gallows"; a "mazorca" (pronounced the same way in Spanish America) is also a corncob, and, in a brutal play on the similarity of these words, the goons who tortured their victims would leave some of them hanging in public places, with corncobs sticking from bodily orifices. With this story and several others of the same sort, as well as her historical biographies and personal recollections of her family's involvement in opposing the dictator, Gorriti has surely earned a place both in the discourse of nation building and in the anti-Rosas school of Argentine literature, though this has not been acknowledged until fairly recently.

Gorriti went to Buenos Aires to live out her final years, still writing and publishing prolifically, founding more women's journals, and remaining involved in the education of young women. Two years before she died she published an unusual cookbook, *Cocina ecléctica* (The Eclectic Kitchen), which is a more interesting text than one might suppose, as many of her contributors were celebrities, and most embedded their recipes in entertaining anecdotes that reveal much about these women's cultural history and about Gorriti's network of friends.[4] Before her death in 1892 she wrote—among other things—some short biographies and her memoirs, *Lo íntimo*. Today she is celebrated as nineteenth-century Argentina's foremost woman writer.

I would like to add one additional note on Gorriti as a precursor to the contemporary literature of women's opposition to terrorism. The Rosas era became a popular topic during and after the recent Dirty War (1976–82), another period of institutionalized terrorism in Argentina, as it was not hard to see the grisly parallels. Like Gorriti, many women artists who protested the activities of the military junta also focused on issues of terrorism and its impact on the family. A famous true story of the Rosas era is that of Camila O'Gorman, who defied society and parental authority by fleeing with her priest/lover; Rosas made it a point to pursue the lovers, who were ultimately caught and executed, in spite of the fact that Camila was pregnant at the time. This event was made into the famous film *Camila* (1984) by María Luisa Bemberg.[6] In a similar vein, the playwright Griselda Gambaro wrote "La malasangre" in 1982,[5] a play that alludes to the brutal relationship between a Rosas-like father and his rebellious daughter. One could cite numerous other examples. There is no doubt that Juana Manuela Gorriti was a groundbreaking precursor in this type of literature.

Notes

1. Harriet Beecher Stowe took much the same approach in *Uncle Tom's Cabin,* in which she foregrounds how destructive slavery is to family life, both black and white.

2. See Doris Sommer, *Foundational Fictions: The National Romances of Latin America* (Berkeley: University of California Press, 1991), esp. ch. 3.

3. On this topic, see the excellent article by Liliana Zuccotti, "Legados de guerra" (The Legacy of War), *El ajuar de la patria: Ensayos críticos sobre Juana Manuela Gorriti,* ed. Cristina Iglesia (Buenos Aires: Feminaria Editora, 1993), 80–93.

4. See my article, "Juana Manuela Gorriti's *Cocina ecléctica*: Recipes as Feminine Discourse."

5. This play has been translated into English twice: "Bitter Blood," by Evelyn Picón Garfield in her volume on *Women's Fiction from Latin America* (Detroit: Wayne State University Press, 1988), 111–57; and *Bad Blood* (*La malasangre*) by Marguerite Feitlowitz (Woodstock, IL: Dramatic Publishing Company, 1994).

6. It is interesting that Bemberg should also turn to Sor Juana in her

1990 film, *Yo, la peor de todas* (I, the Worst of All), to illustrate the silencing and victimization of women by a despotic male hierarchy. See my "Sor Juana and Her World," *Latin American Research Review* 29 (1994): 143–54.

La hija del mashorquero

Roque Alma-negra era el terror de Buenos Aires. Verdugo por excelencia entre una asociación de verdugos llamada Mas-horca y consagrado en cuerpo y alma al tremendo fundador [Rosas] de aquella terrible hermandad, contaba las horas por el número de sus crímenes, y
su brazo, perpetuamente armado de puñal, jamás se bajaba sino para
herir. Su huella era un reguero de sangre, y había huido de él hacia
tanto tiempo la piedad, que su corazón no conservaba de ésta ningún
recuerdo, y los gemidos del huérfano, de la esposa y de la madre, lo encontraban tan insensible, como la fría hoja de acero que hundía en el
pecho de sus víctimas. Cada semejanza con la humanidad había desaparecido de la fisonomía de aquel hombre, y su lenguaje, expresión
fiel del nombre que sus delitos le habían dado, era una mezcla de fe-
rocidad y de blasfemia que hacía palidecer de espanto a todos aquellos
que tenían la desgracia de acercársele.

Sin embargo, entre aquel horrible vocabulario de crueldades y de
impiedad, como una flor nacida en el cieno, había una palabra de bendición que Roque pronunciaba siempre.

—Clemencia—decía aquel hombre de sangre, cuando fatigado con
los crímenes de la noche entraba a su casa al amanecer. Y a este nombre, que sonaba como un sarcasmo en los labios de asesino, una voz tan
dulce y melodiosa que parecía venir de los celestes coros, respondía con
ternura:—¡Padre!—y una figura de ángel, una joven de dieciséis años,
con grandes ojos azules y ceñida de una aureola de rizos blondos salía
al encuentro del mashorquero y lo abrazaba con dolorosa efusión. Era
su hija.

Roque la amaba como el tigre ama a sus cachorros, con un amor
feroz. Por ella hubiera llevado el hierro y el fuego a los extremos del

mundo; por ella hubiera vertido su propia sangre; pero no le habría sacrificado ni una sola gota de su venganza, ni uno solo de sus instintos homicidas.

Clemencia vivía sola en el maldecido hogar del mashorquero. Su madre había muerto hacía mucho tiempo víctima de una dolencia desconocida.

Clemencia la vio languidecer y extinguirse lentamente en una larga agonía, sin que sus tiernos cuidados pudieran volverla a la vida, ni sus ruegos y lágrimas arrancar de su corazón el fatal secreto que la llevaba a la tumba. Pero cuando su madre murió, cuando la vio desaparecer bajo la negra cubierta del ataúd y que espantada del inmenso vacío que se había hecho en torno suyo, fue a arrojarse en los brazos de su padre, los vio manchados en sangre y la luz de una horrible revelación alumbró de repente el espíritu de Clemencia. Tendió una mirada al pasado, y trajo a la memoria escenas misteriosas entonces para ella, y que ahora se le presentaban claras, distintas, horribles. Recordó las maldiciones dirigidas a Roque el Mashorquero, que tantas veces habían herido sus oídos y que ella en su amor, en su veneración por su padre, estaba tan distante de pensar que caían sobre él. Ella, que hasta entonces había vivido en un mundo de amor y de piedad, hallóse un día de repente en otro de crímenes y de horror. La verdad toda entera se mostró a sus ojos, y comparando con su propio dolor el dolor que su madre había devorado en silencio, comprendió por qué había preferido a la vida la eternidad y al lecho conyugal la fría almohada del sepulcro. Pero en el dolor de Clemencia no se mezcló ningún sentimiento de amargura. El alma de aquella hermosa niña se parecía a su nombre: era toda dulzura y misericordia. Su fatal descubrimiento en nada disminuyó la ternura que profesaba a su padre. Al contrario, Clemencia lo amó más, porque lo amó con una compasión profunda; y viéndolo marcharse solo con sus crímenes en un sendero regado con sangre, llevando el odio bajo sus pies y la venganza sobre su cabeza, lejos de envidiar el reposo eterno de su madre, Clemencia deseó vivir para acompañar al desdichado como un ángel guardián en aquella vía de iniquidad, y si no le era posible apartarlo de ella, ofrecer al menos por él a Dios una vida de dolor y de expiación.

Clemencia rechazó con horror el lujo que la rodeaba, porque en él vio el precio del crimen, y olvidando que era joven, olvidando que era bella, y que en el mundo hay goces celestes para la juventud y la belleza, ocultó su esbelto talle, y sus deliciosas formas bajo una larga túnica blanca, cubrió los sedosos rizos de su espléndida cabellera con un tupido velo, acalló los latidos con que su corazón la pedía amor, y se consagró toda entera al alivio de los desgraciados. Sobreponiéndose al profundo horror de su alma, hojeó esas sangrientas listas en que su padre consignaba el nombre de sus víctimas, y guiada por estos fúnebres datos, corría a buscar para adoptarlos a los huérfanos y viudas que el puñal de aquél había dejado sin amparo en el mundo. Empleó para socorrerlos los talentos adquiridos en la esmerada educación que había recibido de su madre: dio lecciones de música y de pintura, y consagró sus horas a un constante trabajo. La pobre niña, llena la mente de lúgubres pensamientos y con el corazón destrozado de dolor, tocaba alegres polkas que sus discípulos danzaban alegres y felices; y en la pavorosa soledad de sus noches, ella, que había dicho un eterno adiós a todas las dichas de la vida, se ocupaba en bordar vaporosos ramilletes en el velo de una desposada o en la transparente y coqueta falda de un vestido de baile, sin que le desanimaran las ideas dolorosas que esos accesorios de una felicidad a que ella no podía ya aspirar, despertaban en su alma; y con el precio de esos trabajos tan llenos de tristes emociones, corría a derramar el consuelo y la paz en el hogar de aquéllas a quienes había sacrificado el hacha de su padre. Como una tierna madre acariciaba e instruía a los niños, velaba a los enfermos con la ardiente solicitud de una hermana de caridad y auxiliaba a los moribundos con una elocuencia llena de unción y piedad.

Enteramente olvidada de sí misma, Clemencia parecía vivir sólo en la vida de los otros. Y sin embargo el mundo la sonreía a lo lejos, le abría los brazos, y le mostraba sus goces. Frecuentemente en sus piadosas correrías, Clemencia oía tras de sí voces apasionadas que exclamaban:

—¡Cuán bella es! ¡Dichoso, mil veces dichoso, aquel que merezca una mirada de esos ojos!

Pero aquellas palabras de galantería y amor en medio del sepulcral silencio de la ciudad desolada, escandalizaban los oídos de Clemencia como cantos profanos entre las tumbas de un cementerio, y ocultando el rostro entre los pliegues de su velo, se apartaba con el corazón oprimido de tristeza y disgusto.

II

Un día al anochecer, Clemencia vio entrar en su casa y dirigirse al cuarto de su padre algunos hombres de fisonomía patibularia, envueltos en largos ponchos bajo cuyos pliegues se veían brillar los mangos de sus puñales. Clemencia previó algo funesto en la presencia de aquellos hombres, y después de haber vacilado algunos instantes corrió a aplicar el oído a la cerradura de una puerta que se abría sobre la habitación de su padre.

Roque, de pie cerca de una mesa, tenía en la mano algunos papeles, y hablaba en voz alta a su auditorio.

—Sí, amigos míos—decía,—¡guerra a muerte a los unitarios![1] ¡guerra a muerte a esos malvados! ¿Vosotros cr[e]éis hacer mucho? Pues sabed que os engañáis. Leed sino la lista de nuestras ejecuciones de este mes y cotejadla con las delaciones que hemos recibido hoy solamente. Leed y veréis que aún queda una inmensa obra al cuchillo de la Mashorca, cuando comparéis el número de los que han caído con el de aquellos que caerán . . . ¡que caerán sí, aunque se escondan bajo el manto de María!

—¡Reina del cielo!—murmuró Clemencia juntando las manos con angustia y volviéndose hacia la imagen de la Virgen, su única compañera en aquella morada solitaria.—Si esa blasfemia ha llegado al pie de vuestro divino trono, no la escuchéis ¡madre buena! desechadla con indulgencia y alumbrad con una sonrisa de compasión al desdichado que camina en las tinieblas.

Al pronunciar estas últimas palabras, Clemencia volvió a oir la voz de su padre que leía:

"A las nueve de esta noche, un hombre embozado se detendrá al pie del obelisco de la plaza de la Victoria, y dará tres silbidos. Ese hombre es Manuel de Puirredón, el incorregible conspirador unitario, amigo de Lavalle[2] y emigrado en Montevideo. La señal es dirigida a la hija de un federal que unida a él secretamente y convertida en su auxiliar más poderoso, le entrega los secretos de su padre e instruído por esa señal del regreso del conspirador, irá a reunírsele para segundar sin duda el infame plan que le trae a Buenos Aires."

—¿Lo oís, camaradas? ¡Y aun están nuestros puñales en el cinto!—exclamó Roque con ira feroz.

—¡Muera Manuel de Puirredón!—gritaron los asesinos desenvainando sus largos puñales.

Clemencia dirigió una mirada por la cerradura a la péndula que estaba enfrente de su padre, y se estremeció.

La aguja marcaba las ocho y cincuenta y cinco.

—¡Cinco minutos para salvar la vida a un hombre! ¡Cinco minutos para preservar a mi padre de un crimen más! ¡Oh! Dios mío, alarga este corto espacio, y presta alas a mis pies.

Y envolviéndose en su largo velo blanco, salió de su casa corriendo, no sin volver muchas veces la cabeza por temor de que los asesinos se le adelantaran, inutilizando el deseo de salvar al desgraciado que sin saberlo se encaminaba a la muerte.

Al llegar al ángulo que forma la calle de la Victoria con la del Colegio, Clemencia divisó un bulto negro que cortando diagonalmente la plaza se dirigía al obelisco.

—¡Es él!—murmuró con voz temblorosa, y corriendo en pos suya alcanzóle en el momento que tocaba ya la verja de hierro.

Muchos paseantes vagaban en aquel sitio halagados por la brisa de la noche, e impedían a Clemencia hablar con el desconocido.

Entonces ella se volvió hacia atrás; pasó cerca de él y tocóle ligeramente la espalda haciéndole una imperceptible seña de seguirle.

El embozado se volvió con impetuosidad y acercándose a Clemencia—¡Emilia! ¡Emilia mía!—exclamó ciñendo apaciblemente el cuerpo de la joven con uno de sus brazos, sin que ella pudiera impedirlo por temor de llamar sobre ellos la atención.

Obligada así a callar, Clemencia, al través de su velo contempló al desconocido, cuyo rostro estaba iluminado en aquel momento por los rayos de la luna. Era un hombre joven y bello como jamás Clemencia había visto otro ni aún en sus poéticos ensueños de dieciséis años. Era alto y esbelto. En todos sus movimientos revelábase esa elegancia fácil, casi descuidada, que sólo dan el uso del mundo y un nacimiento distinguido. La mirada a la vez profunda y lánguida de sus hermosos ojos, tenía un poder irresistible de atracción que aliándose a la mágica armonía de su voz, hacía de aquel hombre uno de esos seres que una vez vistos no pueden olvidarse jamás, y que dejan en nuestra vida una huella imborrable de felicidad o de dolor.

Y el desconocido, bajo el poder de su engaño, repetía al oído de Clemencia:

—Emilia, héme aquí, amada mía, no como un conspirador, a envolverte de nuevo en la ruína de mis quiméricas esperanzas, sino como esposo apasionado a arrebatarte de los brazos de tu padre, y llevarte en los míos, lejos, muy lejos, al fondo de los desiertos, a algún paraje desconocido que tu amor convertirá para mi en un delicioso Edén. Ven, Emilia mía, abandonemos esta patria fatal. Dios la ha maldecido y nuestros esfuerzos y sacrificios para salvarla son vanos. . . .

—¡Oh—continuó el proscrito con voz ahogada y estrechando aún más a Clemencia contra su pecho,—lo ves, Emilia: esta idea despedaza mi corazón . . . pero aquí estás tú para calmar sus dolores y llenarlo de alegría . . .

¿Y nuestro hijo? Qué bello será! Cuánto habrás sufrido al separarte de él en la cruel necesidad de ocultar su existencia! . . .

En aquel momento llegaban a un paraje solitario de la plaza. Clemencia tendió una mirada en torno suyo y separándose precipitadamente de los brazos del desconocido, alzó el velo para hacerle conocer su error.

—¡Cielos!—exclamó él,—¡no es Emilia!

—No, señor; pero si vos os llamáis Manuel de Puirredón, huid de este sitio funesto donde cada segundo es para vos un paso hacia la muerte . . . ¿No lo veis?—continuó ella con terror, señalando un grupo negro al otro extremo de la plaza.—Son ellos, son los puñales sangrientos de la Mas-horca que os acechan. . . . Huid en nombre del cielo, por vuestra esposa, por vuestro hijo. . . . Id con ellos lejos de este antro de fieras a realizar ese hermoso sueño de dicha que halaga vuestra mente. . . . Huid, huid—repitió,—señalando al proscrito una calle sombría y alejándose ella por otra.

Al entrar en su casa Clemencia, fue a postrarse a los pies de la Virgen, y ocultando su rostro bajó el velo de la sagrada imagen, lloró largo tiempo, murmurando entre sollozos palabras misteriosas: quizás algún dulce y doloroso secreto que ella había querido ocultarse a si misma, y que sólo osaba confiar a aquella que guarda la llave del corazón de las vírgenes.

Desde ese día el hechicero y melancólico rostro de Clemencia, palideció más todavía, revistiéndose de una tristeza profunda. ¡Quién sabe que halagüeña visión cruzó por su mente con las palabras apasionadas de ese hombre! ¡Quién sabe que sentimiento hizo nacer su vista en aquel corazón joven y solitario!

Algunas veces con la mirada perdida en el vacío, sonreía dulcemente; pero luego, como asaltada por un amargo recuerdo, movía la cabeza en ademán de dolorosa resignación murmurando en voz baja:

—Hija de la desgracia, heredera del castigo celeste, víctima expiatoria, piensa en tu voto; acuérdate que tu reino no es de este mundo.

Y sumida de nuevo en su mortal tristeza, consagrábase con mayor ardor a la misión de piedad que se había impuesto.

—Clemencia—dijo a su hija un día el mashorquero,—¿por qué te hallo cada vez más triste y meditabunda? ¿quién se atreve a causarte pesadumbre? Nómbralo, por vida mía, y muy luego podrás añadir: ¡Desdichado de él!

—¡Nadie! ¡padre . . . nadie!—respondió ésta estremeciéndose, y levantó instintivamente la mano al corazón, como si hubiese temido que su padre leyera allí algún secreto.

—No . . . tú me engañas. . . . Hace tiempo que advierto lágrimas hasta en tu voz cuando vienes a abrazarme.

—Padre . . . —replicó la joven interrumpiéndolo y fijando en los sangrientos ojos del asesino los suyos azules y piadosos,—¿no lo adivina? Cuando después de una noche de vigilia y ansiedad te veo llegar en fin y salgo a abrazarte, pienso con profundo dolor que los hijos de esos desdichados que diariamente siega el hacha de tu bando, no podrían gozar ya de esa felicidad que Dios me concede a mi todavía. ¡Oh padre! ¿no es este un gran motivo de tristeza y de lágrimas? ¿En medio de esas sangrientas escenas no has llevado alguna vez la mano al corazón, y te has preguntado qué harías tú mismo si vieras una mano armada del puñal bajarse sobre tu hija y degollarla?

—¡Calla . . . ! ¡calla, Clemencia . . . !—gritó el bandido,—¿qué haría? El infierno mismo no tiene una rabia semejante a la que entonces movería el brazo de Roque para vengarte . . . ¡Pero tú estas loca, niña! ¿No sabes que los salvajes unitarios no tienen corazón como nosotros, que amamos y aborrecemos con igual violencia . . . ?

—¡Padre, tú sabes que eso no es cierto! ¿qué dicen pues los gritos desgarradores de esas madres, los gemidos de esas esposas y el triste llanto de esos huérfanos que a todas horas oigo elevarse al cielo contra nosotros? ¿No te dicen que las fibras rotas por tu puñal en el fondo de sus almas son tan sensibles como las nuestras?

—¡Calla—repitió,—calla,—Clemencia! Tienes una voz tan insinuante y persuasiva que me lo harías creer; y entonces ¿qué pensaría el general Rosas de su servidor? ¡Cómo se burlaría Salomón y Cuitiño de su compañero! No . . . ¡Vete! no quiero escucharte, hoy sobre todo que Manuel Puirredón, ese bandido unitario a quien he jurado degollar, vaga entre nosotros invisiblemente y como protegido por un poder sobrenatural . . . ¡Oh! pero en vano me inquieto . . . ¡qué locura! Este corazón está lleno de odio, y ya no cabría en él la piedad . . . Escucha sino esta historia . . .

Hace algunos meses entré a oir misa en la iglesia del Socorro.

—¡Padre! ¡Osasteis entrar en el templo de Dios con las manos manchadas!

—¿De sangre? Sí, por cierto ¿por qué no, si es sangre de unitarios, esos enemigos de Dios?

Entré, como decía, en la iglesia del Socorro. Apenas había comenzado la misa un hombre a cuyo lado me había arrodillado volvióse de repente y habiéndome contemplado un segundo como para reconocerme paseó sobre mí una mirada de desprecio y apartándose con insolente repugnancia, fue a colocarse muy lejos de aquel sitio. Aquella acción me denunció un unitario. El miserable había reconocido a Roque, pero ignoraba lo que era la venganza de Roque.

Mis ojos no se apartaron de él durante la misa y al salir de la iglesia vile entrar al frente de una casa pequeña, casi arruinada.

En la noche de ese día, mientras aquel hombre olvidado del agravio que me había hecho y con dos niños en los brazos estaba tranquilamente al lado de su mujer, ocupada en bordar el ajuar para el tercero que iba a nacer, yo guié a su casa, la Mashorca; y entre los brazos de su esposa y de sus hijos hundí mil veces mi puñal en su corazón salpicando los pañales del que aun no había visto la luz.

—¡Clemencia! ¡Clemencia! ¿qué tienes?

El asesino alargó el brazo para sostener a su hija, que vacilante y trémula lo rechazó con mal disimulado horror.

—Por algún tiempo —continuó él, —creí que sería "eso" que llaman remordimiento el recuerdo imborrable que aquella escena de sangre, de gritos y de lágrimas dejó en mi imaginación; pero ¡ah! era sólo el contento de una venganza satisfecha. El día en que Roque conociera la compasión o el remordimiento, la hoja de esta arma se empañaría y . . . mira como resplandece . . . —dijo el bandido, haciendo brillar su ancho puñal a los ojos de su hija.

Y ocultándolo en seguida entre la faja de su chiripá[3] se alejó, sin duda para volver a su horrible tarea.

Clemencia se sintió anonadada bajo el peso de las espantosas palabras que había escuchado. Débil, quebrantada, exánime fue a caer a los pies de su divina protectora elevando hacia ella las manos en angustiosa plegaria.

A medida que oraba, la esperanza y la fe descendían a su corazón; y cuando se levantó, su frente volvió a iluminarse con la serenidad de la resignación.

—Nunca es tarde para tu infinita misericordia, Dios mío —dijo ella alzando al cielo su mirada. —La hora del arrepentimiento no ha llegado todavía; pero ella sonará.

En seguida visitó el tesoro que guardaba para los desgraciados; tomó consigo una cesta de provisiones y un bolsillo de oro; y a favor de las sombras de la noche, fue a buscar aquella casa de que había hablado su padre.

Reconocióla en la huella del hacha de los bandidos que rompiendo el postigo la habían dejado abierta; Clemencia iba a pasar el umbral de una habitación desnuda y miserable, cuando oyendo una voz que hablaba dentro se detuvo y contempló el cuadro que se ofrecía a su vista.

En un rincón del cuarto, sobre un lecho pobre y desabrigado, yacía una mujer joven, pero pálida y enflaquecida, con un recién nacido entre sus brazos. Más lejos un niño de seis años y otro de cuatro estaban sentados bajo las mantas de una camita suspendida en forma de cuna por cuatro cuerdas reunidas y pendientes de una viga del techo.

La luz opaca de una vela que ardía en el suelo daba a aquella morada un aspecto lúgubre que, unido al recuerdo de la espantosa escena ocurrida allí despedazó de dolor el alma de Clemencia.

—Mamá—decía con voz lamentable el menor de los dos niños,—tengo hambre. ¿Qué has hecho del pan que comimos ayer?

La madre exhaló un profundo gemido al mismo tiempo que el otro niño respondió con acento grave y resignado:

—Lo comimos, Enrique, lo comimos y mamá no tiene dinero para comprar otro, porque está enferma y no puede trabajar. No la atormentes; y durmamos como el pobre angelito que ayer cayó del cielo entre nosotros.

—¡Ay! ¡él tiene el pecho de mi mamá y yo tengo hambre... tengo hambre!—replicaba Enrique llorando.

—¡Dios mío!—exclamó la madre entre sollozos,—si en la sabiduría de tus designios quisiste que el hacha homicida abatierra [sic] el árbol más robusto, yo adoro tu voluntad y me resigno; pero ten piedad de estas tiernas flores que comienzan a abrirse a los rayos de tu sol. ¡Señor! tú que alimentas las avecillas del aire, los gusanos de la tierra y que oyes llorar de hambre a mis hijos ¿no enviarás en su socorro uno de los millares de ángeles que habitan tu cielo...?

—¡Ah! helo ahí—murmuró viendo a Clemencia que arrodillada ante la cama de los niños les presentaba las provisiones que había traido.

La madre juntó las manos y contempló con religiosa admiración a aquella bellísima joven, cuyo blanco velo plegado como una aureola en torno de su frente parecía iluminar las tinieblas que la rodeaban, y que inclinada sobre sus hijos como el genio de la misericordia los cubría con una mirada de ternura y de dolor. La pobre mujer creíala un ángel descendido a su ruego; e inmóvil, temía que un ademán, que un soplo, desvanecieran la divina visión, restituyéndola a la horrible realidad. Y cuando Clemencia se acercó a su lecho, la sencilla hija del pueblo alargó ansiosamente la mano para tocar las suyas y convencerse de que no era una aparición sobre-humana.

—¡Oh! tú, que has venido a derramar el consuelo en esta morada de dolor—exclamó abrazando las rodillas de la joven,—¿quien eres, criatura angelical?

—Soy un ser desventurado como vosotros y vengo a buscar a mis compañeros de dolor. Vengo a deciros: Madre cristiana, confiad en aquél que enjuga toda lágrima y acalla todo gemido. El vela sobre todo de lo alto de su cielo y puede hacer de la más débil criatura un instrumento de su misericordia. ¿Habéis quedado sola y desamparada? Yo estaré cerca de vos y seréis mi hermana querida. ¿Vuestros hijos necesitan de un protector? Yo lo seré. ¿Os halláis falta de todo? He aquí oro para que lo procuréis.

—¡Ah! ¡sois una santa! . . . —dijo la viuda, inclinándose devotamente,—bendecid a mi hijo y dadle un nombre; porque todavía no está bautizado.

Y puso al recién nacido en los brazos de Clemencia.

—Llamadle "Manuel"—dijo ella en voz baja, y al pronunciar este nombre la pálida frente de la virgen se ruborizó, y sus ojos brillaron con extraño fulgor.

—Manuel—continuó, besando al niño con timidez,—yo seré para tí una nodriza solícita y apasionada. Tu madre no tendrá celos, pues para ella serán todas tus caricias; para mí sólo la dicha de poder decir cada día.—Manuel ¡yo te amo!

—¡Ay de mí!—exclamó la pobre madre, cubriendo sus ojos con la mano de Clemencia, y sollozando profundamente,—bien pronto lo seréis todo para él. Mi esposo me llama desde la eternidad. El puñal del asesino no ha podido romper el lazo que unía nuestras almas, y la mía se va, aunque a pesar suyo, y gimiendo amargamente por estas otras almas que se quedan penando en la tierra. Y la infeliz señalaba a los niños con ademán desesperado.

Clemencia la escuchaba con terror. La hija del asesino pensó estremecida de espanto en los crímenes de su padre, cuya imagen nunca se le había presentado tan horrible. Pero sobreponiéndose a las lúgubres ideas que la abrumaban, llamó a la madre al cumplimiento de su deber en la tierra, y a la cristiana a la resignación en la voluntad del cielo.

—Madre mía—dijo el mayor de los niños cuando quedaron solos, —¿cuál de los ángeles del señor es éste que ha venido a visitarnos?

¡Qué hermosos son sus largos cabellos rizados como los de Nuestra Señora del Socorro!

—Y sus ojos, mamá—replicó el más pequeño,—sus ojos azules como el cielo y sus pestañas ¿no es cierto que se parecen a los rayos de esa estrella que nos está mirando por la ventana?

—Sí, hijos míos—dijo la viuda sonriendo tristemente a sus niños, —es un bello ángel que Dios tiene en la tierra para consolar a los infelices.

—¡Ah! es un ángel de la tierra; por eso está tan triste. Yo la he visto llorar mientras arreglaba nuestra cama.

—¿Cuál es el nombre de ese ángel, madre mía?

—Cualquiera que sea, bendigámoslo, hijos míos, y pidamos a Dios que enjugue sus lágrimas como ha enjugado las nuestras—dijo la viuda, haciendo arrodillar a los niños para la oración de la noche.

IV

Clemencia entre tanto se alejaba con lentos y vacilantes pasos. La expresión de su semblante revelaba un profundo desconsuelo. Pensaba en la omnipotencia del mal y en la omnipotencia del bien. Un solo golpe de puñal había bastado a su padre para abrir el insondable abismo de infortunio que acababa de contemplar y ella con toda una vida de sacrificios y abnegación, ¿qué había alcanzado? Aliviar el hambre y la desnudez; curar dolores materiales: para los del alma nada había hallado sino lágrimas. Y a esta idea Clemencia se sintió abrumada por un inmenso desaliento. Pero como siempre cuando temía que su fe vacilara, la virgen elevó su pensamiento a Dios, pidiéndole algún grande sacrificio que la revelase el secreto de hacer descender la felicidad donde reinaba el dolor.

Un nombre pronunciado muchas veces con acento feroz, despertó bruscamente a Clemencia de su triste meditación. Miró en torno suyo, y se encontró entre un grupo de hombres cuyo aspecto siniestro llamó su atención. Embozábanse en largos "ponchos"; y armados todos de puñales guardaban cuidadosamente una puerta. La hija del mashorquero los reconoció. Aquellos hombres eran los compañeros de su padre; aquella casa era la "Intendencia," el sitio consagrado a las ejecuciones secretas, el "in pace" donde los unitarios entraban para no salir jamás, y en cuyas bóvedas el dedo del terror había grabado para ellos la lúgubre inscripción del Dante.[4]

Mientras Clemencia trémula y palpitante de ansiedad procuraba oculta detrás de una columna escuchar lo que hablaban aquellos hombres, un jinete montado en un caballo negro, y cuya espada de largos tiros chocaba ruidosamente contra el encuentro de la lanza que empuñaba, detuvo con una sofrenada y una maldición la fogosa carrera de su corcel; y acercándose al grupo que custodiaba la puerta:

—Teniente Corbalán—gritó con voz ronca y breve—toma veinte hombres y ronda el Bajo, mientras yo hago una batida en Barracas. ¡Por las garras del diablo! Consiento en dejar de ser quien soy si el sol de mañana no encuentra la cabeza de Manuel Puirredón clavada en esta lanza.

Y hundiendo las espuelas en los flancos de su caballo, se alejó como un sombrío torbellino.

Clemencia pálida y helada de espanto cayó sobre sus rodillas. El hombre que acababa de hacer ese horrible juramento era su padre.

—Corbalán—dijo uno de aquellos bandidos,—llévame contigo . . . Quiero matar hombres y no guardar mujeres.

—Si Alma-negra te hubiera entregado la que está en el calabozo de las Tres Cruces, no te habría pesado guardarla para tí—dijo riendo atrozmente otro de ellos.

—¡Ah, viejo tigre! sorprender a la hermosa que esperaba a su galán, atarla como un cordero al arzón de la silla, traerla bajo el poncho a la Intendencia, encerrarla en el calabozo de las Tres Cruces donde hay más de cincuenta sepulturas . . . ¿qué pensará hacer de ella?

—¡Poca cosa! Matarla en lugar de su marido, y matarla con él si logra atraparlo.

Clemencia no escuchó más. Alzóse fuerte y resuelta; acercóse con entereza al jefe de los bandidos, y dando a sus ojos la negra mirada de su padre, levantó el velo y le dijo con voz imperiosa.

—Teniente Corbalán ¿me conocéis?

—¡La hija del comandante!—exclamó el mashorquero descubriéndose.

Los bandidos se apartaron respetuosamente, y la joven sin dignarse añadir una palabra, pasó el umbral y se internó en las sombras del fatídico edificio.

En la obscuridad del lóbrego portal que daba entrada al patio de los calabozos, Clemencia divisó un hombre de pie, inmóvil y apoyado en una alabarda. Vestía el uniforme de gendarme y ella le creyó un centinela; pero al acercarse a él se estremeció.

La joven no tuvo para reconocerlo necesidad de ver su rostro que cubría la ancha manga de una gorra de cuartel.

—¡Desventurado!—murmuró Clemencia al oído de aquel hombre y estrechando su brazo con terror. ¿Qué hacéis aquí? ¿No habéis oído?

—Sí—respondió él cerrándola el paso.—Soy aquel que los asesinos buscan con tan feroz afán. Sus puñales están sobre mi cabeza, pero yo he venido a salvar a mi amada o perecer con ella. Mirad—continuó hiriendo con el pie un objeto sin forma que yacía en tierra,—he matado un centinela, y armado con sus despojos velo aquí para tender a mis pies al primero que atraviese el dintel de esa puerta.

—¡Manuel Puirredón!—dijo Clemencia descubriendo su bello rostro y posando en los ojos del proscrito una mirada inefable, ¿os acordáis?

¡Ella!... exclamó el unitario,—¡el ángel que me salvó!...

—¿Tenéis confianza en mí? Me abandonaréis el cuidado de salvar a aquélla que buscáis?

—¡Ah!—respondió él con un transporte que Clemencia reprimió asustada,—por esas solas palabras, hermosa criatura, heme aquí a vuestros pies. Pedid mi sangre... mi alma... todo os lo daré.

—Alejaos, pues, de esto funesto lugar; trasponed esa puerta fatal, y esperad a vuestra amada donde ella os esperaba poco há.

—¡No! Todo... menos alejarme un paso de aquí.

—¡Oh! ¡Dios mío! ¡quiere perderse!... Pues bien... juradme al menos permanecer inmóvil bajo vuestro disfraz, y no atacar a nadie cualquiera que sea que pase por este sitio.

—¡Duro es hacer esa promesa!... pero, pues lo queréis, ¡sea!

—¡Gracias! ¡gracias!...—exclamó ella estrechando la mano del proscrito, en la que éste sintió caer una lágrima.—Sed feliz, Manuel Puirredón... ¡Adiós!

Y la joven bajando el velo se perdió entre las sombras.

El unitario oyó a lo lejos un ruido áspero de cerrojos y dijo:

—Es la puerta de su calabozo. ¡Emilia! ¡Emilia mía!

Y con la mirada y el oído atento, interrogaba angustiosamente a la noche y al silencio. Y así pasaron con la lentitud de los siglos dos, cinco, diez minutos; y Puirredón, en su mortal inquietud, estaba ya próximo a quebrantar el juramento y a correr tras aquélla que se lo había impuesto.

Al fin allá a lo lejos el blanco velo de Clemencia apareció de repente entre las tinieblas de un lóbrego pasadizo. Puirredón lo vio venir sola y olvidando su promesa, olvidando su peligro, olvidándolo todo, arrojó una exclamación de dolor y corrió a su encuentro. Pero al llegar a ella dos brazos cariñosos rodearon su cuello, y unos labios de fuego ahogaron en los suyos un grito de gozo.

—¡Silencio, amado mío!—dijo una voz querida al oído del proscrito.—Un milagro me ha salvado. La virgen del Socorro ha descendido a mi calabozo para librarme. Sí. Yo la he reconocido en su celeste belleza y en la melancólica sonrisa de su labio divino. Este es su sagrado velo . . . él nos protegerá . . . Huyamos.

Y la mujer encubierta arrastró tras de sí al proscrito.

Cuando los fugitivos llegaban a la puerta vieron avanzar un jinete que haciendo dar botes a su caballo entró en el portal, y arrojándose en tierra desenvainó su puñal y en un silencio feroz se encaminó al patio de los calabozos.

A su vista Puirredón sintió estremecerse entre las suyas la mano de su compañera, y la oyó murmurar bajo su velo con acento de terror!

—¡Alma-negra!

Mas luego traspusieron ambos el umbral maldito, y respiraron el aura embalsamada de la libertad.

Entre tanto Alma-negra atravesó el patio y llegando al calabozo de las Tres-Cruces descorrió los pesados cerrojos y buscó a tientas entre las tinieblas.

Un rayo perdido de la luna menguante deslizándose por la estrecha claraboya de la bóveda, formaba una mancha lívida en el húmedo pavimento, haciendo más densas las tinieblas de aquella espantosa mazmorra. Sin embargo, el ojo ávido del bandido descubrió una forma blanca.

Fuése hacia ella, extendió su mano sangrienta, y palpando el cuello de una mujer, hundió en él su puñal, gritando con rabia:

—Delatora de nuestros secretos, cómplice de los infames unitarios, muere en lugar del conspirador que amas, pero sabe antes que ni tus huesos se juntarán con los suyos porque tu sepulcro será el fondo de este calabozo.

Y hablando así, arrojó una espantosa carcajada.

Al sentirse herida de muerte la desventurada llevó las manos a su cuello dividido, y conteniendo la sangre que se escapaba a torrentes de la herida.

—¡Dios mío!—murmuró,—¡mi sacrificio está consumado! cumplida está la misión que me impuse en este mundo: haced ahora, Señor, que mi sangre lave esa otra sangre que clama a vos desde la tierra.

Al acento de aquella voz Alma-negra sintió romperse su corazón, y los cabellos se erizaron sobre su cabeza. Alzóse rápido y levantando a su víctima corrió a la claraboya y miró al rayo de la luna su rostro ensangrentado.

—¡Clemencia!—gritó el asesino con un horrible alarido.

—¡Padre! . . . ¡pobre padre! . . . eleva al cielo tus miradas, y búscala allí—balbuceó la dulce voz de la joven al exhalar el último aliento.

El bandido cayó desplomado en tierra, arrastrando entre sus brazos el cadáver de su hija degollada . . .

Pero la sangre de la virgen halló gracia delante de Dios, y como un bautismo de redención, hizo descender sobre aquel hombre un rayo de luz divina que lo regeneró.

Notas

1. Los unitarios eran los enemigos políticos de Rosas. Rosas encabezaba el partido federal.

2. El general Lavalle había tratado de apoderarse del gobierno argentino en 1829, pero Rosas le venció en una batalla; después de esta derrota, Lavalle se fue al exilio en el Uruguay.

3. El chiripá es el ancho pantalón de los gauchos.

4. "Abandonad toda esperanza, los que entráis aquí." Del *Inferno* de Dante Alighieri, Canto III.

The Executioner's Daughter

Roque Blacksoul was the terror of Buenos Aires. Executioner par excellence in an association of executioners called "Mas-horca" and devoted heart and soul to the dreadful founder [Rosas] of that terrible fraternity, he measured the hours by the number of his crimes, and his hand, always armed with a dagger, never moved except to wound. His tracks were a pool of blood, and pity had left him so long ago that there was no trace of it left in his heart; the cries of the orphan, the wife, and the mother left him as unfeeling as the cold steel blade he plunged into the breast of his victims. All resemblance to humanity had disappeared from the man's countenance, and his language, faithful expression of the name with which his crimes had endowed him, was a mixture of ferocity and blasphemy that made all those who had the ill fortune to cross his path blanch with fear.

Nevertheless, within that awful storehouse of expressions of cruelty and blasphemy, like a flower which blooms in a swamp, there was one word of goodness which Roque always uttered.

"Clemencia," the bloody executioner would say when he came home at dawn, worn out from the crimes he had committed that night. And at this name, which sounded sarcastic coming from the assassin's lips, a voice so sweet and melodious that it seemed to come from celestial choirs responded tenderly, "Father!" and the angelic figure of a young girl of sixteen, with great blue eyes and a halo of blonde curls, came to meet the executioner and embraced him with painful effusiveness. She was his daughter.

Roque loved her with fierce affection, as a tiger loves his cubs. For her sake he would have taken fire and destruction to the ends of the earth, for her he would have given his own blood; yet he would not have sacrificed one drop of his vengeance nor one of his murderous instincts for her.

Clemencia lived alone in the accursed house of the executioner. Her mother had died long ago, the victim of some unknown ailment. Clemencia had seen her languish and wither away in a slow death, but in spite of her tender care she could not restore her mother to health, nor could Clemencia's pleas and tears wrest from her mother's heart the fatal secret that was taking her to the grave. But when her mother died, and she saw her disappear under the coffin's black lid, and when, terrified at the enormous void in which this left her, she had flung herself into her father's arms, she saw that they were stained with blood, and an awful revelation suddenly flashed in Clemencia's soul. She looked back on the past and remembered scenes that had been mysterious for her at the time, but that now appeared clear, sharp and awful. She recalled the curses hurled at Roque the Executioner that had hurt her ears so many times, and which she, in the love and veneration she felt for her father, could not have conceived were meant for him. She, who until then had lived in a world of love and piety, one day suddenly found herself in another, marked by crimes and horror. The whole truth was revealed to her eyes, and when she compared her own pain to that which her mother had suffered in silence, she understood why the latter had preferred eternity to life and the cold pillow of the grave to the conjugal bed. But no feeling of bitterness mingled with Clemencia's suffering. The beautiful girl's soul was like her name: she was all sweetness and mercy. The awful discovery she had made in no way diminished the tenderness she felt for her father. On the contrary, Clemencia loved him all the more because she loved him with deep compassion, and when she saw him go forth alone to his crimes on a blood-drenched path, with hatred under his feet and vengeance over his head, far from envying her mother's eternal rest, Clemencia wanted to live in order to stand by the wretched man on his road to iniquity like a guardian angel, and, if she could not persuade him to leave this path, she could at least offer God a life of suffering and atonement on her father's behalf.

Clemencia rejected with horror the luxury which surrounded her, for in it she saw the price of crime, and, forgetting that she was young and beautiful, and that in the world there are heavenly pleasures for youth and beauty, she hid her slender figure and delicious curves under a long, white tunic, covered the silken curls of her magnificent hair with a thick veil, quieted the beating of a heart that longed for love, and devoted herself entirely to helping the unfortunate. Controlling her soul's profound horror, she leafed through the bloody lists to which her father consigned the names of his victims, and, guided by these hideous facts, hurried to aid the widows and orphans her father's dagger had left unprotected in the world. In order to help them she used the skills she had acquired from the scrupulous education her mother had given her: she gave lessons in painting and music and dedicated her hours to constant work. The poor girl, whose mind was full of dreadful thoughts and whose heart was rent with pain, played happy polkas which her pupils danced with joy and abandon, and in the terrifying silence of her nights, she, who had bid eternal farewell to all of life's joys, busied herself by embroidering airy bouquets on a bridal veil or the transparent and flirtatious skirt of a ballgown, without having her soul become dispirited by the painful thoughts that these were accessories of a happiness to which she could no longer aspire. With the money she earned by these labors, so full of sad emotions, she hastened to spread consolation and peace in the homes of the victims of her father's axe. Like a tender mother she cuddled and taught the children, watched over the sick with the fervent solicitude of a sister of Charity, and helped the dying with an eloquence full of devotion and piety.

Totally forgetting her own self, Clemencia seemed to exist solely in the lives of others. Yet nevertheless the world smiled on her from afar, opened its arms to her and showed her its pleasures. On her charitable errands Clemencia would often overhear fervent voices exclaim:

"How lovely she is! Fortunate the man who deserves one glance from those eyes!"

But those remarks of gallantry and love uttered in the depths of the aggrieved city's tomblike silence affronted Clemencia's ears like bawdy songs sung among graves in a cemetery, and, shielding her face within the folds of her veil, she drew away, her heart weighed down by sorrow and distaste.

One day at nightfall, Clemencia saw several men of dreadful appearance enter her house and make their way to her father's room. The men were wrapped in long ponchos, under whose folds one could see the handles of their daggers gleam. Clemencia perceived something threatening in the presence of those men, and after vacillating for a few moments, ran to put her ear to the keyhole of a door that opened onto her father's room.

Roque, who stood next to a table, had some papers in his hands, and spoke in a loud voice to his listeners.

"Yes, my friends," he said, "a fight to the death to the Unitarians![1] A fight to the death for those cursed people! You think you're accomplishing a lot? Well, know that you're wrong. Just read the list of our executions for this month and compare it to the denunciations we have received today alone. Read it and you will see that there is still a huge job to be done by the knives of the association of the Mas-horca, especially when you compare the number of the fallen with those who will fall . . . yes, who will fall, even though they hide under the Virgin Mary's cloak!"

"Queen of Heaven," whispered Clemencia, wringing her hands in anguish, and turning toward the image of the Virgin, her only companion in that lonely dwelling. "If this blasphemy has reached the foot of your divine throne, don't listen to it! Good Mother: cast it aside indulgently, and with a smile of compassion enlighten the unfortunate man who walks in darkness."

As she uttered these last words Clemencia again heard her father's voice read:

"Tonight at nine a muffled man will stop at the foot of the obelisk in Victoria Square and whistle three times. This man is Manuel de Puirredón, the incorrigible Unitarian conspirator, Lavalle's[2] friend and exiled in Montevideo. The signal is intended for a Federalist's daughter who has secretly joined him and, converted into his most powerful ally, is handing over her father's secrets. As this signal will tell her of the conspirator's return, she will then join him, doubtlessly to help in the vile plan which brings him to Buenos Aires.

"Do you hear, friends? And our daggers are still in our belts!" exclaimed Roque with ferocious rage.

"Death to Manuel de Puirredón!" shouted the assassins, unsheathing their long knives.

Clemencia shot a look through the keyhole at the pendulum clock in front of her father, and shuddered.

The hand showed eight fifty-five.

"Five minutes to save a man's life! Five minutes to keep my father from committing one more crime! Oh God, make this short time last, and put wings on my feet."

Wrapping herself in her long, white veil, she ran out of the house, not without turning her head many times, in fear that the murderers would get there ahead of her, thus ruining her desire to save the unfortunate man who, without knowing it, was going to his death.

When she got to the corner formed by Victoria and Colegio streets, Clemencia spied a black shape walking diagonally across the square and heading for the obelisk.

"It is he!" she murmured with trembling voice, and running after him, caught up with him just as he reached the iron fence.

Many pedestrians strolled about this place, enjoying the evening breeze, and prevented Clemencia from speaking with the stranger.

Then she turned back; she passed close by him and touched him lightly on the shoulder, making an imperceptible sign to follow her.

The muffled man turned impetuously and, drawing near to Clemencia, exclaimed, "Emilia, my Emilia!" gently embracing the young woman's body with one arm, she being unable to stop this without calling attention to them both.

In this way obliged to silence, Clemencia regarded the unknown man through her veil, whose countenance was at that moment lit by the rays of the moon. He was a young man, and more handsome than any Clemencia had ever envisioned, even in the poetic dreams of a sixteen-year-old girl. He was tall and slender. In all of his movements he showed an easy, almost careless grace, that only experience in the world and distinguished birth can bestow. The deep and yet languid glance of his beautiful eyes had an irresistible force of attraction which, combined with the magic harmony of his voice, made this man one of those beings that once seen, is never forgotten, and who leaves an indelible mark of happiness or pain on our lives.

The stranger, in the throes of deception, repeated into Clemencia's ears:

"Emilia, here I am, my love, not as a conspirator who will once again involve you in the ruin of my fantastic hopes, but as the ardent husband who will tear you from your father's arms and carry you off in mine, far, far away, to the ends of the earth, to some unknown spot which your love will change into a delectable Eden for me. Come, my Emilia, let us leave this fatal homeland. God has cursed it and our attempts and sacrifices to save it are in vain . . .

"Oh," the fugitive went on with a choking voice, and drawing Clemencia even closer to his chest, "you see, Emilia: this idea wreaks havoc on my heart, but you are here to calm its pain and fill it with happiness . . .

"And our son? How handsome he will be! How you must have suffered when you separated from him in the cruel necessity of hiding his existence! . . . "

At that moment they reached a deserted part of the square. Clemencia cast a look around and, drawing back suddenly from out of the stranger's arms, lifted her veil to let him see his mistake.

"Good Heavens!" he said, "It isn't Emilia!"

"No, Sir, but if your name is Manuel de Puirredón, flee from this fateful place as every second you stay here means a step closer to death . . . Don't you see?" she continued, pointing to a dark group at the other end of the square. "It is they, the bloody henchmen of the Mashorca who are going to ambush you . . . Flee, in God's Name, for the sake of your wife and son . . . Take them far away from this savage lair to realize the beautiful dream of happiness your mind envisions . . . Flee, flee," she repeated, pointing out a dark street to the fugitive and disappearing down another.

III

When Clemencia got home she fell at the feet of the Virgin, and, hiding her face under the sacred image's own veil, wept for a long time, while murmuring strange words among her sobs: perhaps some sweet and painful secret she had wanted to hide from herself, and which she only dared to confess to the one who keeps the key to all maidens' hearts.

From this day on Clemencia's enchanting and melancholy face became still paler, and took on a profound sadness. Who knows what pleasant vision crossed her mind, brought on by that man's passionate words? Who knows what feeling the sight of him had awakened in that lonely young heart?

Sometimes, with distracted gaze, she smiled sweetly, but then, as though beset by a bitter memory, shook her head with a movement of painful resignation, murmuring in a low voice:

"Daughter of misfortune, inheritor of heavenly punishment, sacrificial victim, think of your vow and remember that your kingdom is not of this world."

Sunk anew in her definitive sadness, she rededicated herself with even greater fervor to the mission of mercy she had imposed on herself.

"Clemencia," the executioner said to his daughter one day, "why are you continually more pensive and sad? Who dares to cause you grief? Tell me his name, and you can instantly add, 'Poor devil!'"

"No one, Father, no one!" his daughter exclaimed, instinctively lifting her hand to her heart as though fearing that her father could read some secret there.

"No, you are deceiving me . . . For some time now I have even noticed tears in your voice when you come to greet me."

"Father," replied the young woman, interrupting him and looking into his bloodstained eyes with her blue and pious gaze, "can't you guess? When at last you come home after a night of anxiously waiting up for you, and I go to embrace you, I think with great sadness of the children of the unfortunate men cut down by your group, and that those poor beings will never enjoy the happiness that God has still granted me. Oh Father, is this not a good reason for tears and sadness? In the midst of those bloody events, have you never lifted your hand to your heart and asked yourself what you would do if you saw a hand with a dagger descend upon your daughter and cut her throat?"

"Be still, Clemencia, be still!" shouted the outlaw. "What would I do? Hell itself would not equal the rage with which Roque's arm would move to avenge you . . . But you are mad, child! Don't you know that the barbarous Unitarians lack a heart such as ours, we who love and hate with equal intensity?"

"Father, you know that isn't true! What, then, do the mothers' heartrending cries mean, or the sobs of the wives and the sad weeping of the orphaned children which I constantly hear raised to Heaven against us? Don't they tell you that the heartstrings severed by your dagger are as sensitive as our own?"

"Be quiet, Clemencia, be quiet!" he repeated. "You have such a suggestive and persuasive voice that you will have me believing this, and then what would General Rosas think of his servant? How Solomon and Cuitiño would make fun of their compatriot! No! Get out! I don't want to listen to you, above all not today, when Manuel Puirredón, that Unitarian outlaw whose throat I have sworn to cut, walks among us as though invisible and protected by a supernatural force . . . Oh, I am getting upset over nothing. What madness! My heart is full of hatred, and there would be no room for mercy in it. Just listen to this story . . .

"A few months ago I went to hear mass at the Perpetual Help Church."

"Father! You dared to enter God's temple with your hands stained with blood?"

"With blood? Yes, of course, and why not, if it is Unitarian blood, and they are God's enemies?

"Anyway, as I was saying, I went into the Perpetual Help church. Mass had barely begun when the man at whose side I had knelt down, suddenly turned around, and, regarding me for a second as though to place me, threw me a scornful look, and, drawing away with insolent disgust, moved to a spot very far from me. That act betrayed him as a Unitarian. The wretch had recogized Roque, but he had no idea what Roque's vengeance would be.

"I kept my eyes on him during mass, and when he left the church I saw him go into a small, almost ruined house, that was across the street.

"That night, while the man had forgotten his insulting behavior toward me, he sat quietly by his wife's side, holding his two children in his arms. His wife was busy embroidering baby clothes for the third child that was soon expected, while I guided the Mas-horca to his house. While the arms of his wife and children embraced him I buried my dagger countless times in his breast, spattering blood on the clothing of the yet unborn baby.

"Clemencia, Clemencia, what's the matter?"

The murderer reached out his arm to support his daughter, who, trembling and shaking, refused it with ill-concealed horror.

"For a while," he continued, "I thought that the indelible memory that bloody scene, with all its screams and tears, had left in my imagination what is referred to as remorse, but no—it was only the pleasure of satisfied revenge. The day Roque knows compassion or remorse is the day the blade of this knife would be dulled and . . . just look how it shines," the outlaw said, making the wide blade glitter before his daughter's eyes.

And thrusting it quickly into the belt of his wide trousers he left, doubtless to go back to his gruesome task.

Clemencia felt crushed under the weight of the frightful words she had just heard. Feeling weak, broken, and faint she fell at the feet of her divine patroness, raising her hands to her in anguished prayer.

While she prayed hope and faith came into her heart, and when she arose, her face once again shone with serene resignation.

"It is never too late for Your divine mercy, oh Lord," she said, raising her eyes to Heaven. "The hour of repentance has not yet come, but it will toll."

Quickly she went to the fund she kept for the victims. She took a basket of food and a purse of gold with her, and, under cover of night, went to look for the house her father had mentioned.

She recognized it from the marks of the axes the criminals had used to break down the side gate, and had left open. Clemencia was about to cross the threshold of a poor, bare room, when she heard a voice speak inside and held back, contemplating the scene before her eyes.

In one corner, stretched out on a bed so poor it had nearly no covers, lay a pale, thin young woman who held a newborn in her arms.

At a distance a boy of about six and another of four sat under the blankets of a bed that was suspended like a cradle from four ropes attached to a roofbeam.

The faint light of a candle which burned on the floor gave this dwelling a gloomy atmosphere, which, when joined to the memory of the hideous scene which had taken place there, tore Clemencia's soul apart with grief.

"Mother," said the younger of the two children with a sad voice, "I'm hungry. Where is the bread we had yesterday?" The mother let out a deep sigh while the other boy answered with a grave and resigned tone:

"We ate it, Enrique, we ate it and Mother has no more money to buy more because she is ill and can't work. Don't bother her, and let's go to sleep like the little angel that fell down from Heaven here yesterday."

"Oh, he has my mother's breast and I'm hungry, I'm hungry!" wailed Enrique.

"Oh Lord," cried the mother between sobs, "if in the wisdom of Your designs you wished the executioner's axe to fell the strongest tree, I worship Your will and resign myself to it, but have mercy on these tender flowers that are only beginning to open to the sun's rays. Lord! You who feed the birds of the air and the worms of the earth, and hear my children weep with hunger, can't You send one of the countless angels who dwell in Heaven to help them?"

"Ah, here is one," she murmured when she saw Clemencia kneeling by the children's bed and handing them some of the food she had brought.

The mother clasped her hands and with pious adoration looked at the beautiful young girl, whose white veil fell like a halo around her face and seemed to light up the gloom which surrounded them. Bent over the children like a spirit of mercy she gazed at them with a look of tenderness and sorrow. The poor woman held her to be an angel who had come in answer to her prayers and tried to keep as still as possible, fearing that a gesture, a breath would destroy that heavenly vision, bringing her back to her painful reality. And when Clemencia drew near her bed, the simple woman of the people anxiously stretched out her hands to touch Clemencia's, as though to convince herself that she was not a supernatural illusion.

"Oh, you who have come to bring consolation to this unhappy home," she exclaimed, embracing the young woman's knees, "who are you, angelic creature?"

"I am an unfortunate being just like you, and I have come to seek my companions in grief. I have come to tell you this: Christian Mother, trust in the One Who wipes away all tears and quiets all weeping. He watches over everything from on high and can make the weakest creature the instrument of His mercy. Have you been left alone and abandoned? I will be near you and you will be my dear sister. Do your children need someone to protect them? I shall be the one. Do you have need of things? Here is gold so that you can buy them."

"Oh, you are a saint!" said the widow, bending down reverently, "Bless my son and give him a name, for he has not yet been baptized."

And she placed the newborn in Clemencia's arms.

"Call him Manuel," she said in a low voice, and when she said this, the maiden's pale face blushed and her eyes shone with a peculiar brillance.

"Manuel," she continued, kissing the child shyly, "I will be a solicitous and devoted wetnurse for you. Your mother will not be jealous, for all your caresses will be for her. I only want the joy of being able to say to you every day, 'Manuel, I love you!'"

"Oh, Lord!" exclaimed the poor mother, covering her eyes with Clemencia's hands and sobbing hard. "Soon you will be everything to him. My husband calls to me from Eternity. The assassin's knife could not sever the bonds that unite our souls, and mine is about to depart, even though it does not wish to and cries bitterly for these other beings who must remain and suffer on earth." And the unhappy woman pointed to the children with a desperate gesture.

Clemencia listened to her, terrified. With profound horror the assassin's daughter thought about her father's crimes, which had never seemed more awful to her. But, rising above the gloomy thoughts which depressed her, she reminded the mother of her responsibilities on earth, and as a Christian of the need to resign herself to God's will.

"Mother," said the oldest of the children when they were alone again, "which of God's angels is it who has come to see us? How beautiful she is with her long curls, just like Our Lady of Help!"

"And her eyes," replied the youngest, "her eyes are blue like the sky and her eyelashes—isn't it true that they look like the rays of that star that shines in our window?"

"Yes, children," said the widow, smiling sadly at her little ones, "she is a lovely angel whom God has put on earth to console the unfortunate."

"What's the angel's name, Mother?"

"Whatever it is, let us bless it, children, and ask God to dry her tears as He has dried ours," said the widow, making the children kneel for bedtime prayer.

I V

Meanwhile Clemencia walked away with slow, hesitant steps. The expression on her face bore witness to her profound distress. She thought about the omnipotence of good and evil. One blow of her father's dagger had sufficed to create the bottomless abyss of misery she had just witnessed, and she, what had she gained by an entire life of sacrifice and self-abnegation? Alleviate hunger and nakedness, cure some material hurt, perhaps, but for the soul's afflictions the only remedy she had found was weeping. At this thought Clemencia felt overcome by profound dejection. But as she always did when she feared her faith might waver, the maiden lifted up her thoughts to God, asking Him for some great sacrifice that would uncover for her the secret of replacing suffering with happiness.

Clemencia was roused out of her sad reverie by the sound of a name which was uttered often and menacingly. Looking around her, she saw that she was surrounded by a group of men whose sinister aspect aroused her attention. Wrapped in long ponchos and armed with daggers, they were carefully guarding a door. The executioner's daughter recognized them. They were her father's henchmen, the building was "Headquarters," the place devoted to carrying out secret executions, the "R.I.P." where Unitarians entered never to come out again, and on whose vaults the finger of terror had written for them Dante's funereal warning.[3]

While Clemencia, trembling and shaking with anxiety, hid behind a column and attempted to hear what the men were talking about, a rider on a black horse, whose long sword clanked noisily against the handle of the lance he was holding, checked the headlong rush of his mount with a curse, and approached the group on guard at the door.

"Lieutenant Corbalán," he shouted with hoarse, curt voice, "take twenty men and patrol el Bajo, while I raid Barracas. The Devil! I shall renounce who I am if by tomorrow at sunrise Manuel Puirredón's head isn't stuck on this lance!"

Plunging his spurs into his horse's flanks, he departed like a black whirlwind.

White and cold with fear, Clemencia fell to her knees. The man who had just pronounced this terrible oath was her father.

"Corbalán," said one of the bandits, "take me with you. I want to kill men and not keep watch over women."

"If Blacksoul had given you the one who was in the Tres Cruces jail, you wouldn't have minded keeping her for yourself," said another man with savage laughter.

"The old dog! Surprising the lovely lady who was awaiting her gallant gentleman, tying her up like a sheep to his saddle, bringing her to Headquarters under his poncho, and locking her up in the Tres Cruces jail where there are more than fifty graves—what do you suppose he plans to do with her?"

"Not much! Kill her instead of her husband, or kill her with him if he catches him."

Clemencia listened no further. She drew herself up, strong and resolute. She firmly approached the bandits' leader, giving her eyes the same black look as her father's, and spoke in an imperious voice.

"Lieutenant Corbalán, do you know me?"

"The commandant's daughter!" exclaimed the assassin, taking off his hat.

The men drew aside respectfully, and the young woman, without bothering to add another word, crossed the threshold and disappeared into the shadows of the fateful building.

In the darkness of the gloomy portico which gave out onto the patio where the cells were, Clemencia made out a man, standing immobile and leaning on a halberd. He was dressed in a guard's uniform and she took him for a sentinel, but on approaching him she trembled.

The young woman did not need to see his face in order to recognize him, a face which was covered by the wide band of an army cap.

"Poor man!" Clemencia murmured in his ear and clutched his arm in fright. "What are you doing here? Didn't you hear?"

"Yes," he answered, blocking her path. "I'm the one those killers are looking for so desperately. Their daggers are aimed at my head, but I have come to save my beloved or die with her. Look," he went on, kicking at a formless shape that lay on the ground, "I have killed a sentinel, and armed with his things am awaiting the first man to cross this threshold in order to bring him down."

"Manuel de Puirredón!" said Clemencia, uncovering her face and casting an indescribable glance at the fugitive's eyes. "Do you remember?"

"It is she!" exclaimed the Unitarian. "The angel who saved me!"

"Do you trust me? Will you let me take over saving the one you seek?"

"Ah!" he replied with such ecstasy that Clemencia stifled it in fear. "For those words alone, beautiful creature, I fall at your feet. Ask me for my blood, my soul . . . I will give you everything."

"Then get away from this dreadful place; cross that fatal threshold, and wait for your beloved where she was waiting for you a little while ago."

"No! I'll do anything but take even one step away from here."

"Oh, my God! Do you want your doom! Well then, swear to me to keep still in your disguise, and not to attack anyone who walks by here."

"That's a hard promise, but since you wish it, so be it!"

"Thank you, thank you," she said, clasping the fugitive's hand. He felt a tear fall on it. "Be happy, Manuel de Puirredón. Farewell!"

Lowering her veil, the young woman disappeared into the shadows.

The Unitarian heard from afar the harsh sound of the lock, and said, "That's the door to her cell . . . Emilia, my Emilia!"

With eyes and ears alert, he anxiously probed the night and the silence. Two, five, ten minutes crept by at a snail's pace, and in his mortal anxiety Puirredón came close to breaking his oath and running after the one who had exacted it from him.

Finally, there in the distance Clemencia's white veil suddenly appeared among the shadows of the dismal corridor. Puirredón saw her coming alone and, forgetting his promise, forgetting everything, let out an exclamation of pain and ran to meet her. But when he reached her two loving arms encircled his neck and fiery lips sealed the cry of ecstasy that was about to burst from his own.

"Silence, my darling," a beloved voice whispered into the fugitive's ear. "A miracle has saved me. The Virgin of Help came down to my cell to free me. Yes,—I recognized her by her celestial beauty and by the sad smile of her divine lips. This is her holy veil which will protect us. Let us flee!"

Covering her face, the woman dragged the man behind her.

When the fugitives reached the door they saw a rider come up; making his horse prance he entered the gateway, dismounted and unsheathed his dagger, then headed for the cell area in menacing silence.

When they saw him Puirredón felt his companion's hand tremble in his, and under her veil heard her say in a terrified voice, "Blacksoul!"

Then they crossed the accursed threshold together and breathed in the sweet scent of freedom.

Meanwhile Blacksoul crossed the patio, and when he reached the dungeon of Tres Cruces, opened the massive locks and groped about in the dark.

A solitary ray of the waning moon which shone through the narrow skylight of the vault made a livid splash on the damp floor, heightening the dense shadows of the fearful dungeon. Nevertheless, the criminal's sharp eye discerned a white shape.

He went over to it, extended his bloodstained hand, and, feeling a woman's throat, plunged his dagger into it, shouting furiously, "Informer of our secrets, accomplice of the filthy Unitarians, die in place of the conspirator you love, but know ere you do that not even your bones will lie by his because your grave will be the bottom of this cell!"

As he said this he broke into a chilling laugh.

Feeling herself wounded unto death, the unhappy woman brought her hands up to her cleft throat, holding back the blood that gushed in streams from the wound.

"My God!" she whispered, "My sacrifice has been accomplished! The mission I assigned myself here on earth has been completed. Lord, let my blood cleanse this other blood that cries to You from below."

At the sound of her voice Blacksoul felt his heart break and the hair rise on his head. Quickly he stood up, carried his victim over to the skylight, and examined her bloodstained face by the light of the moon.

"Clemencia!" the assassin shouted with a horrible scream.

"Father, poor Father! Raise your eyes to Heaven and look there for mercy," faltered the young woman's gentle voice as she breathed her last.

The criminal fell heavily to the floor, the body of his murdered daughter in his arms.

But the maiden's blood found favor before God, and He, in an act of redemptive baptism, sent down a ray of divine light which reformed her father.

Notes

1. The Unitarians were Rosas's political enemies. Rosas headed the Federalist party.

2. General Lavalle had attempted to take over the Argentine government in 1829, but Rosas defeated him in a battle; after this defeat, Lavalle went into exile in Uruguay.

3. "All hope abandon, ye who enter here." From Dante Alighieri's *Inferno*, Canto III.

Mercedes Cabello
de Carbonera

Mercedes Cabello de Carbonera from Elvira García y García, La mujer peruana a través de los siglos. Serie Historiada de estudios y observaciones. *(Lima: Imprenta Americana, 1924–25).*

*B*orn in 1845 to an upper-class family in the Peruvian provinces, Mercedes Cabello moved to Lima when she was twenty and married a distinguished medical doctor, Urbano Carbonera. Hers was an active and probing intelligence. As university studies were not permitted to women in her time, she read voraciously on her own and began to write at an early age, at first under the pseudonym Enriqueta Pradel (Mazquiarán 98–99). She was widowed after only a few years of marriage (there were no children) and became an active participant in Lima's circle of intellectuals and literary salons. Juana Manuela Gorriti, her close friend, said of her, "She is one of the most remarkable and eminent women of Peru, distinguished for her beauty, intelligence, and erudition" ("Chincha" 65).

Cabello de Carbonera wrote many articles for newspapers and journals, both in Spanish America and in Europe. She is one of the most important essayists in nineteenth-century Latin America, one who, like many other women, spoke out against women's inequality in society and before the law. The importance of women's ever-increasing publications in newspapers and journals cannot be underestimated. As Mary Louise Pratt observed, "Fortunately, their access to literacy, print culture, and the public sphere was established *before* the republican era. They could not be silenced completely" (15). Because she felt her own lack of formal education keenly, Cabello de Carbonera became a fervent advocate for the education of women. She looked at this issue not only in practical terms but in ideal terms as well: as did many women of her time, she felt that educated women contributed to the moral progress of nations. Here, then, is another example of a female perspective in the nation-building process.

Cabello de Carbonera was an outspoken social critic, to which her journalistic articles and also her novels attest. She loathed the materialism and social pretentiousness of the Peruvian upper classes, in which many women unfortunately were the most active participants. Outward show, stylish fashions, and material possessions counted for everything in these social circles. Cabello de Carbonera also spoke out against their sham religiosity, often abetted by the Catholic clergy of Peru.

Among her five novels, *Blanca Sol* (1888), a novel of social realism, is probably the most widely read, and presents a portrait of just such a shallow and hypocritical woman. Blessed with considerable beauty and native intelligence (but almost no education), Blanca had been raised by her mother to covet wealth and social position, and to do anything to get it. She marries a stupid and ugly man she does not love, has six children whom she neglects, and for a while becomes a leader of fashionable Lima society. When her husband goes insane she loses everything, and the book ends with her poised to become the proprietress of a house of prostitution. Cabello de Carbonera has insinuated all along that upper-class women routinely sell themselves into marriage, so that Blanca Sol's ultimate profession is not very different from what she has been doing all her life. Blanca herself realizes this in a moment of reflection: "Her state as a married woman, and wed to a man whom . . . she could not love, presented itself to her with all the frightening reality of her life. Marriage without love, she thought, was nothing more than prostitution sanctioned by society" (118). In spite of the author's stated intentions to condemn her protagonist's sinful end, the final pages of the novel leave little doubt that Blanca will become an eminently successful madam: "She got ready to make many men lose their wits and their money. . . . [I]t was the shamelessness, the insolence of a woman who wished to express by means of her actions what cannot be said by spoken language" (189). Lucía Guerra Cunningham sees in Blanca's end an inversion of the traditional bildungsroman, in which the protagonist finally realizes—and exploits—her true status (41).

Cabello de Carbonera not only wrote novels, she theorized on them. One of her most important essays was "La novela moderna" (1892), in which she lays out the directions she believes this genre should take in Latin America and shows herself very much in touch with French theorists such as Balzac, Zola, and the positivism of Comte. She saw the novel as linked to the experimental sciences and endorsed social realism as the best approach for novels to speak to the emerging young nations of Latin America: "The novel is called upon to collaborate in the solution of the great problems with which science presents it" (iv). With this essay Cabello de Carbonera won major prizes in Buenos Aires and in the 1892 Chicago Exposition.

Gorriti says of her friend that she was a fine cook, and Elvira García y García tells us a number of other personal details about this energetic and efficient woman. She apparently was an avid gardener and sewed beautifully, often making items for the trousseaus of the daughters of impoverished friends. When her husband died her personal fortune disappeared, but she learned how to manage the money she earned by her writing, and even acquired several ranches (García 21). At the end of her life she unfortunately had a nervous breakdown and slipped into permanent mental illness. She died alone, after ten years in what can only be called horrific conditions in Lima's insane asylum.

The brief essay presented in this anthology examines a topic that was very important to many nineteenth-century women: the relative importance of beauty versus intelligence in a woman. It spoke to a woman's destiny as wife and mother and, by implication, to the role of the family as national allegory. Women's literature of this century is full of attacks on the institution of marriage and foregrounds many women's ignorance and powerlessness in the choice of a marital partner, often with disastrous results. Because men and women often barely knew each other before marrying, men could hardly be blamed for preferring an attractive woman to a plain one, but Cabello de Carbonera is quick to point out that to create lasting and happy relationships between marital partners there has to be more than physical attraction. She also shows that the concept of female beauty is both relative and a social construct. Implicit in her opposition of beauty and intelligence in a woman is the idea that the estimation of a woman's beauty depends on the male gaze in general, while appreciation of a woman's mind belonged only to equally intelligent and talented men, thus fitting partners for a lasting relationship. Cabello de Carbonera focused on a woman's domestic role, but at the same time she and her contemporaries "sought to assert themselves as citizens, as social subjects, as agents of history, and as *pensadoras* [thinkers]" (Pratt 15).

This essay was first read in one of Juana Manuela Gorriti's literary gatherings, the so-called *veladas,* and Cabello dedicated it to her hostess and friend, whose drive and intelligence matched her own.

Estudio comparativo de la inteligencia y la belleza en la muger

TRABAJO DE LA SEÑORA MERCEDES CABELLO
DE CARBONERA LEÍDO POR SU AUTORA

A mi querida amiga Juana Manuela Gorriti.

La eminente é ilustre escritora, á quien tengo el honor de dedicar el presente trabajo, fué la que me sujirió este hermoso á la par que difícil tema, comprometiéndome á tratarlo en esta velada. Ella bien sabe que sus deseos, aun los mas pequeños, son para mi órdenes, que en cumplirlas complázcome, y que su inspirada palabra, será siempre un poderoso móvil para mi pluma.

Así, despues de esta breve esplicacion que doy en salvedad de cualquiera interpretacion que sobre el tema pudiera hacerse, procuraré satisfacer á la amiga, llenando al mismo tiempo mi compromiso.

Por fuerza habré de tratarlo lijera y superficialmente, de otro modo, necesario sería al hablar de la belleza, escribir un tratado de estética, para manifestar hasta qué punto la idea de la belleza es relativa, estando sujeta á mil cambios, que ora se relacionan con las modas y las costumbres de un país, ora dependen de otras muchas circunstancias que dificultan y hacen casi imposible poder establecer un principio general, aplicable á todas las épocas y á todos los pueblos. Con mucha razon ha dicho un escritor, que de la belleza se puede decir lo mismo que dijo Pascal de la justicia: "Lo que es á esta parte de los Pirineos belleza, es á la otra fealdad." Prozer-Collard dice: "Lo bello se siente y no se define."

Asi por ejemplo, en los pueblos meridionales, donde parece que el sol tropical hubiera teñido de subidos tintes los ojos y los cabellos y tostado con su calor la tez de los habitantes, allí se toma como el tipo de la belleza, á las mugeres cuyos rúbios cabellos, nos parece que simuláran las hebras del oro, y cuyos ojos celestes, miramos como el reflejo de nuestro azulado y límpido cielo. Al contrario de los pueblos que se alejan del Ecuador, en los que las brumas de un cielo siempre opaco y nebuloso, hace que el sol se muestre avaro de su luz y de su calor, allí se tiene por bella á la muger de ojos negros y pelo de azabache. Así veremos que los Griegos, esos maestros del arte, pintaban á sus Venus con cabellos rubios, y Byron, el inmortal cantor de la belleza, celebraba á las españolas con su color moreno y con sus cabellos de ébano, encontrándolas muy superiores á las inglesas con sus tintes descoloridos.

No hablaré de los pueblos donde los beneficios de la civilizacion no se han dejado sentir, educando el gusto hasta poder formular el tipo de la belleza; entre estos se ve las mayores aberraciones. Hay algunas tribus salvajes, entre las que se usa teñir de negro los dientes con una yerba, y miran como una cosa feísima y propia, segun dicen ellos, de los perros ó de otros animales, el tener los dientes blancos.

Aun mas lijera y superficialmente, será necesario tratar este tema, considerando, que para establecer una comparacion entre la belleza y la inteligencia, preciso es mirar á la muger bajo la seductora y risueña faz que presenta en los salones, considerándola solamente, como un adorno, como un dije, ó si se me permite el calificativo, como una hada que arrebata con su belleza y encanta con su talento.

Forzoso será olvidar la grandiosa mision que la ha sido encomendada por la naturaleza; mision augusta y sublime, de esposa y de madre, en la que la belleza entra por tan poco, y la inteligencia tiene que entrar por tanto. Si hubiera de considerarla bajo de esta última faz, absurdo seria y muy grande, establecer una comparacion entre la importancia de la belleza y la de la inteligencia.

Al tomar á la belleza para ponerla en parangon con la inteligencia, hablaré de ella segun nuestro tipo, es decir, de aquella con ojos de cielo, cabellos de oro, cútis alabastrino, y cuerpo de esbeltas y delicadas formas.

¿Preciso será acaso, que os presente tambien un tipo de la muger inteligente? No, el talento no tiene mas que un solo tipo, y no puede jamás confundirse, ni ocultarse, y si bien es cierto, que entre el vulgo de las inteligencias hay muchas formas y gradaciones, el verdadero talento no tiene mas que una sola forma, una forma única y eterna, puesto que su modelo es Dios.

Para juzgar del poder de la una y de la otra, imaginémonos dos tipos, opuestos el uno del otro; la una dotada de una belleza perfecta y deslumbradora y sin ninguna inteligencia; la otra de una inteligencia poderosa y clara y sin ninguna belleza.

¡Una muger bella! estas palabras nos parece que simbolizan estas otras—Una muger perfecta.

La belleza es la manifestacion mas elocuente que tiene la naturaleza, para despertar en nuestra alma la idea de un Ser infinito, grande y perfecto: he allí por qué en todo corazon noble, existe un culto ferviente para todo lo que es bello; he allí por qué una muger bella nos inspira admiracion y simpatia.

La belleza tiene un lenguaje, una elocuencia que le es propia, peculiar de ella sola. Una muger bella, habla con su mirada, habla con su sonrisa, habla hasta con su frente inmóvil y tersa. Lenguaje admirable que se presta á que cada cual lo traduzca á su deseo; así el hombre soñador y espiritual, lo traduce con su alma, como el hombre material y vulgar, lo interpreta tambien á su modo. Esas son las razones por las que la belleza tiene el privilegio de seducir y fascinar á todos los hombres.

No así la inteligencia, que solo seduce al hombre de talento. El gran Voltaire ha dicho: Solo al genio le es dado comprender al genio.

Sucede con el mérito de una muger inteligente, lo mismo que con el de un hermoso cuadro: mostradle á un hombre torpe y vulgar, un cuadro de gran mérito, en el que, en medio de los tintes vagos y oscuros, se ve sin embargo brillar la idea del autor, es decir, el alma del cuadro; despues de mirarle mucho tiempo, quedará convencido que el cuadro no dice nada, y sin embargo, allí hay una idea, una idea grandiosa, que solo puede comprender el hombre inteligente.

Muchas veces héme preguntado, ¿por qué la belleza no va siempre unida á la inteligencia? ¿Por qué la muger que nos fascina con su hermosura, nos decepciona con su inteligencia, y por qué la que es un encanto para los ojos, suele ser un desencanto para el alma?

Cuántas mugeres conozco, cuya belleza ganaria mucho si enmudecieran; así tendrian solo el lenguaje simbólico de la belleza; ese lenguaje que, como dije ya, tiene el privilegio de que cada cual pueda interpretarlo á su modo; así, sus lábios no serian sus eternos enemigos, que van divulgando á cada momento, que en su cerebro hay tanta incorreccion de forma, como hay en su fisonomia correccion de lineas.

Una belleza sin inteligencia es una ilusion que está muy próxima al desengaño. Es una hada que nos fascina, mientras la miramos á traves del prisma encantador de su belleza; pero que desaparece tan luego que la luz de la razon penetra mas allá de donde miran los ojos.

Una inteligencia sin belleza, es como un rico tesoro oculto entre las escabrosidades de un terreno árido y montañoso, que se esconde para enriquecer al hombre feliz que llega á encontrarlo. Se puede decir que es un magnífico libro encuadernado á la rústica, que los nécios desprecian, solo porque le juzgan mirándole por fuera.

La violeta de los campos por mas que se oculta, la denuncia su perfume; así es la muger inteligente, solo no la encuentra el que es incapaz de comprenderla.

A un hombre de talento, una muger bella puede hacerle concebir la felicidad, solo á una muger inteligente le es dado el realizársela. La primera le hará soñar, la segunda le hará sentir y pensar.

En el turbulento y borrascoso mar de las pasiones, soñar es navegar sin brújula ni timon, á merced de las tempestades; por eso, todo sueño tiene su triste y amargo despertar. Sentir y pensar, es viajar asegurado contra todos los escollos y peligros, atravesando el encantado y risueño paraiso de las dulces emociones, á do mora la verdadera felicidad.

Hé aquí, al fin, llegado el momento de resolver el problema de la importancia de la belleza y de la inteligencia, concediendo la supremacía á una de las dos.

Mi opinion ya la habreis adivinado. Hubiera querido no dejarla comprender, sinó que promoviendo una discusion, someter la solucion de este problema á la ilustrada decision de ustedes, pero ¿cómo establecer un paralelo entre dos cosas tan esencialmente distintas?

¿Cómo comparar lo que constituye la belleza del alma, con lo que solo puede constituir la perfeccion de las formas?

¿Cómo igualar la inteligencia que brilla y perfuma la existencia entera, con la belleza, esa flor primaveral que nace, se colora y resplandece, tan solo en una época de la vida[?]

¿Cómo comparar lo que es efímero y fugaz, como una centella que pasa sin dejar en pos de sí, ni los vestigios de su claridad, con un foco de luz purísima que se irradia sobre nuestra propia existencia y la de todos los seres que nos rodean?

Admiradora entusiasta de todo lo bello, ríndole ferviente culto; pero no he podido encontrar un término siquiera, para establecer una comparacion, entre el mérito de la belleza y el de la inteligencia: así, no creo equivocarme reconociendo la superioridad que tiene la inteligencia sobre la belleza de la muger.

A Comparative Study on Intelligence and Beauty in Women

A PAPER BY SEÑORA MERCEDES CABELLO DE
CARBONERA, READ BY THE AUTHOR

To my dear friend Juana Manuela Gorriti.

The eminent and famous author, to whom I have the honor of dedicating the present paper, was the one who suggested this lovely and yet also difficult topic, making me promise to discuss it during this meeting. She is well aware that her wishes, even the least of them, for me are commands that I enjoy fulfilling, and that her inspired word will always be a powerful impulse for my pen.

So, after this brief explanation which I offer to clarify any interpretation which might be made on this subject, I will attempt to satisfy my friend and at the same time meet my obligation.

Of need I will have to treat it briefly and superficially; to do otherwise when speaking of beauty would necessitate my writing a treatise on aesthetics in order to show to what degree the idea of beauty is relative, being as it is subject to a thousand modifications, at times related to the fashion and customs of a country, at times dependent on many other circumstances which impede and indeed make it almost impossible to establish a general principle which would be applicable to all times and all people. With good reason an author remarked that the same thing could be said of beauty that Pascal said of justice: "What is beauty on this side of the Pyrenees is ugliness on the other." Prozer-Collard says: "What is beautiful is felt and not defined."

For example, it appears that in southern countries, where the tropical sun tints eyes and hair with stronger tones, and by its heat browns people's skin, those women are considered beautiful whose blonde hair resembles strands of gold and whose blue eyes seem to reflect our clear blue sky. On the other hand, in those countries which are far from the equator, in which the mists of a perennially opaque and cloudy sky force the sun to be miserly with its light and heat, there the woman with black eyes and jet hair is considered beautiful. Thus we see that the Greeks, those masters of art, painted their Venuses with blonde hair, while Byron, the immortal bard of beauty, praised Spanish women with their dark skin and ebony hair, considering them far superior to Englishwomen with their faded coloring.

I don't plan to speak of the nations where the benefits of civilization have not yet been felt, [benefits] which educate taste so as to be able to formulate a type of beauty; among these nations one can see the greatest aberrations. There are some savage tribes who use a plant to dye their teeth black, and, according to their own testimony, hold the white teeth of dogs or other animals to be genuinely ugly.

I will have to discuss this topic even more quickly and superficially when I consider that in order to set up a comparison between beauty and intelligence, one must look at a woman with the seductive and smiling countenance she puts on in the salons, regarding her only as a decoration, a trinket, or, if I may be permitted the qualifying noun, as a spirit who enthralls with her beauty and enchants with her talent.

One must of needs forget the great mission that has been entrusted to women by nature, the majestic and sublime mission of wife and mother, in which beauty matters so little and intelligence counts for so much. If a woman is to be considered in this role, it would be absurd in the extreme to establish a comparison between the importance of beauty and of intelligence.

When I take beauty to establish a comparison with intelligence, I will speak of it with our type in mind, that is, the woman with sky-blue eyes, golden hair, alabaster skin, and a body of slender and delicate contours.

Will I also have to establish a type for the intelligent woman? No, for talent has only one type, and can never be mistaken for another, nor hidden, and while it is true that among the masses there are many kinds and gradations of intelligence, true talent has only one form, a unique and eternal form, because its model is God.

To judge the power of one and the other [beauty and intelligence], let us imagine two completely opposite types: one blessed with stunning, perfect beauty and no intelligence at all, and the other with clear, powerful intelligence and no beauty.

"A beautiful woman!"—To us these words seem to symbolize these others: "A perfect woman."

Beauty is the most eloquent manifestation Nature has to awaken in our soul the concept of an infinite, great and perfect Being; this is why there exists in every noble heart a passionate cult to all that is beautiful; this is why a lovely woman inspires admiration and affection in us.

Beauty has a language, an eloquence of its own that is unique to it alone. A beautiful woman speaks with her glance, her smile, even with her firm, smooth brow. An admirable language which lends itself to allow each person to translate it according to his fancy: the dreamy, spiritual man translates it with his soul, just as the coarse materialist interprets it in his way. These are the reasons why beauty has the gift of seducing and bewitching all men.

This is not the case with intelligence, which only seduces the man of talent. The great Voltaire said: "Only genius is able to understand genius."

The merit of an intelligent woman is measured in the same way as that of a beautiful painting: show a great painting to a coarse and vulgar man, one in which among vague, dark hues one can nevertheless see the painter's idea or the painting's soul shine forth; after looking at it at length [this man] will be convinced that the picture says nothing, and yet there is an idea there, a splendid idea that only an intelligent man can understand.

I have often asked myself why beauty and intelligence are not always linked? Why is it that the woman who enchants us with her beauty disappoints us with her intelligence, and why does the one who delights the eye frequently disillusion the soul?

I know many women whose beauty would gain considerably if they kept their mouths shut; in that way they would speak only the symbolic language of beauty, the language which, as I said before, has the advantage that each person can interpret it as he wishes. In that way their mouths would not be their perennial enemies which continually show the world that the flaws within their heads stand in direct contrast to the perfection of their physical features.

Beauty without intelligence is an illusion that is very close to disillusion. It is a spirit that enchants us while we perceive it through the bewitching prism of its beauty, but which disappears as soon as the light of reason penetrates deeper than what the eye can see.

Intelligence without beauty is like a rich treasure concealed in the harshness of an arid, mountainous landscape, a treasure which has been hidden in order to enrich the happy man who finds it. One might compare it to a magnificent book bound in paper, which fools scorn because they look no farther than the cover.

The violet of the field, no matter how it tries to hide, is given away by its scent; it is the same with an intelligent woman: the one who is unable to understand her will never find her.

A beautiful woman can make a gifted man envision happiness, but only an intelligent woman has the power to give it to him. The former will make him dream, the latter feel and think.

In the turbulent and stormy sea of passionate feelings, to dream is to navigate with neither compass nor tiller, at the mercy of the tempest; because of this all dreams have their sad and bitter awakening. To feel and to think is to travel protected against all dangers and pitfalls, and to cross over to the enchanted and smiling paradise of sweet emotions, where true happiness dwells.

I have finally reached the moment to resolve the problem of the importance of beauty versus intelligence, and to assign supremacy to one of the two.

You will have already guessed my opinion. I would have preferred not to have it be understood, but instead have engaged in a discussion, submitting the solution of this problem to your educated decision, but how are we to establish a parallel between two things which are so essentially different?

How is one to compare what constitutes beauty of soul with what makes up perfection of form?

How can one equate intelligence, which illuminates and perfumes an entire lifetime, with beauty, that springtime flower that is born, assumes its color and brilliance, but only in one moment of its life?

How is one to compare that which is ephemeral and fleeting, like a spark which is gone without leaving behind even a trace of its brightness, with a beacon of exceedingly pure light which radiates over our own life and the lives of all those around us?

An impassioned admirer of all things beautiful, I worship them fervently, but I haven't even been able to find the words to set up a comparison between the merits of beauty and intelligence, and thus, I do not believe I am mistaken in recognizing the superiority which intelligence has over beauty in women.

Teresa González de Fanning

Teresa González de Fanning from Elvira García y García, La mujer peruana a través de los siglos. Serie Historiada de estudios y observaciones. *(Lima: Imprenta Americana, 1924–25).*

*T*hat we do not know Teresa González de Fanning's date of death is an indication of how little is known about her, but she was an important member of Lima's circle of women writers and intellectuals in the nineteenth century.

One of the best sources of information about her is the two-volume *La mujer peruana a través de los siglos* (Peruvian Women Across the Centuries), published in 1925 and edited by Elvira García y García, who, it says on the title page, was the director of the Liceo Fanning in Lima. It is obvious from her article that she knew her subject well. García points out that Teresa González de Fanning was known primarily as an educator and writer. She made her first timid forays into the world of literature when she was very young, says García, "with all the scruples and reservations which a woman in our social milieu always has when she launches herself on this exceedingly harsh path" (30).

Even after her marriage to naval Capt. Juan Fanning Teresa continued to write, though, just like Soledad Acosta de Samper after her, often under cover of a pseudonym. In 1880 Fanning was killed in the battle of Miraflores against the Chileans, an encounter that was part of the War of the Pacific (1879–83), after which his widow's formerly comfortable economic position became very precarious. As was the case with so many nineteenth-century women who were forced to make a living, González de Fanning turned to writing and to education to support herself.

She was socially well connected in Lima, and the girls' school she founded soon became one of the best in the city, not so much because it was socially elite, but because it was based on sound pedagogy. García relates that as director of the school González de Fanning always put "education over instruction" (30). In later years, when she had retired from the directorship of the school, she wrote numerous articles about women's education, which were published in Lima in 1905. In so doing González de Fanning was joining in a wider struggle to allow women access to higher education. The basic questions asked in the nineteenth century were the following:

> Were women physically or emotionally capable of meeting the rigorous demands of higher education? Even if they were, was it moral for women to abandon their "natural" sphere of home and hearth to pursue higher education? Must women choose between roles as mothers and wives and activity in the public sphere? (Kimmel 50)

Prose fiction was another outlet for her writing talents, and she published a series of novels, generally under another pseudonym, María de la Luz. Some of these are *Regina* (1886), which was awarded the silver medal in an international competition by Lima's Atheneum, *Lucecitas* (Little Lights) (1893), and *Indómita* (Indomitable) and *Roque Moreno,* both published in 1904.

García points out that because Peruvian society did not heed González de Fanning's advice on the education of women, she became somewhat embittered in old age, especially since she had little patience with "the social farce" and was "truthful to the point of recklessness" (32). Having suffered economic hardship on the death of her husband, González de Fanning was passionate in her pleas to educate women—both intellectually and practically—so that no matter what happened to their men, they would be in a position to support themselves and their families financially. The essay that follows makes this point eloquently, and González de Fanning makes it completely clear how her topic is related to the well-being of the family, society, and the nation. Few of the male essayists of the time who spoke of a woman's domestic destiny as wife and mother thought about the consequences of the husband's death for his family, yet it was a painful reality to many women who suddenly found themselves bereft of spouse and breadwinner and without the skills either to manage the assets they might still have or to earn an independent living. Inserting the feminine point of view into this socioeconomic discourse—as González de

Fanning, Cabello de Carbonera, and Gorriti did—results in a contestatory work that Mary Louise Pratt terms the *gender essay*, "whose topic is the status and reality of women in modern society" (15), and one of whose salient discursive practices is "the analytical commentary on the spiritual and social condition of women" (18). This essay certainly falls into that category. The gender essay, as opposed to the canonical male essays on national identity, has received much less critical attention thus far, but here again it is time the women's voices are also heard.

Trabajo para la muger

DE LA SEÑORA TERESA GONZALEZ DE FANNING
(MARÍA DE LA LUZ) LEÍDO POR RICARDO PALMA[1]

Una nación está tanto mas adelantada en el camino del progreso, cuanto mayor es la suma de moralidad, libertad y cultura de que disponen los miembros que la componen para alcanzar todo el desarrollo y perfectibilidad de que son susceptibles.

Apoyándonos en esta verdad generalmente reconocida, vamos á examinar, si bien muy á la ligera, una de las faces [sic] de la situación moral de la muger en nuestra sociedad, y como resultado de este exámen, á pedir para ella, no la emancipación, no el éjercicio de los derechos políticos, sino pura y simplemente el éjercicio del santo derecho del trabajo. Abrigamos la esperanza de que todos los corazones generosos se pondrán de parte nuestra y en favor de esa pobre esclava de su propia ignorancia y de antiguas y arraigadas preocupaciones.

Para principiar penetremos siquiera sea con la imaginación á la morada donde un recién nacido acaba de ver la primera luz; y observemos como, siendo varon, el padre lo acoge con orgullosa satisfacción y la familia toda lo recibe como una bendición del cielo. Mas, si es muger, qué decepción! se la considera como una nueva carga para los suyos y hasta la tierna madre que tanto ama el fruto de sus entrañas, se conduele al considerar que es una desgraciada mas que viene á soportar las penalidades de la vida y cuya suerte es doblemente incierta y azarosa á causa del sexo á que pertenece.

El niño desde bien temprano ofrece á sus padres mayores dificultades que vencer; en lo general se muestra mas terco, mas indómito, mas dificil de conducir: su educación es incomparablemente mas dispendiosa, pero su sexo lo hace acreedor á que aun á costa de sacrificios, se procure darle no solamente una instrucción tan completa como sea posible, sino además y de preferencia, una profesión que poniéndolo á cubierto de las vicisitudes de la fortuna, lo haga al mismo tiempo un miembro útil de la sociedad y de la familia.

La educación de la muger es mucho mas fácil y limitada. Para ella, el porvenir solo presenta dos caminos practicables: el claustro que hoy dia está ya casi abolido y el matrimonio. Para este esclusivamente se la educa ó por lo menos hácia ese norte se dirigen sus aspiraciones.

Es indudable que la maternidad en el matrimonio es acaso la misión mas santa que ella puede ejercer sobre la tierra y uno de los fines principales para que ha sido creada; pero tambien es cierto que para llenar ese fin, su voluntad entra en parte, solo de una manera secundaria y no es, no puede ser justo que se haga depender esclusivamente su felicidad y su porvenir, de causas hasta cierto punto, independientes de su voluntad, como vamos á demostrarlo.

Nadie nos negará que es el hombre el que tiene la prerogativa de elegir á su compañera y que solo cuando está ya decidido á ligar su suerte, es cuando solicita el consentimiento de la que ha elegido y como la indulgencia social lo absuelve tan fácilmente de las faltas que comete contra la moral, raro es que se apresure á cambiar la independencia y los goces fáciles de su estado de célibe, por los graves deberes é indisolubilidad del matrimonio.

La muger, aunque por naturaleza mas sensible que el hombre, se vé precisada á reprimir los mas vehementes impulsos de su corazón.

En vano será que el amor, ese dulce y espontáneo sentimiento que poetiza la vida y que está en la esencia de nuestro sér, le haga sentir su influjo poderoso; debe esconderlo cuidadosamente so pena de esponerse á la burla, tal vez hasta del mismo que se lo inspiró y que dificilmente se dejará arrebatar el derecho de iniciativa que la costumbre le ha otorgado.

No es necesario recurrir á la estadística, basta la simple observación para adquirir el convencimiento de que en esta capital especialmente, los matrimonios no guardan proporcion con el número de habitantes. Si á esto se agrega la mayor mortalidad de los hombres por la guerra, el abuso de los licores y tantas otras causas, se comprenderá cómo forzosamente tiene que quedar un gran número de mugeres en estado de viudez ó de perpétua soltería.

Estas tristes víctimas del destino, aguardando ver satisfechas sus justas aspiraciones con la venida de ese Mesías que se les había prometido, ven agostarse su juventud y llegar los treinta años, que si para el hombre es como ha dicho un poeta español: "Funesta edad de amargos desengaños," para la muger soltera es la tumba de sus ilusiones y esperanzas.

Aun cuando sienta la vida en toda su plenitud, el porvenir es para ella un desierto árido sin un solo oasis en que reposar. Como el imprudente jugador que aventuró toda su fortuna en una carta y al verla perdida se encuentra sumido en un abismo sin fondo, así la que cifrara toda su ventura en la idea del matrimonio, al ver que esta se desvanece, se siente herida de muerte y desorientada sin saber el rumbo que le conviene seguir.

El mundo, que antes la acogiera con halagos y distinciones cuando se hallaba adornada con las gracias seductoras de la primera juventud, la recibe friamente cuando no la persigue con sus burlas y sarcasmos, porque ha ingresado en el número de las solteronas y todos se creen con derecho para escarnecerla.

Al perder á sus padres que son su natural apoyo, se encuentra de huéspeda en hogar ageno y sin que le sea dado gozar de independencia, porque la educacion y las costumbres se unen para arrebatárselas. Y desgraciada de la que pretendiera arrostrar las preocupaciones sociales! á mas de los inconvenientes que le resultarian del aislamiento, espondria su honra á los ataques venenosos de la calumnia, siempre dispuesta á cebarse en el honor de la muger.

Si agriada por las decepciones y sintiendo hastío de la vida, se acoge como último recurso á la religión, si bien logra calmar en parte sus angustias y llenar el vacío de su existencia, se conquista el despreciativo apodo de beata, que unido al de solterona, acaban de transformarla en un sér antipático y repulsivo, especialmente para los miopes de espíritu que no alcanzan á penetrar los sufrimientos del alma.

Este es á grandes rasgos el porvenir que se les prepara á muchísimas mugeres que no carecen de méritos y virtudes, y de una despejada inteligencia, que si se cultivara, podria aprovecharse en beneficio de la sociedad á que pertenecen y de la cual vienen á ser miembros paralizados, porque se les condena á una absoluta esterilidad y á perpétua dependencia: la dependencia de la debilidad centuplicada por la ignorancia.

Mucho se ha escrito ya y reconocemos que con algun fruto, sobre la necesidad y conveniencia de acrecentar la ilustracion de la muger. Abundando en las mismas ideas nos limitamos, por hoy, á pedir para ella que lo mismo que al hombre, se la enseñe algun arte, profesion ú oficio proporcionados á su sexo y posicion social, que, á la vez que ocupen y desarrollen su inteligencia, le proporcionen cierto grado de independencia á que tiene derecho á aspirar, sobre todo cuando carece del apoyo del ser fuerte que debiera acompañarla en la penosa peregrinación de la vida.

Como nos dirigimos especialmente á las personas de buena intencion y recto juicio, no nos ocuparemos de combatir la vana preocupacion de que la muger solo ha nacido para el desempeño de las tareas domésticas y que redunda en perjuicio de estas, el darle ocupacion y cultura á su inteligencia. Admitir esto, seria colocarla en un nivel muy poco mas elevado que el de las bestias de carga y animales de servicio.

Tampoco seria su debilidad escusa para negarle el derecho de trabajar. No todas las profesiones exigen fuerza física y en cuanto á la moral, está bien probado que la posee.

La fuerza y extensión de su inteligencia bien puede decirse que aun no se conoce, desde que nadie casi ha cuidado desarrollarla sino en muy estrechos límites. Sin embargo, en todos los siglos ha dado, aunque aisladas, brillantes pruebas de que existe. Omitimos citar ejemplos, porque seria á mas de difuso, repetir lo que todos saben.

Seria una insensatez el pretender clasificar por sexos las inteligencias y darle la preferencia ciegamente á la del hombre, que, si bien tiene ciertas cualidades que le hacen superior, en cambio la de la muger la supera en muchas otras. Si se compara la de un hombre inculto con la de una muger medianamente educada, no estará la ventaja de parte del primero, por mas de que pertenezca al sexo privilegiado.

Solicitando inmigracion como un elemento de bienestar y prosperidad para el país, ciertamente que no solo se busca el concurso de las fuerzas materiales, pues las intelectuales son de tanto ó mas valor, que ellas, para hacer floreciente y respetada á una nación. Y esto supuesto ¿es razonable que se dejen en la inercia y el abandono tantas inteligencias que pudieran utilizarse en servicio del bien público y del particular del individuo? ¿Es justo acaso que á seres dotados de una alma inmortal, que aspira á perfeccionarse, se les sujete á una perpétua infancia sin llegar á adquirir nunca su legitimo y natural desarrollo?

Ciertamente que la cultura y el trabajo ya sea manual ó intelectual, solo pueden ser considerados como elementos que deben contribuir á formar la felicidad de la muger; pero que nunca pueden completarla ni menos aun destruir esa irresistible inclinacion que impele á ambos sexos á reunirse, porque ambos son parte de un todo que el matrimonio completa, formando el perfecto ser humano en conformidad con la idea de su divino Hacedor.

Siempre quedará un inmenso vacío que solo Dios podrá llenar en el corazon de las que su fatal destino condene á no conocer jamás los puros goces, las santas fruiciones de esposa y madre, pero para los males del alma, lo mismo que para los del cuerpo, si no se encuentra el remedio que pueda curarlos radicalmente, debe á lo menos buscarse el que, aliviándolos, los haga mas soportables.

Para esos pobres seres condenados á un perpétuo aislamiento, es justamente para los que el trabajo seria un bien mayor y un recurso salvador, y para ellos lo pedimos con mayor instancia.

Dése interés á esas vidas que languidecen en una forzada inercia. Utilícese esa actividad, que bien dirigida puede rendir ópimos frutos. Ábranse nuevos horizontes á las que la injusticia irreflexiva, vilipendia y casi escluye de la comunion social.

Que al perder la esperanza de unir su destino al de un hombre que pudiera labrar su felicidad, no se marque á la inocente víctima de la suerte con el estigma de la burla y el desprecio.

Que no se la condene á una muerte moral tan inmerecida y tanto mas terrible, cuanto que es indefinida.

Que no se la reduzca á la triste condicion de pária de la humanidad.

Si la sociedad fuera justa en sus fallos, el desden y el sarcasmo que emplea con la muger forzadamente célibe, deberia hacerlos recaer y con mayor acritud sobre el hombre que se conserva indefinidamente en tal estado, porque á éste solo el desórden de sus pasiones y un frio egoismo y pésimo cálculo, han podido impedirle que formando una familia llene la misión que el mismo Dios le ha impuesto.

Ojalá que estas consideraciones, que tan desaliñadamente y tan á la ligera apuntamos, pero cuya exactitud nadie podrá negar, lográran fijar la atencion de los padres celosos de la felicidad de sus hijos y los indujeran á tentar una reforma en la educación de la muger.

Ojalá que meditaran sobre el inmenso beneficio que para ella seria en cualquier estado que el porvenir le reserve, si siendo opulenta tuviera una fructuosa ocupacion para distraer sus ocios, si poseyendo una escasa fortuna pudiera acrecentarla para sí ó unir sus esfuerzos á los de su esposo, si lo tiene, para aumentar el bienestar comun, y por último si perteneciendo á la clase pobre ó desheredada pudiera, con ayuda de un inteligente trabajo, hacer mas llevadera la pesada carga de la miseria.

Cuántos bienes se la procurarian si tal sucediera, y de cuántos males se la libertaria!

Teniendo una honrosa ocupacion que la libertara de los azares de la miseria ó del hastío de una vida estéril por falta de un objeto digno que la llene, esperaria tranquila que se presentara el hombre, que, reuniendo las cualidades que ella pudiera apetecer, fuera acreedor á que le entregara sin reserva su corazón y le confiara la felicidad de su vida entera.

Entonces no se apresuraria á aceptar el primer partido que se le presentara, si al dar su mano, su alma hubiera de permanecer insensible ó indiferente á las tiernas afecciones conyugales.

Tal vez entonces no serian tan frecuentes esos matrimonios llamados de razon ó mas bien de conveniencia, que se arreglan por medio de operaciones aritméticas y en los cuales el corazón, como que es ignorante en cálculo, para nada es consultado.

Y acaso desaparecerían esos repugnantes enlaces que no titubeamos en llamar inmorales, de viejos, que casi tocan en la decrepitud, con jóvenes lozanas, que encontrándose en la primavera de la vida, se sacrifican por huir de la miseria porque carecen á la vez de fortuna y de medios honrados y dignos de adquirir la subsistencia.

De ese modo la que tuviera la desgracia de perder con su esposo su sosten y el de sus tiernos hijos, no se veria precisada, tal vez, á mendigar el pan para su alimento ó á prostituirse por huir de la miseria y el desamparo. Apelaría á sus propios recursos y podria ganar su sustento y el de sus hijos, siendo pobre, ó conservaría y adelantaría su fortuna sin tener que recurrir á extraño é inseguro apoyo.

Si al hombre fuerte se cree necesario darle armas para combatir en la penosa campaña de la vida, con cuanta mayor razon la débil muger ha de necesitarlas para que no sucumba y desfallesca [sic]? Se nos dirá que no las ha menester porque en el hombre encuentra el natural apoyo de su debilidad. Pero no nos cansaremos de repetirlo, ese apoyo es incierto y eventual y de ello dan testimonio tantas y tan innumerables huérfanas, viudas y solteras que gimen en el mas completo desamparo ó comen el duro pan de una forzada caridad.

Muchos padres amantes y previsores buscan en las compañias de seguros el medio de afianzar el porvenir de sus hijos. Cuánto mas garantido quedaria éste si se les proveyera de los medios para asegurarlo por sí mismos y hacer frente á las eventualidades de la fortuna ó del destino!

Cuánto ganarian la moral y el progreso sociales, si á la muger se le educara, no solo para esposa, sino tambien para miembro útil de la sociedad á que pertenece!

Cuánto no ganaria la sociedad si se tratára de obtener algun fruto de esas inteligencias que con harta frecuencia, por desgracia, se esterilizan, rindiendo culto á los estravagantes caprichos de la moda ó entregándose por completo á las vanas fórmulas de un exagerado misticismo.

En nombre de tan sagrados intereses, levantamos nuestra humilde voz pidiendo: Trabajo para la muger.

Notas

1. Ricardo Palma (1833–1919). Político y escritor, creador de las llamadas *tradiciones peruanas*, cuentos históricos que se basaban en la época colonial del Perú. Alcanzó gran fama con este género. Era muy amigo de Juana Manuela Gorriti y de su círculo femenino, y participaba activamente en sus *veladas literarias*.

Work for Women

BY SEÑORA TERESA GONZÁLEZ DE FANNING
(MARÍA DE LA LUZ) READ BY RICARDO PALMA[1]

A nation is that much farther down the road to progress the greater the sum of morality, liberty and culture at the disposal of the people who compose it, in order to attain all the development and perfectibility of which these people are capable.

Using this generally accepted truth as our bastion, let us examine, even though very briefly, one of the aspects of the moral situation of women in our society, and, to claim for her, not emancipation, not the exercise of political rights, but pure and simply the exercise of the sacred right to work. We hold to the hope that all generous hearts will rally to our point of view, and in favor of the poor slave of her own ignorance and of old, entrenched prejudices.

To begin, let us enter, albeit only by means of our imagination, the home where a newborn has just seen the light of day, and we will observe that if it is a boy, the father welcomes him with proud satisfaction, and the entire family receives him like a gift from Heaven. But if it is a girl, what a disappointment! She is considered a new burden for the family, and even the tender mother who loves the fruit of her womb is saddened at the thought that there is one more unfortunate soul who has come to bear life's sufferings, and whose fate is doubly uncertain and chancy because of the sex to which she belongs.

From an early age the boy presents his parents with greater difficulties to overcome: in general he tends to be more stubborn, more difficult to lead; his education is incomparably more expensive, but his sex makes him deserving, so that even at the cost of sacrifices an attempt is made to give him not only the best education possible, but, above and beyond, a profession which, by protecting him against the vicissitudes of fate, will simultaneously make him a useful member of society and of the family.

Women's education is much easier and restricted. For her the future holds only two possible paths: the convent, which today is already almost done away with, and marriage. She is educated exclusively toward this end, or at least that is the guiding principle toward which she orients her aspirations.

Undoubtedly motherhood within matrimony is the most sacred mission a woman can perform on earth, and one of the principal reasons for her creation, but it is also true that in order to fulfill this goal her [own] will comes in only partially, in a secondary way, and it is not right—nor can it be—that her happiness and her future should come to depend exclusively on causes that up to a certain point are, as we plan to demonstrate, independent of her will.

No one will deny to us that it is the man who has the prerogative of choosing his mate, and only when he has decided he wants to bind his fate does he solicit the consent of the woman he has chosen; as social indulgence absolves him so easily of the sins he commits against morality, it is rare for a man to rush to exchange the independence and easy pleasures of his celibate state for the serious responsibilities and the indissolubility of marriage.

The woman, although by nature more sensitive than the man, sees herself forced to restrain her heart's most passionate impulses.

Love, that sweet, spontaneous feeling which makes life poetic and is there in the essence of our being, has her feel its powerful influence in vain: she must carefully hide it, or risk exposing herself to mockery, perhaps even from the very man who inspires [this feeling] in her, and who would hardly allow his right to take the initiative (which custom has granted him) to be taken from him.

It is not necessary to consult statistics: simple observation is enough to show that especially in this capital city, there is a discrepancy between the number of marriages and the number of inhabitants. If to this you add the higher mortality rate of men because of war, alcohol abuse and many other causes, one can see why perforce there are a large number of women in states of widowhood or perpetual spinsterhood.

These unfortunate victims of fate, while awaiting the satisfaction of their just aspirations by the arrival of the Messiah who had been promised them, see their youth fade and reach the age of thirty, which, if for a man (in the words of a Spanish poet), is the "doomed age of bitter disillusion," for the single woman it marks the grave of her dreams and aspirations.

Even if she still feels the fullness of life, the future for her is an arid desert without a single oasis which offers repose. Like the reckless gambler who has staked his entire fortune on one card, and who, when he sees that all is lost, feels himself in a bottomless pit, so she, who has invested all her luck in the concept of marriage and sees this fade, feels mortally wounded and disoriented, with no idea which path best to take.

The world, which earlier might have embraced her with compliments and rewards when she was still endowed with the seductive graces of early youth, now greets her coldly, when it is not pursuing her with mockery and sarcasm because she has joined the ranks of the old maids, and all feel entitled to ridicule her.

When a woman loses the parents who are her natural support, she becomes a guest in a strange household without being afforded the pleasure of independence because education and custom unite to take it from her. And woe to her who tries to defy social custom! Besides the problems she would have because of isolation, she exposes her honor to the poisonous attacks of slander, always eager to feed on a woman's honor.

If, soured by disappointment and weary of living, a woman seeks ultimate recourse in religion, if she is partially successful in alleviating her anxieties and filling the emptiness of her existence, she garners for herself the scornful epithet of being overly pious, and this, on top of being an old maid, is enough to make of her a disagreeable and repulsive human being, especially for those who are myopic of spirit and have no way of understanding the agonies of the soul.

This, in broad strokes, is the future which awaits many women who are in no way deficient in merit or virtue or clear intelligence, which, were it cultivated, could be utilized to benefit the society to which they belong, and of which they come to be paralyzed members because they are condemned to absolute sterility and perpetual dependence: the dependence of weakness multiplied a hundredfold by ignorance.

A great deal has already been written, and we grant to some effect, about the need and usefulness of expanding a woman's education. While agreeing with those same ideas, we will for now limit ourselves to asking that she, just like a man, be taught some skill, profession or occupation suitable to her sex and social position, which, while it engages and develops her intellect, simultaneously gives her a certain degree of independence to which she has the right to aspire, above all when she lacks the support of the stronger being who should be at her side on the painful pilgrimage of life.

As we are directing our remarks especially to people of good intentions and sound judgment, we will not waste time combating the foolish notion that a woman is born solely to take care of domestic chores, and that giving her an education and cultivating her intelligence will lead to their neglect. To admit this would relegate her to a level not far above that of beasts of burden and domestic animals.

Nor is a woman's weakness an excuse to deny her the right to work. Not all professions demand physical strength, and with respect to moral fortitude, it has been adequately proven that she possesses it.

It could well be said that the power and range of a woman's intellect is as yet unknown, as practically no one has bothered furthering it outside of very narrow limits. Nevertheless, in all ages there have been examples, albeit isolated ones, of brilliant proof that this intellect exists. We will forgo citing examples because, besides becoming wordy, we would repeat what everyone already knows.

It would be foolhardy to attempt to classify intelligence by gender and blindly give preference to that of the man; although he has some qualities which make him superior, a woman's intellect, on the other hand, surpasses his in many other ways. If one compared the intellect of an uncultured man with that of a moderately educated woman, the former would not have advantage on his side, however much he belonged to the privileged sex.

When looking to immigration as a means to the prosperity and well-being of a nation, one certainly would not look solely for physical strength, as intellectual power is worth as much or more in order to make a nation flourish and earn respect. And this being so, does it make sense to leave so many minds in a state of inertia and abandonment when these might be put to use in the service of both the public and the private good of the individual? Can it be right that human beings endowed with an immortal soul which aspires to perfect itself, should be subjected to perennial infancy without ever attaining their legitimate and natural development?

Certainly culture and work, be it manual or intellectual, can only be considered elements which should contribute to forming a woman's happiness, but they can never completely fulfill her, much less destroy the irresistible inclination that impels the sexes to unite, for both are part of a whole that is completed by marriage, forming the perfect human being in conformity with the idea of his divine Maker.

A huge void only God can fill will always remain in the hearts of those women whose fatal destiny has condemned them never to know the pure pleasures, the sacred fulfillment of wife and mother, but if no remedy can be found to radically cure these ills of the soul as well as of the body, one should at least seek out the balm which, by alleviating them, makes life more bearable.

It is precisely for those poor beings condemned to perpetual isolation that work would be a great good and a saving resource, and we plead for this on their behalf with mounting insistence.

Give interest to lives that languish in forced inertia. Make use of this activity, which, if well directed, will yield abundant fruit. Open new horizons to those women whom unthinking injustice insults, and practically excludes from social association.

When a woman loses hope of uniting her fate to that of a man who could make her happy, don't let the innocent victim of chance be branded with the stigma of mockery and scorn.

Don't let her be condemned to such an undeserved moral death which is that much worse for being indefinite.

Let her not be reduced to the sad condition of a pariah of humankind.

If society were just in its verdicts, the disdain and sarcasm directed against the woman who is forced to be unmarried, should come down even more harshly on the man who remains indefinitely in this state, because only the disorder of his passions, a cold egotism and extremely bad sense have prevented him from founding a family, and thereby fulfilling the mission that God Himself imposed on him.

Hopefully these remarks, which we are penning in so superficial and disorganized a fashion, but whose truth no one can deny, will succeed in attracting the attention of those parents who are concerned about their children's happiness, and will induce them to attempt a reform in women's education.

Let us hope that they will think about the enormous benefit this would mean to [their daughter], in whatever position the future might hold for her—should she be rich, she would have a useful occupation to fill her leisure hours, and if she has a meager fortune she can make it grow for herself or join her efforts to those of her husband, should she have one, in order to augment their common welfare, and last, should she belong to the poor or disinherited class she could, with the aid of intelligent work, make the heavy burden of poverty more bearable.

How much good could be accomplished if this were to happen, and from how much evil it would rescue her!

Were she to have an honest occupation that would free her from the vicissitiudes of poverty or the boredom of a life that has become sterile for lack of the right person to fulfill it, she could wait calmly for the right man to come along, one who possessed the qualities that appealed to her, and who would be the deserving recipient to whom she would unreservedly surrender her heart and entrust the happiness of an entire life.

Then she would not rush to accept the first man who came along, to whom, if she gave her hand, her soul would remain insensitive or indifferent to tender conjugal affections.

Perhaps then we would not have so many so-called arranged marriages, or, better still, "marriages of convenience," which are agreed upon on the basis of mathematical computations and in which the heart, as it is ignorant of calculation, is in no way consulted.

And then perhaps those ghastly marriages would disappear which we do not hesitate to call immoral, between old men, who are practically decrepit, with lovely young women in the springtime of life, who sacrifice themselves to flee from poverty because they have neither money nor any means of earning a living which are either honorable or suitable.

In this way, a woman who might have the misfortune of losing her husband, and with him the support of herself and her children, would perhaps not see herself forced to beg for her daily bread or to prostitute herself in order to escape poverty and homelessness. She could call upon her own resources and, if she were poor, could earn a living for herself and her children, or maintain and increment her fortune without having to rely on outside or uncertain support.

If people think it necessary to give the strong man arms to fight in the hard campaign of life, with what greater reason does a weak woman have need of them so that she will not succumb and perish! We will be told that she doesn't need them because in a man she will find the natural support for her weakness. But we do not tire of repeating that this support is uncertain and chancy, and the proof thereof are the innumerable orphans, widows and spinsters who weep in the most desperate circumstances, or eat the bitter crust of forced charity.

Many loving and farsighted parents look to insurance companies for the means to secure their children's future. How much more secure the latter would be if the children were given the means to secure it for themselves and face the vicissitudes of fortune or destiny!

How much social morality and progress would gain if a woman were educated, not only to be a wife, but also a useful member of the society to which she belongs!

How much society would profit if it attempted to gain some benefit from those minds which unfortunately so often become sterile, either worshiping extravagant whims of fashion or surrendering completely to empty formulas of exaggerated mysticism.

In the name of such sacred interests we lift our humble voice to plead: Give women work.

Notes

1. Ricardo Palma (1833–1919) was a politician and writer who invented the genre known as *Peruvian traditions*, short stories based on Peru's colonial past. He became very famous because of these stories. He was a good friend of Juana Manuela Gorriti's and of her circle of women friends, and participated actively in her literary salon.

Soledad Acosta de Samper

Soledad Acosta de Samper, courtesy of Biblioteca Luis Angel Arango, Bogotá.

Soledad Acosta de Samper is an author waiting to be discovered. One of the most prolific women writers of the nineteenth century, few readers outside of her native Colombia know her name, but it is hoped that this will change in the future.

Her background is both international and distinguished. Born in Bogotá in 1833, she was the only child of Joaquín Acosta, a general and Colombian patriot of the wars of independence, and of Caroline Kemble, of Scottish ancestry. She spent her youth not only in Colombia but also in Ecuador, Washington, D.C., Halifax, Nova Scotia (where her grandmother lived), and Paris, where she was educated and lived for five years. Acosta de Samper was thus at least trilingual, and much better educated than most Colombian women of her time. In 1855 she married José María Samper, a politician, journalist, and prolific writer, and became the mother of four daughters. The family spent more time in Europe and also in Lima, Peru, where Acosta de Samper founded a journal, then returned to Colombia. Two of the daughters later died in an epidemic, and her husband died in 1888, but her active writing career was never interrupted. At one time, when her husband was away on national business, the government confiscated his printing press and the family home. Acosta de Samper kept herself and her children solvent by writing (Otero Muñoz 373). She died in 1913.

Her literary production is astounding, and there is doubtless more that has not been officially cataloged, as she often wrote under pseudonyms and published mainly in newspapers and journals, many of which have likely been lost. According to Flor María Rodríguez-Arenas, her salvaged works form a corpus of 192 texts: 37 novels, 49 short stories, 59 studies, essays, and articles, 21 historical works, 4 plays, 12 travel narratives, 5 journals founded and directed by her, plus

10 translations of essays and novels from English, French, and German (137 n. 2). Paulina Encinales de Sanjinés has shown that in spite of a conservative, moralistic, and religious frame of mind, Acosta de Samper nevertheless did her share to highlight women's participation in Colombia's nation building, sharing González de Fanning's feelings about the need to train women to work and to strive for personal independence:

> Only those who try to degrade the feminine sex in order to debase it, have been able to advance the absurd idea that a woman's only function is to adorn her husband's home. The working-class woman (and even she who belongs to the upper classes) should always learn a lucrative and useful occupation by means of which she might at any time earn a living, so that she knows that she is free and in no way dependent on a man's work. (232 n. 13)

Although Soledad Acosta de Samper belonged to the social and intellectual elite of Colombia (and lived into the twentieth century), during her lifetime it was still extremely difficult for a woman to publish a book in her country. Her husband, José María, obviously very proud of his wife, urged her to collect some of her prose fiction and had it published in Belgium. This collection, *Novelas y cuadros de la vida sur-americana,* came out in Ghent in 1869 and contained the story "Dolores." Apparently the latter was translated into English as *Dolores: The Story of a Leper,* but we do not know when, and to date no one has located this text. For this reason I have done a new translation and have included it in this anthology.

In an effort to get Acosta de Samper better known, some of her works were republished in Colombia in 1988 by the Fondo Cultural Cafetero in a volume entitled *Soledad Acosta de Samper: Una nueva lectura.* It contains an excellent introduction by Montserrat Ordóñez, some critical studies, and a bibliography of Doña Soledad's works, which give the reader an overview of the astounding scope of her interests. Rodríguez-Arenas published an extensive study of Acosta de Samper in 1991, but there is little available on her in English.

"Dolores" is an amazing story, one well worth knowing and appreciating. The content itself is riveting: a beautiful, upper-class young woman—the ideal romantic heroine—contracts leprosy and, after a number of years in which the disease ravages her body and mind, dies. Leprosy was a disease that in Samper's time had a symbolic/moral charge very like AIDS does today, and it is still prevalent in South America. (Gabriel García Márquez and Mario Vargas Llosa mention lepers in their fiction.) Both the Old and the New Testament speak of leprosy and lepers. It was a common disease in Europe but began to disappear on that continent in the sixteenth century. In the Middle Ages it was considered the outward manifestation of an inner corruption of the soul, and lepers were cast out of society to wait for death alone. As Susan Sontag observed, "Nothing is more punitive than to give a disease a meaning—that meaning being invariably a moralistic one" (58). The bacillus that causes leprosy was discovered by the Norwegian Armauer Hansen in 1873–74, shortly before "Dolores" was published, but Acosta de Samper appears to be unaware of this medical breakthrough, for in her story leprosy, although known to be contagious, is primarily considered hereditary.

What we encounter in this text is the radical deconstruction by illness of a beautiful female body, a woman's ultimate marginalization from society, and a surprisingly modern description of the way the human mind copes with terminal illness. Acosta de Samper is skilled in evoking the psychological journey this entails and shows us how this process can, to some degree, even become a liberating one for the doomed heroine (Rodríguez-Arenas 144–47). Not only the plot, but the style in which the story was written, is unusual. Ordóñez points out the stylistic modernity of Acosta de Samper's fragmented narrative, using alternating male and female narrators and interweaving letters and diaries written by the protagonist (*Una nueva lectura* 22).

"Dolores" first appeared in a journal in 1867, the same year that Jorge Isaacs published *María,* Colombia's most important historical romance, and to date one of the most popular novels in all of Latin America (Sommer 172). It is interesting that both novels deal with a woman's terminal illness, a topic of much interest in nineteenth-century Western fiction. Sontag notes that this literature "is stocked with descriptions of almost symptomless, unfrightened, beatific deaths" (15) where "the actual agony is simply suppressed" (29) and "the ultra-virtuous . . . boost[ed] themselves to new moral heights" (41). In a related vein, the critic Lucía Guerra Cunningham observed that "illness should be considered an attribute which beautifies the submissive, weak body to the law of the father and of the husband" (355). The gendered treatment of the terminally ill heroine differs markedly in the works of Isaacs and Acosta de Samper. María, who suffers from epilepsy, expires wordlessly and beautifully within the bosom of her adopted family, whereas Dolores, a social outcast and thus completely alone, records in her diary wild mood swings brought on by the hideous deformation of her body, rage at the Almighty and at her fate, and personal liberation via the writing of her story. In retrospect, it is Acosta de Samper's text that is the more complex and the more compelling for the modern reader, in terms of both content and narrative style.

Dolores
Cuadros de la vida de una mujer

La nature est un drame avec des personnages.[1]

Victor Hugo

—¡Qué linda muchacha! exclamó Antonio al ver pasar por la mitad de la plaza de la aldea de N★★★ algunas personas a caballo, que llegaban de una hacienda con el objeto de asistir a las fiestas del lugar, señaladas para el día siguiente.

Antonio González era mi condiscípulo y el amigo predilecto de mi juventud. Al despedirnos en la Universidad, graduados ambos de doctores, me ofreció visitarme en mi pueblo en la época de las fiestas parroquiales, y con tal fin había llegado el día anterior a N★★★. Deseosos ambos de divertirnos, dirigíamos, con el entusiasmo de la primera juventud, que en todo halla interés, la construcción de las barreras en la plaza para las corridas de toros del siguiente día. A ese tiempo pasó, como antes dije, un grupo de gente a caballo, enmedio del cual lucía, como un precioso lirio enmedio de un campo, la flor más bella de aquellas comarcas, mi prima Dolores.

—Lo que más me admira, añadió Antonio, es la cutis tan blanca y el color tan suave, como no se ven en estos climas ardientes.

Efectivamente, los negros ojos de Dolores y su cabellera de azabache hacían contraste con lo sonrosado de su tez y el carmín de sus labios.

—Es cierto lo que dice usted, exclamó mi padre que se hallaba a mi lado; la cutis de Dolores no es natural en este clima . . . ¡Dios mío! dijo con acento conmovido un momento después, yo no había pensado en eso antes.

Antonio y yo no comprendimos la exclamación del anciano. Años después recordábamos la impresión que nos causó aquel temor vago, que nos pareció tan extraño . . .

Mi padre era el médico de N★★★ y en cualquier centro más civilizado se hubiera hecho notar por su ciencia práctica y su caridad. Al contrario de lo que generalmente sucede, él siempre había querido que yo siguiese su misma profesión, con la esperanza, decía, de que fuese un médico más ilustrado que él.

Hijo único, satisfecho con mi suerte, mimado por mi padre y muy querido por una numerosa parentela, siempre me había considerado muy feliz. Me hallaba entonces en N★★★ tan sólo de paso, arreglando algunos negocios para poder verificar pronto mi unión con una señorita a quien había conocido y amado en Bogotá.

Entre todos mis parientes la tía Juana, señora muy respetable y acaudalada, siempre me había preferido, cuidando y protegiendo mi niñez desde que perdí a mi madre. Dolores, hija de una hermana suya, vivía a su lado hacía algunos años, pues era huérfana de padre y madre. La tía Juana dividía su cariño entre sus dos sobrinos predilectos.

Apenas llegamos a una edad en que se piensa en esas cosas, Dolores y yo comprendimos que el deseo de la buena señora era determinar un enlace entre los dos; pero la naturaleza humana prefiere las dificultades al camino trillado, y ambos procurábamos manifestar tácitamente que nuestro mutuo cariño era solamente fraternal. Creo que el deseo de imposibilitar enteramente ese proyecto contribuyó a que sin vacilar me comprometiese a casarme en Bogotá, y cuando todavía era un estudiante sin porvenir. Considerando a Dolores como una hermana, desde que fui al colegio le escribía frecuentemente y le refería las penas y percances de mi vida de colegial, y después mis esperanzas de joven y de novio.

Esta corta reseña era indispensable para la inteligencia de mi sencilla relación.

Después de permanecer en la plaza algunos momentos más, volvimos a casa. La vivienda de mi padre estaba a alguna distancia del pueblo; pero como se anunciaban fuegos artificiales para la noche, Antonio y yo resolvimos volver al poblado poco antes de que se empezara esta diversión popular.

La luna iluminaba el paisaje. Un céfiro tibio y delicioso hacía balancear los árboles y arrancaba a las flores su perfume. Los pajarillos se despertaban con la luz de la luna y dejaban oír un tierno murmullo, mientras que el filósofo buho, siempre taciturno y disgustado, se quejaba con su grito de mal agüero.

Antonio y yo teníamos que atravesar un potrero y cruzar el camino real antes de llegar a la plaza de N★★★. Conversábamos alegremente de nuestras esperanzas y nuestra futura suerte, porque lo futuro para la juventud es siempre sinónimo de dichas y esperanzas colmadas! Antonio había elegido la carrera más ardua, pero también la más brillante, de abogado, y su claro talento y fácil elocuencia le prometían un bello porvenir. Yo pensaba, después de hacer algunos estudios prácticos con uno de los facultativos de más fama, casarme y volver a mi pueblo a gozar de la vida tranquila del campo. Forzoso es confesar que N★★★ no era sino una aldea grande, no obstante el enojo que a sus vecinos causaba el oirla llamar así, pues tenía sus aires de ciudad y poseía en ese tiempo jefe político, jueces, cabildo y demás tren de gobierno local. Desgraciadamente ese tren y ese tono le producían infinitas molestias, como le sucedería a una pobre campesina que, enseñada a andar descalza y usar enaguas cortas, se pusiese de repente botines de tacón, corsé y crinolina. . . .

Antonio y yo nos acercamos a la casa de la tía Juana que, situada en la plaza, era la mejor del pueblo. En la puerta y sentadas sobre silletas recostadas contra la pared, reían y conversaban muchas de las señoritas del lugar, mientras que las madres y señoras respetables estaban adentro discutiendo cuestiones más graves, es decir, enfermedades, víveres y criadas. Los *cachacos*[2] del lugar y los de otras partes que habían ido a las fiestas, pasaban y repasaban por frente a la puerta sin atreverse a acercarse a las muchachas, que gozaban de su imperio y atractivo sin mostrar el interés con que los miraban.

Me acerqué a la falange femenina con todo el ánimo que me inspiraba el haber llegado de Bogotá, grande recomendación en las provincias, y la persuación de ser bien recibido como pariente. Presenté mi amigo a las personas reunidas dentro y fuera de las casa, y tomando asientos salimos a conversar con las muchachas. . . .

Propuse entonces que fuéramos todos los que estábamos reunidos en casa de la tía Juana a dar una vuelta por la plaza.

La tropa femenina se formó en columna y los del sexo feo, desplegándonos en guerrilla, dábamos vuelta a su rededor. La simpatía es inexplicable siempre: en breve Antonio y Dolores se acercaron el uno al otro y trabaron al momento una alegre conversación.

La plaza estaba cubierta de mesas de diferentes juegos de lotería, *bisbis, pasa-diez, cachimona*, etc., en los que con la módica suma de un cuartillo se apuntaban todos aquellos que querían probar la suerte. En otras mesas y bajo de toldos algunos tomaban licores de toda especie: *chicha* de coco, *guarapo*, anisado, mistela, y hasta brandi y vino no muy puros; mientras que otros encontraban el *ideal* de sus aspiraciones en suculentos guisos, *ajiacos*, pavos asados y *lechonas* rellenas con ajos y cominos. Más lejos se veían orchatas, aguas de lulos, de moras, de piña, *guarruz* de maíz ye de arroz, que se presentaban en sus botellas tapadas con manojitos de claveles o rosas. Los bizcochuelos cubiertos con batido blanco o canela, los huevos *chimbos*, las frutas acarameladas, las cocadas, los panderos, las arepitas de diversas formas, y todo el conjunto de golosinas que lleva compendiosamente el nombre de colación, yacían en bandejas de varios tamaños y colores, en hileras sobre manteles toscos pero limpios. . . .

Después de haber inspeccionado las mesas de la plaza, en las cuales campeaba la alegría popular, nos dirigimos hacia un baile de *ñapangas*[3] o *cintureras*. Era tal la compostura de estas gentes, que las señoras gustaban ir a verlas bailar, sin temor de que sus modales pudiesen ser tachados. Se había anunciado este baile como muy ruidoso y en extremo concurrido; así fue que hallamos una multitud de curiosos que rodeaban la puerta o prendidos de las ventanas se asomaban a la sala. Sin embargo, al vernos llegar se hicieron a un lado, y las señoritas se situaron al pie de las ventanas y nosotros detrás de ellas. . . .

Las *ñapangas* vestían enaguas de fula azul con su arandela abajo, camisa bordada de rojo y negro, pañolón rojo o azul y sombrerito de paja fina con lazos de cinta ancha. Algunas se quitaban los sombreros para bailar y descubrían sus profusas cabelleras negras partidas en dos trenzas que caían por las espaldas terminando en lazos de cinta.

Los hombres, casi todos con pretensiones a ser los cachacos de la sociedad, fumaban y tomaban copitas de aguardiente, fraternizando con los músicos, quienes situados en la puerta interior de la sala templaban sus instrumentos.

—¡Arriba, don Basilio! exclamaron varias voces desde la puerta, al momento que empezaban a tocar un alegre *bambuco*: ¡la pareja lo aguarda!

Y todas las miradas se dirigieron a un hombre de unos cuarenta años, grueso, lampiño, de cara ancha, frente angosta y escurrida hacia atrás: su mirada torva y la costumbre de cerrar un ojo al hablar le daban un aire singularmente desagradable.

—Nos vamos a divertir esta noche si baila don Basilio, dijo Antonio.

—Cállate, le contesté, que si te oye no te perdonará jamás; ese hombre es presuntuoso y vengativo.

—Bailo, exclamó don Basilio con aire importante, si Julián me acompaña.

—¡Adelante, Julián! gritaron los cachacos; y sacando a Julián de enmedio de ellos los obligaron a que diera la mano a una alegre y desenvuelta *ñapanga*, cuyos negros ojuelos hacían contraste con un ramo de azahares que llevaba en la cabeza. Entre tanto don Basilio tiraba a otra de la mano diciéndole al oído palabras que la hicieron sonrojarse, y adelantándose con aire complacido se situó frente a ella y empezó a bailar el bambuco. La muchacha, joven y ligera, daba vueltas en torno de su pareja poniendo en ridículo el grueso talle y toscos ademanes de su galán, el cual parecía un enorme oso jugando con una gatita. Aunque afeminado y lleno de afectación, Julián formaba con la otra muchacha un cuadro más agradable.

Pero mientras acaban de bailar, digamos quiénes eran estos personajes, uno de los cuales figura en esta relación.

Basilio Flores era hijo de una pobre campesina de los alrededores de Bogotá. Su genio vivo y natural talento llamaron la atención a un rico hacendado en cuyo terreno su madre cultivaba su sementerilla de papas y maíz. El hacendado lo llevó a su casa y le enseñó a leer en sus ratos de ocio; y encantado con la facilidad que el muchacho tenía para aprender, se propuso sacar de él un buen dependiente, sobre quien pudiese, con el tiempo, descargar una parte de sus complicados negocios. Lo envió, pues, a un colegio en donde pronto hizo grandes adelantos. Tenía Basilio 18 años cuando estalló la guerra de la independencia, y el español que lo protegía creyó necesario emigrar. Antes de partir llamó al muchacho con mucho sigilo y le exigió bajo juramento que cuando se calmasen las revueltas públicas sacase una suma que había enterrado en un sitio de la casa de su habitación y que con ella lo fuese a buscar a España.

La situación del país impedía que se tuviese comunicación alguna con la madre patria, y enmedio de las emociones políticas que lo rodeaban el protegido del español seguramente olvidó la recomendación de su patrón. . . .

Cuando volvió a reinar alguna paz en el país se supo que, entre los españoles que habían salido prófugos, el patrón de Basilio, después de haber vagado por las costas de Colombia y enfermádose en las Antillas, apenas había tenido tiempo de llegar a España y morir sin dar sus últimas disposiciones. . . .

Basilio volvió a la capital diciendo haber heredado a [un] incógnito pariente, y haciendo alarde de su riqueza trató de introducirse en la sociedad distinguida, pero fue rechazado con desdén.

Disgustado, pero decidido a poner todos los medios que tenía a su alcance para hacer olvidar su origen, partió para Europa y permaneció algunos años en París. Sin relaciones ni disposición, se entregó a los vicios y acabó de corromper el escaso corazón con que la naturaleza lo había dotado. . . .

Resuelto a crearse una carrera brillante en su país, volvió con mil proyectos ambiciosos, y muy pronto se hicieron notar sus artículos en los periódicos de uno y otro partido. Poseía una memoria muy feliz, una instrucción regular y cierta elocuencia irónica, aunque superficial, con que se engaña fácilmente. Se firmaba B. de Miraflores, y decían que en París había pasado por *barón*. Hablaba francés e inglés con bastante corrección y siempre adornaba su conversación con frases y citas de autores extranjeros. Se vestía con un lujo extravagante y de mal gusto, y daba almuerzos en que desplegaba un boato charro con que alucinaba al vulgo.

Pero, desgraciadamente, si tenía memoria para algunas cosas la había perdido completamente para otras, y durante su viaje olvidó a la pobre madre, única persona que lloraba su ausencia. A su regreso de Europa no quiso verla ni dejarse visitar por ella (¡eso lo podría desacreditar!) pero fingiendo la generosidad que distingue a los nobles corazones, enviaba, por medio de un joven que le servía de *factotum*, una pensión mensual a "la pobre estanciera que le había servido de nodriza," según decía arqueando las cejas.

Deseando, al cabo de algunos años, *faire une fin*,[4] como él decía, propuso casamiento sucesivamente a las señoritas más ricas, bellas y virtuosas de Bogotá: naturalmente todas lo desdeñaron hiriendo su amor propio, lo que hizo recordar la famosa máxima de que: "de la calumnia siempre queda algo." Y tarde o temprano se vengó de ellas.

Desalentado en sus proyectos matrimoniales entró de lleno en la política; pero aquí también lo aguardaban desengaños. Sus antecedentes poco claros, su lenguaje acerbo y mordaz y sus malas costumbres lo hicieron despreciable entre los hombres de algún valer en todos los partidos. No pudiendo hacerse apreciar y admirar se hizo temible, y juró burlarse de la sociedad y vengarse de todos los que lo habían humillado. Se alió con los hombres más corrompidos de uno y otro partido y logró por medio de intrigas formarse cierta reputación entre los escritores públicos del país. . . .

La carrera política de nuestro héroe no podía ser completa si no agregaba un lauro más a su gloria: quería ser diputado. En las provincias del centro y del Magdalena era demasiado conocido para ser popular, y le aconsejaron que fuese a las provincias del Sur, donde podría ganarse a los lectores con algunos discursos *bien* sentidos. Este era el motivo que había llevado a *don* Basilio de Miraflores a mi pueblo, en el que se detuvo de paso al saber que se preparaban fiestas.

Julián era el tipo de cierta clase de cachacos que desgraciadamente se han hecho muy comunes en los últimos años; aumentando sus malas cualidades en cada generación y perdiendo las pocas buenas que los distinguían.

Hijo de un rico propietario de las provincias del Sur y educado en Bogotá, en cuyos colegios había permanecido siete años, no había sufrido nunca aquella heróica pobreza que forma el carácter del estudiante. Su tez blanca y rosada, su talle flexible y su mirada lánguida le habían granjeado la admiración de las señoritas de Bogotá, mientras que la riqueza conocida y la posición que ocupaba su familia le habían ganado el corazón de las madres de familia. Durante los siete años de colegio y los dos más en que permaneció *repasando* lo que había estudiado, como escribía a sus padres, aprendió a hablar algo en francés y tal cual frase en latín; de historia, sabía la de las novelas de Dumas; muy poco de filosofía y menos de geografía. . . . [B]ailaba todas las danzas conocidas y hablaba con gravedad del tedio de su existencia, de la pérdida de sus ilusiones y de su adolorido corazón; pero al ver la frescura de su fisonomía y la alegría de su aspecto, se comprendía que su salud no había sufrido con tamañas desgracias y tantas pérdidas irreparables. ...

Inspirado por el baile y la ruidosa música, don Basilio recordó los tiempos de su mocedad y adornó los últimos compases del bambuco con varios saltos en tosca imitación del *cancán* de los famosos bailes de "Mabille" y "Valentino."

—¡Bravo! le gritaron los cachacos, y al concluir se acercaron para ofrecerle una copa de licor por vía de refrescante. ...

En ese momento los instrumentos tocaron un valse del país y todos los jóvenes se apresuraron a sacar parejas entre las *ñapangas* más agraciadas. Algunos usaban ruana y todos bailaban con el sombrero puesto y el cigarro en la boca.

Las señoritas que acompañábamos miraban en silencio aquella escena, y se sentían naturalmente vejadas y chocadas al ver que los jóvenes que las visitaban eran tratados de igual a igual por aquellas mujeres.

—Vámonos, dijeron, y se quitaron de las ventanas.

Antonio y yo acompañamos a las señoras hasta sus respectivas casas y volvimos a tomar el camino de nuestra habitación.

El corazón tiene a veces presentimientos que no podemos explicarnos. No sé por qué la suerte de Dolores me preocupaba aquella noche: recordaba mil causas que debían hacerla feliz, y con todo no podía desechar una aprehensión sin motivo que me molestaba sin comprenderla. Antonio, por su parte, sentía los primeros síntomas de una gran pasión: las tempestades que se desarrollan en el corazón siempre se anuncian por un sentimiento de melancolía dolorosa. La dulzura del sentimiento no inspira sino cuando uno ha perdido ya el poder de voluntad y ama sin reflexionar.

Antonio sufría; yo me sentía triste, y ambos volvimos a casa en silencio.

En los días siguientes concurrimos a los encierros y corridas de toros y los bailes por la noche. Antonio se mostraba completamente subyugado por los encantos de Dolores, y cada vez que nos hallábamos juntos no se cansaba de elogiarme sus gracias y hermosura. Recuerdo que una vez casi se enfadó conmigo porque le cité riendo aquel proverbio latino: "No es la naturaleza la que hace bella a la mujer, sino nuestro amor."

Dolores recibía los homenajes de Antonio con su buen humor e inagotable alegría. Ella no podía estar nunca triste y perseguía con alegres chanzas a los que se mostraban melancólicos. Mi amigo correspondía a su genio vivo contestándole con mil chistes y agudezas propias del cachaco bogotano. El amor entre estos dos jóvenes era bello, puro y risueño como un día de primavera. En donde quiera que se reunían comunicaban su innata alegría a cuantos los rodeaban. No he visto nunca dos personas más adecuadas para amarse y saber apreciar sus mutuas cualidades. No hay duda que es un grave error el que encierra aquel axioma de que los contrastes simpatizan. Eso puede dar cierto brillo, animación y variedad a un sentimiento fugaz, a una inclinación pasajera; pero entre personas que aman verdaderamente es preciso una completa armonía, armonía en sentimientos, en educación, en posición social y en el fondo de las ideas. La tranquilidad moral es el resultado de la armonía, y ése debe ser el principal objeto del matrimonio, en lo que debe consistir su bello ideal.

Don Basilio pronto descubrió que Dolores, además de ser bella y virtuosa, poseía una dote regular, e inmediatamente puso sitio ante aquella nueva fortaleza; creyó que no sería mal *negocio* encontrar en su viaje una diputación y una novia. El caudal de su difunto *tío* empezaba a desaparecer muy de veras y no quería ver llegar la vejez unida a la pobreza. Le confió a Julián su propósito diciendo:—Una sencilla *villageoise* es una conquista fácil de obtener . . . Además es bella, y la podré presentar en Bogotá sin bochorno; y añadía con su acostumbrada fatuidad, citando a un autor francés: "Elle a d'assez beaux yeux . . . pour des yeux de province."[5]

—Pero, observaba Julián, ¿no ve usted que ya tiene un rival en Antonio?

—Mejor, mejor, joven inexperto ¿no sabe usted que el gran Corneille dijo:"A vaincre sans péril on triomphe sans gloire?"[6]

Un día le presentó a Dolores una composición rimada que le dedicaba, en la cual declaraba su ardiente amor en versos glaciales: tenía tantas citas que casi no se encontraba una palabra original; mezclaba la mitología con la historia antigua invocando a Venus y a Lucrecia, a Minerva y a Virginia, y acababa diciendo: "que, guiado por el destino, había montado en el Pegaso para caer a sus pies."[7] A instancias de la tía Juana, Dolores nos mostró a Antonio y mí la sonora composición, y naturalmente no escaseamos nuestras burlas.

Después de haber permanecido algunos días en N★★★ don Basilio siguió su marcha en busca de popularidad, bien persuadido de que allí no podría conseguir nada, y comprendiendo que Dolores le preparaba, si los provocaba, unos *nones* como los que él estaba enseñado a recibir. Fácil nos era ver que partía furioso con Antonio y yo, pues, no habíamos ocultado nuestras burlas, y que se prometía hacérnoslas pagar algún día.

Las fiestas se habían concluido. Cada cual de los que habían ido a ellas fueron dejando el lugar de uno en uno.

El día antes del de la partida de Antonio promoví un paseo en que debían reunirse las principales personas que se hallaban todavía en el pueblo. A algunas horas de N★★★ corre un caudaloso río sombreado por altísimos árboles, y muy cerca de él se halla la casa de un trapiche que ofrece recursos y lugar en que dejar las cabalgaduras. Este es el sitio predilecto de los que organizan los paseos de todas las inmediaciones.

A las siete de mañana, como veinte personas aguardábamos a la puerta de la casa de tía Juana a que saliera Dolores. Pronto se presentó ésta montada en un brioso caballo, con su traje largo, sombrerito redondo, velillo al viento, la mirada brillante y ademán gracioso. Después de atravesar bulliciosamente las calles tomamos un angosto camino orillando potreros, y allí se fueron formando grupos según las simpatías de cada uno. Yo dejé que Antonio buscase el lado de Dolores, acordándome de que no sé qué autor ha dicho que el tiempo más a propósito para una declaración es cuando uno anda a caballo. Y efectivamente, la animación del paseo, el aire libre que sopla en torno, la facultad de apurar o detener el caballo, de atrasarse, o adelantarse sin aparente motivo, de hablar o callar de repente, volver la cabeza o buscar la mirada de su compañera, todo esto da ánimo y presenta fácilmente ocasiones de aislarse aún enmedio de una numerosa concurrencia. Sin embargo, Antonio callaba ese día, y la fisonomía de ambos se velaba por momentos con una dulce melancolía; acaso porque pensaban que debían separarse aquella tarde.

Acompañamos a las señoras hasta la orilla del río, y mientras que ellas se bañaban, nos reunimos en el trapiche conversando y riendo alegremente. Antonio no recobró, sin embargo, animación hasta que nos volvimos a reunir todos con la parte femenina de la concurrencia en el punto en que se había preparado el almuerzo. El campo estaba bellísimo: la fragancia de las flores, el susurro de los insectos, el murmurante río que bajaba entre lucientes piedras a nuestro lado, el rumor del viento entre las hojas de los árboles que se balanceaban sobre nuestras cabezas, y toda aquella vida y movimiento de la naturaleza tropical, nos hacían gozar y convidaban al reposo y a la dicha perezosa del vivir . . . Antonio y Dolores se habían alejado insensiblemente de los demás y se sentaron al pie de una gran piedra cubierta de amarillento musgo. Dolores tiraba al río con distracción los pétalos de un ramo de flores que llevaba en la mano; y mientras que el agua salpicaba la dorada arena a su pies, ambos miraban con interés la suerte de aquellas florecillas en la espumosa corriente. Algunas bajaban lentamente y se detenían muy pronto sobre la blanda orilla: otras, arrastradas con ímpetu por el agua, se engolfaban de improviso en un remolino y desaparecían al punto: otras salían al principio con rapidez y alegremente, pero al llegar a una concavidad formada por las piedras, tropezaban allí y no pudiendo salir, se impregnaban de agua y se consumían poco a poco; por último, las más afortunadas se unían en grupos y salían a la mitad del río, descendiendo por medio de la corriente sin encontrar tropiezo alguno.

—¿Ven ustedes la filosofía de ese espectáculo? dije acercándome de improviso a los dos.

Antonio y Dolores se estremecieron como si se los hubiera interrumpido; y en efecto, ellos se comunicaban sus pensamientos con una mirada y se hablaban en su mismo silencio.

—¿Qué filosofía? preguntaron.

—La que encierra esa flor que Dolores tira a la corriente. Ella es la imagen de la Providencia y cada uno de esos pétalos lo es de una vida humana. ¿Cuál suerte preferirías tú, Dolores? La de las que pronto se retiran a la playa sin haber tenido emociones; la de las que se precipitan a la corriente y se pierden en un remolino . . .

—¿Yo? . . . no sé. Pero las que me causan pena son aquellas que se encuentran encerradaas en un sitio aislado y sin esperanza de salir . . . Mira, añadió, cómo se van hundiendo poco a poco y como a pesar suyo.

—Yo, decididamente, señor filósofo, dijo Antonio fijando la mirada en la de Dolores, prefiero la suerte de las que bajan de dos en dos por la corriente de la vida.

Las mejillas de mi prima se cubrieron de carmín y levantándose turbada se unió a los demás grupos de amigas.

Las risas y conversaciones, los cantos y armonía de los tiples y bandolas, el baile en el patio del trapiche y el buen humor general, nada de esto pudo animar a Dolores. Estaba contenta, dichosa tal vez por momentos, pero se veía en su frente una sombra y cierta modulación dolorosa suavizaba el timbre de su voz. Antonio estaba en aquella situación en que los enamorados se vuelven taciturnos y atolondrados, sin poder hacer otra cosa que contemplar el objeto amado, sin poder atender sino a lo que *ella* dice, ni admirar a otra persona u objeto; estado de ánimo sumamente fastidioso para todos, menos para la que inspira y comprende tal situación.

Volvimos al pueblo por la noche; estaba muy oscura no obstante que las estrellas lucían en el despejado cielo. Al atravesar un riachuelo en un punto peligroso se creyó necesario que cada hombre fuese al lado de una señora. El caballo de Dolores se asustó al resbalar en las piedras, y si Antonio no la hubiese sostenido con un brazo y afirmándola nuevamente en el galápago, al brincar el caballo la habría hecho caer al agua. Cuando Antonio se encontró nuevamente en tierra, seguramente se le conoció el susto y la emoción que había sentido en aquel lance, y su voz temblaba al contestar a mi pregunta. Entonces comprendí cuán verdadera y tiernamente amaba a Dolores. El amor sincero no es egoísta; y nunca es más cobarde el corazón que cuando la persona amada está en peligro, aunque éste parezca insignificante para los demás.

¡Media hora después se separaron, tal vez para simpre, aquellos dos seres que habían nacido para amarse tan profundamente!

Luego a solas me confió Antonio que no había podido hablar a Dolores de su amor, que siendo tan vehemente y elevado, no había hallado palabras con que expresarlo. Me rogó que le dijera a mi prima en nombre suyo que no había pedido su mano formalmente porque su posición no se lo permitía aún; pero teniendo esperanzas de ser correspondido me pedía la suplicara que no lo olvidase.

El mismo día que partió Antonio para Bogotá, la tía Juana volvió a su hacienda con Dolores. Yo había visto la despedida de Dolores y Antonio, y aunque ella tenía la sonrisa en los labios comprendí que necesitaría algún consuelo. Así, al domingo siguiente me dirigí muy temprano a la hacienda, llamada Primavera, situada en una llanura al pie de altos cerros cubiertos de bosques y vestida principalmente de ganados y extensos cacaotales.

Cuando llegué, mi tía estaba ausente y la casa completamente silenciosa. Me desmonté y entregando mi caballo a un sirviente, atravesé el patio que antecedía a la casa y me dirigí al retrete de Dolores en el cual me dijeron se encontraba.

El sitio favorito de mi prima era un ancho corredor hacia la parte de atrás de la casa y con vista sobre una semi-huerta, semi-jardín. . . . La pajarera de Dolores era afamada en los alrededores: en una gran jaula que ocupaba todo el ángulo del corredor había reunido muchos pájaros de diversos climas, que se habían enseñado a vivir unidos y en paz. . . . Enmedio de sus flores y pájaros Dolores pasaba el día cosiendo, leyendo, y cantando con ellos. Desde lejos se oía el rumor de la pajarera y la dulce voz de su ama.

Ese día todo estaba en silencio. El calor era sofocante, y la naturaleza parecía agobiada y abochornada por los rayos de un sol de fuego que reinaba solo en un cielo despejado. Los pájaros callaban y sólo se oía el ruido del chorro de la alberca que corría sin cesar bajo su enramada de flores. Desde lejos vi a Dolores vestida de blanco y llevando por único adorno su hermoso pelo de matiz oscuro. Recostada sobre un cojín al pie del asiento en que había estado sentada, apoyaba la cabeza sobre el brazo doblado, mientras que la otra manecita blanca y rosada caía inerte a su lado. Detúveme a contemplarla creyéndola dormida, pero había oído el ruido de mis espuelas al acercarme, y se levantó de repente, tratando de ocultar las lágrimas que se le escapaban y cogiendo al mismo tiempo un papel que tenía sobre su mesita de costura.

—¿Qué es esto, prima? le pregunté señalándole el papel, después de haberla saludado.

—Estaba escribiendo y . . .

—¿A quién?

—A nadie.

—Cómo, ¿Antonio ya logró . . . ?

—No, Pedro, me contestó con dignidad; él no me pidió tal cosa, ni yo lo haría.

—Dolores, le dije tomando entre mis manos la suya fría y temblorosa ¿no te juró Antonio que te amaba locamente, como me lo dijo mil veces? ¡Confiésame que te suplicó que le guardaras tu fe!

—No; me hizo comprender que me prefería tal vez, pero nunca me dijo más.

—¿Y esa carta?

—¡No es carta!

—Misiva, pues, dije riéndome, epístola, billete, como quieras llamarla.

—¿No quieres creerme? Toma el papel; haces que te muestre lo que sólo escribía para mí.

Y me presentó un papel en que acababa de escribir unos preciosos versos, que mostraban un profundo sentimiento poético y cierto espíritu de melancolía vaga que no le conocía. Era un tierno adiós a su tranquila y feliz niñez y una invocación a su juventud que se le aparecía de repente como una revelación. Su corazón se había conmovido por primera vez, y ese estremecimiento la hacía comprender que la vida del sufrimiento había empezado.

Avergonzada y conmovida bajaba los ojos a medida que yo leía. Su tez blanca y rosada resaltaba aun con mayor frescura en contraste con su albo vestido y cabello destrenzado. Un temor vago me asaltó a mí también, como a mi padre, al notar el particular colorido de su tez; pero esa impresión fue olvidada nuevamente para recordarla después.

Pasé el día en casa de mi tía, cumplí la recomendación de Antonio y me persuadí de que ella lo amaba también. Debía volver a Bogotá en esos días: estaba impaciente y deseaba tener la dicha de ver otra vez a mi novia después de mes y medio de ausencia.

Al tiempo de despedirme quisieron acompañarme hasta cierto punto del camino para que Dolores me mostrara un lindo sitio al pie de la serranía, que ella había *descubierto* algunos días antes en uno de sus paseos.

Dolores se manifestaba muy risueña y festiva. El amor que la animaba formaba como una aureola en torno suyo. ¿Qué importa la ausencia si hay seguridad de amar y ser amado? Al llegar a una angosta vereda que había hecho abrir por enmedio del monte, tomó la delantera. Yo la seguía, admirando su esbelto talle y su gracia y serenidad para manejar un brioso potro que sólo con ella se había mostrado obediente y dócil.

Pocos momentos después llegamos a un sitio más abierto: un riachuelo cristalino bajaba saltando por escalones de piedras y reposaba en aquel lugar entre un bello lecho de musgos y de temblantes y variados helechos. Altísimos árboles se alzaban a un lado del riachuelo, impidiendo con su tupida sombra que otros arbustos creciesen a su lado. Varios troncos viejos y piedras envueltas en verde lama cubrían el suelo, alfombrado por una suave arena dorada. Empezaba a caer el sol y la sombra de aquel sitio producía un delicioso fresco. Bandadas de pájaros vistosos, entre los que charlaban numerosos loros y pericos, llegaban a posarse en las altas copas de los árboles, dorados por los últimos rayos del sol.

Nos desmontamos, y sacando mi tía algunos dulces y un coco curiosamente engastado en bruñida plata, nos invitó a que tomásemos un refrigerio campestre.

—Qué bello sería pasar su vida aquí, ¿no es cierto? exclamó Dolores.

—¿Sola? contesté sonriéndome.

No replicó sino con sólo una mirada tierna que se dirigía a mi amigo ausente, y continuó conversando alegremente. ¡Pobre niña! . . . pero feliz todavía en su ignorancia de lo porvenir.

PARTE SEGUNDA

La douleur est une lumière qui nous éclaire la vie.[8]

Balzac

Dos meses después de haber llegado a Bogotá recibí de Dolores su primera carta, la que he conservado con otras muchas como recuerdos de mi prima, cuyo claro talento fue ignorado de todos menos de mí.

"Querido primo," me decía: aguardaba recibir noticia de tu lle-

gada para escribirte, y después, cuando quise hacerlo, los acontecimientos que han tenido lugar en casa y en mi vida, me lo habían
impe-dido . . . No sabía si debería confiarte el horrible secreto que
he descubierto; pero el corazón necesita desahogarse, y sé bien que
eres no solamente mi hermano sino un amigo muy querido que
simpatiza con mis penas. No hace mucho que leía que lo que hace
las amistades indisolubles y duplica su encanto, es aquel sentimiento
que falta al amor: la seguridad. ¡Oh! la amistad es lo único que
puede ahora consolarme, ya que otro sentimiento me será prohibido
. . . No hace mucho, ¿te acuerdas? veía el mundo bello, alegre, encantador; todo me sonreía . . . pero ahora, ¡gran Dios! . . . ¡un terre-
moto ha cubierto de ruinas el sitio en que se levantaba el templo de
mis esperanzas!

Perdóname, Pedro, esta palabrería con que procuro retardar la
confesión de mis penas: esto sólo te demuestra el terror que me
causa ver escrito lo que casi no me atrevo a pensar.

Pero, ¡valor! empezaré.

Algunos días después de tu partida me dirigía una tarde a la pieza
de mi tía, cuando al pasar por el corredor del patio de entrada, oí
que un viejo arrendatario que vivió en los confines de la hacienda
preguntaba por ella. Llevaba una carta en la mano, y al saber que era
para mi tía la tomé y me preparaba a entregársela, cuando al notar
que el viejo Simón la había llevado dio un grito diciendo:—Tira esa
carta, Dolores, ¡tírala!

Yo hice instintivamente lo que mandaba y la dejé caer. Mi tía
hizo entonces que me lavara las manos, y mandando llevar un
brasero, no tomó la carta en sus manos sino después de haberla
hecho fumigar.

Yo estaba tan admirada al ver aquella escena, que casi no acertaba
a preguntar la causa de los súbitos temores de mi tía; al fin la cosa
me pareció hasta chistosa y exclamé riéndome:—¿Está envenenado
ese papel, tía? El viejo Simón tendrá sus rasgos a lo Borgia,[9] como en
la historia que leíamos el otro día?

—No te burles, hija mía, me contestó con seriedad: el veneno que
puede contener ese papel es más horrible que todos los que han in-
ventado los hombres.

Al decir estas palabras, acabó de leer la carta y tirándola al brasero, la vio consumirse lentamente.

—Es preciso que me explique usted este misterio . . .

—En esto no creas que hay misterio romántico, me dijo con acento triste, interrumpiéndome. ¿No sabes que en las inmediaciones de N*** hay lazarinos? Uno de esos desgraciados me ha enviado esa carta.

—¿Y quién es?

—¡Quién! un infeliz a quien he mandado algunos socorros y vive en una choza arruinada no lejos de la de Simón.

—¡Pobrecito! Y vive solo como todos ellos! Solo, enmedio del monte, sin que nadie le hable ni se le acerque jamás. Vivirá y morirá aislado sin sentir una mano amiga . . . ¡Dios mío! qué horrible suerte, ¡qué crueldad!

Y se me apretaba el corazón con indecible angustia.

—La sociedad es muy bárbara, tía, añadí; rechaza de su seno al desgraciado . . .

—Así es, me contestó, ¿pero qué remedio? Se dice que esa espantosa enfermedad se comunica con la mayor facilidad. ¿No es mejor en tal caso que sufra uno solo en vez de muchos? Por mi parte, Dolores, te confieso que el aspecto de un lazarino me espanta y querría más bien morir que acercármele.

—¿Y cómo conoció usted a ese infeliz? ¿Por qué lo protege, tía? Mucho me ha interesado: el sobrescrito de la carta estaba muy bien puesto . . . y aún me parece que la letra no me es enteramente desconocida.

—¿Por qué lo protejo, me preguntas? ¿No se ha de procurar siempre aliviar a los que sufren?

Mi tía cortó la conversación bruscamente. Aunque en los subsiguientes días no hablamos del episodio de la carta; esto me había impresionado mucho. El invierno entró con toda la fuerza con que tú sabes se desencadenan las lluvias en estos climas. Estábamos completamente solas en la hacienda: nadie se atrevía a atravesar los ríos crecidos y los caminos inundados para venirnos a visitar. A veces me despertaba en medio de la noche al ruido de una fuerte tempestad, y al oír caer la lluvia, el trueno rasgar el aire y mugir el viento contra las ventanas bien cerradas, y sintiéndome abrigada en mi pieza y rodeada de tantas comodidades, mi espíritu se trasportaba a las chozas solitarias de esos parias de nuestra sociedad: los lazarinos. Veía con la imaginación a esos infelices, presas de terribles sufrimientos, enmedio de las montañas y de la intemperie, y solos, siempre solos . . .

Una noche había leído hasta muy tarde, estudiando francés en los libros que me dejaste: procuraba aprender y adelantar en mis estudios, educar mi espíritu e instruirme para ser menos ignorante: el roce con *algunas* personas de la capital me había hecho comprender últimamente cuán indispensable es saber. Me acosté pues tarde, y empezaba a dormitar cuando creí oír pasos en el patio exterior y como el cuchicheo de dos voces que hablaban bajo. Mi perro favorito, que pasa la noche en mi cuarto, se levantó de repente y se salió por ventana abierta al corredor, y un momento después oí que se abalanzaba sobre alguien en el patio. La voz de mi tía lo hizo retirarse. ¡Cosa extraña! ¡mi tía que se recogía a las ocho, andaba por los corredores de la casa a media noche! Me levanté resuelta a indagar esto y entreabrí la puerta que daba al corredor extremo. Entonces oí una voz de hombre que decía por lo bajo: '¡Adiós, Juana!' Esta voz me causó grande estremecimiento: creí soñar . . .

—Aguárdese un momento, contestó mi tía, voy a traerle el retrato que mandé hacer para usted por un pintor quiteño que por casualidad estuvo aquí ahora días.

Al decir esto sentí que la tía Juana entró a su cuarto y aprovechándome de la oscuridad, salí al corredor prontamente y me situé en un ángulo desde donde, agazapada, pude ver un bulto que aguardaba inmóvil enmedio del patio.

El temor y la vaga aprehensión que había sentido al oír la voz del desconocido desaparecieron al ver que no era una fantasma, un sueño de mi imaginación. Sin embargo, no podía comprender que la tía Juana tuviera *citas* a media noche y regalara su retrato! . . . Era cierto que poco antes le rogué que se hiciese retratar por un pintor de paso que hizo el mío también. Un momento después volvió, y apoyándose sobre la baranda del corredor dijo, atando a una cuerda un paquete envuelto:—No está tan parecida como yo quisiera; y cuando el bulto se acercó, añadió: va también [el libro] la 'Imitación de Cristo,' de Dolores, que se la cambié por una nueva.

No sabe usted cuánto provecho me hará esto, exclamó con voz conmovida el desconocido . . . ¡Oh! ¡pobre hija mía! . . . ¡su retrato!

Esa voz, ese acento me heló la sangre, y por un momento no sé lo que pasó por mí. Una idea increíble, un terror horrible me dejó como anonadada. Me puse en pie, fría, temblando.

Váyase pronto, Jerónimo, contestó mi tía, he oído un ruido del lado del cuarto de Dolores y . . .

Nada más oí. Había conocido la voz de mi padre y mi tía lo nombró. ¡Mi padre, que yo creía muerto hacía seis años! No reflexioné en el misterio de aquella aparición, y bajando las gradas del corredor que caían al patio corrí hacia el bulto, y acercándome le eché los brazos al cuello. Al ver mi acción, tanto mi tía como mi padre, pues él era, dieron un grito de horror: éste último se separó de mí con desesperación, se cubrió la cara con la *ruana* en que estaba envuelto y quiso huir; yo pugnaba por seguirlo, y mi tía que había bajado detrás de mí me detuvo.

—Dolores, gritaba ésta, Dolores, no te acerques, ¡por Dios! . . . ¡está lazarino!

¿Lazarino? ¡qué me importa! Mi padre no ha muerto y quiero abrazarlo.

No te puedes figurar la escena que hubo entonces . . . al fin mi tía logró que mi padre se fuera, y llamando a las sirvientas me llevó por fuerza a mi cuarto; y allí quitándome los vestidos que tenía los hizo tirar al patio para ser quemados al día siguiente.

No consentí que mi tía me dejase hasta que no me refiriera la causa de este acontecimiento y me hiciera saber inmediatamente porqué se hallaba mi padre oculto y en aquel estado . . . Conversamos largo tiempo y no me quedé sola sino cuando empezaban a entrar los primeros rayos de la aurora por la ventana abierta. Me levanté entonces y recostándome contra la ventana contemplé el bello paisaje que se extendía a mis ojos. . . . ¡El día, el paisaje, los rumores campestres eran bellos y admirables! . . . pero yo veía todo triste y sin animación. La faz de mi vida ha cambiado; ya nada puede ser risueño para mí. ¡Mi padre vive, pero vive sufriendo!

¿No es cierto, Pedro, que el lázaro es una enfermedad horrorosa? Al saber cuál es la herencia que me aguarda, todos tratarían de retirarse de mi lado y procurarían descubrir en mí los síntomas precursores; ¡estaría condenada a vivir aislada! Mi padre que me amaba con ternura no quiso que esa mancha empañase mi frente, y por eso resolvió desaparecer. Ha vivido escondido en los más recónditos rincones de la provincia y hace apenas un año que mi tía y tu padre saben dónde se halla . . . ¿Pero, yo podré vivir contenta lejos de mi desgraciado padre? ¿Sería justo que engañase a los demás ocultando la enfermedad a que la suerte puede condenarme? Mi padre me ha hecho saber que de ningún modo permitirá que se sepa que él existe . . . En tu última carta me dices que Antonio tiene esperanzas de alcanzar más pronto de lo que creía una posición que le permita pedir mi mano. Ya es tarde, primo mío: es preciso que renuncie a esa idea . . . ¡que me olvide! Mi desdicha no debe encadenarlo. No le digas nunca la causa, pero hazle perder la esperanza. Me creerá variable, ingrata . . . pero ¿qué puedo hacer? Este sacrificio es grande, muy grande, pero no tiene remedio.

Adiós. Escríbele palabras de consuelo a la que sufre tanto.

—Dolores

Al cabo de algunos días recibí esta otra carta:

Me escribes, querido primo, y tus palabras han sido para mí un verdadero consuelo: ¡gracias, oh, mil gracias! Me preguntas con interés los pormenores de la desaparición de mi padre y cómo vivió tanto tiempo oculto, sin que nadie adivinase ni pudiese sospechar que vivía.

He reunido todo lo que acerca de este particular he podido descubrir, y procuraré explicarte las cosas como pasaron.

Tú sabes que desde que murió mi madre, mi padre había concentrado en mí todo su afecto y me cuidaba con la ternura de una mujer. Tenía yo doce años, cuando sintiendo mi padre algunas novedades en su salud que lo alarmaron partió para Bogotá. Allí consultó varios médicos que le dijeron que los síntomas que sentía eran los de una enfermedad incurable y horrorosa: el lázaro. Desesperado, volvió para N★★★ sin determinar la conducta que debía seguir. Pero al llegar a las márgenes del Magdalena, su espíritu exaltado le presentó la imagen del suicidio como la única salida menos mala y el solo remedio que tenía su situación. Se desmontó y en un momento de demencia se precipitó al río con la intención de dejarse ahogar. Pero tú recordarás que mi padre era muy buen nadador. El instinto natural y el apego que se tiene a la vida lo obligaron a no dejarse consumir, y aunque exánime arribó al otro lado. Allí lo amparó un infeliz que vivía en una triste choza en la orilla de río. ¡Qué casualidad! su protector estaba también lazarino, y vivía en aquellas soledades manteniéndose con algunos socorros que le enviaban del vecino pueblo y el producto de un platanal y otras sementerillas que cultivaba y mandaba a vender a las inmediaciones con sus dos hijos que lo acompañaban. Mi padre permaneció con él algunos días y concibió la idea de huir del mundo para siempre, y ocultando sus padecimientos no dejarle esa misteriosa herencia a su hija.

Con el producto de una cantidad de oro y algunas joyas que llevaba entre el bolsillo vivió algún tiempo en aquellos desiertos. Pronto se separó del lazarino. ¿Vivir bajo el pie de igualdad con un ser vulgar no es la peor de las desgracias? Compró pues una choza en el monte y allí vegetó solo, aislado y profundamente desgraciado más de cinco años. Algunas veces bajaba a las márgenes del Magdalena, visitaba al lazarino y estudiaba en él los progresos y estragos que hacía el mal que ambos padecían. Otras ocasiones, vestido como campesino, penetraba de noche a los pueblos más cercanos y preguntaba por la suerte de su familia. ¡Cuántas veces no podía tener noticia alguna y se volvía desconsolado a su montaña!

Un día bajó a la choza de su compañero en infortunio, y encontró a los dos muchachos llorando en el quicio de la puerta.

El lazarino había muerto. Ese espectáculo conmovió a mi padre y les propuso que lo siguieran a su desierto. Ellos, una niña de doce años y un muchacho de catorce, aceptaron su oferta con gratitud. Hacía muchos meses que mi padre no había sabido nada con certeza de su familia, y estaba sumamente inquieto; por otra parte, la muerte del lazarino le hizo comprender que la suya podía estar cercana, y no pudo menos que desear verme por la última vez.

Emprendió, pues, viaje hacia N★★★, viaje penosísimo al través de aquellas desiertas llanuras de pajonales interminables, acompañado por los dos muchachos.

En los confines de la hacienda de mi tía había una choza abandonada, y allí eligió su domicilio. Sus compañeros no sabían quién era él y así pudo mandar sin cuidado una carta dirigida a tu padre, revelándole su existencia y pidiéndole noticias de su familia. Ya te puedes figurar la admiración que semejante revelación le causaría a tu padre. Nunca se había tenido la menor duda de que el mío no se hubiese ahogado al atravesar imprudentemente el Magdalena. Cuando aquel se persuadió de la verdad consultó con la tía Juana lo que debía hacer: su primer impulso había sido buscar a mi infeliz padre y llevarlo nuevamente a su casa, aunque él rehusase seguirlo. Pero tú sabes el horror que mi tía le tiene a esa enfermedad, y de ningún modo accedió a la propuesta. Decía (me aseguran que en esto tenía razón) que teniendo yo por herencia predisposición a ese mal, era preciso precaverme en lo posible de todo contagio. Convinieron en que de la hacienda se le enviaría todo lo que necesitaba, pero que viviría lejos de todos sus parientes y su existencia continuaría ignorada por todos. Mi padre, ¡oh infeliz! nunca había tenido otra pretensión que la de verme ocultamente y de lejos . . . . ¿Te acuerdas de la tarde en que te despediste de nosotros? él se hallaba oculto entre las breñas a orillas del riachuelo; nos contemplaba alegres y el eco de nuestra risa llegaba hasta sus oídos.

Me dicen que su enfermedad está el último período . . . que sufre horriblemente; pero no me es permitido verlo ni aliviarlo. Vivo ahora siempre triste, retraída: mi carácter ha cambiado totalmente. Dime ¿qué ha dicho Antonio? ¿Me olvida con facilidad? . . . Preguntas necias, ¿no es cierto? Hablemos de ti: me dices que tu matrimonio no podrá ser tan presto como pensabas, pero tú al menos vives en una atmósfera de esperanza. Hemos sido hermanos: a ti te toca la dicha, a mí . . . No, Dios sabe lo que hace: habrá medido mis fuerzas y resignación. Adiós . . .

Estas noticias de N★★★ me entristecieron mucho. El estado de dolor mórbido a veces, exaltado otras que revelaban las cartas de Dolores me alarmó. Escribí a mi padre aconsejándole que procurasen distraerla, pues ese pensamiento continuo en una cosa tan dolorosa podía presdisponerla más que todo a que estallase en ella la enfermedad de su padre. Una reflexión me consolaba: rara vez se han visto casos de que los hijos de los lazarinos sufran la enfermedad: casi siempre salta una generación para aparecer en los nietos. Sin embargo, comprendía y aprobaba su noble conducta al desear romper con Antonio. Yo no me atrevía a quitar repentinamente las esperanzas a mi amigo; lo veía tan feliz que me parecía una crueldad inútil apagar aquel fuego y vida, aquel vigor y energía que animaban sus trabajos y lo hacían triunfar de todas las dificultades.

Así se pasaron varios meses. Al fin recibí la noticia de la muerte del padre de Dolores: escribió ella algunas líneas en que me manifestaba su angustia. No podía llorar públicamente la pérdida que había hecho, ni vestirse de luto, pues él le había hecho saber en sus últimos momentos que quería que su sacrificio sirviera al menos para preservar a su hija de las miradas recelosas de una sociedad que sabría lo que ella debía esperar al conocer la causa de su muerte.

Viéndola tan abatida, mi tía quiso distraerla y la llevó hasta el Espinal.[10] Ambas me escribieron entonces rogándome que fuese a verlas por algunos días, ya que estaban más cerca de Bogotá.

Accedí a ese deseo y fuí a pasar una semana con ellas. ¡Cómo podía prever las consecuencias que esa visita tendría para mí!

Nada podía consolar a Dolores; estaba pálida y en todos sus movimientos se veía la profunda pena que la agobiaba. Entonces me volvió a pedir encarecidamente que desengañase a Antonio, pero me hizo prometer que jamás le diría la causa del rompimiento que ella deseaba.

A mi vuelta procuré hacer comprender a Antonio la repugnancia que Dolores manifestaba por el matrimonio, y lo imposible que sería que se realizasen sus esperanzas. Esta era una obra ardua, y frecuentemente no tenía valor para desconsolarlo enteramente.

Por otra parte mis proyectos matrimoniales habían tomado un aspecto que me causaba mucha desconfianza en lo porvenir. Don Basilio se había hecho presentar en casa de mi novia como aspirante a la mano de Mercedes, quien le mostraba siempre un ceño esquivo; pero los padres lo acogían con cierta atención que me disgustaba. Poco a poco descubrí que a medida que se acataba a don Basilio se me trataba con mayor indiferencia. Una vez me dijo Mercedes que estaba muy triste porque sus padres habían tenido malos informes de mí; que ella me había defendido, pero no podía impedir un viaje que se preparaba con dirección a Chiquinquirá.[11] Hacía muchos años que su madre había hecho una promesa a la Virgen, pero hasta entonces no le ocurrió cumplirla, sin duda con la intención, me decía Mercedes, de separarnos. Quise tener una explicación acerca de los informes que de mí habían tenido, pero Mercedes no me lo permitió, asegurándome que no sabía cuáles eran los cargos que se hacía, y que, cuando ella averiguase de qué se me acusaba yo podría defenderme mejor.

Comprendí que ésta debía ser obra de don Basilio y prometí esperar. A los pocos días la familia de Mercedes partía para Chiquinquirá. Durante las primeras semanas de su ausencia estuve profundamente abatido y mi mayor gusto era conversar largamente con Antonio de nuestras mutuas penas. Mercedes me escribía con frecuencia, pero al fin me dijo que no volverían a Bogotá tan pronto como habían pensado; que su madre había deseado quedarse algunos meses en San Gil con la familia que tenía allá. Cada vez que recibía una carta de Mercedes era motivo de fiesta para mí, pero al fin empezaron a escasear, bajo pretexto de que su madre le había prohibido que me escribiese. Entonces todavía amaba y me creía amado, y aunque sufría mucho en aquel tiempo lo recuerdo con ternura: "todos los demás placeres no equivalen a nuestras penas," decía un autor francés. Pero poco a poco me fui enseñando a su silencio y ya no deseaba sus cartas con tanta impaciencia. No sé por qué motivo dieron en esos días en Bogotá muchos bailes y tertulias: asistí a ellos y confieso que no estuve triste. Sin embargo, llevaba siempre en el alma un malestar, una pena oculta que revestía la memoria de Mercedes.

Se habían pasado cuatro meses sin recibir noticia alguna de ella cuando un día llegó a mis mano una carta suya, y comprendí con profunda tristeza que mi corazón ya no sentía la dicha de antes. Mercedes me decía que habiéndole dicho a su padre que debían volver a Bogotá porque ya se cumplía el plazo en que se debía verificar nuestro matrimonio, éste le había notificado que con su consentimiento nunca sería mi esposa. No le quiso explicar la causa de su resolución, pero añadió que tenía seguridad de que bastaría una ausencia prolongada para que mutuamente nos olvidásemos. La carta de Mercedes era sumamente afectuosa, tal vez más que ninguna otra; pero con aquel magnetismo, aquella intuición que hay entre dos personas que se aman y que queda aún después de haberse amado; con esa revelación del alma, digo, que se comprende sin poderse explicar, sentí hasta en sus expresiones más cariñosas cierto despego y frialdad. La cadena de sentimientos y simpatías estaba a punto de romperse entre los dos. Desde ese día empecé a resignarme a su ausencia y a familiarizarme con la posibilidad de que nuestra suerte podía ser desunida.

Un negocio importante del padre de Mercedes trajo a toda la familia a Bogotá por fin. Apenas supe su llegada imprevista mi corazón se galvanizó por un momento y me dirijí inmediatamente a su casa. ¡Triste desengaño! aquella impresión fue pasajera y pronto me sentí otra vez tranquilo. Sin embargo, hacía un esfuerzo para pensar que al verla sería otra vez dichoso, y al entrar a la casa repasaba con la imaginación todas las soñadas escenas con que antes había revestido la esperanza que ahora iba a ser colmada. Llegué, la vi bella como siempre, pero en sus ojos se había apagado la luz que faltaba en los míos. Nos hablamos: yo procuré ocultar mi indiferencia; ella estaba distraída . . . Al despedirme se apoderó de mí un pesar inmenso. ¡Es tan desalentador sentir el corazón vacío, sin emociones ni entusiasmo!

No quería tener ninguna explicación con ella y temía que hubiera entre nosotros una reconciliación que ya no se deseaba. Así me fui retirando de su casa, y aunque ella no podía menos que notar la frialdad que había en nuestras relaciones nada me dijo. La vi más hermosa que nunca, cubierta de galas, en el teatro y en tertulias: oí hablar de las conquistas que había hecho y de los pretendientes que tenía, entre los cuales se hallaban en primer lugar don Basilio y Julián que había vuelto a Bogotá; pero en lugar de los celos y la pena que antes hubiera sentido al verla tan obsequiada, mi corazón permaneció tranquilo. Había perdido la facultad de sentir aquellos nobles celos que son el síntoma del amor. No hay duda que hay celos, o más bien cierta envidia, en un corazón que no ama, pero no puede haber amor vehemente sin ellos.

¡Pobre Mercedes! A veces procuraba llamarme a su lado y encubría su indiferencia cuando le era posible, como yo la mía. Yo estaba muy triste entonces: el corazón humano, sin exceptuar el mío, me parecía tan pequeño, variable e indigno, bien que en lo íntimo de él guardase el recuerdo de la mujer que amé como un ángel, ¡pero que se había convertido para mí en un ser débil, fútil, y fácilmente llevado por la voluntad ajena! A veces la conciencia me acusaba de haber cambiado yo también. Era cierto, pero no había empezado a sentirme indiferente sino cuando advertí en ella despego. Su silencio y sus vacilaciones durante nuestra separación me la habían mostrado bajo otra luz, y el antiguo ideal había desaparecido para mí.

Fluctuaban mis sentimientos en este vaivén anárquico, en que nada espera uno ni desea, cuando recibí otra carta de Dolores, carta que me llenó de aprehensión penosísima. Luego que la leí, tomé la resolución de partir al día siguiente para N★★★. La misma noche fuí a despedirme de Mercedes.

Estaba muy abatido, y en esa situación el ánimo está dispuesto a aceptar con agradecimiento cualquiera simpatía. Creo que si Mercedes me hubiera acogido aquella noche como en otro tiempo, tal vez habría recuperado su imperio sobre mi corazón. Cuánta gratitud hubiera tenido hacia ella al ser inspirado por el sentimiento que creía ser el mayor bien dado a los mortales: ¡el amor!

Subí muy conmovido las escaleras de su casa; mi voz tembló al saludarla.

La tertulia estaba completa como la de casi todas las noches. En un lado de la sala y alrededor del piano había un grupo compuesto de Mercedes y algunas amigas: una de ellas tocaba una pieza, mientras que don Basilio disertaba sobre la ópera de donde había sido tomada: Julián volvía las hojas del papel de música y miraba lánguidamente a Mercedes. Al lado opuesto, el padre de ella jugaba tresillo con dos o tres amigos de don Basilio, sencillos congresistas de provincias lejanas, que vestían casacas muy apretadas, cuellos muy tiesos, trabillas muy tirantes, por último *usaban* unas manos tan negras y toscas, que se conocía cuáles habían sido sus antecedentes.

Noté que mi llegada produjo impresión. Todos los ojos se fijaron en mí con curiosidad y se interrumpieron las conversaciones empezadas. Mercedes me recibió desdeñosamente, volteándome la espalda después de haberme saludado ligeramente y sin mirarme. El dueño de casa apenas me contestó y toda la concurrencia me recibió con frialdad. Enmedio del silencio general causado por mi llegada don Basilio se dirigió a mí y dijo con voz sonora y su acostumbrada pedantería: —"Hablando del rey de Roma," etc., o más bien como dicen los ingleses: "*Talk of the devil. . . .*" Se hablaba de usted, joven, hace un momento. Y añadió mirando a todos con aire significativo ¿ha tenido usted últimamente noticias de sus interesantes parientas a quienes conocí el año pasado en N★★★?

No sé qué le contesté. Un momento después, acercándome a Mercedes le dije que venía a despedirme porque tenía que ausentarme algunos días.

—Naturalmente, me contestó sonrojándose con suma contrariedad.

—¿Por qué naturalmente? Usted no sabe a dónde voy . . .

—¿Cómo no he de adivinar? . . . El engañado puede a veces abrir los ojos.

—¿El engañado?

—O la engañada, si usted gusta.

—Explíquese, Mercedes.

—Lo haré. Sepa usted que hoy ya comprendo la falsedad de la conducta de usted, y tenga por seguro que entre nosotros acabó todo compromiso.

—¿Y de qué soy culpable, por Dios?

—Ahora no tengo tiempo para explicarme. Bástele saber que lo sé todo . . . y añadió con ironía: ¡comprendo que usted quiera ir a visitar a la persona que prefiere!

—No entiendo.

—¿No? Pues, entonces hágame el favor de saludar a su prima Dolores de mi parte.

—Mercedes, usted es muy injusta, y no sé quién ha podido inventar semejante . . .

Ella no pudo menos que volver lo ojos hacia don Basilio al interrumpirme diciendo:—No sé por qué se ha tomado usted la pena de venir a despedirse. Entre usted y yo no hay ni puede haber simpatía: yo no me intereso en sus asuntos particulares.

Inmediatamente comprendí que todo esto era obra de don Basilio. Mi orgullo se exaltó, y no quise humillarme pidiendo explicaciones.

—Ya veo, le contesté mirando a mi rival, ya veo que mi dignidad me impide defenderme; la fortaleza está en manos del enemigo y sería inútil procurar rechazar las calumnias que ciertas personas saben inventar.

Y saludando con aire altivo a Mercedes y a toda la concurrencia salí de la sala seguido por la mirada maligna y la perversa sonrisa de don Basilio. En la puerta me alcanzó Julián, y ofreciéndome la mano me dijo:—No crea usted, Pedro, que yo he tenido parte en la conspiración que comprendo se había preparado contra usted, pues yo soy enemigo de estas cosas y tengo verdadero aprecio por usted.

Le agradecí este acto de espontaneidad y nos separamos.

Atravesé las calles que me separaban de casa, y odio, deseo de vengarme, profunda humillación al verme vencido por ese aventurero de pluma, desprecio por Mercedes que servía de instrumento, todo esto bullía en mi mente y hacía latir mi corazón. Enmedio de todo recordaba que al salir había visto que la mirada de Mercedes me siguió, humedecida y melancólica . . . No volví a verla sino años después y ¡en qué circunstancias!

Al llegar a casa me dijeron que alguien me aguardaba: era Antonio. Al acercarme para saludarlo dio un paso atrás y rechazando mi mano dijo con destemplanza:—Deseo primero saber si le doy la mano a un amigo o a un traidor a la amistad!

—¡A un traidor! . . . ¿yo Antonio?

—¡Usted!

—Explícate . . . ¡Esto me faltaba! exclamé con desaliento. Esto me faltaba para volverme loco . . . Vengo de casa de Mercedes que rompió conmigo definitivamente.

—¿Y no dijo la causa?

—Me dio a entender que creía en una calumnia . . .

—¡Calumnia! tal vez ella tenía razón . . . ¡Pedro, Pedro! todavía me queda una esperanza: ¡tu lealtad de tantos años! Dime la verdad, añadió tuteándome otra vez; es tan triste perderlo todo en un día . . . contéstame ¿amabas acaso a Dolores antes de conocerla yo? O en tu viaje al Espinal, ahora cuatro meses . . . ¡Oh! ¡dime la verdad!

—Te juro en nombre de nuestra vieja amistad y por todo lo que hay más sagrado, que Dolores ha sido siempre solamente una hermana para mí.

—No sé qué creer . . . He estado pensando mucho en tu conducta últimamente y es inexplicable. Desde que estuviste en el Espinal has procurado siempre disuadirme de mis proyectos con respecto a Dolores, y no me permites que hable de ella; todo esto con cierto aire misterioso que no puedes ocultar y sin decirme la causa de tan extraño cambio. El amigo Durán me dijo también en días pasados que ya nadie veía a Dolores, que vivía siempre retirada en su hacienda . . . En estos días han circulado aquí rumores acerca de ella y de ti que no acierto a repetirlos . . . ¡Dime si esto es verdad!

—¿Qué verdad? pregunté angustiado y sin saber qué contestar.

—Dime si . . . ¡tú debes casarte con ella?

—Esa es una infame mentira forjada por don Basilio; ¡y que tú, Antonio, hayas podido dar oídos a esto!

—¡Por don Basilio! . . .

Y un momento después añadió:

—Tienes razón, Pedro, debe ser mentira entonces. Me admiro cómo no lo había pensado antes. Me dijeron aquí que pensabas irte mañana para N***: no espero más tiempo: no quiero creer en la repugnancia de Dolores por el matrimonio: ¿no me has dicho que me ama? Pues bien, tú mismo llevarás una carta pidiendo la mano de tu prima, y de cualquier modo haremos el matrimonio. Este es el mejor modo de contestar a semejante calumnia.

—Eso no puede ser! exclamé sin pensar en las consecuencias de mis palabras.

—¿Por qué?

—Ella dice que jamás se casará.

Antonio me miró sin contestarme y yo añadí:—Hay en su vida un misterio que no puedo revelar.

—¿Un misterio?

—Sí.

—Un misterio en la vida de una mujer no puede ser bueno. Exijo que se me diga en qué consiste. Yo no soy héroe de novela, y si se me engaña que sea con algo verosímil.

—No tengo libertad para revelártelo: Dolores me ha exigido el secreto.

—¡El secreto! ¡Y yo que empezaba a creerle! . . .

Y levantándose, se caló el sombrero con aire decidido, y con voz temblorosa de rabia me impuso silencio diciendo:—Basta ya. Nadie se burla de mí impunemente. No me replique usted; no quiero cometer una falta aquí; yo mandaré amigos que arreglen el asunto entre los dos.

—¡Un desafío!

—Así lo entiendo ¿acaso la cobardía es otra de las cualidades que lo distinguen a usted?

—La cólera te ciega, Antonio, contesté procurando guardar mi razón. Entre los dos no puede haber desafío. ¡Esto es hasta ridículo! Escúchame: te he dado mi palabra de que en esto hay una horrible equivocación.

—¿Qué pruebas me puede usted dar para creer que sus palabras son verídicas, puesto que asegura que Dolores no puede casarse?

—El tiempo . . .

—¡El tiempo! . . . ¡Usted es un cobarde!

-¡No permito que nadie me diga semejante cosa!

—Entonces acepta mi reto, o contesta a mi pregunta.

-Antonio, exclamé, haciendo el último esfuerza para no perder mi serenidad, Antonio, esto es absurdo. Si las circunstancias lo exigen, separémonos, ¡pero no como enemigos!

Antonio fuera de sí ya, se acercó con el brazo levantado.

—¡Cobarde e hipócrita! gritó.

Entonces olvidé toda consideración, y mostrándole la puerta dije:—Salga usted. Arregle las cosas como quiera y para cuando quiera.

Al día siguiente a las seis de la tarde me llevaban desmayado para la casa en que vivía. Cuando volví a recuperar mis sentidos me encontré tendido en la cama. Era de noche, y sentada a los pies de la cama vi dormida a la casera: traté de hablar y moverme, pero un dolor agudísimo en el pecho me obligó a estarme quieto. Estaba solo, sin pariente ni amigo que se condoliera de mí; la caridad de los dueños de casa era mi único amparo. Recordé entonces lo que me había sucedido: me ví nuevamente al frente de Antonio detrás de las colinas de San

Diego: cada uno de nosotros tenía una pistola en la mano: Julián me servía de testigo. La expresión de la fisonomía de Antonio era temible: me miraba con todo el odio nacido de su anterior cariño. En ese momento olvidé todo sentimiento religioso, todo recuerdo de mi padre ... un profundo desaliento de la vida me dominaba; deseaba verdaderamente morir en aquel momento. Le apunté a Antonio, pero la memoria de Dolores y de su pena al saber que yo habría causado su muerte me hizo volver a mejores sentimientos y disparé al aire; pero al mismo tiempo sentí una fuerte conmoción y sin saber cómo, me encontré en el suelo ... No recordaba más.

Volví a perder el juicio y por muchos días estuve entre la vida y la muerte. Cuando mis ojos se abrieron nuevamente a la luz y a la razón encontré a mi lado a mi padre, que acababa de llegar de N*** sin haber tenido noticia del estado en que me hallaba.

La siguiente carta de Dolores hará comprender mejor que otras explicaciones la causa del viaje imprevisto de mi padre.

No sé si recibiste una carta que te escribí hace algunos días. Es posible que se haya extraviado o que no hubieras entendido lo que en ella te decía. Ahora pienso explicarte con más claridad la causa del desorden de mi espíritu: estoy en completa calma y me creo capaz de abarcar con ánimo mi situación ... ¡Con ánimo! ¡gran dios! En calma ... ¡qué ironía! ... no, Pedro estoy loca, desesperada.

He tenido momentos de verdadera demencia ...

Sin embargo, quiero vencer la repugnancia, el horror que siento. Es preciso referírtelo todo.

Desde que estuve en el Espinal empecé a sentir mucho malestar, una agitación de nervios constante y una completa postración de ánimo. Sentía por turnos y en algunas horas, frío, calor, fuerza, debilidad, valor, desaliento, temor, audacia, en fin los sentimientos más contradictorios y las sensaciones más diversas. Al volver a N*** consulté a tu padre: me hizo varias preguntas y leí en su semblante la mayor emoción y desconsuelo a medida que le refería los síntomas del extraño mal que padecía. El pobre tío procuró infundirme valor asegurándome que esas novedades provenían de mis recientes penas.

Mi tía se empeñó en que consultase con otros médicos, pero yo no quería que me viese nadie. Al fin viendo que mi salud no mejoraba, llamaron sin consultarme a varias personas de los alrededores que pasan aquí por médicos, y su experiencia, si no el diploma, los hace dignos del título de doctores que les dan.

Se reunieron, pues, un día en la hacienda. Yo me presenté temblando, pero me acogieron con tanta bondad y me trataron con tan alegres chanzas, que fui perdiendo en presencia de ellos el horrible temor que me asaltaba. Antes de separarme comprendí que esos señores debían reunirse en la sala para dar su opinión. Quise saber la verdad y resolví oír ocultamente la consulta. Me retiré a mi cuarto, pero saliendo inmediatamente entré a una alcoba vecina de la sala y separada de ésta sólo por un cancel.

Me había tardado algunos momentos y cuando llegué a mi observatorio ya estaba empezada la conversación.

—¡Pobre niña! decía uno de ellos; me parece que no hay esperanza . . .

—El lázaro está en su segundo período apenas, repuso otro, y creo que se podría hacer algún esfuerzo.

—Eso apenas retardaría por algunos días más . . .

—Es cierto, dijeron todos, no hay ya remedio . . .

No supe qué más dijeron, ni lo que pasó por mí. Había procurado hacerme fuerte y ver con serenidad el mal que podía, que debía esperar. Pero al tener la seguridad de que era cierto lo que sólo temía, al encontrarme cara a cara con el espectro que había presentido, al contemplar de repente el horror de mi situación, no pude resistir a semejante dolor, y aunque no perdí el sentido, me tiré al suelo dominada por una completa postración de espíritu. No lloraba, ni me quejaba: mi desesperación no admitía desahogo. Un sollozo prolongado en el corredor me hizo volver en mí. Conocí la voz de mi tía, salí . . . al menos, pensé, ¡podremos llorar juntas! Guiada por el mismo interés que me animaba, también había querido conocer el fallo de los médicos, y al oír sus palabras no había podido resistir a su emoción.

Me le acerqué, pero al levantar los ojos y verme a su lado no pudo reprimir cierto movimiento de repugnancia que corrigió inmediatamente con una tierna mirada.

—Hija mía, me dijo alargándome la manos, ven, abrázame.

Pero su primer movimiento había sido como una puñalada para mí: no lo pude olvidar, y huyendo entré a mi cuarto sin querer oírla, y me encerré. ¡Me sentía sola, completamente abandonada en el mundo! Después de esto no recuerdo más. Parece que mi tía, cansándose de llamarme y no teniendo contestación alguna se había alarmado, y auxiliada por tu padre forzaron la puerta y ¡me encontraron loca!

Sí, Pedro: fue tal mi desesperación que perdí el juicio por algunos días. Cuando volví a la razón y contemplé la horrible existencia que me aguardaba, en lo primero que pensé fue en escribirte. Tú has sido siempre un amigo en cuya simpatía creo; un hermano, cuyo apoyo ha sido mi consuelo siempre. A ti apelé: no recuerdo qué te decía; todavía había en mi mente una nube de demencia. Tu padre me dice que no ha perdido completamente la esperanza, y parte para Bogotá a consultar él mismo los mejores médicos del país. Si hubiera esperanza, ¡Dios mío! . . . ¡si hubiera esperanza!

La carta a que se refería Dolores era la que había determinado mi partida para N★★★, partida que se había interrumpido trágicamente.

Apenas pude levantarme quise acompañar a mi padre a casa de los mejores médicos de Bogotá, quienes nos dieron algunos medicamentos con los cuales decían haberse mejorado notablemente varios lazarinos. Mi padre regresó a N★★★. Yo me quedé solo, triste, enfermo todavía, desalentado y sin proyectos ya para lo porvenir.

En eso supe que un rico capitalista partía enfermo para Europa y deseaba llevar un médico que lo asistiera durante su viaje. Me le ofrecí y me aceptó con gusto: pero antes de partir no pude resistir al deseo de ir a abrazar a mi padre y ver a mis parientes. Por otra parte deseaba arreglar las pocas propiedades de que podía disponer para tener algunos recursos con que subsistir algunos años en Europa.

Llegué inesperadamente a N★★★, y después de haber pasado algunas horas con mi padre fui a casa de la tía Juana. Estaba sola y muy triste: la enfermedad de Dolores no tenía ningún alivio. Me decía que no quería vivir sino en la hacienda; y prorrumpiendo en llanto la pobre tía añadió que no se dejaba ver de nadie, y no permitía que se le acercasen. Yo traté de consolarla diciendo que iría a verla y procuraría dulcificar sus pensamientos y mejorar su género de vida.

Al principio mi prima rehusó verme, pero cuando le hice saber que partía pronto para un viaje tan lejano accedió a mi deseo.

Estaba sentada en un sillón y el cuarto muy oscuro: así con su vestido blanco se veía como un espectro entre las sombras. No quería que yo me acercase a ella; pero usando de mis prerrogativas de primo y hermano le tomé las manos por fuerza y abriendo de improviso una ventana quise contemplar los estragos que aquel mal había hecho en ella.

Estaba ya empezando el tercer período de la enfermedad. La linda color de rosa que había asustado a mi padre, y que es el primer síntoma del mal, se cambió en desencajamiento y en la palidez amarillenta que había notado en ella en el Espinal: ahora se mostraba abotagada y su cutis áspera tenía un color morado. Su belleza había desaparecido completamente y sólo sus ojos conservaban un brillo demasiado vivo. Comprendí que ya no tenía esperanzas de mejoría, pero procuré ocultar mi sorpresa: ciertamente no esperaba encontrar en ella semejante cambio. Al principio permaneció callada, pero cuando le expliqué las penas de la tía Juana, me confió que su aparente despego y el deseo de aislarse provenían de un plan que había ideado y que tenía la determinación de llevar a cabo.

—Quiero que mi tía se enseñe a nuestra separación, pues no pienso vivir más tiempo a su lado.

—¿Y dónde te irás?

—Viviré sola. Mi tía tiene un horror, una repugnancia singular al mal que sufro, y sé que vivirá martirizada. Por otra parte, es tal el temor que me causa una voz extraña . . . veo a la humanidad entera como un enemigo que me persigue, que me acosa, y he resuelto separarme de todo el que me tema.

—¿Pero cómo?

—¿No recuerdas aquel sitio tan lindo donde nos despedimos la última vez que estuviste aquí?

—¿La quebradita?

—Allí quiero mandar hacer una casita y acompañada por los muchachos que sirvieron a mi padre hasta sus últimos momentos (ellos no me tienen repugnancia) viviré aislada, pero en mi soledad estaré tranquila.

—Esa es una locura, Dolores ¿cómo sería tu vida enmedio del monte? no, eso no puede ser.

—En lugar de disuadirme, Pedro, ténme lástima y ayúdame a llevar a cabo mi propósito, Si no, añadió apretándose las manos con ademán desesperado, si no, huiré, me iré sola al monte y moriré como una fiera de los bosques. Mira: he sentido mayor desesperación al comprender que inspiro horror. ¡Dios mío! si no me permiten vivir sola, ocultarme a todos los ojos, no sé qué haré . . . no es difícil quitarse uno la vida.

El estado de exasperación en que se hallaba la pobre joven no admitía razonamientos y tuve que ofrecerla mi cooperación a su plan.

—¿Y Antonio? preguntó al cabo de un momento de silencio y haciendo un esfuerzo para serenarse.

—No lo he visto, ¿acaso no has sabido? . . .

—Sí, tu padre me lo refirió todo. ¡Yo he sido la causa de tus penas y peligros, y sin embargo ni un consuelo, ni una señal de gratitud has recibido de mí! Perdóname: las penas nos hacen egoístas. Te confesaré mi debilidad: me llena de espanto la idea de que Antonio me recuerde con repugnancia.

—¿Pero no es peor que te tenga en mal concepto?

—Sí, es cierto; no lo había pensado. ¡Que lo sepa todo!

Y al decir esto prorrumpió en amargo llanto.

—Dile también a Mercedes lo que quieras, añadió.

—Ya Mercedes no es nada para mí. No quiero darle explicaciones: ella debió haber tenido fe en mi lealtad.

Dolores me miró un momento.

—Tú no la amaste nunca, pues cuando uno ama no tiene orgullo: no puede haber resentimiento duradero, ni pique, ni mala voluntad respecto del ser amado.

—No hablemos más de ella. Mercedes tiene otros pretendientes y yo ni la recuerdo.

Me despedí prometiéndole hablar con mi tía, lo que efectivamente hice, procurando hacerle comprender que la vida de Dolores dependía de que hiciese su voluntad.

Algunos días después me reuní con mi compañero en Honda y bajamos el Magdalena sin novedad, embarcándonos en Santamarta a principios del siguiente mes.

PARTE TERCERA

Sólo busco en la selva más lejana
Tétrico albergue, asilo tenebroso
No pisado jamás de huella humana.

Vicenta Maturana

Je meurs, et sur ma tombe, ou lentement j'arrive,
Nul ne viendra verser des pleurs.[12]

Gilbert

Durante los primeros meses de mi permanencia en Europa recibí varias cartas de mi padre en que me daba cuenta de la salud de Dolores. Empeoraba cada día, y al cabo de algunos meses ya todos habían perdido completamente las esperanzas. A pesar de los esfuerzos que hacían, consultando a los médicos más afamados del país, la horrible y misteriosa enfermedad continuaba con su mano desoladora destruyendo la belleza y aún la figura humana de mi infeliz prima. Ella vivía oculta, sin aire y sin luz, rogando que le permitiesen huir lejos de aquella atmósfera que la sofocaba.

Al fin entre otras cartas recibí la siguiente, de Dolores:

¡Ya no hay remedio, mi querido Pedro! Hace dos meses que he muerto para el mundo y me hallo en esta soledad. Tú escucharás con paciencia mis quejas, ¡oh! ¡ténme piedad!

Pero no, ¿por qué quejarme? la Providencia es ciega, y hay momentos . . . No me atrevo a leer lo que hay en el fondo de mi alma. Voy a referirte cómo fue mi despedida de mi tía y la llegada aquí. Si mi carta es incoherente, perdónamela: ¡mi espíritu cede a veces a tantos sufrimientos!

No sé si tú lo sabías, pero fueron tantas mis instancias, que al fin logré que se empezara a construir una casita, una pequeña choza, aunque aseada y cómoda, en el sitio que indiqué. Yo misma quise ir a mostrar el lugar exacto en que debía quedar. Sin embargo se pasaron meses antes de que la acabasen, y aunque yo rogaba que la concluyeran pronto, conocí que mi tía no podía resolverse a esta separación. Pero fatigada ya de rogar, amenacé seriamente que me huiría de la casa y conseguí mi deseo.

Yo permanecía oculta siempre y hablaba con mi tía y tu padre al través de la reja de la ventana de mi cuarto, y por entre las rendijas de mi puerta.

Un día me vinieron a decir que la casa estaba concluida y habían llevado los muebles necesarios, mis pájaros y algunas flores. Mi pobre tía se había esmerado en que tuviese cuantas comodidades podía apetecer. Tu padre me vino a decir, después de hacerme algunas recomendaciones higiénicas, que entre lo que habían llevado a mi futura casa se hallaba un pequeño botiquín y una relación sobre el modo de usarlo. 'Ahí encontrarás todo, me dijo, según la marcha de la enfermedad hasta, hasta. . . .' Al pronunciar estas palabras el buen anciano que tanto me había mimado prorrumpió en sollozos. Yo había entreabierto la puerta para hablar con él más cómodamente, y al oír aquella señal de vivísimo dolor, sentí en mi corazón una desesperación indomable, y abriendo la puerta enteramente me hinqué en el suelo exclamando con angustia:—¡Oh! tío, tío . . . usted tiene en su poder el hacerme penar menos; ¡oh! por Dios, deme un remedio . . . un remedio que acorte mi vida!

Tu padre se cubrió la cara con las manos y no me contestó. Pero en eso oí que mi tía venía por el corredor e inmediatamente me volvió el juicio, y haciendo un esfuerzo de voluntad violento me levanté y entrando a mi pieza cerré la puerta. Pero ella me había visto y me gritó golpeando en la puerta:—¡Dolores, Dolores! este sacrificio es demasiado grande, tú no puedes dejarme así.

Tuve una debilidad de un instante; pero eso ya pasó, le contesté con voz segura:—mañana me quiero ir a la madrugada, pero ruego por última vez que a mi salida nadie se me acerque.

Esa noche dormí tranquila. Ya había pasado la agitación y me sentía fuerte ante mi resolución. Antes de aclarar el día me vinieron a decir que mi caballo estaba preparado. Me levanté, y saliendo de mi cuarto atravesé el corredor en que estaba mi pajarera y ví por última vez el jardín, la alberca, los árboles . . . todo, todo lo que me recordaba mi feliz niñez y los sueños de mi corta juventud. No quise pensar, ni detenerme: la luz fría y triste del amanecer empezaba a iluminar los objetos que tomaban un aspecto fantástico. Mi perro favorito me siguió dando saltos de alegría.

El mayordomo, que debía acompañarme hasta mi choza y dos o tres sirvientes más me esperaban en el patio. Yo no quise aceptar el apoyo de nadie y de un salto monté a caballo.

—¡Adios! dije con voz ahogada dirigiéndome a los criados, díganle a mi tía . . .

No pude añadir otra cosa, y azotando con las riendas al caballo, que es muy brioso, salí como un relámpago del patio seguida por el mayordomo. No sé qué sentí entonces. Mi vida entera en sus más íntimos pormenores pasó ante mi imaginación, como dicen sucede a los que se están ahogando. Creo que iba a perder el sentido y dejarme caer del caballo, cuando un grito ahogado por la distancia me hizo detener mi cabalgadura, y mirando hacia atrás vi venir a mi tía que había montado y me seguía.

—¡Hija mía, Dolores! me dijo al acercarse. ¿Creías que yo permitiría que salieras de mi casa como una criminal sin que te acompañara siquiera hasta tu destierro?

—Perdón, tía; sí lo creí, y me desgarraba el corazón esta idea; pero como usted me había ofrecido no volverme a ver . . .

—Sí, sí lo dije. ¿Pero cómo dejar de verte, de hablarte por la última vez?

Dejé volar mi pañuelo al viento para ver de dónde venía y poniéndome del lado opuesto le contesté:—Una sola vez y al aire libre no podrá serle funesto. Prométame, sin embargo, que no se me acercará; si no me lo ofrece, juro, tía, que pondré en acción mi amenaza y me iré lejos de aquí: me ocultaré y moriré en el fondo del monte.

—Tía, añadí después, ésta es nuestra última conversación. Hablemos con toda la cordura y resignación que puede tener un cristiano en su lecho de muerte. No permitamos que nos interrumpan lágrimas, y no seamos débiles. El sacrificio indispensable está hecho;

aceptémoslo como una prueba enviada por la Providencia. Cuando lleguemos a orillas del monte me adelantaré sin decir nada. No pronunciemos la palabra adiós; ambas necesitamos de un valor que nos abandonaría si nos despidiésemos.

Así se hizo. Conversamos tranquilamente, en apariencia, del modo como arreglaría mi vida, pero teníamos el corazón despedazado. Cuando llegamos al estrecho camino que recordarás, me adelanté en silencio y al cruzar por la vereda que conduce a mi choza volví involuntariamente la cara: al través de los árboles vi a mi tía que se había detenido y me miraba partir con profunda pena. ¡Probablemente no la volveré a ver jamás! . . .

Por mucho tiempo no volví a recibir noticias de Dolores: mi padre me decía apenas que continuaba en su soledad y había prohibido que nadie se le acercase. Una vez me escribió lleno de tribulación. Parece que un día le vinieron a decir que Dolores estaba sumamente indispuesta: él se hallaba en la hacienda de mi tía y no pudo evitar que supiese lo que decían de Dolores. La tía Juana se alarmó y quiso a todo trance, y sin acordarse de su promesa, acompañar a mi padre a la choza de mi prima.

Llegaron hasta la casa, sin ser vistos, compuesta de una salita y una alcoba; separábala de la cocina y despensa un patiecito lleno de flores, y entre los bejucos que enredaban en el diminuto corredor colgaban jaulas llenas de pájaros. Penetraron a la salita, adornada con varios muebles y muchos libros sobre las mesas. Al ruido que hicieron al entrar, Dolores salió de la alcoba sin precaución alguna. Estaba tan desfigurada que mi tía dio un grito de espanto y se cubrió la cara con las manos. Dolores se detuvo un momento, y al ver la expresión de la fisonomía de sus tíos pasó cerca de ellos sin decir nada y tomó la puerta. Mi padre la siguió llamándola y la vio internarse en el monte. Viendo que no contestaba corrió hacia el sitio en que había desaparecido: caminó por la orilla de la quebrada, llamándola a cada paso, hasta que llegó a un sitio más abierto; pero el monte espeso se cerraba completamente más arriba, y la quebrada encajonándose entre dos rocas, no podía atravesarse sino llevando el agua hasta las rodillas. Dolores no parecía ni contestaba: mi padre creyó que había tomado otra senda y volvió a la casa para consultar con los sirvientes de mi prima. Ellos no la habían visto nunca salir así, pero inmediatamente corrieron a buscarla. Mi tía estaba tan conmovida e inmutada, que mi padre le aconsejó que volviera a la hacienda mientras que él se quedaría buscando a Dolores.

Se pasaron horas y no era posible encontrarla. Los sirvientes y todos los peones de la hacienda se pusieron en movimiento, pero llegó la noche, la que pasó también sin noticia alguna. Los primeros rayos del sol encontraron todavía a mi padre lleno de angustia, pues además de la desaparición de Dolores, mi tía se había enfermado gravemente.

Mejor será trascribir ahora una parte de la carte que recibí de Dolores, dándome noticia de lo sucedido.

. . . Creí, Pedro, que nunca volverías a saber de mí . . . quise morir, amigo mío, y no pude lograrlo. En días pasados me sentía muy enferma, tanto material como espiritualmente: mi postración era horrible y pasé días sin hablar ni tomar casi alimento alguno. Isidora y su hermano probablemente se alarmaron al verme en ese estado, y dieron aviso a la familia: no he querido preguntarles cómo llegaron repentinamente a mi choza tu padre y mi tía Juana. Al verme, fue tal el horror que se pintó en sus semblantes, que comprendí en un segundo que yo no debía hacer parte de la humanidad, y sin saber lo que hacía salí de la casa. Creo que perdí el juicio: me parecía oír tras de mí la carrera de cien caballos desbocados que me perseguían, y oía el ladrar de innumerables perros . . . Subí desalada por la orilla de la quebrada, y al llegar a un sitio más inculto atravesé sus aguas sin sentir que me mojaba ni pensar que me hería en los espinos del monte. Al fin se me acabaron las fuerzas y me detuve. Ya no oía los gritos ni las carreras de los que creí me perseguían y me encontré sola en medio de la montaña: no había más ruido que el zumbido de los insectos, el trinar de los pájaros y el chasquido de las hojas secas al romperlas con los pies. Estaba completamente exánime: no sé si me dormí o me desmayé, pero caí al suelo como un cuerpo inerte. Cuando volví en mí la oscuridad era casi completa en el fondo del bosque. ¿Qué hacer? La muerte se me presentó como un descanso. Me levanté para buscar un precipicio, pero la montaña en aquel sitio está en un declive suave del cerro y no hallé lugar alguno que fuera a propósito.

No sentía dolor ninguno (tú sabes que a consecuencia de la enfermedad se pierde la sensibilidad cutánea) y sin embargo me había desgarrado y estaba inundada de sangre y los vestidos hechos pedazos. Después de haber vagado largo tiempo llegué a un sitio más abierto en donde al pie de algunos árboles altísimos se veían anchas piedras cubiertas de musgo. Se sentía allí un fresco delicioso: me recosté sobre una piedra y levanté los ojos al cielo. La noche había llegado, y a medida que el suelo se cubría de sombras el cielo se poblaba de estrellas. Las lámparas celestes se encendían una a una como cirios en un altar. ¡Cuántas constelaciones, qué maravillosa titilación en esos lejanos soles, qué inmensidad de mundos y de universos sin fin . . . ! Poco a poco la misteriosa magnificencia de aquel espectáculo fue calmando mi desesperación. ¿Qué cosa era yo para rebelarme contra la suerte? Esos rayos de la luz morían antes de llegar a mi rincón, y sin embargo parecían mirarme con compasión . . . ¡Compasión! ¿todos no me tienen horror? No, hay tal vez algún ser que me recuerde todavía con ternura: te diré la verdad; la memoria de Antonio me salvó, y creí comprender como por intuición que no me había olvidado. ¿No bastaría la seguridad de su lejana simpatía para vivir resignada? No me creas ingrata: también te recordé; tú al menos no te mostraste espantado al verme.

La noche estaba estrellada pero muy oscura. Me sentía sin valor para pasarla entera en medio de aquella selva. Al desaparecer la agitación nerviosa que me animaba, sentí una gran postración y deseaba encontrar un sitio seguro en que pudiera recostarme sin temor. Recordé que había subido por la quebrada, y por la vista de las estrellas que tanto había contemplado en mi soledad me orienté. Busqué un lucero que brilla siempre en el confín del cielo al caer el sol, y me dirigí hacia un lado en que debía hallarse la choza de una pobre tullida que vivía en el monte con un hijo tonto. A poco comprendí que había encontrado un angosto sendero y procuré seguirlo. No sé cómo no me picaron mil animales venenosos que se arrastraban por el suelo, colgaban de las ramas y volaban chillando en torno mío. Desapareció la estrella tras de los árboles y la noche se hacía cada vez más oscura: había perdido los zapatos, y los pies rehusaban llevarme más lejos, cuando oí el ladrido de un perro: ¡qué música tan deliciosa fue aquella para mí! Algunos pasos más lejos encontré la choza y defendiéndome del perro con un palo que había tomado en el monte y me servía de bastón, empujé el junco que servía de puerta y despertando a la tullida pedí licencia para acostarme en un rincón.

Pasé la noche como una miserable, despertándome sobresalta[da] a cada momento, pero el cansancio me hacía dormir otra vez. Cuando amaneció, el tonto se levantó y encendiendo fuego enmedio del rancho, puso una olla sobre tres piedras que había allí e hizo un caldo con yucas, plátanos y carne salada. Yo permanecía en mi rincón sin moverme, hasta que habiéndome brindado un plato con hirviente caldo comprendí que mi mayor debilidad provenía de la falta de alimentos. Acepté y tomé con gusto lo que me ofrecían y al acabar rompí el plato como por descuido y tiré la cuchara.

A medida que subía el sol el calor aumentaba en el rancho y al fin salí a la puerta a respirar el aire. Mi vestido enlodado y hecho pedazos, los cabellos desgreñados y mi aspecto indudablemente terrible causaron impresión a los dueños de casa. Imposible que me reconocieran, aunque en otro tiempo había visitado algunas veces a la enferma. Pero aunque no sabían quien era, la tullida adivinó la enfermedad de que padecía y me dijo con dulzura que sería mejor que me fuera a sentar en el alar . . . Comprendí la repugnancia que inspiraba aún a aquellos desgraciados y me salí profundamente humillada. Deseaba mandar decir a mis parientes que no volvería otra vez a mi choza hasta que no me ofreciesen solemnemente que jamás irían a ella. El tonto no podía hablar claro ¿cómo mandar a decir lo que deseaba? Busqué un lápiz que llevaba en el bolsillo y que por casualidad no se había perdido en mi huida, y la tullida me dio un pedacito de papel que el tonto había llevado con unos remedios enviados por la tía Juana. Sobre un tronco de árbol caído que había cerca de la casa, puse el papelito y con mano trémula escribí algunas líneas y se las di al tonto para que las llevase a la hacienda, prometiendo pagarle bien.

Esa tarde llegaron mis dos sirvientes. Isidora me trajo ropa y Juan un caballo ensillado y una carta de tu padre en la que me decía que mi tía estaba gravemente enferma a causa de las penas que yo les había dado: por último me ofrecía no intentar verme sin mi consentimiento.

Volví a mi choza a cuidarme . . . sí, ¡me cuidé! ¡Oh triste humanidad! ¿No era mejor dejarme morir? Siempre encontramos en nuestro corazón este amor a la vida, y por lo mismo que es miserable como que nos complacemos en conservarla . . . Sí, Pedro: mientras yo cuidaba mi horrible existencia, mientras recuperaba fuerzas para seguir viviendo, mi pobre tía moría de resultas del terror, de la aprehensión y de la angustia que yo le había causado. Parece que se le declaró una fiebre violenta y al cabo de dos días sucumbió sin conocer a nadie, pero asediada por mi recuerdo y llamándome sin cesar. Acaso me creerás insensible, desnaturalizada, al ver que puedo hablar tranquilamente de la muerte de la que me quiso tanto. No sé qué decir: no me comprendo a mí misma y creo que hasta he perdido la facultad de sentir. Nunca lloro: la fuente de las lágrimas se ha secado; no me quejo, ni me conmuevo. Deseo la muerte con ansia, pero no me atrevo a buscarla y aun procuro evitarla.

Mi espíritu es un caos: mi existencia una horrible pesadilla. Mándame, te lo suplico, algunos libros. Quiero alimentar mi espíritu con bellas ideas: deseo vivir con los muertos y comunicar con ellos.

La carta de Dolores me impresionó vivamente. Comprendí que su carácter tan dulce había cambiado con el sufrimiento, y esto me dio la medida de sus penas. Busqué algunos libros buenos y se los envié. Durante los siguientes años recibí apenas algunas breves cartas de Dolores: el fondo de ellas era de una tristeza desgarradora a veces, con cierta incredulidad religiosa y odio al género humano en sus pensamientos, que me llenaban de pena. Mi padre me escribía que nunca la había vuelto a ver, pero que mandaba una persona todas las semanas a llevarle lo que podía necesitar y recoger noticias de ella.

Antonio se había arrepentido de su conducta ligera conmigo, y continuábamos una correspondencia muy activa. El primer golpe de dolor al comprender la horrible suerte de Dolores y la imposibilidad de que jamás fuera suya; ese rudo golpe no fue para él causa de desaliento: su carácter enérgico no permitía eso, y al contrario procuró vencer su pena dedicándose a un trabajo arduo y a un estudio constante. Pronto se hizo conocer como un hombre de talento, laborioso y elocuente, y alcanzó a ocupar un lugar honroso entre los estadistas del país.

Había pasado varios años estudiando en Europa y me preparaba a volver a la patria, cuando llegó la noticia de la muerte de mi padre. No diré lo que sentí entonces . . . Dolores me escribió también manifestándome la desolación en que había quedado.

Aunque al principio me repugnaba la idea de visitar mi hogar vacío, no pude resistir al deseo de volver al lado de Dolores y me embarqué.

Llegué a Bogotá de paso, pero allí me detuvo Antonio para que asistiese a su matrimonio. Se casaba con una señorita de las mejores familias de la capital, rica y digna de mucha estimación. Inmediatamente le escribí a Dolores la causa de mi detención, participándole la noticia del brillante matrimonio que hacía Antonio.

El matrimonio fue rumboso si no alegre. La novia no era bella; pero sus modales cultos, educación esmerada y bondad natural, hacían olvidar sus pocos atractivos. Cuando, después de la ceremonia me despedí de Antonio en la puerta de su casa, me entregó una carta para Dolores; carta que había escrito ese día, y en sus ojos vi brillar una lágrima, último tributo a sus ensueños juveniles.

Ocho días después llegaba a las cercanías de N★★★ y en vez de entrar al pueblo me dirigí inmediatamente por un camino extraviado al rincón del valle en que vivía Dolores. Al llegar a la vereda que años antes había pasado con mi prima, mi imaginación me trajo otra vez el recuerdo del esbelto talle de Dolores, su brillante mirada y alegres palabras: oía de nuevo el eco de su argentina risa que me parecía vibraba todavía en aquellas soledades. ¡Cómo había cambiado mi vida desde entonces! Mi tía había muerto, mi pobre padre también, mi novia era la esposa de otro (no sé si he dicho, que casó con don Basilio) y en fin, mi prima, la alegre niña de otro tiempo, era un ser profundamente desgraciado. No había querido entrar al pueblo que tenía para mí tan tristes recuerdos, y nada sabía de Dolores.

Cuando me acerqué al sitio en que debía hallarse la choza de mi prima, sentí cierto rumor que me admiró. Bajo un árbol estaban varios caballos ensillados: piqué el mío y llegué a la puerta de la casita a tiempo que salían de ella el cura y varios vecinos de N★★★.

—¡Qué encuentro tan casual! dijo el cura al reconocerme y deteniéndome en la puerta.

Era un respetable anciano que había sido cura de mi pueblo desde mi infancia.

—¿Dolores está adentro? pregunté después de haberle saludado.

—¡Dolores! No sabía usted acaso . . . ?

—¿Qué? Deseo hablarla.

—No, no entre, me contestó tomándome la mano.

—¿Qué ha sucedido?

—¡Pobre niña! me dijo con voz conmovida: ¡esta mañana dejó de padecer!

—¡Dios mío! exclamé sintiendo que hasta el último eslabón que me ligaba a los recuerdos de mi provincia había desaparecido; y entonces comprendí cuán necesario había sido para mí ese afecto.

Sentándome en silencio en el quicio de la puerta de la casa de Dolores, escondí la cara entre las manos. Los que rodeaban al cura se alejaron por un sentimiento de delicadeza; el cura se sentó a mi lado.

—Su muerte fue la de una cristiana, dijo el buen sacerdote. Hace algunos días me mandó rogar que viniera a verla; que no había necesidad de que me acercase, pues hablaría conmigo al través de la puerta de su alcoba. Vine varias veces y ayer se confesó y recibió lo auxilios de la religión. Esta mañana me fueron a decir que se estaba muriendo, y hasta entonces no pude verla: ¡no le diré a usted cuán cambiada estaba!

—Ahora, añadió al cabo de un momento, habiéndola visto expirar volvía a la parroquia para disponer el entierro.

Yo cumplí con mi deber. Asistí al entierro. Había dispuesto que la enterrasen en el patio de la casita y mandó que todo aquello quedase inhabitado.

Entre sus papeles hallé un testamento a mi favor y varias composiciones en prosa y verso. He aquí algunos fragmentos de un diario que llevaba y que hacen comprender mejor su carácter y los horribles padecimientos morales que sufría, sus vacilaciones y su desesperación.

23 de junio 1843.

Hace un año que sufro sola, aislada, abandonada por el mundo entero en este desierto. ¡Oh! si hubiera alguien que se acordara de mí ¿cómo no me hubieran de llegar ráfagas de consuelo que inspiraran resignación a este corazón desgarrado? A lo lejos en la llanura corren y se divierten. Mañana es día de San Juan, aniversario de las fiestas de N★★★. ¡Las fiestas! ¡qué de recuerdos me traen a la memoria! Hoy encontré por casualidad un ramo de jazmines secos ¿podrá creerse que este ser monstruoso que aparece ante mí al acercarme al espejo es la bella niña a quien fueron regaladas estas flores? Antonio, Antonio, tú a quien amo en el secreto de mi alma, cuya memoria es mi único consuelo, Antonio, ¿te acordarás acaso todavía de la infeliz a quien amaste? ¡Si supieras cómo me persigue tu imagen! Resuena tu nombre en el susurrante ramaje de los árboles, en el murmullo de la corriente, en el perfume de mis flores favoritas, en el viento que silba, entre las páginas del libro en que me fijo, en la punta de la pluma con que escribo; veo tus iniciales en el ancho campo estrellado, entre las nubes al caer el sol, entre la arena del riachuelo en que me baño . . . ¡Dios Santo! que este amor sea tan grande, tan profundo, tan inagotable, y sin embargo mi corazón ardiente yace mudo para siempre!"

Diciembre 8 de 1843.

La vida es un negro ataúd en el cual nos hallamos encerrados. ¿La muerte es acaso principio de otra vida? ¡Qué ironía! En el fondo de mi pensamiento sólo hallo el sentimiento de la nada. Si hubiera un Dios justo y misericordioso como lo quieren pintar ¿dejaría penar una alma desgraciada como yo? ¡Oh! muerte, ven, ¡ven a socorrer al ser más infeliz de la tierra! Soledad en todas partes, silencio, quietud, desesperante calma en la naturaleza . . . El cielo me inspira horror con su espantosa hermosura: la luna no me conmueve con su tan elogiada belleza: el campo me causa tedio: las flores me traen recuerdos de mi pasada vida. Flores, campos, puros aromas, armonías de la naturaleza que son emblemas de vida ¿por qué venir a causar tan hondos sentimientos a la que ya no existe? . . .

Mayo de 1844.

. . . Espantoso martirio . . . la enfermedad no sigue su curso ordinario. ¿Viviré aun muchos años? Hay noches en que despierto llena de agitación: soñé que al fin pude conseguir una pistola; pero al quererme matar no dio fuego y en mi pugna por dispararla desperté . . . Otras veces imagino que estoy nadando en un caudaloso

río, y me dejo llevar dulcemente por las olas que van consumién-
dome; pero al sentir que me ahogo, me despierta un intenso
movimiento de alegría.

Febrero de 18[45.][13]

    Recibí hoy una carta de Pedro que me ha consolado. Hay todavía
alguien, además de mi buen tío, que se acuerda de mí . . . Había
dicho que esta carta me había consolado . . . ¡mentira! La he vuelto
a leer y me ha causado un sufrimiento nuevo. Me habla de su vida
tranquila, de sus estudios y proyectos para lo porvenir. Los hombres
son los seres más crueles de la creación: se complacen en hacernos
comprender nuestro infortunio. En los siglos de la edad media,
cuando se le declaraba lázaro a alguno, era inmediatamente considerado como un cadáver: lo llevaban a la iglesia, le cantaban la misa de
difuntos y lo recluían por el resto de sus días como ser inmundo . . .
Pero al menos ellos no volvían a tener comunicación con la sociedad; morían moralmente y jamás llegaban a sus oídos los ecos
de la vida de los seres que amaron. Y yo, yo que me he retirado al
fondo de un bosque americano, hasta aquí me persigue el recuerdo
. . . ¿Amar qué es? Amar es sentir gratas emociones: los médicos
dicen que el lazarino ha perdido el sistema nervioso ¿para qué siento
yo, por qué recuerdo con ternura los seres que amé? . . .

Abril de 1845.

    . . . ¡Dios, la religión, la vida futura! ¡Cuestiones insondables!
¡Terribles vacilaciones de mi alma! ¡Si mi mal fuera solamente físico,
si tuviera solamente enfermo el cuerpo! Pero cambia la naturaleza
del carácter y cada día siento que me vuelvo cruel como una fiera
de estos montes, fría y dura ante la humanidad como las piedras de
la quebrada. Hay momentos en que en un acceso de locura vuelo a
mis flores, que parecen insultarme con su hermosura, y las despe-
dazo, las tiro al viento: un momento después me vuelve la razón, las
busco enternecida y lloro al encontrarlas marchitas. Otras veces mi
alma se rebela, no puede creer en que un Dios bueno me haga
sufrir tanto, y en mi rebeldía niego su existencia: después . . . me
humillo, me prosterno y caigo en una adoración sin fin ante el Ser
Supremo. . . .

Septiembre de 1845.

Siempre el silencio, la soledad, la ausencia de una voz amiga que me acaricie con un tono de simpatía. ¡La eterna separación! ¿Podrá haber idea más aterradora para un ser nacido para amar?

1 de enero de 1846.

Atravieso una época de desaliento y de letargo completo. He vivido últimamente como en sueños . . . No estoy triste ni desesperada. Siento que en mi corazón no hay nada: todo me es indiferente: la vida es el sufrimiento, la muerte . . . todo pasa y se mezcla en las tinieblas de mi alma, y nada me llega a conmover. ¡Una emoción! una emoción aunque fuera de pena, de miedo, de espanto (lo único a que puedo aspirar) sería bendecida por mí como un alivio: ¡tal es el estado en que me encuentro! Es peor esto que mi loca desesperación de los tiempos pasados. Vegeto como un árbol carcomido: vivo como una roca en un lugar desierto. . . .

Marzo de 1846.

A veces me propongo estudiar, leer, aprender para hacer algo, dedicarme al trabajo intelectual y olvidar así mi situación: procuro huir de mí misma, pero siempre, siempre el pensamiento me persigue, y como dice un autor francés: "*Le chagr[i]n monte en croupe et galope avec moi.*"[14]

La mujer es esencialmente amante, y en todos los acontecimientos de la vida quiere brillar solamente ante los seres que ama. La vanidad en ella es por amor, como en el hombre es por ambición. ¿Para quién aprendo yo? Mis estudios, mi instrucción, mi talento, si acaso fuera cierto que lo tuviera, todo esto es inútil, pues jamás podré inspirar un sentimiento de admiración: estoy sola, sola para siempre. . . .

6 Septiembre de 1846.

Ya todo acabó para mí. Pronto moriré: mi mano apenas puede trazar estas líneas con dificultad. ¡Cuánto había deseado este día! pero ¿por qué no he tenido la dicha de morir antes, cuando tenía una ilusión? Acaso soy injusta; pero este golpe aflojó, por decirlo así, la última cadena que me ligaba a la existencia. Recibí una carta de Pedro fechada en Bogotá: ¡pobre primo mío! pensé al abrirla; pronto podré oír tu voz; y también por él tendré alguna noticia directa de Antonio . . . Mi corazón latía con una dulce emoción y me sentía desfallecer. Me senté a orillas del riachuelo que corre murmurando cerca de mi habitación. ¡Con cuánto gusto había visto llegar al sirviente que trajo la carta! La imagen de Antonio vagaba en torno mío. . . .

Después de leer las primeras líneas una nube pasó ante mis ojos. Pedro me daba parte del matrimonio de Antonio ¡el matrimonio de Antonio! ¿Por qué rehusaba creerlo al principio? ¿No es él libre para amar a otra? Sin embargo, la desolación más completa, más agobiadora se apoderó de mí: me hinqué sobre la playa y me dejé llevar por toda la tempestad de mi dolor. Me veía sola, ¡oh! cuán sola, sin la única simpatía que anhelaba. Todo en torno mío me hablaba de Antonio, y sólo su recuerdo poblaba mi triste habitación. No había rincón de mi choza, no había árbol o flor en mi jardín, ni estrella en el azul del cielo, ni pajarillo que trinara, que no me dijera algo en nombre de él. Mi vida hacía parte de su recuerdo; ¿y ahora? El ama a otra ¡qué absurda idea! ¡a cuántas no habrá amado desde que nos separamos! ¡Cosa rara! esto no me había preocupado antes, y ahora esta idea no me abandona un momento. Como que mi alma esperaba este último desengaño para desprenderse de este cuerpo miserable. Comprendo que todos los síntomas son de una pronta muerte. ¡Gracias, Dios mío! Dejo ya todo sufrimiento; pero *él* es mi pensamiento en estos momentos supremos: ¡oh! ¡*él* me olvidará y será dichoso!

FIN

Notas

1. "La naturaleza es un drama con personajes."
2. Un *cachaco* es un joven elegante, de Bogotá o del centro del país.
3. Una *ñapanga* es una mujer mestiza.
4. Hacer un buen partido; casarse bien.

5. "Ella tiene bastante bonitos ojos . . . para ojos de provincia."

6. "El que vence sin peligro, triunfa sin gloria."

7. Venus es la diosa del amor; Lucrecia, matrona romana, es el modelo de la fidelidad conyugal; Minerva es la diosa de la sabiduría; Virginia es la heroína de la novela popular *Paul et Virginie* (1787) de Bernardin de St. Pierre; Pegaso es el caballo alado de la mitología griega.

8. "El dolor es una luz que nos aclara la vida."

9. Los Borgia (o Borja), era una famosa familia de origen español en los siglos XV y XVI, uno de cuyos miembros llegó a ser santo (San Francisco Borja), pero otros, como el Papa Alejandro VI, y su hijo, Cesare, tenían pocos escrúpulos y fama de eliminar a sus enemigos por medio del veneno.

10. El Espinal es un pueblo pequeño al suroeste de Bogotá, en la provincia de Tolima.

11. Chiquinquirá, unos 140 km al norte de Bogotá, tiene un culto importante a una Virgen milagrosa.

12. "Me muero, y sobre mi tumba, a la cual lentamente me acerco,/ Nadie vendrá a verter sus lágrimas."

13. El original dice "1864," lo cual tiene que ser un error.

14. "La tristeza monta a la grupa y corre al galope conmigo."

Dolores
Scenes from a Woman's Life

FIRST PART

La nature est un drame avec des personnages.[1]
Victor Hugo

"What a lovely girl!" exclaimed Antonio when he saw a group of people on horseback cross the center of the plaza of the village of N★★★, people who had come from a ranch for the purpose of attending the village festival, slated for the following day.

Antonio González was my classmate and favorite childhood friend. When we said good-bye at the university, both having graduated with our doctorates, he offered to come and visit me in my hometown at the time of the religious festival, and with that end in mind had arrived in N★★★ the previous day. As we were both anxious to have a good time, we oversaw with all the enthusiasm of early youth (which can muster interest in everything) the construction of the barriers in the plaza for the following day's bullfights. Just then, as I said before, a group on horseback went by, in whose midst there shone like a lovely lily in a field the area's most beautiful flower: my cousin Dolores.

"What strikes me the most," added Antonio, "is such a white complexion, and a soft tint you don't see in this hot climate."

In effect, Dolores's black eyes and long, jet black hair stood out against her rosy skin and the crimson of her lips.

"What you say is true," exclaimed my father, who happened to be at my side. "Dolores's skin is not normal for this climate . . . Good Heavens!" he said with a troubled voice a moment later. "I hadn't thought of that before."

Antonio and I didn't understand the old man's comment. Years later we would remember the impression that his vague fear caused in us, a fear that seemed so strange. . . .

My father was the doctor in N★★★ and in any other more civilized place he would have been famous for his practical knowledge and his charity. Contrary to the norm, he had always wanted me to follow in his same profession, with the hope, he said, that I would be a better-educated doctor than he.

An only child, satisfied with my lot, spoiled by my father and dearly cherished by numerous relatives, I had always considered myself very fortunate. At that time I was in N★★★ only temporarily, taking care of some business so that soon I could formalize my engagement to a young lady I had met, and with whom I had fallen in love in Bogotá.

Among all my relatives I had always been Aunt Juana's favorite; she was a most respectable and wealthy lady who had taken care of me and overseen my childhood from the time I lost my mother. Dolores, one of her sister's children, had been living with her for several years, as the girl had lost both of her parents. Aunt Juana shared her affection between her favorite niece and nephew.

Hardly had we reached the age when one begins to think of these matters, when Dolores and I realized that the good lady's dearest wish was to arrange our engagement, but human nature prefers the difficult to the smooth path, and both of us tacitly attempted to make it clear to her that our mutual affection was only fraternal. I think that the desire to thwart this project once and for all contributed to my urgent desire to get married in Bogotá at a time when I was still a student without a clear future. As I regarded Dolores as a sister, from the time I went off to high school I wrote to her often, describing the ups and downs of my student life, and later my plans as a young man and a fiancé.

This short summary is indispensable for understanding my simple tale.

After staying in the plaza a little while longer we returned home. My father's house was a little distance from the village, but as there were to be fireworks that night, Antonio and I decided to return to town a little before this popular spectacle was to begin.

The moon lit up the landscape. A warm, delicious breeze ruffled the trees and brought out the flowers' scent. Birds awakened with the moonlight and twittered gently, while the philosophical owl, ever silent and gloomy, complained with his unlucky call.

Antonio and I had to cut through a horse pasture and cross the main road before reaching N★★★'s plaza. We talked happily of our hopes and future plans, because for youth the future is always synonymous with happiness and fulfilled expectations! Antonio had chosen the more difficult but also more brilliant career of law, and his evident ability and easy eloquence promised him a fine future. As for myself, after doing some practical training with one of the best-known professors, I planned to get married and return home to enjoy quiet country life. I have to confess that N★★★ was really no more than a large village, no matter how much its inhabitants minded having it called that, for it gave itself the airs of a city and back then had a governor, judges, a city council and the other trappings of local government. Unfortunately these trappings and pretensions were the source of countless problems, much like those of a simple country girl, who, used to going barefoot and wearing short skirts, suddenly puts on high-heeled boots, a corset, and crinolines. . . .

Antonio and I went to Aunt Juana's house, which was located on the plaza and was the finest in town. Many of the local young ladies sat on low chairs in the doorway and against the walls, laughing and chatting, while their mothers and respectable ladies sat inside discussing more serious matters, such as ailments, food, and maids. Dandies from the village and from other places who had come for the festival strolled up and down in front of the doorway without daring to approach the girls, while the latter reveled in their glory and fine appearance without revealing the interest with which they regarded the young men.

I approached the female phalanx with all the high spirits that came from having arrived from Bogotá, something that carried considerable weight in the provinces, and the knowledge that as a relative I would be well received. I introduced my friend to everyone inside and outside the house, and, taking chairs, we went outside to talk to the girls. . . .

I then suggested that all of us who were from Aunt Juana's house should take a stroll around the plaza.

The female contingent formed a line, and we of the unfair sex took up guerrilla positions, patrolling the outskirts of the group. Attraction is always inexplicable: very soon Antonio and Dolores were drawn to each other and immediately began an animated conversation.

The plaza was full of tables offering different games of chance, at which for the modest sum of a penny everyone who wished to could try his luck. Around other tables and under tents people were drinking a variety of alcoholic beverages: fermented coconut juice, cane liquor, anise and fruit-flavored spirits, and even rather bad wine and brandy. Others satisfied their heart's desire with succulent food: soups, roast turkey, and suckling pigs stuffed with garlic and cumin. There were also tropical fruit drinks, some of blackberry and pineapple, and beverages made with corn or rice, proffered in bottles stoppered with bunches of carnations or roses. Cookies with white or cinnamon icing, almond and egg desserts, candied fruit, coconut macaroons, dry biscuits and little griddle cakes in a variety of shapes; the whole assortment of delicacies commonly known as "snacks" was spread out on trays of various colors and sizes, arranged in rows on coarse but clean tablecloths. . . .

After having inspected the tables in the plaza, where rustic enjoyment reigned, we went to the mestizas' dance. So colorful were these women that ladies liked to go and see them dance, without fearing that their reputations might be compromised. As this dance was supposed to be very noisy and extremely crowded, we found a great number of curious onlookers around the door or glued to the windows that gave onto the dance floor. Nonetheless, when they saw us coming they stepped aside so that the girls could stand by the windows, and we men behind them. . . .

The mestizas wore blue silk skirts with a frill on the bottom, a red and black embroidered blouse, a red or blue shawl, and a small hat of fine straw with wide ribbon ties. Some of the women took off their hats to dance, exposing their thick black hair to view, hair that was parted into two braids, the ends tied up with ribbons, and which hung down their backs.

The men, practically all of whom had pretensions of being social dandies, smoked and drank small glasses of aguardiente,[2] chatting with the musicians who sat by the inner door of the room while they tuned their instruments.

"Hey, Don Basilio!" several voices shouted from the doorway, just as the band began to play a sprightly *bambuco*. "Your partner's waiting for you!"

All eyes focused on a man of some forty years of age, heavyset, beardless, broad of face, with a narrow brow which slanted backward, an irritable look, and the habit of closing one eye when he spoke, all of which combined to give him a singularly disagreeable appearance.

"If Don Basilio dances tonight we're going to have some fun," said Antonio.

"Quiet," I answered. "If he hears you he'll never forgive you. That man is conceited and vengeful."

"I'll dance," exclaimed Don Basilio with self-importance, "if Julian will dance, too."

"Go on, Julian," the dandies shouted, and, hauling Julian out of their midst they made him give his hand to a cheerful and spirited mestiza, whose little black eyes contrasted with a sprig of orange blossoms she wore in her hair. Meanwhile Don Basilio pulled another woman by the hand, whispering things in her ear that made her blush, and, stepping out with a complacent air, stood in front of her and began to dance the *bambuco*. The girl, who was young and light, circled around him, mocking the thick waist and awkward gestures of her swain, so that he looked like a huge bear playing with a kitten. Although he was effeminate and very affected, Julian and the other girl made a much better pair.

But while they finish dancing, let us tell you who these people are, one of whom is important to this story.

Basilio Flores was the son of a poor country woman from the outskirts of Bogotá. His cleverness and natural aptitude came to the attention of a rich landowner, on whose property Basilio's mother cultivated her plot of potatoes and corn. The landowner took him home, and in his free time taught Basilio to read; pleased at the facility with which the boy learned, he determined to make a good employee out of him, onto whose shoulders he could in time shift some of the burden of his complicated business dealings. He sent him to a school where the boy quickly made great strides. Basilio was eighteen when the War of Independence broke out, and his Spanish protector felt obliged to emigrate. Before leaving he secretly summoned the boy, and made him promise under oath that when things calmed down, Basilio should dig up a sum of money that had been buried somewhere in the house where he lived, and use it to travel to Spain to fetch his master.

Circumstances in the country made any kind of communication with the motherland impossible, and, in the midst of the political turmoil which engulfed him, the Spaniard's protégé doubtless forgot his patron's request. . . .

When some sort of peace finally returned to the nation, it came to light that, among the Spaniards who had fled the country, Basilio's master, who had wandered about the Colombian coast, and had fallen ill in the Antilles, had barely had time to reach Spain before he died, leaving no will. . . .

Basilio went back to the capital claiming to have been an unknown relative's inheritor, and, making a great show of his wealth, attempted to enter good society but was rejected with disdain.

Angry, yet determined to use all the means at his disposal to gloss over his origin, he left for Europe and lived in Paris for several years. Lacking connections and ability, he surrendered to vice, and managed to corrupt the meager heart with which nature had endowed him. . . .

Resolved to forge a brilliant career for himself in his own country, he returned with a thousand ambitious projects, and very soon the articles he wrote for the newspapers of this or that political party began to attract attention. He had a very good memory, an average education, and some ironic, though superficial eloquence, the kind that deceives people easily. He signed himself B. de Miraflores, and there were people who said that in Paris he made himself out to be a baron. He spoke French and English fairly correctly, and always embellished his conversation with phrases or quotations by foreign authors. He dressed with extravagant luxury and bad taste, and gave luncheons where he flaunted the gaudy ostentation with which he dazzled the masses.

But unfortunately, if he had a good memory for some things, it failed him completely in others, and during his trip abroad he forgot about his poor mother, the only person to weep for his absence. On his return from Europe he refused to see her, nor did he permit her to come to his house (this might discredit him!), but pretending a generosity that distinguishes noble hearts, by means of a young man who served as his factotum he sent a monthly pension to "the poor country woman who had been his wet nurse," as he said, arching his eyebrows.

When, after a few years he wanted to *faire une fin*,[3] in his words, he successively proposed marriage to the richest, prettiest, and most virtuous young ladies of Bogotá society; naturally all scorned him and wounded his self-esteem, which brings to mind the famous maxim: "When it comes to insults, there is always a legacy." And sooner or later he got even with them.

Discouraged in his marital plans, he turned wholeheartedly to politics, but here, too, disappointments awaited him. His more than humble origin, his coarse, biting tongue, and his bad habits made him undesirable among men of any worth in all the political parties. Unable to make himself esteemed and admired, he made men fear him, and swore to mock society and take revenge on all those who had humiliated him. He allied himself with the most corrupt men of any party, and by means of intrigue succeeded in forging some sort of reputation among the well-known public writers of the nation. . . .

Our hero's political career would not be complete if he were unable to add yet one more laurel to his crown: he wanted to be elected to the national government. In the central and the Magdalena provinces he was too well known to be popular, and was advised to go to the southern provinces, where he might be able to win over his readers by some impassioned articles. This was the reason why *Don Basilio de Miraflores* had come to my town, in which he stayed on when he found out about the coming festival.

Julian belonged to a certain type of dandy that unfortunately has become very common of late, their bad traits worsening with each generation while losing the few good ones they had.

The son of a rich landowner of the southern provinces and educated in Bogotá, in whose preparatory schools he had spent seven years, he had never experienced the heroic poverty that molds a student's character. His pink and white complexion, willowy build, and languid gaze had captured the admiration of the young ladies of Bogotá, while word of his wealth and of the social position of his family won the hearts of their mothers. In the course of his seven years of preparatory school, and a further two in which, according to what he wrote his parents, he was *reviewing* what he had studied, he learned to speak a smattering of French and one or two sentences in Latin; in history he knew Dumas's novels, very little philosophy and even less geography. . . . [He] could dance all the latest dances, and spoke with great seriousness about the tedium of his life, the loss of his illusions, and his wounded heart, but when one saw his fresh face and cheerful demeanor, it was clear that his health had not been impaired by great misfortune or numbers of irreparable losses. . . .

Spurred on by the dance and the loud music, Don Basilio recalled his own youth, and embellished the last strains of the *bambuco* with various leaps which were clumsy imitations of the cancan, performed at the famous Mabille and Valentino balls.

"Bravo!" the dandies shouted to him, and when he finished came over to offer him a glass of liquor as refreshment. . . .

At that instant the musicians struck up a popular waltz and the young men hurried to find partners from among the prettiest mestizas. Some men wore *ruanas*,[4] and all danced with hats on and cigarettes in their mouths.

The young ladies whom we had escorted looked on in silence, naturally feeling affronted and shocked to see that the young men who called upon them were treated very familiarly by those women.

"Let's go," they said and left the windows.

Antonio and I saw the ladies to their respective homes and ourselves resumed the road to our lodging.

At times the heart has premonitions that we cannot explain. I don't know why Dolores's fate worried me so that night: I thought of many things that should make her happy, but in spite of that I could not shed an apprehension that had no motive but that bothered me without my understanding why. For his part Antonio was feeling the first symptoms of a great love: the storms that develop in a heart always begin with a sense of painful melancholy. The sweetness of love is not felt until one has already lost one's willpower and loves unthinkingly.

Antonio suffered, I felt sad, and both of us returned home in silence.

The following days we went to the penning of the bulls and to the bullfights, and in the evenings to dances. Antonio was completely enthralled by Dolores's charms, and any time we were together never wearied of praising her grace and beauty to me. I remember that once he nearly got angry with me because I laughingly quoted the Latin proverb that says, "It is not Nature which makes a woman beautiful, but our love."

Dolores received Antonio's attentions with her good humor and irrepressible happiness. She was unable to be sad, and went after those who appeared melancholy with good-natured barbs. My friend matched her lively character by countering with many jokes and witticisms characteristic of the Bogotá dandy. The love between those two young people was as beautiful, clear, and smiling as a spring day. Wherever they were, they communicated their innate happiness to all around. I have never seen two people more suited to fall in love, and to appreciate each other's mutual qualities. There is no doubt that the axiom which says that opposites attract is a serious error. It may lend a certain glitter, liveliness, and variety to a fleeting sentiment, but between people who love deeply there has to be complete harmony: harmony of feelings, upbringing, social position, and the background of one's ideas. The result of this harmony is moral peace, and this should be the principal goal and beautiful ideal of matrimony.

Don Basilio soon discovered that Dolores, besides being pretty and virtuous, had a fair-sized dowry, and immediately began to lay siege to this new fortress; he thought it would not be bad *business* to garner both a political post and a bride on his trip. The late *uncle's* fortune was beginning to disappear at an alarming rate and he had no desire to grow old in a state of poverty. He confided his plan to Julian, saying: "A simple *villageoise* is an easy conquest . . . Besides, she's pretty, and I could show her in Bogotá without embarrassment," adding with his usual fatuousness by quoting a French writer: "Elle a d'assez beaux yeux . . . pour des yeux de province."[5]

"But," observed Julian, "don't you see that you have a rival in Antonio?"

"Better yet, my young novice. Don't you know that the great Corneille said, 'A vaincre sans péril on triomphe sans gloire?'"[6]

One day he gave Dolores a poem dedicated to her, in which he declared his torrid love in glacial verses: it had so many quotes there was hardly an original word in it, he jumbled mythology with ancient history when he invoked Venus and Lucrece, Minerva and Virginia, and ended by saying, "that led by fate, I mounted Pegasus to fall at your feet."[7] On Aunt Juana's urging Dolores showed the ringing verses to Antonio and me, and naturally we did not spare our jokes.

After having stayed in N*** for several days, Don Basilio continued his journey in search of popularity, totally convinced that there was nothing to be gained in our town, and realizing that if he asked for it, Dolores was set to give him the kind of *no* he was accustomed to receiving. It was not hard for Antonio and me to see that he was furious with us when he left, for we had openly made fun of him, something he promised himself he would make us pay for some day.

The festival was over. One by one the people who had come for it began to leave.

The day before Antonio's departure I organized an outing to which the most important people who were still in town were to come. A few hours from N*** flows a good-sized river shaded by very tall trees, and nearby is the house of a sugar mill that offers refreshments and a place to leave the horses. This is the favorite destination for anyone hereabouts who organizes excursions.

At seven in the morning some twenty of us were waiting at the entrance of Aunt Juana's house for Dolores to come out. She soon appeared, mounted on a spirited horse, with her long habit, round little hat with flying veil, bright look, and charming air. After noisily clattering through the streets we took a narrow path along some horse pastures, and there groups formed according to each person's preference. I let Antonio ride alongside Dolores, recalling that some writer once said that the best time for a declaration of love is when one is on horseback. And indeed, the liveliness of the outing, the fresh air blowing, the ability to spur on or rein in your horse, to ride ahead or stay back for no apparent reason, of speaking or falling silent, to turn your head or catch your companion's eye—all this enlivens things and easily presents opportunities for being alone, even in the midst of a large group. Nonetheless, that day Antonio was silent, and both their faces were at times shadowed by a sweet melancholy, perhaps because they were thinking of having to separate that very afternoon.

We accompanied the ladies to the riverbank, and while they were bathing we gathered in the sugar mill, talking and laughing happily. But Antonio never recovered his spirits until we rejoined our group's female contingent when lunch was ready. The landscape was extraordinarily beautiful: the scent of the flowers, the buzzing of the insects, the murmuring river that on our side flowed downstream among glistening rocks, the sound of the wind in the leaves of the trees that fluttered over our heads—all the life and motion of tropical nature made us revel in it, enticing one to leisure and the lazy joy of living . . . Antonio and Dolores had imperceptibly drawn apart from the others and were seated at the base of a huge rock covered with yellow moss. Dolores was distractedly tossing the petals of a bunch of flowers she held in her hand into the river, and while the water splashed the golden sand at her feet, both of them regarded with interest the fate of those little blossoms in the foaming current. Some floated slowly downstream, and soon came to rest on the soft bank; others, swept away forcefully by the river, were suddenly caught in a whirlpool and immediately disappeared; others initially sailed off quickly and joyfully, but when they came to a cavity the rocks had formed, ran into each other, and, unable to escape, became waterlogged and sank little by little; in the end, the most fortunate ones clung together, and made their way into the middle of the river, floating downstream without encountering any obstacles whatever.

"Do you see the philosophy behind this event?" I asked, suddenly coming upon the two of them.

Antonio and Dolores started as though they had been interrupted, and in fact communicated their thoughts to each other with a glance, speaking through their very silence.

"What philosophy?" they asked.

"The one in the flower Dolores is casting into the stream. It is the symbol of Providence, and each one of the petals is a human life. What fate would you like, Dolores? That of the blossoms which quickly come to rest on the sand without ever having felt any emotions? That of those that are swept away by the current and are swallowed up in a whirlpool?"

"I? I don't know. But those I feel sorry for are the ones that are trapped in a lonely place, and have no hope of getting out . . . Look," she added, "how they sink little by little, and seemingly against their will."

"I, most assuredly, Sir Philosopher," said Antonio, catching Dolores's eye, "prefer the fate of those who float down the river of life two by two."

My cousin's cheeks flushed crimson, and getting up in a fluster, she went to rejoin the other groups of her girlfriends.

Laughter and conversation, songs and the harmony of guitars and mandolins, a dance in the patio of the sugar mill and general good spirits, none of this could cheer Dolores. She was content, momentarily even happy, but there was a shadow in her face and a kind of sad tone modulated the timbre of her voice. Antonio was in that state in which people in love fall silent and are bewildered, unable to do anything but gaze at their beloved, hear what *she* has to say, not see anything or anyone else—a state of mind which is extremely annoying to everyone except the woman who inspires these feelings and understands the situation.

We returned to town at night; it was very dark, in spite of the stars which sparkled in the cloudless sky. While crossing a stream at a dangerous point, we thought it a good idea for each man to cross beside one of the ladies. Dolores's horse shied when it slipped on the rocks, and if Antonio had not caught her with one arm and sat her back in her saddle, her horse's lunge would have thrown her into the water. When Antonio finally regained the bank, one could plainly see the fright and emotion he had felt in that endeavor, and his voice shook when he answered my question. It was then I realized how tenderly and truly he loved Dolores. True love is not selfish, and the heart is never more fearful than when the beloved person is in danger, even though it might not seem all that serious to others.

Half an hour later they parted, perhaps forever, those two people who had been born to love each other so deeply!

Later, when we were alone, Antonio confided to me that he had not been able to speak to Dolores of his love, for as it was so strong and noble, he had found no words to express it. He asked me to tell my cousin for him that he had not formally asked for her hand because his present position did not yet allow him to do so, but as he had hopes that she felt the same way, asked me to beg her not to forget him.

The same day Antonio left for Bogotá, Aunt Juana returned to her ranch with Dolores. I had witnessed Antonio and Dolores's parting, and although she had a smile on her lips I understood that she might need some comforting. And so, very early the following Sunday, I rode off to the ranch, which was called Springtime, and was located on a plain at the foot of some high, forested hills, a plain where livestock and extensive cacao plantings flourished.

When I got there my aunt was out, and the house absolutely quiet. I dismounted and, giving my horse to a servant, crossed the patio in front of the house and headed for the room in which I was told Dolores could be found.

My cousin's favorite place was a wide passageway toward the rear of the house, with a view over a combined garden and orchard. . . . Dolores's aviary was famous round about: in a great cage which took up the entire corner of the passageway she had collected from all over many birds who had been taught to live together peacefully. . . . Among her flowers and birds Dolores spent the days sewing, reading, and singing along with them. From afar one heard the sound of the aviary, and the gentle voice of its mistress.

On that day everything was still. The heat was asphyxiating, and Nature seemed oppressed and scorched by the rays of a fiery sun which ruled by itself in a cloudless sky. The birds were silent, and the only sound that one heard was that of a stream of water from the pond, which flowed unceasingly under the arbor of flowers. From afar I could see Dolores, dressed in white, her lovely dark hair her only adornment. Resting on a pillow at the foot of the chair on which she had been seated, she leaned her head on her folded arm, while her other small hand, rosy and white, lay inert at her side. I stopped when I spied her, thinking her asleep, but she had heard the jingle of my spurs when I approached, and suddenly stood up, attempting to hide the tears that sprang to her eyes, and simultaneously picking up a paper she had put on her little sewing table.

"What's this, cousin?" I asked her, pointing to the paper after having greeted her.

"I was writing, and . . . "

"To whom?"

"To no one."

"What? Has Antonio already managed . . . ?"

"No, Pedro," she answered with dignity, "he hasn't asked me any such thing, nor would he."

"Dolores," I said, taking her cold, trembling hand between my own, "didn't Antonio swear to you that he loved you madly, just like he's told me thousands of times? Confess that he asked you to be true to him!"

"No; he indicated that perhaps he liked me somewhat, but never told me any more than that."

"And this letter?"

"It isn't a letter!"

"Message, then," I said laughing, "epistle, note, whatever you want to call it."

"You won't believe me? Take it; you're making me show you what I wrote only for myself."

And she gave me the page whereupon she had just written some beautiful verses which showed deep poetic sensitivity, and a kind of vague melancholy spirit I did not know she possessed. It was a tender farewell to her peaceful, happy childhood, and a prayer to her youth, which suddenly seemed like a revelation to her. Her heart had been touched for the first time, and that trembling had made her understand that a life of suffering had begun.

Embarrassed and moved, she dropped her eyes as I read. Her rosy white skin stood out with greater freshness against her white dress and loose hair. A vague fear gripped me, as it had my father, when I noted the particular coloration of her skin, but this impression was again forgotten, only to be recalled later.

I spent the day at my aunt's house, attended to Antonio's request, and was convinced that she loved him, too. About that time I had to return to Bogotá: I was restless, and longed for the joy of seeing my fiancée again after an absence of a month and a half.

When I was leaving the two ladies wanted to accompany me up to a certain point in the road, so that Dolores could show me a pretty spot at the base of the hills, which she had *discovered* a few days before on one of her outings.

Dolores was most happy and joyful. The love that vitalized her formed a kind of halo around her. What does absence matter if we are sure we love and are loved in return? When she reached a narrow trail she had had broken through the wilderness, she rode on ahead. I followed her, admiring her slender figure and the grace and sureness with which she controlled a spirited colt that had shown itself obedient and docile only with her.

A few moments later we reached a more open place: a crystalline stream leaped down stony steps and came to rest in a lovely bed of moss and of quivering, variegated ferns. Extremely tall trees rose on one side of the stream, their dense shade preventing other shrubs from growing beside them. A number of old trunks and stones encased in green moss covered the earth, carpeted by a soft, golden sand. The sun was beginning to set and the shade in that spot produced a delicious coolness. Groups of colorful birds, among which chattered many parrots and parakeets, flew up to land in the high crowns of the trees, gilded by the sun's last rays.

We dismounted, and my aunt, who brought out some sweets and a coconut curiously set in polished silver, invited us to share in a rustic repast.

"How lovely it would be to spend one's life here, wouldn't it?" exclaimed Dolores.

"Alone?" I answered, smiling.

Her only reply was a tender glance that was meant for my absent friend, then she continued talking gaily. The poor girl! . . . But still happy in the ignorance of what was to come.

La douleur est une lumière qui nous éclaire la vie.[8]

Balzac

Two months after I had gotten back to Bogotá I received Dolores's first letter, which I have kept along with many others as mementos of my cousin, whose truly gifted nature no one knew but I.

"Dear Cousin," she wrote me,

I was awaiting news of your arrival before I wrote you, and later, when I wanted to write, the events which have taken place at home and in my life prevented me from doing so . . . I didn't know if I should confide the terrible secret I have discovered to you, but the heart needs to let go, and I well know that you are not only my brother but a very beloved friend who will feel compassion at my troubles. Recently I read that what makes friendships last and doubles their joy is a feeling that love does not have: security. Oh! Friendship is the only thing that can comfort me now, as other feelings will be forbidden me. Not long ago, remember? I saw the world as beautiful, happy, enchanting; everything smiled on me . . . but now, great God, an earthquake has strewn with ruins the place where the temple of my hopes once stood!

Forgive me, Pedro, for this chatter with which I am trying to put off confessing my troubles; this itself will indicate to you the terror I feel when I see in writing that which I hardly dare even to think.

But courage! I shall begin.

A few days after your departure I was going to my aunt's room one afternoon, when I went by the passageway of the entrance patio, and heard that an old tenant who lived within the borders of the ranch was asking for her. He had a letter in his hand, and when I found out it was for my aunt I took it, and was about to hand it to her, but when she found out that it was old Simon who had brought it, she screamed, "Throw that letter away, Dolores, throw it away!"

Instinctively I did as she asked and dropped it. My aunt then had me wash my hands, and, ordering a brazier brought to her, did not pick up the letter in her own hands until she had had it fumigated.

I was so surprised at seeing this that I could barely ask the reason for my aunt's sudden fear; in the end the whole thing even seemed funny, and I exclaimed, laughing,

"Is the paper poisoned, Aunt? Is old Simon like the Borgias,[9] as in the story we read the other day?"

"Don't joke, my dear," she answered me seriously, "for the poison this letter might contain is far more dreadful than any men have invented."

As she said these words she finished reading the letter, and, tossing it on the brazier, watched it slowly go up in flames.

"You have to explain this mystery to me . . . "

"Don't think there's any romantic mystery here," she interrupted me with a sad tone. "Don't you know that there are lepers on the outskirts of N★★★? One of those unfortunate beings sent me this letter."

"And who is it?"

"Who indeed? A poor wretch whom I have sent some help and who lives in a tumbledown cabin not far from old Simon's."

"The poor man! And he lives alone the way they all do? Alone, right in the wilderness, with no one to speak to him nor ever approach him. He will live and die in isolation, without the touch of a helping hand . . . My God, how cruel, what an awful fate!"

And my heart ached with unspeakable anguish.

"Society is very cruel, Aunt," I added. "It casts out the unfortunate man from its bosom . . . "

"That's the way it is," she answered me, "but what is there to do? Apparently this ghastly disease is terribly contagious. Given that, isn't it better for one to suffer than many? As for me, Dolores, I confess that the very sight of a leper horrifies me, and I would rather die than get close to one."

"And how did you get to know this poor man? Why do you help him, Aunt? This really interests me, for the address was beautifully written . . . and the handwriting even looks familiar to me."

"Why do I help him, you ask? Shouldn't one always help those who suffer?"

My aunt abruptly ended the conversation. Although during the following days we did not talk about the business of the letter, it had impressed me greatly. Winter came with all the fury with which you know the rains fall here in this climate. We were completely alone on the ranch; no one dared cross the swollen rivers and flooded roads to come and see us. Sometimes I awoke in the middle of the night at the noise of a tremendous storm, and when I heard the rain fall, thunder rip the air, and the wind moan against the tightly shut windows, and when I felt secure in my room, surrounded by so much comfort, my spirit flew to the lonely huts of those pariahs of our society: the lepers. In my imagination I saw the poor wretches, beset by terrible suffering, in the midst of the wilderness and the storm, and alone, always alone . . .

One night I had read until very late, studying French in the books you left me; I tried to learn and progress in my studies, to educate my spirit and teach myself so as to be less ignorant: contact with *certain* people from the capital city had lately made me realize how indispensable it is to be educated. I thus went to bed late, and was just falling asleep when I thought I heard steps in the outside patio, and something like the whispering of two voices speaking in low tones. My favorite dog, who spends the night in my room, suddenly jumped up and went out the open window to the passageway; a moment later I heard him leap up on someone in the patio. My aunt's voice made him stop. How strange! My aunt, who usually went to bed at eight, was wandering about corridors of the house at midnight! I got up, determined to find out what was going on, and slightly opened the door which went out into the farthest passage. Then I heard a man who said in a low voice, "Good-bye, Juana!" This voice caused me to tremble greatly; I thought I was dreaming . . .

"Wait a moment," answered my aunt, "and I will bring the portrait I had done for you by a painter from Quito who happened by here a few days ago."

After saying this I heard Aunt Juana go into her room, and, under cover of darkness, I quickly slipped into the corridor and hid in a corner from which, by crouching down, I could see a shape that stood motionless in the center of the patio.

Fear and a vague apprehension I had felt when I heard the

stranger's voice vanished when I saw he was no ghost, no figment of my imagination. Nevertheless, I could not understand how Aunt Juana could have *appointments* at midnight and give away her portrait! It was true that a short time previously I had asked her to have her portrait done by an itinerant painter who did mine as well. A moment later she returned, and, leaning on the railing of the corridor, tied a string around a wrapped package while saying, "It's not as good a likeness as I would have wished," and when the shape drew nearer, she added, "I'm also giving you Dolores's [book] *Imitation of Christ*, which I replaced with a new one."

"You don't know how much good this will do me," the stranger said with feeling. "Oh, my poor daughter! Her portrait!"

The voice, the tone froze my blood, and for a moment I don't know what happened to me. An incredible idea, a horrible terror left me feeling as though I had been struck down. I stood up, cold and trembling.

"You must go soon, Jerome," my aunt replied, "I heard a noise from Dolores's room and . . . "

I heard no more. I had recognized my father's voice and my aunt called him by name. My father, whom I had thought dead for six years! I thought no further about the mystery of that apparition. Racing down the corridor steps which led to the patio, I ran toward the figure, and when I reached him, threw my arms around his neck. When they saw what I had done, both my aunt and my father let out cries of horror: the latter pushed me away in desperation, covered his face with the *ruana* in which he was wrapped, and attempted to flee. I fought to run after him, but my aunt, who had followed me down, stopped me.

"Dolores," she shouted, "Dolores, don't go near him! Good God, he's a leper!"

"A leper? What do I care? My father isn't dead, and I want to put my arms around him."

You can't imagine the scene that followed. My aunt finally got my father to leave, and, calling the servants, forcibly took me to my room. There she took off my clothes and had them thrown out onto the patio to be burned the next day.

I did not allow my aunt to leave me until she had told me the cause of this incident, and explained to me on the spot why my father was hiding and in that state . . . We spoke for a long time, and I was finally alone only when the first rays of dawn appeared through the open window. Then I got up, and, leaning against the window, regarded the beautiful landscape that lay before my eyes. . . . The day, the landscape, the farmyard sounds were so lovely and so good! . . . But to me everything looked sad and lifeless. My whole life has changed; nothing can be happy for me again. My father is alive, but he lives a life of suffering!

Isn't it true, Pedro, that leprosy is a hideous disease? When people find out what a legacy awaits me, everyone will try to avoid me, and attempt to discern my first symptoms. I will be condemned to live in isolation! My father, who loved me tenderly, did not want this stain to mar my life, and so he decided to disappear. He has lived hidden away in the farthest reaches of the region, and it has only been for a year or so that my aunt and your father have known where he was . . . But I, can I live happily far from my unhappy father? Is it right to deceive everyone else by hiding the disease to which fate may condemn me? My father has made it clear that under no circumstances will he allow it to be known that he exists . . . In your last letter you tell me that somewhat sooner than he had anticipated Antonio hopes to get a position that would allow him to ask for my hand. It's too late, cousin: he has to give up this idea . . . Let him forget me! My misfortune should not tie him down. Do not ever tell him the reason, but make him forget his hopes. He will think I am inconstant and ungrateful . . . but what can I do? This is a very, very great sacrifice, but there's no other way.

Farewell. Write some comforting words to one who suffers greatly.

Dolores

A few days later I received this other letter:

You have written me, dear cousin, and your words have been a real comfort to me—many, many thanks! You have asked with concern for details as to the disappearance of my father, and how he lived hidden away for so long without anyone suspecting nor guessing that he was alive.

I have collected everything I have been able to find out about this matter, and will try to explain to you how things happened.

You know that ever since my mother died, my father bestowed all his affection on me, and cared for me with a woman's tenderness. I was twelve years old when my father discovered some changes in his health that disturbed him, and went to Bogotá. There he consulted various doctors who told him that the symptoms he had were those of a ghastly and incurable disease: leprosy. Desperate, he started for N*** without knowing what he was going to do. But when he reached the banks of the Magdalena, his distraught spirit presented him with the idea of suicide as the best way out, and the only solution to his plight. He dismounted, and in a moment of madness threw himself into the river with the intention of letting himself drown. But you will recall that my father was a very good swimmer. Natural instinct and the will to live made him not succumb, and, although exhausted, he reached the other side. There he was taken in by an unfortunate soul who lived in a poor hut on the riverbank. What a coincidence! His savior was also a leper, and lived in that desolate spot; he managed to exist thanks to some help with which a neighboring town provided him, as well as the harvest from a banana tree and other crops which he grew and sold in the surrounding area by means of his two children who lived with him. My father stayed with him for a few days; he thought of fleeing from the world for ever, and, by hiding his affliction, avoid passing on this secret legacy to his daughter.

With the assets of some gold and jewels he had in his possession, he lived for a while in that desolate area. He soon took leave of the leper. To live as an equal with a common person, is that not the worst tragedy of all? So he bought a cabin in the mountains and there vegetated alone, isolated and deeply afflicted for over five years. Sometimes he went down to the banks of the Magdalena to visit the leper, and observed in him the progress and ravages of the disease from which they both suffered. On other occasions, dressed as a peasant he would roam about the neighboring towns at night, asking how his family was. How often he failed to find out anything at all, and returned disconsolate to his wilderness!

One day he went down to his fellow sufferer's cabin, and found the two children weeping in the doorway.

The leper had died. This event moved my father deeply, and he asked the children to follow him into his exile. They, a girl of twelve and a boy of fourteen, gratefully accepted his offer. For many months my father had not heard anything definite about his family, and was extremely uneasy; besides, the leper's death made him realize that his own might not be far off, and he could not resist wanting to see me for the last time.

So, accompanied by the two children, he began the trek to N★★★, a terribly difficult journey through desolate plains of interminable grassy fields.

There was an abandoned cabin within the boundaries of my aunt's ranch, and there he chose to live. His companions had no idea who he was, and thus he could send a letter to your father with no difficulty, revealing his existence to him, and asking him for word of his family. You can well imagine the surprise which such a revelation would cause your father. There had never been the slightest doubt but that my father had died while rashly crossing the Magdalena. When he was convinced of the truth he went to talk to Aunt Juana as to what he should do; his first impulse had been to look for my unfortunate father and take him home again, even though the latter might refuse to go with him. But you know the extreme aversion my aunt has to this disease, and would in no way agree to the plan. She said (and I have been assured that in this she was right), that as I had a hereditary propensity for contracting this disease, it was essential to protect me as much as possible from any contagion. They agreed that they would send him anything he needed from the ranch, but that he would live far from all of his family and his existence would continue to be concealed from everyone. My father, poor man, never had had any other wish than to see me secretly and from afar . . . Do you remember the afternoon you came to say good-bye to us? He was hidden in the bramble thicket at the bank of the stream; he saw us so happy and the echo of our laughter reached his ears.

I am told that his illness is in the last stages . . . that he is suffering terribly, but I am not permitted to see nor to help him. I am living in a state of perennial sadness and withdrawal; my character has changed completely. Tell me, what has Antonio said? Has he forgotten me easily? . . . Silly questions, aren't they? Let's talk about you: you tell me that your wedding will not be as soon as you thought, but you at least live in a state of hope. We have been like brother and sister: you will attain happiness, and I . . . No, God knows what He is doing: He will have taken measure of my strength and my obedience. Farewell . . .

This news from N★★★ made me very unhappy. The at times morbid, at times overwrought state of suffering revealed by Dolores's letters alarmed me. I wrote to my father, advising him to try to get her mind off this, because constant fixation on such a painful matter could predispose her more than anything else to having her father's disease break out in her. One thought consoled me: rarely had there been cases in which the children of lepers caught the disease; it almost always skips a generation, and appears in the grandchildren. Nevertheless, I understood and approved of her noble conduct at wishing to break with Antonio. I did not dare dash my friend's hopes suddenly; I saw him so happy that it seemed a useless act of cruelty to quench the fire and life, the vigor and energy which vitalized his work and made him overcome all obstacles.

Several months went by like this. At last I received word of the death of Dolores's father: she wrote a few lines in which she gave vent to her grief. She could not openly weep for the loss she had sustained, nor put on mourning, for in his last moments he had let her know that he wanted his sacrifice to be of at least some use in protecting his daughter from the suspicious glances of a society that would know what awaited her when it learned the cause of his death.

Seeing her so depressed, my aunt wanted to cheer her up and took her to El Espinal.[10] The two of them thereupon wrote me, asking me to come and see them for a few days, now that they were a little closer to Bogotá.

I consented to this request, and went to spend a week with them. How was I to foresee the consequences this visit would have for me!

Nothing could console Dolores: she was pale, and in all of her gestures one could see the deep sorrow that distressed her. She then begged me insistently to tell Antonio that things were over, but made me promise that I would never tell him the reason for the break she desired.

On my return I tried to make clear to Antonio the aversion Dolores felt toward the prospect of matrimony, and the impossibility of realizing his hopes. This was a difficult task, and I often lacked the courage to distress him too much.

On the other hand, my own marital plans had taken a turn that caused me to feel a great deal of doubt about the future. Don Basilio had had himself introduced in my fiancée's house as a suitor for Mercedes's hand; she had always regarded him with a disdainful frown, but her parents treated him with the sort of attention I did not like at all. Little by little I began to realize that while Don Basilio was treated with growing respect, I was shown increasing indifference. One time Mercedes told me that she was very sad because her parents had heard some bad things about me; she had come to my defense, but could not prevent an upcoming trip to Chiquinquirá[11] that was being organized. Her mother had made a vow to the Virgin many years ago, but up until then had not considered fulfilling it; as Mercedes told me, it was doubtless with the intention of separating us. I wanted an explanation as to what had been said about me to them, but Mercedes would not allow it, assuring me that she did not know of what I was being accused, and that when she found out the charges I would be able to defend myself better.

I realized that this must be Don Basilio's doing, and promised to wait. A few days later Mercedes's family left for Chiquinquirá. During the first weeks of her absence I was deeply dejected, and my greatest pleasure was to have long talks with Antonio about our respective heartaches. Mercedes wrote me often, but finally told me that they would not be returning to Bogotá as soon as they had thought, as her mother wanted to stay a few months in San Gil with relatives she had there. Whenever I received a letter from Mercedes it was cause for celebration for me, but gradually they became fewer and fewer, under the pretext that her mother had forbidden her to write me. Back then

I was still in love and believed myself loved in return, and though I was very unhappy at the time, remember it fondly; as a French writer said, "None of our other pleasures can compare with our sorrows." But gradually I became used to her silence, and did not wait for her letters with my previous impatience. I don't know the reason why there were so many balls and functions given in Bogotá during that time, but I attended them, and confess that I was not unhappy. Nevertheless, deep down I was always uneasy, with a hidden pain that clung to the memory of Mercedes.

Four months had passed with no word at all from her, when one day a letter from her arrived and I realized with deep sorrow that my heart no longer felt the joy of previous times. Mercedes told me that when she told her father they ought to be returning to Bogotá because the time had come when our engagement was to be formalized, he had informed her that she would never become my wife with his consent. He refused to give her an explanation for his decision, but added that he was sure a prolonged separation would suffice to have us forget about each other. Mercedes's letter was extremely affectionate, perhaps more than any other one of hers, but with the attraction, the intuition that exists between people who love each other and which remains even after they have stopped being in love, I mean with that revelation of the soul that is understood without the possibility of explanation, I felt a certain disdain and coldness even in her most loving phrases. The bond of feeling and intimacy between us was about to snap. From that day on I became resigned to her absence, and used to the idea that our paths might diverge.

At last some important business of her father's brought the whole family back to Bogotá. Hardly had I learned of her unexpected arrival than my heart beat high for an instant, and I immediately went to her house. What a sad disappointment! The excitement was fleeting, and I calmed down again very quickly. Nevertheless, I made an effort to think that when I saw her my old joy would return again, and when I entered her house I recalled all the imagined scenes with which I had embellished the hopes that now were to be fulfilled. I arrived, found her as lovely as ever, but in her eyes as in mine the old spark had died. We spoke, I attempted to hide my indifference, and she was distracted. When I said good-bye a deep sorrow took hold of me. How depressing it is to feel your heart empty, with neither emotions nor enthusiasm!

I wanted no explanation from her, fearing there might be a reconciliation between us that was no longer desirable. So I withdrew from her house, and though she could not fail to notice the chill in our relationship, she said nothing to me. I saw her at the theatre and at functions, lovelier than ever and beautifully dressed; I heard of the conquests she had made and the suitors she attracted, among whom Don Basilio and Julian, who had returned to Bogotá, figured most prominently, but instead of the jealousy and hurt I would have felt earlier at seeing her thus courted, my heart remained calm. I had lost the ability to feel the noble jealousy that is symptomatic of love. Though doubtless a heart which does not love can feel jealousy, or perhaps a certain envy, there can be no passionate love without jealousy.

Poor Mercedes! At times she tried to coax me to her side and hid her indifference when she could, as I did mine. During that time I felt very sad: the human heart, my own not excepted, seemed to me so small, fickle, and despicable, though in its inner reaches it still retained the memory of the woman I had loved like an angel, but who in my opinion had changed into a weak, trivial person, easily swayed by the will of others! At times my conscience accused me of having changed as well. This was true, but I had not begun to feel indifferent until I sensed the coolness in her. Her silence and her vacillations during our separation had revealed her to me in another light, and for me the old ideal had disappeared.

My feelings were fluctuating in those uncontrolled mood swings, in which one neither wants nor hopes for anything, when I received another letter from Dolores, a letter which filled me with the most painful apprehension. As soon as I had read it I resolved to leave for N★★★ the following day. That same evening I went to say good-bye to Mercedes.

I was very distressed, and in that frame of mind would gratefully have accepted any sign of friendship. I think if Mercedes had received me that evening the way she did in former times, she might have recovered her hold over my heart. How grateful I would have been to her had she been inspired by the emotion I held to be the greatest good given to humankind: love!

I was very troubled when I went up the steps to her home; my voice shook as I greeted her.

The function was well attended, as it was almost every evening. In one part of the living room around the piano stood a group made up of Mercedes and some of her girlfriends; one of them was playing a piece, while Don Basilio pontificated about the opera from which it came. Julian turned the pages of the music and gazed languidly at Mercedes. Across the room her father was playing cards with two or three of Don Basilio's friends, country bumpkin politicians from distant provinces who sported very tight jackets, very stiff collars, very taut gaiters, and to top it off had such coarse, black hands that it was quite obvious who their forebears had been.

I saw that my entrance had caused a stir. All eyes turned on me curiously, and conversations in progress broke off. Mercedes received me disdainfully, turning her back once she had extended a cursory greeting without looking at me. The master of the house barely acknowledged me, and the entire crowd treated me coldly. In the midst of the silence produced by my arrival Don Basilio turned to me, saying with resonant voice and his usual pedantry:

"Well, well, the man of the hour, etc., or better yet, 'Talk of the devil,' as the English say. You were being spoken of just a moment ago, young man." And, looking at everyone meaningfully, he added, "Have you had any news lately of your interesting relatives whom I met in N★★★ last year?"

I don't know what I answered. A moment later I went up to Mercedes and told her that I had come to say good-bye because I had to be away for a few days.

"Naturally," she answered, flushing with marked annoyance.

"Why naturally? You don't even know where I'm going . . ."

"How could I fail to guess? The man being deceived can sometimes open his eyes."

"The man deceived?"

"Or the woman, as you wish."

"Explain yourself, Mercedes."

"I will. I want you to know that I now understand how false your conduct has been, and you can be sure that any relationship between us is over."

"And of what in Heaven am I guilty?"

"I haven't time to explain now. It suffices for you to know that I'm aware of everything." And she added ironically, "I understand your wanting to visit the person you prefer!"

"I don't understand."

"No? Well then, do me the favor of saying hello to your cousin Dolores for me."

"Mercedes, you're quite unfair, and I have no idea who could have made up such a . . . "

She could not help looking at Don Basilio as she interrupted me and said, "I don't know why you even bothered to come to say goodbye. There is nothing between us, nor can there ever be; I'm not interested in your private affairs."

I immediately realized that this was all Don Basilio's doing. My pride flared, and I had no desire to be humiliated by asking for an explanation.

"Well, I see," I answered her while looking at my rival, "I see that my dignity prevents my defending myself; the fortress is in enemy hands and it would be pointless to try to rebut the falsehoods that certain people know how to fabricate."

Paying my respects disdainfully to Mercedes and to the other guests, I left the room, followed by the malignant look and perverse smile of Don Basilio. In the doorway Julian caught up with me, and, offering me his hand, said, "Pedro, please don't think I had a hand in this conspiracy which I gather has been set up against you, because I am against this sort of thing, and hold you in genuine esteem."

I thanked him for this spontaneous gesture and we parted.

I crossed the streets between me and my home, and hatred, a longing to get even, profound humiliation at seeing myself bested by this windbag, disdain for Mercedes who was his instrument—all of this seethed in my head and made my heart pound. In the midst of it all, I remembered that when I had left Mercedes had looked after me with a misty, saddened glance . . . I did not see her again for many years and then, under what circumstances!

When I got home I was told that someone was waiting for me: it was Antonio. When I went up to greet him he stepped back and pushed my hand away, saying harshly, "The first thing I want to know is if I am shaking hands with a friend or a traitor to friendship!"

"A traitor! . . . I, Antonio?"

"You!"

"Explain yourself . . . This is the last straw!" I said with dismay. "This is just what I needed to go absolutely mad . . . I've just come from Mercedes's house, who has definitively broken off our relationship."

"And she didn't say why?"

"She gave me to understand that she believed a lie . . . "

"A lie! But maybe she's right . . . Pedro, Pedro! I still have one hope left: your loyalty of so many years' standing! Tell me the truth," he added, speaking to me more familiarly, "for it is so heartbreaking to lose everything in one day . . . Answer me: were you perhaps in love with Dolores before I met her? Or when you went to El Espinal, four months ago now? Oh, tell me the truth!"

"I swear to you by our old friendship and by all I hold sacred that Dolores has always been only a sister to me."

"I don't know what to believe . . . Lately I've been thinking a great deal about your behavior and it's inexplicable. From the time you went to El Espinal you have constantly tried to dissuade me from my plans with respect to Dolores, and you won't let me speak of her at all. And all this with a kind of mysteriousness you can't hide, and without telling me the reason for such a startling change. My friend Durán also told me that of late no one has seen Dolores anymore, that she was living in constant seclusion at her ranch. Lately rumors have begun to circulate here about her and you that I can't bring myself to repeat . . . Tell me if this is true!"

"What's true?" I asked him, disconcerted and not knowing what to answer.

"Tell me if . . . are you going to marry her?"

"That's an outrageous lie fabricated by Don Basilio. I'm amazed that you, Antonio, would have even listened to it!"

"By Don Basilio?"

A moment later he added, "You're right, Pedro, then it must be a lie. I'm amazed I hadn't thought of it before. They told me here that you were planning to leave for N✱✱✱ tomorrow; I won't wait any longer. I refuse to believe in Dolores's aversion to marriage; didn't you tell me she loved me? Well then, you yourself will take along a letter asking for your cousin's hand, and we'll get married any way we can. That's the best way to answer a lie like that."

"That cannot happen!" I exclaimed, without thinking about the consequences of my words.

"Why?"

"She says she will never marry."

Antonio looked at me without answering and I added, "There is a secret in her life I cannot reveal."

"A secret?"

"Yes."

"A secret in a woman's life cannot be good. I demand that you tell me what it's about. I'm not a hero in a novel, and if people are going to deceive me it had better be with something plausible."

"I am not at liberty to reveal it to you; Dolores has made me keep the secret."

"The secret! And I was beginning to believe you!"

Getting up, he firmly put on his hat, and, in a voice that shook with anger, silenced me by saying, "That's enough. No one makes a fool of me and gets away with it. Don't answer me because I don't want to do anything rash here. I will send friends to arrange the matter between us."

"A challenge!"

"That's the way I see it. Is cowardice perhaps another one of your distinguishing characteristics?"

"Anger is blinding you, Antonio," I answered, trying to keep my reason. "There can't be a challenge between the two of us. This is totally ridiculous! Listen to me: I have given you my word that this is a terrible misunderstanding."

"What proof can you give me to make me believe what you say is true, given that you say Dolores can't get married?"

"Time . . . "

"Time! . . . You're a coward!"

"I will not have anyone call me that!"

"Then accept my challenge or answer my question."

"Antonio," I cried, making a last effort not to lose my temper. "Antonio, this is absurd. If circumstances demand it, then let us part, but not as enemies!"

Antonio was already beside himself and approached with raised arm.

"Coward and hypocrite!" he shouted.

Then I forgot all restraint, and, showing him the door, said, "Get out. Set things up for when and where you want."

The following day at six in the evening I was carried unconscious to the house where I lived. When I came to I was lying in bed. It was nighttime, and I saw my landlady asleep at the foot of the bed; I tried to speak and to move, but an extremely sharp pain in my chest forced me to lie still. I was alone, with neither a relative nor a friend to feel sorry for me; my only comfort was the kindness of my landlords. Then I remembered what had happened to me: I saw myself once again facing Antonio behind the San Diego hills. Each of us had a pistol in his hand, and Julian was serving as my second. The expression on Antonio's face was fearsome: he regarded me with all the hatred born of his earlier affection. At that moment I forgot all religious feeling, all memory of my father . . . profound despair with regard to life held sway over me; at that instant I truly wanted to die. I aimed at Antonio, but the thought of Dolores and of her sorrow when she found out I had caused his death appealed to my better nature, and I fired into the air. But simultaneously I felt a strong jolt, and without knowing how, found myself on the ground: I remembered nothing more.

I lost consciousness again, and for many days hovered between life and death. When I opened my eyes again to light and consciousness I found my father at my side, who had just arrived from N*** without having received word of the state I was in.

The following letter from Dolores will explain better than anything else the reason for my father's unexpected journey.

I don't know if you received a letter I wrote you a few days ago. It may have gotten lost, or you might not have understood what I was telling you in it. Now I plan to explain to you more clearly the reason for the turmoil within my soul; I am completely calm and able, I think, to face my situation with courage. "With courage"— great God! "Calm" . . . what irony! No, Pedro, I'm crazy, desperate. I have had moments of true madness.

Nevertheless, I want to overcome the revulsion, the horror I feel. I must tell you everything.

From the time I was at El Espinal I began to feel very ill, a constant nervous agitation and total depression. In the space of a few hours I would feel alternating heat, cold, strength, weakness, courage, despair, fear, bravery—in short, the most contradictory emotions and disparate feelings. When I returned to N*** I went to see your father: he asked me some questions, and in his face I could read the greatest agitation and sorrow as I described the symptoms of the strange disease afflicting me. Poor Uncle tried to give me courage, assuring me that these changes were a result of my recent trials.

My aunt insisted that I consult other doctors, but I didn't want anyone to examine me. Finally, seeing that my condition was not improving, without consulting me they called in some local persons who hereabouts pass for doctors, for their experience, rather than a diploma, makes them worthy of the title of doctor that people give them.

They all met then, one day at the ranch. I appeared before them trembling, but they received me with such kindness and treated me with such good humor, that in their presence I began to forget about the awful terror that haunted me. Before I left them, I gathered that these gentlemen were to convene in the living room to give their opinions. I wanted to know the truth, and decided to eavesdrop on their session. I withdrew to my room, but, leaving immediately, slipped into a bedroom which adjoins the living room and is separated from it only by a screen.

This took me a few minutes, and when I reached my vantage point their conversation had already begun.

"The poor girl!" one said. "It seems to me there's no hope . . . "

"The leprosy is scarcely in its second phase," another replied, "and I think some effort should be made."

"That would only slow it down for a few more days . . . "

"That's true," they all agreed. "There's no cure any longer."

I didn't find out what else they said, nor knew what came over me. I had made an effort to be strong, and to face with serenity the illness that I could—should—expect. But when I was certain something was true that [up to then] I only feared, when I was face-to-face with the specter that had filled me with foreboding, when I suddenly grasped the horror of my situation, I could not fight the excruciating pain, and, though I did not faint, I threw myself on the floor in the throes of complete spiritual anguish. I neither wept nor lamented: my desperation tolerated no release. A deep sob in the hallway made me come to. I recognized my aunt's voice and left the room . . . at least, I thought, we can cry together! Guided by the same desire that impelled me, she, too, had wished to know the opinion of the doctors, and when she heard their words had not been able to control her feelings.

I approached her, but when she raised her eyes and saw me at her side she could not repress a kind of revulsive shudder, which she immediately mediated with a tender look.

"My dear," she said, holding out her hands, "come, give me a hug."

But her first reaction had been like a knife thrust for me: I could not forget it, and fleeing to my room without wanting to hear her, locked myself in. I felt alone, completely abandoned in the world! After that I don't remember anything. Apparently my aunt, exhausted from calling me and not getting a response, became frightened. With your father's she help broke open the door, and found me deranged!

Yes, Pedro, my despair was such that I lost my mind for several days. When I recovered my reason, and thought about the horrible existence that awaited me, the first thing I thought about was writing to you. You have always been a friend in whose kindness I have believed, a brother whose support has ever been my consolation. I cried out to you: I can't recall what I told you because my mind was still clouded by madness. Your father tells me that he has not given up hope completely, and is leaving for Bogotá to consult in person with the finest doctors in the nation. If only there were hope, dear God! . . . if only there were hope!

The letter to which Dolores referred was the one that had impelled me to go to N★★★, a departure which had been tragically interrupted.

No sooner was I up again than I insisted on accompanying my father to the practices of Bogotá's best doctors, who gave us some remedies by means of which, they said, a number of lepers had significantly improved. My father went back to N★★★. I was left alone, sad, still ill, discouraged, and now with no set plans for the future.

At this point I heard of a wealthy businessman who was ill, and en route to Europe; he wanted to take along a doctor to attend him during his trip. I offered him my services, and he gladly accepted me, but before my departure I could not resist the desire to go and embrace my father and see my relatives. Furthermore I wanted to put the little property I had in order, so that I would have some funds on which to live in Europe for several years.

I arrived unexpectedly in N★★★, and, after spending a few hours with my father, went to Aunt Juana's house. She was alone and very sad: there was no help for Dolores's affliction. She told me that Dolores only wanted to live on the ranch, and, bursting into tears, the poor aunt added that she let no one see her or come near her. I tried to comfort her, saying that I would go and see Dolores, to try to cheer her thoughts and improve her way of life.

At first my cousin refused to see me, but when I told her that soon I was leaving on a trip very far away, she gave in to my wish.

She was seated in an armchair, and the room was very dark, so that in her white dress she looked like a ghost among the shadows. She did not want me to come near her, but, taking advantage of my privileged status as cousin and brother, I forcibly took her hands, and, suddenly opening a window, insisted on seeing the damage the malady had done to her.

The third phase of the disease was already beginning. The lovely rosy color that had alarmed my father, and is the first symptom of the illness, had now blanched and changed into the yellowish pallor I had noted in her in El Espinal; [her face] was swollen and the rough skin had a purple color. Her beauty had completely disappeared, and only her eyes still retained an unnatural brightness. I realized that she no longer had any hope of getting better, but attempted to hide my surprise: I surely had not counted on seeing such a change in her. At first she remained silent, but when I described Aunt Juana's grief to her, she confided in me that her apparent indifference and the desire to isolate herself were part of a plan she had devised, and was determined to put into action.

"I want my aunt to get used to our separation, for I do not plan to live with her any longer."

"And where will you go?"

"I shall live alone. My aunt is horrified and singularly repulsed by the illness I have, and I know that she would live like a martyr. Besides, a stranger's voice causes me such terror . . . I look on all of humanity as an enemy that pursues me, that lies in wait for me, and have resolved to part company from all who fear me."

"But how?"

"Don't you remember the lovely spot where we said good-bye the last time you were here?"

"The little stream?"

"I want to have a small house built there, and, accompanied by the young people who served my father until his last moments (they are not repulsed by me), I will live alone, but I will be content in my solitude."

"This is madness, Dolores. What would your life be out in the wilderness? No, you can't do that."

"Instead of dissuading me, Pedro, have pity on me and help me carry out my plan. If you don't," she added, wringing her hands with a desperate gesture, "I'll run away, I'll go into the wilderness alone, and die like a wild forest animal. Look: my greatest despair comes from knowing I produce horror in people. My God! If I am not allowed to live alone, to hide from all eyes, I don't know what I'll do . . . it isn't hard to end one's life."

The poor young woman's state of despair was such that there was no room for reason, and I had to offer her my help with her plan.

"And Antonio?" she asked after a moment of silence, making an effort to regain her composure.

"I haven't seen him. Perhaps you didn't know?"

"Yes, your father told me everything. I have been the cause of grief and danger to you, and you have never received any comfort nor sign of gratitude from me! Forgive me: suffering makes one an egotist. I'll confess my most vulnerable point to you: I am terrified at the thought that Antonio should remember me with loathing."

"But isn't it worse that he should think ill of you?"

"That's true; I hadn't thought about that. Let him know everything!"

On saying that she burst into bitter tears.

"Tell Mercedes anything you want as well," she added.

"Mercedes doesn't mean anything to me anymore. I don't want to give her any explanation: she should have had faith in my constancy."

Dolores looked at me for a moment.

"You never loved her at all, because when one loves one is not proud: it's impossible to harbor lasting resentment, or pique, or ill will toward one you love."

"Let's not discuss her further. Mercedes has other suitors and I don't even think about her."

I said good-bye, promising to speak with my aunt, which indeed I did, attempting to make her understand that Dolores's life depended on doing what she wanted.

A few days later I joined my companion in Honda, and we sailed down the Magdalena without incident, boarding our ship in Santa Marta the beginning of the following month.

THIRD PART

In the remotest of forests I seek
But a gloomy shelter, a shadowy refuge
Where man's footstep has never trod.

Vicenta Maturana

Je meurs, et sur ma tombe, ou lentement j'arrive
Nul ne viendra verser des pleurs.[12]

Gilbert

During the first months of my stay in Europe I received various letters from my father, in which he gave me an account of Dolores's health. She was getting worse every day, and at the end of several months' time everyone had totally given up hope. In spite of their efforts and consultations with the nation's most renowned doctors, the destructive hand of this horrible and mysterious disease continued to ravage the beauty and even the human body of my unhappy cousin. She lived hidden away, without air or light, begging for permission to flee from the atmosphere which was stifling her.

Finally, among other letters I received the following one from Dolores:

There's no help anymore, my dear Pedro! For two months now I have been dead to the outside world, and find myself in this solitude. You will listen patiently to my troubles; oh, have pity on me!

But no—why complain? Providence is blind, and there are times . . . I don't dare read what is at the bottom of my soul. I'll tell you how my parting from my aunt was, and the arrival here. If my letter is incoherent, forgive me: at times my spirit gives way under so much suffering!

I don't know if you knew this, but I insisted so long that finally I got them to begin to construct a small house, a little cabin, but clean and comfortable, on the site I had picked. I wanted to go myself and show them the exact spot where it should be built. Nevertheless, months went by before it was finished, and even though I begged that it be completed quickly, I realized that my aunt could not bring herself to this separation. Tired of pleading, however, I seriously threatened to run away from home, and got what I wanted.

I always stayed hidden away, and spoke with my aunt and your father through the grille over the window of my room, or though the crack in the door.

One day they came to tell me that the house was finished, and that the necessary furniture, my birds, and some flowers had been taken over there. My poor aunt had gone to great pains to see that I had all the comforts I might want. After making some suggestions as to personal hygiene, your father came to tell me that among other things that had been taken to my future home, there was a small medical kit and instructions as to its use. "There you will find everything," he told me, "that should see you through the different stages of the disease, until, until . . . " When he said these words, the dear old man who had cared for me so much burst into tears. I had opened the door a bit to speak with him more easily, and when I heard the sound of that intense pain, I felt an overwhelming despair in my heart; opening the door completely, I knelt down on the floor and cried out in anguish, "Oh, Uncle, Uncle . . . you have it in your power to ease my suffering; oh, for God's sake, give me something . . . something to shorten my life!"

Your father covered his face with his hands, and did not answer me. But then I heard my aunt coming down the hall, and I immediately came to my senses; by an enormous effort of will I stood up, went into my room, and closed the door. But she had seen me, and, while pounding on the door, shouted, "Dolores, Dolores, that's too great a sacrifice; you can't leave me like this!"

I felt a momentary weakness, but it passed and I answered her with a firm voice: "I want to leave tomorrow at dawn, and I am asking for the last time that no one come near me when I go."

That night I slept well. My agitation had gone, and I felt strong in the face of my decision. Before dawn broke people came to tell me that my horse was ready. I got up, and, leaving my room, crossed the hall where I had my aviary, took a last look at the garden, the pond, the trees . . . everything that reminded me of my happy childhood and the dreams of my brief youth. I refused to think, or linger: the cold, sad light of dawn began to illuminate things, which took on a fantastic appearance. My favorite dog followed me, leaping joyfully.

The foreman, who was to accompany me to my cabin, and two or three other servants were waiting for me in the patio. I wanted no one's help and with one bound leapt into the saddle.

"Good-bye," I said with a choked voice, as I spoke to the servants, "tell my aunt . . . "

Unable to say another thing, I lashed the horse with the reins, and, as he is very spirited, I shot out of the patio like lightning, followed by the foreman. I don't know what I felt then. My whole life, in its most intimate details, went through my mind, the way they say happens to people who are drowning. I thought I was going to faint and fall off the horse, when a faraway cry, muffled by distance, made me rein in my mount, and, looking behind me, I saw my aunt, who had gotten on a horse and was following me.

"Dolores, my darling!" she said when she reached me. "Do you think I would let you leave my house like a criminal without accompanying you to your place of exile?"

"I'm sorry, Aunt; I did think so, and my heart broke at the thought, but as you had promised not to see me again . . ."

"Yes, yes, I did say that. But how could I not see you or speak to you for the last time?"

I let my handkerchief flutter in the wind to see from whence it blew, and, placing myself in the opposite direction, answered her: "Only once, and out in the open air can't hurt you. Promise me, though, that you won't come near me; if you don't, I swear, Aunt, I'll carry out my threat and go far, far away; I'll hide, and die in the depths of the wilderness."

"Aunt," I added, "this is our last conversation. Let us speak with all the judiciousness and resignation a Christian can muster on his deathbed. Let no tears interrupt us, and don't let's break down. The essential sacrifice has been made; let us accept it as a test sent us by Providence. When we reach the edge of the mountain I will go on ahead without saying anything. We will not utter the word 'good-bye'; we both need a strength we would lose were we to say farewell."

And that's what we did. We spoke with apparent calm of how I would organize my life, but our hearts were broken. When we reached the narrow trail you will recall, I rode ahead in silence, and, when I crossed the path that leads to my cabin I involuntarily turned my head; through the trees I saw that my aunt had stopped, and was looking after me with deep sorrow. I will probably never see her again!

For a long time I received no other word from Dolores; my father told me only that she continued in her isolation, and had forbidden anyone to come near her. On one occasion he wrote me in a very troubled state. It seems that one day he was told that Dolores was extremely ill; he was at my aunt's ranch and could not keep her from finding out what was being said about Dolores. Aunt Juana became alarmed, and, forgetting about her promise, insisted on accompanying my father to my cousin's cabin at all cost.

Without being seen they reached the house, which consisted of a small living room and a bedroom; a tiny, flower-filled patio separated the latter from the kitchen and the pantry, and among the vines which trailed in a diminutive corridor hung cages filled with birds. They went into the living room, which held several pieces of furniture and many books on the tables. When she heard them come in, Dolores came out of the bedroom without taking any precautions. She was so disfigured that my aunt let out a horrified shriek, and covered her face with her hands. Dolores paused a moment; when she saw the expression on the faces of her aunt and uncle, she passed them by without a word, and went out the door. My father followed her, calling her name, and saw her vanish into the forest. As she did not answer, he ran to the place where she had disappeared; he walked along the edge of the stream, continually calling her name, until he got to a clearing. The dense forest closed in completely farther up the hill, and the stream, compressed between two boulders, could not be crossed without getting wet up to one's knees. Dolores neither appeared nor answered; my father thought she had taken another path and went back to the house to consult with my cousin's servants. They had never seen her leave like this, and immediately ran to look for her. My aunt was so upset and worried that my father urged her to return to the ranch while he stayed behind to look for Dolores.

Hours passed, and it was impossible to find her. The servants and all the ranch hands joined in, but night came and went without any news of her. The first light of dawn found my father still filled with anguish, for besides Dolores's disappearance, my aunt had fallen gravely ill.

At this point it would be better to transcribe part of the letter I received from Dolores, in which she told me what had happened.

. . . I thought, Pedro, that you would never hear from me again . . . I wanted to die, dear friend, and I couldn't make it happen.

Lately I had felt very ill, in body and in spirit: I was horribly weak, and spent days without speaking or eating much of anything.

Isidora and her brother were probably alarmed at seeing me in this state, and notified the family; I have not wanted to ask them how it was that your father and Aunt Juana suddenly appeared at the cabin. When they saw me the expression of horror on their faces was such that in a second I understood that I was no longer a member of the human race, and without knowing what I was doing, I left the house. I think I went mad: I seemed to hear the hoofbeats of a hundred runaway horses that were after me, and heard the baying of countless dogs . . . Hurriedly I climbed up the bank of the stream, and, when I reached a particularly wild spot, waded through the water without feeling myself getting wet, or realizing that I was getting scratched by the hawthorns in the forest. At last my strength gave out and I stopped. I no longer heard the shouts or the running of those I thought were after me, and found myself alone in the midst of the wilderness: the only sound was the buzzing of the insects, the trill of the birds, and the crunching of the dry leaves when I walked on them. I was completely exhausted; I don't know if I went to sleep or fainted, but I fell to the ground as one dead. When I came to it was almost totally dark there in the heart of the forest. What to do? Death seemed to me a release. I got up to look for a cliff, but up there the mountain is a gentle, hilly slope, and I found no appropriate place.

I felt no pain at all (you know that one of the consequences of the disease is that your skin loses feeling), but nevertheless I was badly scratched, covered with blood, and my clothes were in tatters. After having wandered about for a long time, I came to a clearing where broad, moss-covered rocks lay at the feet of some very tall trees. It was deliciously cool there; I lay down on one of the rocks and looked up at the sky. Night had fallen, and as darkness fell on the earth the sky became covered with stars. The heavenly lanterns lit up one by one, like candles on an altar. So many constellations, such wonderful sparkling in those faraway suns, such an immensity of worlds and endless universes . . . ! Little by little the mysterious magnificence of that spectacle assuaged my despair. Who was I to rebel against fate? Those rays of light were dying before they ever reached my remote spot, yet still seemed to look on me with compassion . . . Compassion! Isn't everyone horrified by me? No, perhaps there is some person who still remembers me tenderly. I'll tell you the truth: Antonio's memory saved me, as I think I knew by intuition that he had not forgotten me. Wouldn't the certainty of his distant affection be enough for me to live on with resignation? Don't think me ungrateful: I remembered you, too; you, at least, did not appear to be horrified when you saw me.

The night was starry, but very dark. I did not feel I had the courage to spend the whole night in the heart of that wilderness. When the nervous excitement which stirred me up had abated, I felt tremendous exhaustion, and wanted to find a safe spot where I could lie down without being afraid. I recalled that I had gone upstream, and oriented myself by the stars at which I had gazed so long in my solitude. I looked for a bright star that always shines on the horizon when the sun goes down, and went in a direction in which I would find the hut of a poor paralyzed woman who lives there in the wilderness with a retarded son. I soon realized I had come across a narrow path, and attempted to follow it. I don't know why I wasn't bitten by the thousands of poisonous animals that crawled on the ground, hung from branches or flew shrieking round about me. The star vanished behind the trees, and the night became progressively darker; I had lost my shoes, and my feet refused to carry me any further when I heard a dog bark: what a delightful sound for me! A few steps farther on I found the hut; warding off the dog with a stick I had found in the forest and was using as a cane, I pushed aside the rushes that served as a door and, waking the invalid woman, I asked permission to curl up in a corner.

I spent the night in misery, constantly waking up in a fright, but my weariness made me fall asleep again. When dawn came, the retarded boy got up, lit a fire in the center of the hut, placed a pot on three stones lying there, and made a soup from yucca, bananas, and salted meat. I remained motionless in my corner until he offered me a plate of hot soup, and realized that the major part of my weakness stemmed from a lack of food. I accepted and ate heartily what they put before me; when I finished I broke the bowl as though by accident and threw away the spoon.

As the sun rose it got hotter in the hut and at last I went to the door to get some air. My muddy, ragged dress, disheveled hair, and undoubtedly dreadful appearance had an effect on the owners of the house. There was no way for them to recognize me, although in previous times I had visited the sick woman on several occasions. But although they did not know who I was, the paralyzed woman guessed the nature of the illness which afflicted me, and gently told me that it would be better if I sat outside the hut on the ground . . . I was aware of the revulsion I caused even in those unfortunate beings and went out, completely humiliated. I wanted to let my relatives know that I would not return to my cabin again until they solemnly promised me they would never return there. The retarded boy could not speak intelligibly, so how could I get my message across? In my pocket I found a pencil which by chance had not been lost during my flight, and the paralyzed woman gave me a scrap of paper the retarded boy had brought along with some medicines sent by Aunt Juana. I placed the paper on the trunk of a fallen tree which lay near the house, and with a shaking hand wrote a few lines, then gave them to the boy to take to the ranch, promising to pay him well.

That afternoon my two servants arrived. Isidora brought me clothes, and Juan a saddled horse and a letter from your father, in which he told me that my aunt was gravely ill, on account of the grief I had caused them; in the end he promised not to try to see me without my consent.

I returned to my cabin to take care of myself . . . yes, I took care of myself! Oh unhappy humanity! Wasn't it better to let myself die? In our hearts there is always this love of life, and as miserable as it is, we take pleasure in prolonging it . . . Yes, Pedro: while I took care of my horrible existence, while I regained strength to keep on living, my poor aunt was dying as a result of the fright, the worry, and the anguish I had caused her. Apparently she developed a violent fever and died two days later without recognizing anyone, but haunted by my memory and continually calling my name. Perhaps you think me insensitive, unnatural when you see that I can speak calmly of the death of someone who loved me so dearly. I don't know what to say: I don't understand myself, and think that I may have lost the ability to feel. I never cry; I think the source of my tears has dried up. I never complain, nor am I moved. I long anxiously for death, but don't dare seek it out, and even attempt to avoid it.

My spirit is chaos, my existence a ghastly nightmare. I beg you to send me some books. I want to nourish my spirit with beautiful thoughts; I want to live with the dead, and communicate with them.

Dolores's letter made a deep impression on me. I saw that her particularly sweet character had changed because of her suffering, and that helped me assess the extent of her troubles. I got together some good books and sent them to her. During the years that followed I received only a few short letters from Dolores: their essence was at times one of wrenching sadness, and there was a certain lack of religious faith and a hatred of humankind in her thoughts that filled me with sorrow. My father wrote me that he had never seen her again, but that every week he sent a person with things she might need and to bring word of her.

Antonio had repented of his thoughtless conduct toward me, and we continued a very active correspondence. The first painful shock when he grasped Dolores's awful fate and the impossibility of her ever being his were not enough to discourage him: his vigorous character would not allow that. On the contrary, he attempted to get over his sorrow by throwing himself into his demanding work and constant study. He was soon known as a man of talent, hardworking and eloquent, and succeeded in attaining an honorable place among the nation's statesmen.

I had spent several years studying in Europe and was preparing to return home when I received word of my father's death. I cannot express what I felt at that point . . . Dolores wrote me as well, describing the bereavement in which she had been left.

Although at first I loathed the idea of visiting my empty home, I could not resist the desire to return to Dolores's side, and took passage home.

I was just passing through Bogotá, but Antonio detained me there in order to attend his wedding. He was marrying a young woman of one of the city's best families, wealthy, and very respected. I wrote Dolores immediately, explaining the reason for my delay, and telling her the news of Antonio's brilliant match.

The wedding was sumptuous, though not joyful. The bride was not beautiful, but her cultured manners, polished education, and natural goodness made one forget her lack of physical charms. After the ceremony, when I was saying good-bye to Antonio at the door of his house, he gave me a letter for Dolores, a letter he had written that day, and in his eyes I saw a single tear glisten, the last tribute to his youthful dreams.

Eight days later I reached the outskirts of N★★★, and instead of going into town, immediately took the little-traveled road to that corner of the valley where Dolores lived. When I reached the path I had taken years ago with my cousin, my imagination brought back to me once again Dolores's slender figure, her brilliant eyes and lighthearted words; once more I heard the echo of her silvery laugh which to me still hovered in that desolate spot. How my life had changed since then! My aunt had died, my poor father as well, my fiancée was someone else's wife (I don't know if I've told that she married Don Basilio), and finally my cousin, that happy girl of former times, was a profoundly unfortunate human being. I had not wanted to go to the town which held such sad memories for me, and I knew nothing of Dolores.

When I approached the place where my cousin's cabin should have been, I heard a certain sound which astonished me. Several saddled horses stood under a tree; I spurred my own, and reached the door of the little house just as the priest and several people from N★★★ were leaving.

"What an amazing coincidence!" said the priest when he recognized me and detained me in the doorway.

He was a respected old man who had been the village priest ever since I was a child.

"Dolores is inside?" I asked, after I had greeted him.

"Dolores? But didn't you know . . . ?"

"What? I want to speak with her."

"No, don't go in," he answered, taking my hand.

"What's happened?"

"Poor girl!" he said with a shaken voice. "This morning her suffering came to an end."

"My God!" I exclaimed, feeling that the last link that bound me to the memories of this place had disappeared, and then I realized just how essential this attachment had been for me.

Sitting down in silence on the threshold of Dolores's house, I hid my face in my hands. The people surrounding the priest moved away out of respect for my feelings; the priest sat down beside me.

"Her death was a Christian one," said the good clergyman. "A few days ago she asked me to come to see her, saying that there was no need to come near her because she would speak to me through her bedroom door. I came several times, and yesterday she made her final confession and received the last rites. This morning I was told that she was dying; up to that point I had not been able to see her, and I won't tell you how greatly she had changed!

"Now," he said a moment later, "having been present when she died, I was just going back to the parish to make arrangements for the burial."

I did my duty. I went to the funeral. She had asked to be buried in the patio of her little house, and ordered that all was to be left uninhabited.

Among her papers I found a will leaving everything to me, and some works in prose and verse. Here are a few fragments of a diary she kept, which help one to understand her character better, as well as the terrible moral suffering she underwent, her misgivings and her despair.

June 23, 1843

For a year now I have been suffering alone, isolated, abandoned by the whole world in this wilderness. Oh! If there were only someone to remember me, how could I not feel bursts of consolation that would inspire this tormented heart to resignation? Far away, down on the plain, people run about and enjoy themselves. Tomorrow is Saint John's day, the anniversary of the festival in N***. The festival! What memories come to mind! Today by chance I found a bouquet of dried jasmine—is it possible that this monstrous being that appears before me when I draw near the mirror is the pretty girl to whom these flowers were given? Antonio, Antonio, you whom I love in the secret recesses of my soul, whose memory is my only consolation, Antonio, do you perchance still remember the unhappy girl you loved? If you knew how your image haunts me! Your name resounds in the whispering branches of the trees, in the murmuring of the stream, in the scent of my favorite flowers, in the wind that whistles, among the pages of the book I am reading, in the tip of the pen with which I write; I see your initials in the wide, starry sky, among the clouds at sunset, in the sand of the brook in which I bathe . . . Holy God! That this love should be so great, so deep, so boundless, and yet my burning heart lies mute forever!

December 8, 1843

Life is a black coffin into which we find ourselves locked. Is death perhaps the beginning of another life? What irony! In the depths of my thoughts I only find a sensation of nothingness. If there were a God Who was as just and merciful as people are wont to describe Him, would He let an unfortunate soul like me suffer? Oh, Death, come, come to the aid of the unhappiest being on earth! Solitude everywhere, silence, stillness, Nature's maddening calm! . . . The sky with its ghastly beauty fills me with horror, I am not moved by the moon and its highly exalted loveliness, the countryside bores me, flowers remind me of my past life. Flowers, earth, pure scents, harmonies of Nature which are emblems of life: why come and arouse deep feelings in one who no longer exists? . . .

May 1844

. . . Awful martyrdom . . . the illness is not following its normal course. Will I live many more years? There are nights I wake up totally agitated: I dreamt I finally got hold of a pistol, but when I tried to kill myself it wouldn't go off, and in my struggle to get it to fire I woke up . . . Other times I dream I am swimming in an abundantly flowing river, and I let myself be carried gently by the waves which are engulfing me, but when I feel I am drowning, an intense rush of joy awakens me.

February 18[45][13]

Today I received a letter from Pedro which consoled me. There still is someone, aside from my good uncle, who remembers me . . . I said that the letter consoled me: that's a lie! I reread it and it caused me new pain. He tells me of his quiet life, his studies, and his plans for the future. Men are creation's cruelest beings: they take pleasure in making us aware of our misfortune. In the Middle Ages, when a person was declared a leper, he was immediately considered a corpse: he was taken to the church, the funeral mass was sung, and he was shut away the rest of his days like a filthy being . . . But at least they never again had any contact with society; morally they were dead, and never heard echoes of the lives of the persons they held dear. Yet I, I who have withdrawn to the depths of an American wilderness: even here memory follows me . . . What does it mean to love? To love is to have pleasant feelings. Doctors say lepers have lost their nervous system. Then for what purpose do I feel? Why do I tenderly recall the people I loved?

April 1845

. . . God, religion, future life! Unfathomable questions! Terrible vacillations of my soul! If my disease were only physical, if it were only my body that was sick! But the nature of one's character changes, and every day I feel I have become cruel, like the animals in this wilderness, cold and hard toward humanity like the rocks in the stream. There are times when in a fit of madness I rush to my flowers which seem to insult me with their loveliness, and I shred them, I throw them to the winds; a moment later my reason returns, I tenderly look for them and weep when I find they are withered. Other times my soul rebels: it cannot believe that a good God would make me suffer so much, and in my rebellion I deny His existence; afterward . . . I humble myself, I throw myself on my knees, and fall into endless adoration of the Supreme Being . . .

September 1845

Ever the silence, the loneliness, the absence of a friendly voice which might caress me with an affectionate tone. Eternal separation! Can there be a more terrifying concept for one who was born to love?

January 1, 1846

I am going through a time of discouragement and total lethargy. Lately I have lived as though in dreams . . . I am neither sad nor desperate. I feel that in my heart there is nothing: I am indifferent to everything; life is suffering, death . . . everything passes, and mingles in my soul's shadows; nothing can move me. One feeling! One feeling, even if it were of sorrow, fear, horror (the only thing to which I can aspire) would be blessed by me as a consolation: such is the state I am in! This is worse than my maddened desperation in the past. I vegetate like a worm-eaten tree; I live like a stone in some deserted spot . . .

March 1846

At times I intend to study, read, learn, in order to do something, devote myself to intellectual tasks, and thus forget my condition; I try to flee from myself, but always, always, thought pursues me, and, as a French writer said, "Le chagrin monte en croupe et galope avec moi."[14]

Woman is essentially a loving being, and in all of life's events wants only to shine before those whom she loves. In her, vanity is for the sake of love, as in man it is for ambition. For whom do I learn? My studies, my education, my gifts, even if it is true that I have them, all of this is useless, for I can never inspire a feeling of admiration: I am alone, forever alone . . .

September 6, 1846

Everything is over for me now. I am going to die soon: even with an effort my hand is scarcely able to write these lines. How I had longed for this day! But why was I not fortunate enough to die sooner, when I [still] had a dream? Perhaps I am unjust, but this blow, so to speak, undid the last link that chained me to life. I received a letter from Pedro, dated in Bogotá. My poor cousin, I thought on opening it, soon I will hear your voice, and through him, too, I will have some direct news of Antonio . . . My heart beat with sweet emotion and I felt faint. I sat down by the banks of the stream which runs burbling near my room. How happy I had been to see the servant who brought the letter! Antonio's image hovered around me . . .

After reading the first lines a cloud passed before my eyes. Pedro told me of Antonio's wedding. Antonio's wedding! Why did I initially refuse to believe it? Is he not free to love another? Nevertheless, the most awful, overwhelming grief came over me: I knelt down on the beach and let myself be swept away by the gale force of my pain. I envisioned myself alone, oh, so alone, bereft of the only affection for which I longed. Everything around me spoke of Antonio, and his memory alone dwelt in my sad abode. No corner of my hut, no tree or flower in my garden, no star in the blue heaven, no singing bird failed to tell me things in his name. My life was part of his memory, and now? He loves another woman. What an absurd idea! How many others will he most likely have loved since we parted! How strange! Earlier this did not bother me, and now I can't relinquish this idea for one moment. It was as though my soul were waiting for this last disillusionment in order to depart this miserable body. I understand that all of these symptoms portend a speedy death. Thank you, dear God! I am about to end all my suffering, but *he* is all I think about in these final moments. Oh! *He* will forget me and be happy!

THE END

Notes

1. "Nature is a play with characters."
2. Liquor; literally "burning water."
3. Make a good match.
4. A type of poncho.

5. "Her eyes are quite pretty . . . for provincial eyes."

6. "He who wins without danger, triumphs without glory."

7. Venus is the goddess of love; Lucrece, a Roman matron, is the symbol of conjugal fidelity; Minerva is the goddess of wisdom; Virginia is the heroine of the popular novel *Paul et Virginie* (1787), written by Bernardin de St. Pierre; Pegasus is the winged horse of mythology.

8. "Pain is a light which illuminates our life."

9. The Borgias (or Borjas) were a famous Spanish family of the fifteenth and sixteenth centuries, one of whose members became a saint (Saint Francis Borgia); others, such as Pope Alexander VI and his illegitimate son, Cesare, had few scruples, and were known to do away with their enemies by poison.

10. El Espinal is a small town southwest of Bogotá, in the province of Tolima.

11. Chiquinquirá, due north of Bogotá, is a town where there is a cult to a miraculous Virgin.

12. "I am dying, and over my grave, to which I am slowly borne / No one will come to shed tears."

13. The date in the original is 1864, which is an error.

14. "Suffering leaps up behind my saddle and gallops along with me."

Works Cited

Acosta de Samper, Soledad. *Novelas y cuadros de la vida sur-americana.*
Gante: Imprenta de Eug. Vanderhaegen, 1869.
———. *Una nueva lectura.* Introd. Montserrat Ordóñez. Bogotá: Fondo
Cultural Cafetero, 1988.
Alzate-Cadavid, Carolina. "Cristóbal Colón e Isabel de Guevara: Voz
narrativa y autoridad." Unpublished paper. October 1993.
Antoni, Claudio G. "A Comparative Examination of Style in the Works
of Madre Castillo." Diss. City University of New York, 1979.
Arenal, Electa, and Stacey Schlau. *Untold Sisters: Hispanic Nuns in Their
Own Works.* Trans. Amanda Powell. Albuquerque: University of New
Mexico Press, 1989.
Auerbach, Emily. *Sor Juana Inés de la Cruz.* The Courage to Write Series.
With Electa Arenal, Nina M. Scott, and Margarita Zamora. Audio-
cassette. University of Wisconsin–Madison, 1997.
Bénassy-Berling, Marie-Cécile. *Humanismo y religión en Sor Juana Inés de
la Cruz.* Trans. Laura López de Belair. México: Universidad Nacional
Autónoma de México, 1983.
Benítez-Rojo, Antonio. "Power/Sugar/Literature: Toward a Reinterpre-
tation of Cubanness." Trans. Jorge Hernández Martín. *Cuban Studies*
16 (1986): 9–31.
Berg, Mary. "Viajeras y exiliadas en la narrativa de Juana Manuela Gor-
riti." *Mujeres y cultura en la Argentina del siglo XIX.* Ed. Lea Fletcher.
Buenos Aires: Feminaria Editora, 1994. 69–79.
———. "Rereading Fiction by 19th-Century Latin American Women
Writers: Interpretation and Translation of the Past into the Present."
Translating Latin America: Culture as Text. Ed. William Luis and Julio
Rodríguez Luis. Binghamton, NY: Center for Research in Transla-
tion, 1991. 127–33.
Bergmann, Emilie L. "Sor Juana Inés de la Cruz: Dreaming in a Double
Voice." *Women, Culture, and Politics in Latin America.* Ed. Emilie
Bergmann et al. Berkeley: University of California Press, 1990.
151–72.

Bravo-Villasante, Carmen. *25 mujeres a través de sus cartas*. Madrid: Editorial Almena, 1975. 27–31.

———. *Una vida romántica: La Avellaneda*. Madrid: Instituto de Cooperación Iberoamericana, 1986.

Cabello de Carbonera, Mercedes. *Blanca Sol*. Lima: Torres Aguirre, 1888.

———. "Estudio comparativo de la inteligencia y la belleza en la mujer." Juana Manuela Gorriti. *Veladas literarias de Lima, 1876–1877*. Tomo 1. Veladas 1–10. Buenos Aires: Imprenta Europea, 1892. 207–12.

———. "La novela moderna: Estudio filosófico." 1892. 2d ed. Lima: Ediciones Hora del Hombre, 1948.

Castillo, Francisca Josefa de. "Madre Castillo's *Afectos espirituales*. Trans. and comm. Kathleen Jeanette Jarvis. Master's thesis. University of Texas at Austin, 1985.

———. *Obras completas de la Madre Francisca Josefa de la Concepción del Castillo*, según fiel transcripción de los manuscritos originales que se conservan en la Biblioteca Luis-Angel Arango. 2 vols. Introducción, notas e índices elaborados por Darío Achury Valenzuela. Bogotá: Talleres Gráficos del Banco de la República, 1968.

Cotarelo y Mori, Emilio. *La Avellaneda y sus obras: Ensayo biográfico y crítico*. Madrid: Tipografía de Archivos, 1930.

Crow, John A. *The Epic of Latin America*. 1946. 3d ed. Berkeley: University of California Press, 1980.

Cruz, Sor Juana Inés de la. *Inundación castálida*. Ed. Georgina Sabàt de Rivers. Madrid: Editorial Castalia, 1982.

———. *Obras completas*. 4 vols. Vols. 1–3, ed. Alfonso Méndez Plancarte. Vol. 4, ed. Alberto G. Salceda. México: Fondo de Cultura Económica, 1951–57.

Dekker, Rudolf, and Lotte van der Pol. *The Tradition of Female Transvestism in Early Modern Europe*. New York: St. Martin's Press, 1989.

De la Maza, Francisco. *Sor Juana Inés de la Cruz ante la historia*. Rev. Elías Trabulse. México: Universidad Nacional Autónoma de México, 1980.

Dugaw, Diane. *Warrior Woman and Popular Balladry, 1650–1850*. Cambridge: Cambridge University Press, 1989.

Encinales de Sanjinés, Paulina. "La obra de Soledad Acosta de Samper ¿Un proyecto cultural?" *Mujeres latinoamericanas: Historia y cultura. Siglos XVI al XIX*. 2 vols. Ed. Luisa Campuzano. Tomo II. La Habana: Fondo Editorial Casa de las Américas, 1997. 227–32.

Epple, Juan Armando. "Mercedes Cabello de Carbonera y el problema de la novela moderna en el Perú." *Doctores y proscritos*. Ed. S. Muñoz. Minneapolis: Institute for the Study of Ideologies and Literature, 1987. 233–53.

Erauso, Catalina de. *Historia de la monja alférez Doña Catalina de Erauso, escrita por ella misma*. 1829. Ed. Joaquín María Ferrer. Madrid: Tipografía Renovación, 1918.

———. *Lieutenant Nun: Memoir of a Basque Transvestite in the New World*. Trans. Michele Stepto and Gabriel Stepto. Boston: Beacon Press, 1996.

———. *The Nun Ensign*. Trans. James Fitzmaurice-Kelly. Also *La monja alférez*, a Play in the Original Spanish, by Juan Pérez de Montalbán. London: T. Fisher Unwin, 1908.

———. *Vida i sucesos de la Monja Alférez: Autobiografía atribuida a Doña Catalina de Erauso*. Ed. Rima de Vallbona. Tempe, AZ: ASU Center for Latin American Studies, 1992.

Figarola Caneda, Domingo, y Doña Emilia Boxhorn. *Gertrudis Gómez de Avellaneda: Biografía, bibliografía e iconografía, incluyendo muchas cartas, inéditas y publicadas, escritas por la gran poetisa o dirigidas a ella, y sus memorias*. Madrid: Sociedad General Española de Librería, 1929.

Fitzmaurice-Kelly, James. Introduction. *The Nun Ensign*. Trans. James Fitzmaurice-Kelly. Also *La monja alférez*, a Play in the Original Spanish, by Juan Pérez de Montalbán. London: T. Fisher Unwin, 1908. xv–xl.

Fletcher, Lea, ed. *Mujeres y cultura en la Argentina del siglo XIX*. Buenos Aires: Feminaria Editora, 1994.

———. "Patriarchy, Medicine, and Women Writers in Nineteenth-Century Argentina." *The Body and the Text: Comparative Essays in Literature and Medicine*. Ed. Bruce Clark and Wendell Aycock. Lubbock: Texas Tech University Press, 1990. 91–110.

Franco, Jean. *Plotting Women: Gender and Representation in Mexico*. New York: Columbia University Press, 1989.

———. "Writers in Spite of Themselves: The Mystical Nuns of Seventeenth-Century Mexico." *Plotting Women: Gender and Representation in Mexico*. New York: Columbia University Press, 1989. 3–22.

Garber, Marjorie. "Foreword: The Marvel of Peru." *Lieutenant Nun: Memoir of a Basque Transvestite in the New World*. Trans. Michele Stepto and Gabriel Stepto. Boston: Beacon Press, 1996. vii–xxiv.

García y García, Elvira, ed. "Mercedes Cabello de Carbonera." *La mujer peruana a través de los siglos: Serie historiada de estudios y observaciones*. 2 vols. Lima: Imprenta Americana, 1924–25. II: 18–22.

———. "Teresa González de Fanning." *La mujer peruana a través de los siglos: Serie historiada de estudios y observaciones*. 2 vols. Lima: Imprenta Americana, 1924–25. 2: 29–32.

Glantz, Margo. *Sor Juana Inés de la Cruz: ¿Hagiografía o autobiografía?* México: Editorial Grijalbo, 1995.

Gómez de Avellaneda, Gertrudis. *Cartas inéditas existentes en el Museo del Ejército*. Ed. José Priego Fernández del Campo. Madrid: Fundación Universitaria Española, 1975.

———. *Diario íntimo*. Ed. Lorenzo Cruz de Fuentes. Buenos Aires: Ediciones Universal, 1945.

———. *Obras de doña Gertrudis Gómez de Avellaneda*. 6 vols. Habana: Imprenta A. Miranda,1914.

———. *Sab* and *Autobiography*. Trans. and ed. Nina M. Scott. Austin: University of Texas Press, 1993.

———. "Women." ["La mujer."] Trans. Nina M. Scott. *Rereading the Spanish American Essay: Translations of 19th- and 20th-Century Women's Essays*. Ed. Doris Meyer. Austin: University of Texas Press, 1995. 25–39.

González de Fanning, Teresa. *Educación femenina: Colección de artículos pedagógicos, morales y sociológicos*. Lima: "El Lucero," 1905.

———. "Trabajo para la muger." Juana Manuela Gorriti. *Veladas literarias de Lima: 1876–1877*. Buenos Aires: Imprenta Europea, 1892. 286–93.

Gorriti, Juana Manuela. "Chincha." Trans. Mary G. Berg. *Rereading the Spanish American Essay: Translations of 19th- and 20th-Century Women's Essays*. Ed. Doris Meyer. Austin: University of Texas Press, 1995. 61–66.

Guerra, Lucía. "Estrategias femeninas en la elaboración del sujeto romántico en la obra de Gertrudis Gómez de Avellaneda." *Revista Iberoamericana* 51 (July-Dec. 1985): 707–22.

Guerra Cunningham, Lucía. "La modalidad hermética de la subjetividad romántica en la narrativa de Soledad Acosta de Samper." Acosta de Samper, *Una nueva lectura*, 353–67.

———. "Mercedes Cabello de Carbonera: Estética de la moral y los desvíos no-disyuntivos de la virtud." *Revista de Crítica Literaria Latinoamericana* 26 (1987): 25–41.

——. "Visión marginal de la historia en la narrativa de Juana Manuela Gorriti." *Ideologies and Literature* 11 (Fall 1987): 59–76.

Guevara, Isabel de. "Carta de Doña Isabel de Guevara a la princesa gobernadora Doña JUANA . . . " *Cartas de Indias.* Madrid: Imprenta de Manuel G. Hernández, 1877. 619–21.

HarperCollins Study Bible. New Revised Standard Version. Gen. ed. Wayne A. Meeks. New York: HarperCollins, 1989.

Harter, Hugh A. *Gertrudis Gómez de Avellaneda.* Boston: Twayne, 1981.

Hinds, Harold E., Jr. "Life and Early Literary Career of the Nineteenth-Century Colombian Writer Soledad Acosta de Samper." *Latin American Women Writers: Yesterday and Today.* Ed. Yvette E. Miller and Charles M. Tatum. Pittsburgh: Latin American Literary Review, 1977. 32–41.

Iglesia, Cristina. "Prólogo." *El ajuar de la patria: Ensayos críticos sobre Juana Manuela Gorriti.* Ed. Cristina Iglesia. Buenos Aires: Feminaria Editora, 1993. 5–10.

Johnson, Julie Greer. *Women in Colonial Spanish American Literature: Literary Images.* Westport, CT: Greenwood Press, 1983. 169–83.

Karttunen, Frances. *Between Worlds: Interpreters, Guides, and Survivors.* New Brunswick: Rutgers University Press, 1994.

Kimmel, Michael S. "The Struggle for Gender Equality: How Men Respond." *Thought and Action* 8 (Winter 1993): 49–76.

Kirkpatrick, Susan. *Las Románticas: Women Writers and Subjectivity in Spain, 1835–1850.* Berkeley: University of California Press, 1989.

Lavrin, Asunción. "Female Religious." *Cities and Society in Colonial Latin America.* Ed. Louisa Schell Hoberman and Susan Migden Socolow. Albuquerque: University of New Mexico Press, 1986. 165–95.

——. "*Lo femenino:* Women in Colonia Historical Sources." *Coded Encounters: Writing, Gender and Ethnicity in Colonial Latin America.* Ed. Francisco Javier Cevallos-Candau, Jeffrey A. Cole, Nina M. Scott, and Nicomedes Suárez-Araúz. Amherst: University of Massachusetts Press, 1994.

León, Fray Luis de. *La perfecta casada.* Duodécima edición. Madrid: Espasa Calpe, 1983.

Leonard, Irving A. *Baroque Times in Old Mexico.* Ann Arbor: University of Michigan Press, 1959.

Lewis, Bart L. "Art, Society and Criticism: The Literary Theories of Mercedes Cabello de Carbonera and Clorinda Matto de Turner." *Letras Femeninas* 10 (1984): 66–73.

Lockhart, James, and Enrique Otte, eds. *Letters and People of the Spanish Indies: The Sixteenth Century*. London: Cambridge University Press, 1976. 15–17.

Lopreto, Gladys. "Isabel de Guevara: La primera feminista." *Todo es Historia* 34 (March 1991): 43–49.

Luciani, Frederick. "The Burlesque Sonnets of Sor Juana Inés de la Cruz." *Hispanic Journal* 8 (1986): 85–95.

Ludmer, Josefina. "Tretas del débil." *La sartén por el mango: Encuentro de escritoras latinoamericanas*. Ed. Patricia Elena González and Eliana Ortega. Río Piedras, Puerto Rico: Ediciones Huracán, 1984. 47–54. This essay has also been published in English as "Tricks of the Weak" in Stephanie Merrim's *Feminist Perspectives on Sor Juana Inés de la Cruz*, 86–93.

McKnight, Kathryn Joy. *The Mystic of Tunja: The Writings of Madre Castillo, 1671–1742*. Amherst: University of Massachusetts Press, 1997.

———. "Nexos del discurso femenino y la vida conventual de Sor Juana Inés de la Cruz y Sor Francisca Josefa de la Concepción de Castillo." *Memoria del Coloquio Internacional Sor Juana Inés de la Cruz y el pensamiento novohispano. 1995*. Toluca: Instituto Mexiquense de Cultura, 1995. 241–52.

———. "Sister Acts: Subject, Voice and Intertextuality in the Works of Madre Castillo (1671–1742)." Diss. Stanford University, 1992.

———. "Voz, subjetividad y mística en la Madre Castillo: Tres elementos de una escritura femenina conventual." *Texto y Contexto* 17 (Sept.-Dec. 1991): 66–96.

Marín, Luis. *Daughters of the Conquistadores: Women of the Viceroyalty of Peru*. Dallas: Southern Methodist University Press, 1983.

Marrero-Fente, Raúl. "De retórica y derechos: Estrategias de la reclamación en la carta de Isabel de Guevara." *Hispania* 79 (Mar. 1996): 1–7.

Martin, Leona. "Las veladas literarias de Juana Manuela Gorriti: Un momento dorado del feminismo hispanoamericano." *Mujeres latinoamericanas: Historia y cultura. Siglos XVI al XIX*. Ed. Luisa Campuzano. Tomo II. La Habana: Fondo Editorial Casa de las Américas, 1997. 219–26.

Martínez-San Miguel, Yolanda. "Sujetos femeninos en *Amistad funesta* y *Blanca Sol*: El lugar de la mujer en dos novelas latinoamericanas de fin de siglo XIX. *Revista Iberoamericana* 52 (Jan.-Mar. 1996): 27–45.

Mazquiarán de Rodríguez, Mercedes. "Mercedes Cabello de Carbonera." Trans. Alicia Valero Covarrubias. *Escritoras de Hispanoamérica: Una guía bio-bibliográfica.* Ed. Diane Marting. (Ed. de la edición en español, Montserrat Ordóñez.) Bogotá: Siglo XXI Editores, 1991. 98–108.

Masiello, Francine. "Between Civilization and Barbarism: Women, Family and Literary Culture in Mid-Nineteenth-Century Argentina." *Cultural and Historical Grounding for Hispanic and Luso-Brazilian Feminist Literary Criticism.* Ed. Hernán Vidal. Minneapolis: Institute for the Study of Ideologies and Literature, 1989. 517–66.

———. "Disfraz y delincuencia en la obra de Juana Manuela Gorriti." *El ajuar de la patria: Ensayos críticos sobre Juana Manuela Gorriti.* Ed. Cristina Iglesia. Buenos Aires: Feminaria Editora, 1993. 62–71.

Meehan, Thomas C. "Una olvidada precursora de la literatura fantástica argentina: Juana Manuela Gorriti." *Chasqui* 10 (Feb.-May 1981): 3–19.

Merrim, Stephanie. "Catalina de Erauso: From Anomaly to Icon." *Coded Encounters: Writing, Gender and Ethnicity in Colonial Latin America.* Ed. Francisco Javier Cevallos-Candau, Jeffrey A. Cole, Nina M. Scott, and Nicomedes Suárez Araúz. Amherst: University of Masssachusetts Press, 1993. 177–205.

Merrim, Stephanie, ed. *Feminist Perspectives on Sor Juana Inés de la Cruz.* Detroit: Wayne State University Press, 1991.

Meyer, Doris, ed. *Reinterpreting the Spanish American Essay: Women Writers of the 19th and 20th Centuries.* Austin: University of Texas Press, 1995.

Mignolo, Walter. "Cartas, crónicas y relaciones del descubrimiento y la conquista." *Historia de la literatura hispanoamericana.* Tomo I: *Epoca colonial.* Ed. Iñigo Madrigal. Madrid: Cátedra, 1982. 57–75.

Miller, Beth. "Gertrude the Great: Avellaneda, Nineteenth-Century Feminist." *Icons and Fallen Idols: Women in Spanish American Literature.* Ed. Beth Miller. Berkeley: University of California Press, 1983. 201–14.

Miller, Martin C. "Clorinda Matto de Turner and Mercedes Cabello de Carbonera: Societal Criticism and Morality." *Latin American Women Writers: Yesterday and Today.* Ed. Yvette E. Miller and Charles M. Tatum. Pittsburgh: Latin American Literary Review Press, 1975. 25–32.

Mizraje, María Gabriela. "Juana Manuela Gorriti: Cuentas pendientes." *Mujeres y cultura en la Argentina del siglo XIX.* Ed. Lea Fletcher. Buenos Aires: Feminaria Editora, 1994. 47–60.

Moraña, Mabel. "Orden dogmático y marginalidad en la *Carta de Monterrey* de Sor Juana Inés de la Cruz." *Hispanic Review* 58 (1990): 205–25.

Morison, Samuel Eliot. *Christopher Columbus: Admiral of the Ocean Sea.* Boston: Little, Brown, 1942.

Mújica, Elisa. *Sor Francisca Josefa del Castillo.* Bogotá: Procultura, 1991.

Myers, Kathleen A. 1998. "Broader Canon, Interdisciplinary Approaches: Recent Works in Colonial Latin American Literary Studies." *Latin American Research Review* 33.2 (1998): 258–70.

Netchinsky, Jill Ann. "Engendering a Cuban Literature: Nineteenth-Century Antislavery Narrative (Manzano, Suárez y Romero, Gómez de Avellaneda, A. Zambrana)." Diss. Yale University, 1986.

Niño Dios, Sor María Antonia del. *Flor de santidad: La Madre Castillo.* Tunja: Academia Boyacense de Historia, 1993.

Otero Muñoz, Gustavo. "Doña Soledad Acosta de Samper." Acosta de Samper, *Una nueva lectura,* 369–76.

Ordóñez, Montserrat. "One Hundred Years of Unread Writing: Soledad Acosta, Elisa Mújica and Marvel Moreno." *Knives and Angels: Women Writers in Latin America.* Ed. Susan Bassnett. London: Zed Books, 1990. 132–44.

———. "Soledad Acosta de Samper: Una nueva lectura." Acosta de Samper, *Una nueva lectura,* 11–24.

Pagés-Rangel, Roxana. *Del dominio público: Itinerarios de la carta privada.* Amsterdam: Teoría Literaria: Texto y Teoría 20, 1996.

Paz, Octavio. *Sor Juana Inés de la Cruz o Las trampas de la fe.* Barcelona: Seix Barral, 1982. English translation by Margaret Sayers Peden, *Sor Juana or The Traps of Faith.* Cambridge, MA: Harvard University Press, 1988.

Perry, Mary Elizabeth. *Gender and Disorder in Early Modern Seville.* Princeton: Princeton University Press, 1990.

Picon Garfield, Evelyn. *Poder y sexualidad: El discurso de Gertrudis Gómez de Avellaneda.* Amsterdam: Teoría Literaria: Texto y Teoría 12, 1993.

Plà, Josefina. *Algunas mujeres de la conquista.* Asunción, Paraguay: Newprint, 1985.

Poot Herrera, Sara, ed. *Sor Juana y su mundo: Una mirada actual.* México: Universidad del Claustro de Sor Juana, 1995.

Poot Herrera, Sara, and Elena Urrutia, eds. *"Y diversa de mí misma/entre vuestras plumas ando": Homenaje internacional a Sor Juana Inés de la Cruz.* México: El Colegio de México, 1993.

Pratt, Mary Louise. "'Don't Interrupt Me': The Gender Essay as Conversation and Countercanon." *Reinterpreting the Spanish American Essay: Women Writers of the 19th and 20th Centuries.* Ed. Doris Meyer. Austin, TX: University of Texas Press, 1995. 10–26.

Quintana, Isabel A. "Juana Manuela Gorriti y sus mundos." *El ajuar de la patria: Ensayos críticos sobre Juana Manuela Gorriti.* Ed. Cristina Iglesia. Buenos Aires: Feminaria Editora, 1993. 72–79.

Robledo, Angela. "La pluralidad discursiva como mecanismo de afirmación personal en *Su vida* de Francisca Josefa de Castillo y Guevara." *¿Y las mujeres? Ensayos sobre literatura colombiana.* Ed. María Mercedes Jaramillo, Angela Inés Robledo, and Flor María Rodríguez-Arenas. Antioquia: Universidad de Antioquia, 1991. 65–73.

Rodríguez-Arenas, Flor María. "Soledad Acosta de Samper, pionera de la profesionalización de la escritura femenina colombiana en el siglo XIX: *Dolores, Teresa la limeña, y El corazón de la mujer.*" *¿Y las mujeres? Ensayos sobre literatura colombiana.* Ed. María Mercedes Jaramillo, Angela Inés Robledo, and Flor María Rodríguez-Arenas. Antioquia: Otraparte, Editorial Universidad de Antioquia, 1991. 133–75. Bibliografía de Soledad Acosta de Samper: 289–307.

Sabàt de Rivers, Georgina. "Sor Juana Inés de la Cruz." *Historia de la literatura hispanoamericana.* Tomo I: *Epoca colonial.* Ed. Luis Iñigo Madrigal. Madrid: Ediciones Cátedra, 1982. 275–93.

Schlau, Stacey. "Madre Castillo." *Spanish American Women Writers: A Bio-Bibliographical Source Book.* Ed. Diane Marting. New York: Greenwood Press, 1990. 156–64.

———. "Madre Francisca Josefa de Castillo (1671–1742)." *Escritoras de Hispanoamérica: Una guía bio-bibliográfica.* Ed. Diane Marting. (Ed. de la edición en español, Montserrat Ordóñez.) Bogotá: Siglo Veintiuno Editores de Colombia, 1991. 161–69.

Schulman, Ivan A. "The Portrait of the Slave: Ideology and Aesthetics in the Cuban Antislavery Novel." *Annals of the New York Academy of Sciences* 292 (1977): 356–67.

Schurz, William Lytle. "The Woman." *This New World.* New York: Dutton, 1954. 276–338.

Scott, Nina M. "Juana Manuela Gorriti's *Cocina ecléctica*: Recipes as Feminine Discourse." *Recipes for Reading: Community Cookbooks, Stories, Histories.* Ed. Anne L. Bower. Amherst: University of Massachusetts Press, 1997. 189–99, 260–63.

———. "'La gran turba de las que merecieron nombres': Sor Juana's

Foremothers in 'La Respuesta a Sor Filotea.'" *Coded Encounters: Writing, Gender and Ethnicity in Colonial Latin America*. Ed. Francisco Javier Cevallos-Candau, Jeffrey A. Cole, Nina M. Scott, and Nicomedes Suárez-Araúz. Amherst: University of Massachusetts Press, 1994. 206–23.

———. "Ser mujer, ni estar ausente,/No es de amarte impedimento": Los poemas de Sor Juana a la Condesa de Paredes." *"Y diversa de mí misma/entre vuestras plumas ando": Homenaje internacional a Sor Juana Inés de la Cruz*. Ed. Sara Poot Herrera and Elena Urrutia. México: El Colegio de México, 1993.

———. "Shoring up the 'Weaker Sex': Avellaneda and Nineteenth-Century Gender Ideology." *Reinterpreting the Spanish American Essay: Women Writers of the 19th and 20th Centuries*. Ed. Doris Meyer. Austin: University of Texas Press, 1995. 57–67.

Serrano y Sanz, Manuel. *Apuntes para una biblioteca de escritoras españolas desde el año 1401 al 1833*. Tomo I, Segunda Parte. Madrid: Establecimiento Tipolitográfico "Sucesores de Rivadeneyra," 1903.

Sommer, Doris. *Foundational Fictions: The National Romances of Latin America*. Berkeley: University of California Press, 1991.

———. "Sab c'est moi." *Foundational Fictions: The National Romances of Latin America*. Berkeley: University of California Press, 1991. 114–37.

Sontag, Susan. *Illness as Metaphor*. New York: Farrar, Straus and Giroux, 1977.

Stepto, Michele. Introduction and Translators' Note. *Lieutenant Nun: Memoir of a Basque Transvestite in the New World*. Trans. Michele Stepto and Gabriel Stepto. Boston: Beacon Press, 1996. xxv–xlviii.

Tieffemberg, Silvia. "Isabel de Guevara o la construcción del yo femenino." *Filología* 24 (1989): 287–300.

Trabulse, Elías. *La memoria transfigurada: Tres imágenes históricas de Sor Juana*. México: Universidad Claustro de Sor Juana, 1996.

Trueblood, Alan. *A Sor Juana Anthology*. Cambridge, MA: Harvard University Press, 1988.

Vallbona, Rima de. "Realidad histórica y ficción en *Vida y sucesos de la monja alférez*." Diss. Middlebury College, 1981.

Varela, Consuelo, ed. *Los cuatro viajes: Testamento*. By Cristóbal Colón. Madrid: Alianza Editorial, 1986.

Volek, Emil. "Cartas de amor de la Avellaneda." *Cuadernos Hispanoamericanos* (Madrid) 511 (Jan. 1993): 103–13.

Yeager, Gertrude. "Juana Manuela Gorriti: Writer in Exile." *The Human Factor in Latin America: The Nineteenth Century*. Ed. William H. Beezley and Judith Ewell. Wilmington, DE: Scholarly Resources, 1989. 114–27.

Yo, la peor de todas. Dir. María Luisa Bemberg. GEA Cinematográfica, 1990. Available with English subtitles.

Zaldívar, Gladys, y Rosa Martínez de Cabrera, eds. *Homenaje a Gertrudis Gómez de Avellaneda: Memorias del simposio en el centenario de su muerte*. Miami: Ediciones Universal, 1981.

Index